REMEMBERING SOCIAL MOVEMENTS

Remembering Social Movements offers a comparative historical examination of the relations between social movements and collective memory.

A detailed historiographical and theoretical review of the field introduces the reader to five key concepts to help guide analysis: repertoires of contention, historical events, generations, collective identities, and emotions. The book examines how social movements act to shape public memory as well as how memory plays an important role within social movements through 15 historical case studies, spanning labour, feminist, peace, anti-nuclear, and urban movements, as well as specific examples of 'memory activism' from the 19th century to the 21st century. These include transnational and explicitly comparative case studies, in addition to cases rooted in German, Australian, Indian, and American history, ensuring that the reader gains a real insight into the remembrance of social activism across the globe and in different contexts. The book concludes with an epilogue from a prominent Memory Studies scholar.

Bringing together the previously disparate fields of Memory Studies and Social Movement Studies, this book systematically scrutinises the two-way relationship between memory and activism and uses case studies to ground students while offering analytical tools for the reader.

Stefan Berger is Professor of Social History and Director of the Institute for Social Movements at Ruhr-Universität Bochum, Germany. He is also executive chair of the Foundation History of the Ruhr, and an honorary professor at Cardiff University in the UK. His books on social movements include (with Holger Nehring) *The History of Social Movement in Global Perspective* (2017).

Sean Scalmer is Professor of History at the University of Melbourne, Australia. His books on social movements and politics include *Dissent Events* (2002), *Activist Wisdom* (2006), *Gandhi in the West* (2011), *On the Stump* (2017), and *Democratic Adventurer* (2020).

Christian Wicke is Assistant Professor of Political History at Utrecht University, the Netherlands. He wrote *Helmut Kohl's Quest for Normality* (2015). He recently edited (with Ulf Teichmann) an issue of *Arbeit-Bewegung-Geschichte* on the relationship between 'old' and 'new' social movements (2018/III).

Remembering the Modern World
Series Editors: David Lowe and Tony Joel

The *Remembering the Modern World* series throws new light on the major themes in the field of history and memory in a global context. The series investigates relationships between state-centred practices and other forms of collective and individual memory; looks at the phenomenon of anniversaries and national days in the context of global and national identities; shows how some cities and sites play active roles in generating acts of remembrance and asks why some phenomena and events are remembered more widely and easily than others.

Titles in the series:

Remembering the Second World War
Edited by Patrick Finney

Remembering Independence
Carola Lentz and David Lowe

Remembering the Holocaust in Educational Settings
Edited by Andy Pearce

Remembering Women's Activism
Sharon Crozier-De Rosa and Vera Mackie

Remembering Asia's World War Two
Edited by Mark R. Frost, Daniel Schumacher and Edward Vickers

Remembering Social Movements
Activism and Memory
Edited by Stefan Berger, Sean Scalmer and Christian Wicke

For more information about this series, please visit: https://www.routledge.com/Remembering-the-Modern-World/book-series/RMW11

REMEMBERING SOCIAL MOVEMENTS

Activism and Memory

Edited by
Stefan Berger, Sean Scalmer
and Christian Wicke

Routledge
Taylor & Francis Group

LONDON AND NEW YORK

First published 2021
by Routledge
2 Park Square, Milton Park, Abingdon, Oxon OX14 4RN

and by Routledge
605 Third Avenue, New York, NY 10158

Routledge is an imprint of the Taylor & Francis Group, an informa business

© 2021 selection and editorial matter, Stefan Berger, Sean Scalmer and Christian Wicke; individual chapters, the contributors

The right of Stefan Berger, Sean Scalmer and Christian Wicke to be identified as the authors of the editorial material, and of the authors for their individual chapters, has been asserted in accordance with sections 77 and 78 of the Copyright, Designs and Patents Act 1988.

All rights reserved. No part of this book may be reprinted or reproduced or utilised in any form or by any electronic, mechanical, or other means, now known or hereafter invented, including photocopying and recording, or in any information storage or retrieval system, without permission in writing from the publishers.

Trademark notice: Product or corporate names may be trademarks or registered trademarks, and are used only for identification and explanation without intent to infringe.

British Library Cataloguing-in-Publication Data
A catalogue record for this book is available from the British Library

Library of Congress Cataloging-in-Publication Data
Names: Berger, Stefan, editor. | Scalmer, Sean, editor. |
Wicke, Christian, editor.
Title: Remembering activism : social movements and memory /
edited by Stefan Berger, Sean Scalmer and Christian Wicke.
Subjects: LCSH: Social movements—Historiography. |
Social movements—Case studies. | Protest movements—Case studies. |
Collective memory—Political aspects.
Classification: LCC HM881 .R45 2021 (print) |
LCC HM881 (ebook) | DDC 303.48/4—dc23
LC record available at https://lccn.loc.gov/2020057618
LC ebook record available at https://lccn.loc.gov/2020057619

ISBN: 978-0-367-54156-9 (hbk)
ISBN: 978-0-367-54155-2 (pbk)
ISBN: 978-1-003-08783-0 (ebk)

Typeset in Bembo
by codeMantra

CONTENTS

List of figures vii
List of contributors ix

1 **Memory and social movements: an introduction** 1
   Stefan Berger, Sean Scalmer and Christian Wicke

2 **The ascension of 'comfort women' in South Korean colonial memory** 26
   Lauren Richardson

3 **The past in the present: memory and Indian women's politics** 41
   Devleena Ghosh and Heather Goodall

4 **History as strategy: imagining universal feminism in the women's movement** 60
   Sophie van den Elzen and Berteke Waaldijk

5 **'The memory of history as a *leitmotif* for nonviolent resistance' – peaceful protests against nuclear missiles in Mutlangen, 1983–7** 83
   Richard Rohrmoser

6 **Atomic testing in Australia: memories, mobilizations and mistrust** 95
   David Lowe

7 'The FBI Stole My Fiddle': song and memory in US
  radical environmentalism, 1980–95　　　　　　　　　　　　　113
  Iain McIntyre

8 Memory 'within', 'of' and 'by' urban movements　　　　　　133
  Christian Wicke

9 Memory as a strategy? – dealing with the past in
  political proceedings against communists in 1950/60s
  West Germany　　　　　　　　　　　　　　　　　　　　156
  Sarah Langwald

10 'We believe to have good reason to regard these
   comrades, who died in March, to be ours.' The
   remembrance of the *Märzgefallenen* by workers'
   organizations during the Weimar Republic　　　　　　　　180
   Jule Ehms

11 Memory as political intervention: labor movement
   life narration in Australia, Jack Holloway and
   May Brodney　　　　　　　　　　　　　　　　　　　　199
   Liam Byrne

12 Remembering the movement for eight hours:
   commemoration and mobilization in Australia　　　　　　219
   Sean Scalmer

13 The memory of trade unionism in Germany　　　　　　　240
   Stefan Berger

14 Protest cycles and contentious moments in memory
   activism: insights from postwar Germany　　　　　　　　260
   Jenny Wüstenberg

15 Social movements, white and black: memory struggles
   in the United States South since the Civil War　　　　　　280
   W. Fitzhugh Brundage

16 Afterword: the multiple entanglements of memory
   and activism　　　　　　　　　　　　　　　　　　　　299
   Ann Rigney

Index　　　　　　　　　　　　　　　　　　　　　　　　*305*

FIGURES

8.1	Juanita Nielsen community centre	148
8.2	Kelly's Bush, Green Bans memorial plaque	149
8.3	1979 mural by activist artists Merilyn Fairskye and Michiel Dolk and the Woolloomooloo residents action group	150
8.4	Jack Mundey at Miller's Point	151
13.1	Silke Wagner: Glückauf. bergarbeiterproteste im ruhrgebiet	254
14.1	Heimkehrermahnmal in Friedland near Göttingen: 'Memorial built by the federation of homecomers, POWs and Relatives of the missing 1967'	263
14.2	Members of the Marburg History workshop next to the Marburger Jäger regiment during a commemorative ceremony	266
14.3	Center for Human Rights Memory in Cottbus, staged to show how guards humiliated prisoners by rifling through their belongings in their cells	269

CONTRIBUTORS

Stefan Berger is Full Professor of Social History and Director of the Institute for Social Movements at Ruhr-Universität Bochum. He is also Executive Chair of the Foundation History of the Ruhr, and an Honorary Professor at Cardiff University in the UK. He has worked on social movements, nationalism, memory, industrial heritage, deindustrialization, and the history of historiography, and is currently finishing a monograph on historical writing since the 1980s. He is the author of *The Past as History. National Identity and Historical Consciousness in Modern Europe* (2015) and editor (with Jeff Olick) of a six-volume *Cultural History of Memory* (2020), as well as editor (with Holger Nehring) of *The History of Social Movements: A Global Perspective* (2017).

Liam Byrne was awarded his PhD by the University of Melbourne in 2017. In 2018 he began work with the Australian Council of Trade Unions, and in 2019 was appointed as its Historian.

Jule Ehms is a PhD candidate at the Institute of Social Movements (Bochum), working on syndicalist union work during the Weimar Republic. She studied philosophy and history at the Martin-Luther-Universität Halle/Wittenberg and the University of Notre Dame. Furthermore, she is interested in history of knowledge, political theory and Marxism, and history of social movements.

W. Fitzhugh Brundage has been the William B. Umstead Professor of History at the University of North Carolina at Chapel Hill since 2002. He has written on lynching, socialism, historical memory, African American popular culture, and the history of torture in the United States. He is currently completing a book on prisoner of war camps during the American Civil War.

Devleena Ghosh is Professor of Social and Political Sciences in the Faculty of Arts and Social Sciences at the University of Technology Sydney. Her areas of research and publication include environmental, postcolonial, and gender studies in South Asia and Australia. Her publications include *Colonialism and Modernity* (with Paul Gillen, 2007) and *Teacher for Justice: Lucy Woodcock's Transnational Life* (co-authored with Heather Goodall and Helen Randerson, 2019). She has edited numerous volumes on environmental and gender studies (Women in Asia: Shadowlines, 2012; Water, Borders and Sovereignty in Asia and Oceania 2008 with H. Goodall and S.H. Donald; The Cultures of Trade 2007 with S. Muecke). Her article 'Burma-Bengal Crossings: Intercolonial Connections in Pre-Independence India' in *Asian Studies Review* won the Wang Gung-Wu award for 2016.

Heather Goodall is Professor Emerita of History at the University of Technology Sydney. Her projects include those on Indigenous histories and environmental history in Australia, on twentieth-century decolonization in India and Australia, and on maritime history in the eastern Indian Ocean. Her historical analyses have drawn on intersectional and gendered approaches using oral history as well as archival and image methodologies. Her publications include 'Port Politics: Indian Seamen, Australian unionists and Indonesian Independence, 1945–1947', in *Labour History* (2008); *From Invasion to Embassy*, (1996); *Beyond Borders: Indians, Australians and the Indonesian Revolution, 1939–1950* (2018); *Isabel Flick: The Many Lives of an Extraordinary Aboriginal Woman* (co-authored with Isabel Flick, 2004); *Rivers and Resilience* (co-authored with Allison Cadzow, 2009); and *Teacher for Justice: Lucy Woodcock's Transnational Life* (co-authored with Helen Randerson and Devleena Ghosh, 2019). Lucy Woodcock (1889–1968) was an Australian unionist, feminist, and peace and refugee advocate who travelled to India, China, and Japan.

Sarah Langwald is a PhD candidate in Contemporary History at the Ruhr University Bochum. She is also part of the editorial team of the historical journal *Arbeit – Bewegung – Geschichte*. In her doctoral thesis, she investigates the criticism of the use of political justice against (alleged) communists in 1950/60s West Germany in the context of the Cold War. Her main research interests are legal history, politics of history, and labour history.

David Lowe holds a Chair in contemporary history at Deakin University Australia. His recent research interests include the uses of history by politicians; remembering conflict and political transitions; the international students as a factor in cultural diplomacy; and the history of Australia's foreign and aid policies, including overseas diplomatic representation. His recent books include (with Carola Lentz) *Remembering Independence* (Routledge, 2018) and, edited with Cassandra Atherton and Alyson Miller, *The Unfinished Atomic Bomb: Shadows and Reflections* (2018). He is currently writing an international history of the Colombo Plan for aid to South and Southeast Asia during the 1950s and 1960s.

Iain McIntyre is a Melbourne-based researcher with an interest in the history of social and labour movement tactics and strategy as well as music, fiction, and other forms of (un)popular culture. His recent books include *Sticking It to The Man: Revolution and Counterculture in Pulp and Popular Fiction, 1950–80* (2019) and *On The Fly!: Hobo Literature and Songs* (2018).

Lauren Richardson is Director of the Japan Institute and Lecturer in the Department of International Relations at the Australian National University. Previously she taught Northeast Asian Relations at the University of Edinburgh, and she received her PhD from the Department of Political and Social Change at the ANU. Her research focusses on the role of non-state actors in shaping diplomatic interactions in Northeast Asia, particularly Japan-South Korea relations. Her publications have focussed on the South Korean anti-nuclear movement and the role of Buddhists in Sino-Japanese rapprochement, and she is currently completing a book manuscript entitled *Reshaping Japan-Korea Relations: Transnational Advocacy Networks and the Politics of Redress*.

Ann Rigney is Professor of Comparative Literature at Utrecht University, the Netherlands. She has written widely on theories of cultural memory and on the evolution of memory cultures since the early nineteenth century. Her many publications include *The Afterlives of Walter Scott: Memory on the Move* (2012), and (co-edited with C. De Cesari) *Transnational Memory: Circulation, Articulation, Scales* (2014). She currently directs the research project *Remembering Activism* funded by the European Research Council (ERC); www.rememberingactivism.eu.

Richard Rohrmoser studied English, History, and Political Science in Augsburg, Malmö, and Ottawa (2008–15). He received his PhD from the University of Mannheim (2019) and his main fields of research are social movements, protest, and the Cold War. Currently, he works on a second book project on the history and the characteristics of the German 'Antifa'.

Sean Scalmer is Professor of History at the University of Melbourne, Australia. His books on social movements and political history include *Dissent Events* (2002), *Activist Wisdom* (2006), *Gandhi in the West* (2011), and *On the Stump* (2017). His most recent book is *Democratic Adventurer: Graham Berry and the Making of Australian Politics* (2020). He is a member of the Editorial Working Party for the journal *Labour History*, and a co-editor of the journal *Moving the Social: Journal of Social History and the History of Social Movements*.

Sophie van den Elzen is a PhD Candidate at Utrecht University. She is currently completing a study of cultural memories of slavery and antislavery in nineteenth-century women's rights contention in Europe. She studied comparative literature at Utrecht University, University of Toronto, and UC Berkeley.

Berteke Waaldijk is a scholar of history and gender studies. She holds the chair 'Language and Culture Studies' at the Faculty of Humanities at Utrecht University and is part of the Graduate Gender Programme. Her research is focussed on gender, culture, and citizenship. She publishes on history and gender of Social Work in the Netherlands and in Europe, on colonial culture and citizenship, on history of Dutch Women's movements, and on gender, history, and philosophy of the humanities. She works on projects on teaching and learning related to European Gender Studies and the Liberal Arts Programme at Utrecht University.

Christian Wicke is Assistant Professor in Political History at Utrecht University. He has worked on nationalism, memory, industrial heritage, deindustrialization, and social movements and is currently pursuing a comparative study of urban movements. He is the author of *Helmut Kohl's Quest for Normality* (2015) and has co-edited *Industrial Heritage and Regional Identities* (with Stefan Berger and Jana Golombek, 2017).

Jenny Wüstenberg is Associate Professor of Twentieth Century History and Director of the Centre for Public History, Heritage, and Memory at Nottingham Trent University. She received her PhD from the University of Maryland, College Park and has since then held academic positions at American University, the Free University Berlin, the Commission at the Federal Ministry of Justice for the Investigation of its Nazi Past, and York University in Toronto. Her research interests revolve around memory activism and politics in Germany, Europe, settler colonial societies, and in transnational networks. Her most recent project examines the comparative remembrance of family separation policies. Wüstenberg is also the cofounder and co-president of the Memory Studies Association.

1

MEMORY AND SOCIAL MOVEMENTS

An introduction

Stefan Berger, Sean Scalmer and Christian Wicke

Social movements rely on collective memories to assert claims, mobilize supporters and legitimize their political visions. Social movements also help to shape collective memories. But though frequently intertwined in practice, scholars have rarely pondered the relationship between 'memory' and 'activism' in any depth. Individual scholars have certainly identified the import of 'memory activists'[1] or 'heroes of memory'[2] in the transformation of shared understandings of the past. Likewise, the role of memory in the maintenance of an insurgent movement's collective identity has also been widely recognized, even if few studies have begun to consider its actual place in mobilization.[3] Overall, there has been, until very recently, little attempt to consider 'memory' and 'activism' in an integrated, systematic and comparative fashion.[4]

In part, this failure is a product of the distinct history of the separate institutionalization of scholarship on 'activism' and 'memory'. Scholars working on 'activism' have often been inspired by the dissent of the 1960s and 1970s. The sub-discipline of social movement studies, with a strong focus on the new social movements emerging in the wake of 1968, has been the key arena for research on activism. 'Memory studies', by contrast, emerged out of the cultural turn in the humanities during the 1980s. Its original concentration on national memory is indebted to the crisis of national historical master narratives. Pierre Nora's concept of the 'realms of memory' is a cunning attempt to resurrect a national historical master narrative after poststructuralism had effectively undermined such master narratives.[5] Even where memory scholarship was not tied to attempts to stabilize or re-invent national history, it was fascinated by traumatic events such as wars and genocides that had led to major national and transnational debates and controversies, and thus to some extent democratized official interpretations of the past. Social movement studies and memory studies have over the last three decades developed as distinctive sub-disciplines. Each is defined by exclusive scholarly associations and journals. Each has their canons of exemplary scholarship. Each uses their own 'master concepts' and hegemonic methods. All of this has ensured that studies of 'memory' and 'social movements' have been pursued in parallel rather than connected fashion; there has so far been little mutual borrowing or intellectual exchange across borders that at times appeared rather impermeable. This is somewhat surprising, as social movements have had great agency in shaping historical cultures and public memory.

'Social movement studies' boasts three dedicated international journals in the English language alone: *Mobilization*, founded in 1996; *Social Movement Studies*, launched in 2002; and *Interface: a Journal for and about Social Movements*, an online journal that has been published since 2009. Two research committees of the International Sociological Association (ISA) – RC47: Social Classes and Social Movements, and RC48: Social Movements, Collective Action and Social Change – were formally recognized by the ISA in the early 1990s. Major English-language publishers have established book series – for example, Cambridge University Press, University of Minnesota Press, University of Chicago Press, Amsterdam University Press. A succession of textbooks has been published, and major universities (as well as many minor ones) now offer courses in the field, undergraduate and postgraduate.

The consolidation of social movement studies as a sub-discipline has, however, also been accompanied by an intellectual narrowing. Interest in collective action and social movements has a very long lineage, and has been widely shared among historians, as well as social scientists. In celebrated works published from the later 1950s, British Marxist scholars Edward Thompson, George Rudé and Eric Hobsbawm identified the importance of collective action as a motor of history, and ventured influential hypotheses on the long-term trajectory of protest forms.[6] As 'social movement studies' has developed, however, it has cohered much more closely and exclusively within the disciplines of sociology and political science. Historical studies have become increasingly marginal. There have been exceptions to the rule, such as the work of historical sociologists like Sidney Tarrow, Charles Tilly and Craig Calhoun.[7] However, the study of social movements is in need of a much deeper historical perspective. Reflecting this need, historians interested in social movements have recently established a distinctive book series, *Palgrave Studies in the History of Social Movements*, edited by Stefan Berger and Holger Nehring, and their own academic journal, *Moving the Social: Journal of Social History and the History of Social Movements*, edited by Stefan Berger and Sean Scalmer.

The 'fathers' of 'social movement studies' (despite the presence of important female scholars, above all, Donatella della Porta, the recognized 'founders' are all men) were all sociologists of various kinds. Broadly speaking, research initially developed around two competing approaches. First, a 'European' school, best exemplified by Alain Touraine and Alberto Melucci, was distinguished by its interest in so-called 'new social movements' (such as environmentalism and feminism) that were alleged to succeed the labour movement as primary social actors.[8]

Students concerned with these movements were marked by close interest in consciousness and in the constitution of the subject. Distinct from this European approach, there also developed an 'American' school, propelled by the Stakhanovite productivity of Charles Tilly and by his leading collaborators such as Sidney Tarrow and Doug McAdam.[9] It was wider in its temporal range but less concerned to trace the underlying social basis and phenomenology of collective actors, and much more concerned with political organizations, relationships and processes.

The combination of competition and cooperation among these scholars and their peers has propelled a series of splits, regroupings and reconfigurations. In consequence, the investigation of social movements has for some years principally been organized around a handful of central processes: the mobilization of protest (through formal organizations and alternative political structures); the production of collective identities; the 'framing' of protest demands and arguments; the interactions between movements and other pertinent actors (especially opponents and the state); the presence and influence of movement networks (often transnational in scope); the nature and transformation of contentious performances; or some combination of part or all of the above. Even if collective identity has been considered as an important feature of social movements in this crowded field, the study of 'memory' has only recently begun to find a place of its own. Nicole Doerr has asked how social movement activists have constructed collective memories in order to further their activism in wider society and build strong internal collective identities.[10] The analysis of forms of collective action can benefit enormously from paying attention to the role of subjectivities and memory in underpinning the activities of social movements.[11] Ron Eyerman has produced a preliminary survey of the work on how social movements use memory and history in order to build strong collective identities in 2015.[12] Lorenzo Zamponi has been looking at the role of memory in the construction of media narratives of Spanish and Italian student movements.[13] Priska Daphi has been exploring the relationship between identity, narrative and memory in the European Global Justice Movement.[14] Priska Daphi and Lorenzo Zamponi have published a special issue of *Mobilization* on the topic of social movements and memory.[15] Donatella della Porta and her collaborators have looked at the impact of memory on forms of democracy in contemporary southern Europe.[16] Lara Leigh Kelland has published an account of how forms of memory work have been crucial for a great variety of US-based social movements, including civil rights, black power, women's, gay liberation and red power movements.[17] A comparison of right-wing populist movements in contemporary Europe has shown that the success or failure of those movements is strongly linked to public memory cultures commemorating fascist movements in the twentieth century.[18] Ann Rigney's current project *Remembering Activism: The Cultural Memory of Protest in Europe* (REACT) is trying to further fill this gap.[19] Yifat Gutman and Jenny Wüstenberg, whose work in this field has been mentioned,[20] are currently preparing a handbook of memory activism that will for the first time attempt to present an overview of scholarship concerned with protest and its relationship with memory.

Why has it taken so long for social movement studies to discover memory? The acknowledged founders of sociology – so-called 'classical' thinkers like Karl Marx, Max Weber and Emile Durkheim – were remarkable not simply for distinguished works of analysis, but for their minting of specialized concepts to explain social processes. Later work claiming authority within the discipline has typically sought to extend these concepts, or else to develop some rival conceptual language. The most prestigious thinkers concerned with 'social movements' have largely conformed to this pattern: positioning their studies within broader intellectual traditions (for example, emphasizing a challenge to Marxian approaches),[21] developing relatively elaborate conceptual schema or sometimes drawing upon and adapting recent theoretical approaches (Latour's 'actor network theory'; Bourdieu's 'field theory', Deleuzian analysis; Lefebvre's rhythmanalysis).[22] Memory plays no major explanatory role in this wider sociological canon, regardless of the fact that one of the founding fathers of memory studies, Maurice Halbwachs, was a sociologist.[23] Deprived of strong theoretical legitimacy, the import of memory into social movement studies has, for a long time, escaped the attention of students of particular movements and campaigns.

There are other reasons too. Since the rise of the 'survey' and then of procedures of statistical sampling, the field of applied sociology has also been marked by an expansion of quantitative approaches, a process heightened by the rise of the computer.[24] Besieged and somewhat defensive, 'qualitative' social scientists have been forced to assert the equal rigour of their analyses, and the 'scientific' status of their scholarship. This could be interpreted as a somewhat inhospitable context for memory studies. It has encouraged qualitative sociologists to treat the interview transcript as a relatively transparent data source, providing the raw material for analysis. The procedures of 'grounded theory' have been developed to guide the researcher in movement from '(interview) text' to 'analysis'.[25] Dedicated computer programs have aided the process, allowing for the identification of key themes and tropes. In these ways, testimony about the past has been incorporated into the operation of a 'normal science'. By contrast, historians using the interview as a method – typically identifying as 'oral historians' rather than as 'qualitative' social scientists – have been less pressured to establish the 'scientific reliability' of their informants. This, in turn, has liberated a more reflexive consideration of the vagaries and the limits of 'memory'.[26] And it has thereby provided one important inspiration for the development of 'memory studies'.

A third reason why social movement studies has found it so difficult to forge a positive relationship with memory studies has to do with its temporal orientation. The discipline of sociology emerged and grew on a promise that it might understand the problems of emergent industrial societies. It is present- and future-oriented. Reflecting such a perspective, the journal *Social Movement Studies* was launched with the assertion that social movements play an 'increasingly key role' as 'the dynamic and oppositional forces within global socio-economies'.[27] Most scholars working on protest and collective behaviour have been excited to explore the relationship between the 'social movement' and contemporary change.

Studies of recent rather than temporally distant mobilizations have predominated, and these have certainly tended to draw greater interest than historical studies.[28] The most influential theorists in social movement studies have sought to proclaim the possibility that still unfolding campaigns embody prospects of incipient transformation: first, 'new social movements' of the 1960s and 1970s; more recently, 'global movements'.[29] And with their quest for novelty and eyes fixed ahead, students of social movements have been very slow to develop a close interest in how the 'past' is recalled.

'Memory studies', in turn, has also been slow in developing an interest in social movements. While heritage studies in particular over the last years have opened new perspectives into the relations between official memory and civil society activism,[30] memory studies has been marked predominantly by its own emphases, preoccupations and oversights. There are a range of scholarly journals focussing on memory studies today, above all the appropriately named *Memory Studies* that came into existence in 2008 and is widely regarded as the lead journal in the field. In 2016 a Memory Studies Association was founded, and it has held hugely successful and well-attended conferences since. In 2019 almost 2,000 memory scholars assembled in Madrid to discuss a wide variety of different subjects.[31] Specifically concerned with history is the journal *History and Memory* founded in 1989 with the explicit aim of encouraging research into the question how the past has shaped the present through a wide variety of memorialization practices and how our perception of the past is always moulded by present-day agendas. Today virtually all major academic publishing houses have book series on memory studies. As a field of study, memory studies comes onto the scene of academic scholarship around two decades later than social movement studies. It is not rooted in 1968 but rather in the 1980s, when questions of national identity were coming to the fore again in politics as well as scholarship. Pierre Nora's path-breaking 'realms of memory' project, referred to above, provided in effect a new national master narrative for France at a moment in time when the republican master narrative was perceived to be in deep crisis. It was the starting point of a remarkable career of one of the most successful paradigms in humanities research over recent decades. Rediscovering the forgotten Halbwachs, Nora opened the curtain for a vast amount of research that was primarily concerned with the memory of the nation,[32] especially where this memory was held to be particularly traumatic and related to war and genocide.[33] Thus, for example, the Holocaust and controversies over the colonial legacies of racism have shaped memory studies to a considerable extent.[34] The double emphasis on trauma[35] and national memory has produced a range of blind spots for memory studies, as subjects that were neither central to national recollection nor necessarily traumatic were only rarely dealt with.[36] Social movements were one such topic.

Yet, the production of 'social', 'collective' or 'cultural' memory has been strongly intertwined with the history of social movements. Social movements have had, for example, the capacity to manipulate official memory, in demanding 'official apologies' for atrocities committed by political regimes in the past.[37]

They also have at various times and places been successful in constructing forms of 'counter-memory' through street protests, the creation of counter-monuments, the toppling of existing monuments (something very much to the fore in the discussions we are witnessing in many countries across the globe as we are putting the final touches to this introduction in the summer of 2020) or the curation of alternative exhibitions.[38] And they have been influential in making collectives forget – a process that is as important as remembering, as scholars ranging from Ernest Renan to Paul Ricoeur have taught us.[39] And social movements have not only used and forged memory, but memory has also been a key motivation for the formation of social movements.[40]

Next to Halbwachs the art historian Aby Warburg and his concept of 'social memory'[41] served memory scholars to understand memory not as something that was biologically inherited but as something that required a cultural transmittance that we can shape. As Andreas Huyssen put it: '[the] past is not simply there in memory ... it must be articulated to become memory'.[42] Memory studies was to adopt social constructivist positions wholesale.[43] Jan and Aleida Assmann became two of the most influential theorists of memory, in particular with their distinction between three levels of memory: individual memory, where conception of time operates very subjectively; 'communicative memory', which operates in any social group, where its members are still alive; and 'cultural memory', which is connected to the institutionalization of communicative memory in museums, heritage initiatives, monuments and public discourses about the past.[44] The forging of memory by and through state power has often caught the attention of scholars in memory studies.[45] However, as this volume will demonstrate, social movements as civil society actors were also important in shaping public discourses about the past and thus have become, time and again, carriers of cultural forms of memory and forgetting, as Guy Beiner reminded us in his recent memory history of the Ulster Rebellion.[46] Other historians have pointed out that political activists have made frequent references to the past in order to legitimize visions for the future – think, for example, of Joan Derk van der Capellen's lecturing on the parallels between the eighteenth-century American Revolution and the sixteenth-century Batavian Revolution or Jacques-Pierre Brissot reminding the Genevans during the same age of revolutions of their heritage of William Tell who had lived in the fourteenth century.[47] Already before the French Revolution, the citizens of several European cities used the memory of past rights in order to justify political entitlements and to construct a strong sense of place identity.[48] Nineteenth- and twentieth-century national movements, which can also be understood as social movements, have invariably referenced their visions for the future with interpretations of the past.[49] Historians have contributed to the study of the memory of 1968,[50] and they have looked at the importance of memorializing the civil rights movement in the US.[51] The study of terrorism in Italy has also been enriched by perspectives from memory studies.[52] How different conceptions of historical time have influenced a variety of social movements, such as the Madres in Argentina, and how forms of transitional justice have been blind to the conflicts produced by such different ideas of historical time have been the subject of an intriguing analysis by Berber Bevernage.[53] In future an even stronger focus on social movements and their constructions of the past would arguably contribute further to a better understanding of the political 'dynamics of cultural memories'.[54] If we take, for example, the role of social movements in the production of heritage, a rich field for further examination opens up. As memory activism in the form of industrial-heritage movements becomes institutionalized, memory often becomes part of branding campaigns for place identities, touristified and commodified for profit.[55] The touristification of the past, memory activists have argued, may also involve the banalization of remembrance, as for instance the site of the Berlin Holocaust memorial illustrates, where visitors have frequently behaved disrespectfully.[56]

If social movements are conscious of their own role in the political process, and if their representatives are highly articulate, they are far more likely to leave memory work that, in turn, can influence and has to be deconstructed by historians. As Richard Vinen has pointed out in relation to 1968, activists dominate the memory literature on 1968 and they are not shy in securing their special place in history. Vinen has shown that 'the leading figures in 68 often had a highly developed sense of themselves as historical actors and as people who would one day be the object of historical research'. This was reinforced by 1968ers subsequently working as historians seeing 'politics and historical research as intertwined'. This affected the way we think of 68. By contrast, Vinen points out, working-class protest in and around 1968 is rarely present through ego-documents of workers: 'Students in 68 are portrayed in words, frequently their own words, but workers are often remembered in pictures'.[57]

While we have identified above some attempts to begin to think social movements and memory together, this collection is a response to the relative scarcity of such attempts to examine the 'memory'-'activism' relationship, and its editors see themselves in line with those who wish to change this. Previous and current research on the relationship between social movements and memory has disclosed several concepts and approaches that may be useful to both fields. Here we grant sustained attention to five areas of research that seem to us to hold special potential for a more integrated and cross-disciplinary treatment of memory activism: repertoires of contention, historical events, generations, collective identities and emotions.

The concept of a 'repertoire of contention' was first advanced by Charles Tilly 40 years ago.[58] Seeking to describe and explain the changing ways in which people made collective claims, Tilly observed that though people might act in an almost limitless range of ways (from throwing dynamite to composing a letter), in practice campaigners in a particular time and place typically employed only a small number of tactics. The 'repertoire' was this cluster of preferred performances. It was limited, it was learned, and like the repertoire of a jazz musician, it was open to improvisation, at the margins.[59] Tilly's principal studies of the 'repertoire' of contention focussed on long-term shifts in the dominant forms of collective action in Great Britain and France, especially over the eighteenth and early nineteenth centuries. To schematize, he divined a shift from an 'old' repertoire of contention that was 'parochial' (concentrated in a single community), 'bifurcated' (taking different forms, depending on whether issues were predominantly local or national) and 'particular' (varying greatly), to a 'new repertoire' of performance that was 'cosmopolitan' (spanning many localities), modular (easily transferable between places) and 'autonomous' (beginning on the claimants' own initiative). This was a transformation embodied in the replacement of the grain seizure by the demonstration. It was, according to Tilly, integral to the rise of the modern social movement.[60] In his later work Tilly somewhat moderated this binary treatment of the repertoire. He conceded that there were 'many repertoires' rather than just two, arguing more carefully that this 'exaggerated division' served only as a 'useful guide' to a more 'complex history'.[61] More recent scholars have largely elaborated this pluralism using the term 'repertoire' to describe more particular and limited clusters of performance: the Gandhian repertoire,[62] suicide protest,[63] cyberactivism,[64] 'carnivalized politics',[65] disruption,[66] 'slutwalks',[67] parades,[68] and so on.

But if the concept is widely and creatively used, then the historical processes that underpin the making and alteration of a repertoire have not always been rigorously examined.[69] Perhaps responding to such a deficit, a new vein of scholarship has recently emerged, specifically concerned with the import of 'strategy' and 'strategic interaction'. This research has introduced a fresh conceptual language (of 'players' and 'arenas') as an alternative to the familiar language of 'social movements'. It has emphasized that the strategic choices of 'players' are based on 'meaning' and 'emotions', and not simply on rational calculation of 'means' and 'ends'. And its leading practitioners have signalled an openness to close ('micro') studies (such as those advanced by historians) rather than to abstract structural analyses.[70] They have not, however, granted 'memory' any direct consideration notwithstanding isolated studies that have asked how social memory has underpinned community-making using affective means in strategic ways to support specific political aims. One example here would be Ruth Cardoso's study on how popular movements in the city of Sao Paulo have used memory to build a sense of belonging to specific neighbourhoods that, in turn, strengthened demands for improving those neighbourhoods.[71] Another would be how the transfer of repertoires of contention from western and southern Europe to Romania was limited by a host of local factors in relation to social movements mobilizing on behalf of students, against the government and against business interest in Romania after 2011.[72]

Notwithstanding such oversight, scholarly examinations of the 'repertoire of contention' offer one potentially fruitful point of connection between 'memory studies' and 'social movement studies' and indeed, one recent intervention has already advocated such a possibility.[73] If an actor's preferred political performances rest greatly on habit and custom, then they are largely conveyed through remembrance: processes of sharing and story-telling, personal testimonies, influential texts (whether handbooks, memoirs or histories) that convey lessons concerning the appeal of rival tactics. Scholars working specifically on social movements have not granted such processes very direct or sustained attention. Experts in the study of memory can here provide a model and a guide.

The likelihood of successful collaboration in such a quest is heightened by conceptual similarities between the fields. Like students of the 'repertoire of contention', leading figures in 'memory studies', such as Ann Rigney, have emphasized the principle of 'scarcity': of the enormous number of past experiences only a few are in practice recollected.[74] Like students of the repertoire, 'memory' scholars, such as Michael Rothberg, have identified the process by which one actor's successful strategy is borrowed or exploited by others seeking public recognition (a process that Rothberg calls 'multi-directional memory').[75] Some of the chapters in this volume pursue such connections. We hope our collective work encourages more research of this kind.

Notwithstanding an abiding preoccupation with structure (reflective of the influence of sociology), students of social movements have also evinced considerable interest in the 'event' as an object of research. Charles Tilly pioneered an influential research method that organized data collection around the occurrence of 'contentious events', reported in major public sources, such as newspapers. He also reflected explicitly on the relationship between these 'event catalogues' and broader social theories.[76] More ambitiously, historian and political scientist, W.H. Sewell Jr., has argued in a series of influential publications for the value of an 'event-ful sociology', registering the centrality of 'historical events' to processes of structural change.[77] A 'historical event', Sewell has suggested, can be analytically distinguished from the flow of everyday experiences as: '(1) a ramified sequence of occurrences that (2) is recognized as notable by contemporaries, and that (3) results in a durable transformation of structures'.[78] The catalytic power of historical events lies in their capacity to touch off unpredictable ruptures in the distribution of resources, access to political power and cultural understanding.[79] They rearticulate broader power structures and incite more events.[80] But they are also symbolically loaded: characterized by heightened emotion, punctuated by ritual, distinguished by collective creativity: a 'historical event' is not simply a happening, for 'symbolic interpretation' is also 'part and parcel' of what grants it a transformative capacity.[81]

Sewell demonstrated the potential of these insights in an extended analysis of the taking of the Bastille as an 'historical event'. In Sewell's handling, this 'event' could be considered 'historical' for its pivotal role in the creation of the modern concept of 'revolution'. The liberation of the King's prisoners was one thing. The linking of popular violence with the concept of popular sovereignty a second. The King's subsequent yielding of effective power to the National Assembly a third. Cumulatively, they can be understood as a transformation of political structures – a major historical event.[82] Sewell's presentation is notable for its attention to culture and time. It was only in the days after the liberation of the prisoners, he argues, that orators, journalists, politicians and 'the crowd itself' reinterpreted the rising as a culturally significant moment, seizing on the political theory of 'popular sovereignty' as a means to 'explain' and to 'justify' the popular violence.[83] But notwithstanding the richness of this examination, the student of memory will be struck perhaps more forcefully by the relative truncation of Sewell's symbolic examination. The invention of 'revolution', in his treatment, is completed in 1789. There is no attention to the ways in which the taking of the Bastille was recalled or rearticulated in new combinations in future months and years. The ways in which 'memory' might consolidate or undermine new political schema lie outside his purview. The 'interpretation of events' is treated as a relatively immediate action, not a long-term, collective and contentious process in its own right.[84] Closer attention to the processes through which occurrences are remembered, reshaped and exploited would enrich our understanding of the ways that they become significant. Students of memory have independently grappled with these issues, developing such concepts as 'memory events'[85] and 'impact events'.[86] Further examination of these questions offers one obvious basis for a richer cross-disciplinary research.

Next to utilizing repertoires of contention and historical events, those intent on bringing memory studies and social movement studies closer together might also think of generation as a useful concept. Many forms of social protest have been described as generational. Thus in German contemporary history, for example, there has been much talk about a 1945 generation, a 'sceptical generation', a 1968 generation and a 1989 generation.[87] In Spain, the recent iaioflautas movement explicitly used their grandparents' identity in order to draw attention to the democratic deficits of the transition period between Francoism and the post-Francoist democracy in Spain.[88] Generational factors have also been examined in relation to the question whether particular generational cohorts remember the women's movement differently in the US.[89] Studies on the generational memory within left-wing movements in the US and France revealed not only a whole host of amnesias but also important memory strains active in mobilizing left-wing protest cultures in both countries.[90] Anna Wiemann's study on the Fukushima protests in Japan highlighted the way in which activists disassociated themselves from the violent protests of social movements in 1960s Japan.[91] She thereby pointed not only to the importance of generational continuity but also discontinuity. Attention to generational memory would be one way of thinking the construction of the past together with the history of protest, especially if one generation of memory activists is referencing the work of previous generations of memory activists. Of course, the scholar who wishes to bring together memory and social movements has to be careful not to reduce every political conflict to generation thereby sidelining other issues such as class, race, gender and other issues relevant to the formation of social movement memories. Yet, with Karl Mannheim we can nevertheless assert that the concept of generation 'is one of the indispensable guides to an understanding of the structure of social and intellectual movements'. Mannheim already emphasized the importance of memory for the constitution of generations. For him generations were not concrete communities but rather constructions within a particular timeframe of distance to actual experience that was communicated as joint tradition and heritage. In particular at times of significant social change, Mannheim argued, a generation was some kind of historical community sharing an imagined destiny. Even if generations' representations of personal and collective pasts would be reformed in accordance with the conditions of the changing present, memories of the past would be crucial in understanding the politics of the past, including the politics of social movements.[92]

Next to the concept of 'generation', the concept of 'collective identity' constitutes a kind of golden bridge between social movement studies and memory studies. Like generation, collective identity is in some respects a deeply problematical concept. Indeed, it has been described as a 'plastic word' by Lutz Niethammer.[93] Yet if we approach 'collective identity' as a construction rather than an essence, then we can see how collective identities were forged with the help of particular memories. This has also been true for the collective identities of social movements.[94] In social movement studies, collective identity has often been seen as necessary and constitutive to the formation and endurance of social movements.[95] To Alberto Melucci the collective identity of social movements consisted predominantly of a process of formalizing boundaries between the social movement network and the outside world which emerged from the relatively concentrated exchanges and internal debates within the movement. The sense of belonging of social movement members, developed in the course of their struggles, was the result of a convergence between interests and practices among individuals.[96] In memory studies, Halbwachs already pointed to the intrinsic relationship between collective memory and collective identity. Individual memory had always been intermingled with the social: you might think you are alone, but you never are in your perceptions of the past which are collectively constructed. Halbwachs showed that our individual memory is fundamentally shaped by group belongings and the associated 'collective memory', which is a key basis for 'collective identity'. Dieter Rucht has pointed out that the mechanisms according to which social movements operate rely on such memory and identity work.[97] This has been the case not just for new social movements but also for the nineteenth-century labour movement. Especially in its Marxist variant, it constructed a collective identity of class that was based partly on strong memory work. Class identity, forged to some extent through memory, was the precondition for successful revolutions and the implementation of a socialist future. Even at the beginning of the twenty-first century some Marxist theorists, such as Oskar Negt and Alexander Kluge, argued that class identities would forge a comprehensive proletarian public sphere countering the bourgeois one.[98] Similarly, historians of youth subcultures have pointed to the importance of collective identities of youth that were built on the construction of common memories.[99] And the forging of the Stonewall myths in LGBTQ circles was crucially based on memorial practices that were institutionalized nationally and internationally over time.[100]

Finally, we would like to suggest that social movement studies and memory studies can be brought closer together by paying attention to developments in the field of history of emotions.[101] Social movement scholars have long pointed out that social movement activists do not only follow rational calculations.[102] Emotional processes, as manifested, for example, in ritual practices, have been at least equally important in explaining social movement action.[103] A wide range of emotions such as shame, sorrow, anger, hatred, happiness and love have influence not only the way in which social action has been remembered but also the way in which such memories have then been transformed again into social action. As the history of emotions has recently moved from a concern with the discursive construction of emotions to the bodily basis of emotions, so scholars interested in the role of emotions in both memory and social movement work could usefully ask how subjectivities were linked to political performances and memory work in the realm of social movements.[104] The history of emotions allows for the unpacking and deconstruction of memories of selves and memories contributing to the forging of collective identities. Transferred to the fields of memory and social movement studies, the study of emotions would allow us to problematize the construction of identities and collective selves through emotional memory work. If we take, for example, the history of the French revolution, Bill Reddy has argued that it is impossible to understand that seminal event in world history without paying due attention to changes in the navigation of emotions that took place between the 1660 and the 1780s.[105] Turning grief into anger and transforming anger into political demands was a strategy followed by many social movements, for example, the movement to make medication available more readily to those suffering from AIDS.[106] Emotional dynamics were often crucial in allowing social movements to acquire critical mass of supporters and to mobilize the media on their behalf. As the attention space of the media is extremely limited, the strength of emotional mobilization through social movements is vital in positing the concerns of social movements on the scale of what the media regard as important news. The emotional dynamics of social movements have both internal appeal and external effects.[107] If social movement studies have been rediscovering the history of emotions, the same can be said for memory studies, where scholars have discussed to what extent emotional memories can be deemed accurate,[108] what role emotions have played in forms of disputed memories,[109] and to what extent emotions are important to agonistic memory regimes,[110] to mention but a few examples in a rich field of enquiry. Overall then, the scene seems to be set for a greater dialogue in which ways social movement studies and memory studies are dealing with the role of emotions in their respective sub-fields.

The case studies of this volume

Having pointed out some of the fruitful ways of conceptually combining memory studies and social movement studies in the future, in the final part of this introduction we would like to draw out some of the challenges and promises of combining those two fields of studies as they present themselves in the contributions to this volume.

We have not sought to impose a uniformity of approach on individual contributions, but rather to present a diversity of cases and methods. The cases are drawn from a variety of national and cultural contexts: Europe – especially Germany – Australia, the US, India, South Korea, Japan, China. They also range across many different kinds of social movements: the women's movement; the anti-nuclear movement; the environmental movement; the labour movement (in its reformist and revolutionary wings); memory activists in post-war Germany; African-Americans and Southern whites in the US, struggling to shape their polity. They extend from the nineteenth century to the contemporary period. And they consider how activists shape public memory and how memory is mobilized within social movements.

Notwithstanding such diversity, we do not claim comprehensiveness. The chosen case studies are especially drawn from two national contexts – Germany and Australia. This relative geographical concentration is partly an expression of the identities of editors (German and Australian). But it is also a reflection of the vibrancy of memory politics in these societies. Marked by traumatic histories of genocide, war and colonialism, they have also been shaped by strong social movements and by major public controversies over the past (the so-called 'Historikerstreit' in Germany and the 'History Wars' in Australia). This makes them especially fecund soil for the student of 'memory and activism'.

While the chapters that follow give the particularities of various national contexts due attention, they are not offered primarily as contributions to national histories. We hope and expect that they will be of special interest to students of social movements and of memory, whatever their national affiliations and expertise. And we hope still more fervently that our explorations here will elicit further research into a still more diverse range of historical cases.

The collection is made up of 14 substantial case studies. The first, Lauren Richardson's chapter, shows how the so-called 'comfort women' of South Korea forged a powerful social movement which, by the 1990s, enabled them to write their memories of victimhood into the national South Korean memory of Japanese colonialism in the Second World War. She demonstrates that the framing strategies of the movement were key to its success. By framing their claims in the universalist language of human rights,[111] the women could write themselves into the burgeoning democracy movement in South Korea that looked favourably on rights-based political claims. The movement could also link itself very successfully to a transnational discourse that condemns violence against women. It is a good example of how a social movement was capable of transforming national memory when both the national and the transnational frames have been favourable to such transformation. Richardson uses the case of the Chinese 'comfort women' as counter-example to the success of their Korean counterparts, as she argues that both the domestic and transnational frameworks, dictatorship and non-acceptance of a global human rights discourse, have meant

14 Stefan Berger et al.

that the Chinese movement has not been able to gain much attention or even to form itself into an effective movement to date. However, Richardson also shows clearly how it takes two to tango, for the 'comfort women's' calls for financial redress from Japan so far have gone unheeded, as Japan's government and the majority of Japan's public opinion does not share the narrative of Japanese perpetratorship that is being pronounced by the Korean women.

Devleena Ghosh and Heather Goodall, in their chapter, deal with another social movement for women, the Indian women's movement and its long struggle for greater emancipation of Indian women. They demonstrate how memory activism was crucially important for the movement both after Indian independence, when memories of the earlier struggles of the movement served to underpin the conviction that independence did not bring the envisioned emancipation for women and fell far short of women activists' expectations. In subsequent decades the memory activism of members of the women movement served the purpose of strengthening the internal identity of the women's movement and in presenting a narrative of ongoing struggle and progress that helped to mobilize new generations of women on behalf of the movement. Thus, almost over the entire course of the second half of the twentieth century, memory activism was a vital ingredient of the women's movement of India.

Sophie van den Elzen and Berteke Waldijk also deal with the memory of the women's movement – in the form of histories that have been produced by activists from within the movement. They can show how such histories have contributed vitally to forging the memory of the movement – thus relativizing the gulf that is sometimes wrongly put between history and memory by both theorists of memory and theorists of history. The texts the authors have chosen construct feminism as an explicitly global movement that posited solidarity across national, racial, class, age and other boundaries. They focus in particular on strategies that sought to overcome racial boundaries within feminist movements. In contrasting the narrative strategies in histories produced by feminists before the First World War with texts that were produced from the 1980s onwards, the authors highlight efforts in the later period to overcome exclusions of race and class that still often characterized the histories written by white middle-class feminist authors around the turn of the twentieth century.[112]

If the first three chapters deal with memory issues in the women's movement, the following chapter underlines how memory activism was also crucial in the peace movement. Richard Rohrmoser in his chapter underlines the importance of the memory of the Second World War for the German peace movement of the 1980s. In fact, both the peace movement and those in favour of stationing new nuclear missiles on German territory argued with history and memory in order to justify their respective positions. As the author argues, the verdict of the constitutional court in 1995 on the legitimacy of peaceful resistance to the stationing of new missiles vindicated the memory activism of the peace movement as the court seemed to follow the logic of their memory-based arguments and memory-driven actions in the 1980s. Like the previous chapter this one also demonstrates how history and understandings as well as representations of history can serve as a powerful memory discourse.

The chapter on joint British-Australian atomic bomb testings in Australia by David Lowe highlights the role of the memory of the terrible environmental and human costs of those tests as a powerful resource of the anti-nuclear, environmental and aboriginal social movements in Australia. He peels back the layers of memory of different groups and institutions, official state memory as well as the memory of diverse groups from within civil society to highlight the role of popular Australian nationalism and the impact of colonial legacies on the memory of atomic bomb testing that had been initially combined with strong utopias about Australia's future role in world politics and its access to nuclear weapons and a nuclear-powered future. Social movements, Lowe shows, very successfully remediated the official government investigation report on the nuclear testing in order to establish a particular narrative highlighting the environmental and human costs of the tests, which serve as negative counterfoil to the aims of the anti-nuclear, environmental and aboriginal social movements in Australia.

Environmentalism and memory already looms large in Lowe's chapter and it moves centre stage with Iain Mcintyre's chapter on the role of song in the memory of the US-American environmental movement Earth First between 1980 and 1995. Drawing on diverse traditions of protest songs, both from the US and internationally, song, sometimes deliberately commemorating specific events, became a powerful means of memorializing the movement and providing strength and re-assurance to its members. Consciously and unconsciously the Earth First activists built lines of traditions to earlier activists inside and outside the US, from the First World War to American folk song, Native American songs and European radical and popular protest songs ranging back to the pre-industrial era. Song, as McIntyre underlines, was also a powerful way of highlighting the plight of nature in the industrial era and of harking back to a glorified pre-industrial past that was often treated with high doses of nostalgia in the song culture of the movement. Songs are an important repertoire of social movement memory.[113]

From Environmentalism we move to urban social movements in the chapter by Christian Wicke comparing the Green Bans in Sydney with the urban social movement trying to protect traditional working-class housing in the Ruhr area of Germany. In both cases, heritage activism played an important role in the prevention of urban renewal measures. Wicke suggests three different perspectives on the relations between collective memory and social movements: the role of memory within social movements, how social movements are publicly remembered, and how historical cultures have been shaped by social movements. He demonstrates that these three sets of social movement memory are in practice intertwined, and that this connection is dependent on movement leadership, as particular activists assume greater agency in generating and prolonging memory.

As Wicke shows in his chapter, the discovery of postindustrial aesthetics and rediscovery of West Germany's working-class past in the context of the radical student movement and the emergence of new social movements paved the way for the conservation of industrial heritage in the Ruhr from the late 1960s. Sarah Langwald's chapter, however, highlights the stark anti-Communism of the previous decade in West-German history and the attempts of a small band of activists to use the memory of anti-fascism in order to counter the prevalent anti-Communism in mainstream West-German society during the 1950s and into the 1960s. Looking at trials of Communists in West Germany, she shows how the defence of the accused Communists tried to mediate between the Communist memory of the National Socialist past and the judges' memory – with many judges having already served as judges under National Socialism. The judges' insistence on juridifying the trials, Langwald argues, was one way of deflecting from their own perpetratorship in the years before 1945. While the Communist defendants, with the help of the East-German government, attempted to de-mask the judges, the left-liberal attorneys, often with the help of the liberal media in West Germany, attempted to open a space where the National Socialist past could be discussed more widely in German society, thereby helping to pave the way for a different memory discourse in Germany that was to break the long silence about the complicity of West German elites in the barbarous Nazi regime.

In the following chapter we stay with the German labour movement but move backwards in time, to the Weimar Republic. Jule Ehms here asks about the memory of those workers who had died in the defence of the republic against the right-wing Kapp Putsch in March 1920. Often that memory was closely connected to longer-term memorial practices within the labour movement going back to the pre-First World War years, when the labour movement regularly remembered those who had fallen in the German revolution of 1848/9 and the victims of persecution under the Anti-Socialist Laws between 1878 and 1890. While initially the divided labour movement in Weimar remembered the victims of right-wing violence together, very soon the memory politics of Social Democrats, Communists and Anarcho-Syndicalists began to diverge sharply. The memory of those who died in March 1920 was now underpinning very different narratives about the republic and the attitude of the left towards the republic – foreshadowing the lack of unity in the defence of Weimar in the early 1930s. Memory in this chapter is revealed as a potential divisive force within social movements that does not only unite but also underpins splits and divisions.

The next three chapters of the book all stick with labour movement memory. Liam Byrne uses autobiographical accounts of two prominent Australian Labour leaders to show how they carried out memory battles as interventions in contemporary Australian politics in the 1960s. He focusses on the memory of the famous 1916 referendum on conscription, which ended with the trade unions playing a decisive role in bringing about a 'no' vote for conscription – against the wishes of the Labor government at the time, which led to the ousting of the then Labor Prime Minister from the party and a party split. In the debates, 50 years later, surrounding conscription for the Vietnam War in the 1960s, two completely contradictory accounts of 1916 were published by the Labour reformist Jack Holloway and the Communist radical May Brodney, who both had been opposed to conscription in 1916. Byrne underlines how their memory narratives were active interventions in the politics of the 1960s showing how different wings of the labour movement used different memory narratives in order to push through particular policies also against other wings of the same movement. The Australian story from the 1960s thus nicely mirrors the story from Weimar Germany by Jule Ehms.

Sean Scalmer's chapter examines the place of 'memory' in an earlier period of Australian labour history: the struggle for the eight-hour day. Male craftworkers in Australia won the eight-hour day from the later 1850s, subsequently celebrating their achievements in annual mass processions of increasing scope and sophistication. Scalmer recovers the elaborate form of this memory politics and argues for its import to successful industrial mobilization, as other sections of the workforce also sought to win this key demand. He suggests that the annual processions served to assert publicly the value of the eight-hour standard, to draw attention to the (increasing) number of beneficiaries, to demonstrate the strength of the movement, to establish the worthiness and skills of Australian workers, to promote their unity, and to convey to labour's supporters the value of ongoing political and industrial struggle. His chapter also considers the place of generations in the memory of the eight-hour struggle, as a self-identified generation of 'eight-hour pioneers', sought to win greater recognition with the movement, and to imprint their achievements on Australian public culture.

Stefan Berger, in his chapter on the memory of the German trade union movement, provides an overview of the role that memory played as a resource for the trade unions from Imperial Germany to the present day. He argues that memory played an important role for the identity and self-assurance of the union movement in Germany until the 1970s. In Imperial Germany it was tied to the memorialization of struggles and of persecution, but with the clear perspective that ultimately victory would be theirs. In Weimar they celebrated the move of reformist trade unionism to the centre of German society – with important laws recognizing trade unions and giving them a say over social and industrial policy. After the disastrous National Socialist years, the memory of ideological divisions of trade unionism led to the formation, for the first time in German history, of a united free trade union movement in West Germany. Up until the 1970s the memory of important struggles and victories as well as defeats served as inspiration for the movement to continue on its path to improve the situation of their members and ensure better working and living conditions. However, with the economic crisis of the 1970s and the erosion of the prospects for further advances as well as the attacks on trade unionism itself, the future suddenly began to look much less bright and trade unions, focussing on defending themselves, hardly referred to memory as a resource anymore – a situation that played in the hands of its adversaries, as Berger argues.

The penultimate chapter in this volume sticks with Germany but looks at the long-term changes to German memory politics vis-à-vis its National Socialist past. It highlights the importance of organized memory activism in sustaining momentum behind the agenda of changing the paradigm of how to remember German fascism. In other words – social movements from the heart of civil society were key to long-term changes in German memory culture. However, Jenny Wüstenberg also highlights what she calls, with Aristide Zolberg, 'moments of madness', that is, specific 'impact events' (Anne Fuchs), which crystallize change and have a major transformative quality with regard to memory regimes. The dialectic between longer-term movement activities and event-based changes leads her to discuss different temporalities, which account for changes in memory paradigms brought about by memory activism.

Fitzhugh Brundage also considers long-term memory politics in a magisterial examination of the contest over history, memory and slavery in the South of the US. Placing contemporary struggles over monuments – such as the events in Charlottesville in 2017 – in a longer historical context, Brundage surveys the struggle over the Southern past from the aftermath of the Civil War until the present. In a three-step analysis, he first traces the efforts of white southerners – white clerics, Confederate veterans, white southern women – to sacralize the Civil War and to celebrate Confederate heroism and sacrifice, further establishing how this shaped the public spaces of the South and the character of its civic life. Brundage then considers the efforts of black southerners to remember and to promote black history, through the celebration of notable holidays, public processions, and especially through work within black public schools and colleges. Finally, he traces a white counter-mobilization that gathered strength from the 1980s, acting as a defender of Confederate 'heritage', and winning the increasing support of the Republican party and its elected officials. Brundage's contribution showcases the process of contentious struggle over 'memory', as well as the special value of an historical perspective on contemporary forms of memory activism.

In a stimulating epilogue, Ann Rigney – an eminent figure in memory studies – offers a rich commentary on the papers that also raises questions for further research. Overall, the chapters in this volume should be read as case studies highlighting how fruitful the bringing together of social movement studies and memory studies can be in a diversity of different ways. Methodologically, they show how a wide range of written, oral and visual material, ranging from written documents in state archives, reports by government commissions, legal documents, newspaper and other media coverage, interviews, ego-documents, such as autobiography, social movement archives, museums, monuments, as well as songs, film and television can all be used very effectively to explore the interrelationships between memory and social movements. Memory clearly had a huge role to play in the formation and endurance of social movements, and inversely, social movements made active use of memory politics in order to achieve their goals and ambitions. Examining the relationship between social movements and memory further in years to come will surely yield rich results.

Notes

1 Carol Gluck, 'Operations of Memory: 'Comfort Women' and the World,' in *Ruptured Histories: War, Memory, and the Post-Cold War in Asia*, eds. Sheila Miyoshi Jager, and Rana Mitter (Cambridge, MA: Harvard University Press, 2007), 47–77, here: 57; good examples of studies on memory activism are Jenny Wüstenberg, *Civil Society and Memory in Post-War Germany* (Cambridge: Cambridge University Press, 2017); and Yifat Gutman, *Memory Activism: Reimagining the Past for the Future in Israel/Palestine* (Nashville, TN: Vanderbilt University Press, 2017).
2 Alexander Etkind, *Warped Mourning: Stories of the Undead in the Land of the Unburied* (Stanford, CA: Stanford University Press, 2013), Chapter 9.
3 Erik Neveu, 'Memory Battles over May 68,' in *Conceptualizing Culture in Social Movement Research*, eds. Britta Baumgarten, Priska Daphi, and Peter Ulrich (London: Palgrave Macmillan, 2014), 275–299, here: 277, 295.
4 As noted in: Timothy Kubal and Rene Becerra, 'Social Movements and Collective Memory,' *Sociology Compass* 8, no. 6 (2014): 865; Frederick C. Harris, 'It Takes a Tragedy to Arouse Them: Collective Memory and Collective Action during the Civil Rights Movement,' *Social Movement Studies* 5, no. 1 (2006): 19–43, here: 19.
5 Pierre Nora, *Les Lieux de Mémoire* (7 vols.) (Paris: Gallimard, 1984–92).
6 Most notably, a shift from what Hobsbawm called 'primitive' rebellions to the modern social movements (Eric Hobsbawm, *Primitive Rebels: Studies in Archaic Forms of Social Movement in the 19th and 20th Centuries* (Manchester: Manchester University Press, 1959)) and what Rudé called a transformation from 'pre-industrial' to 'industrial' collective action (George Rudé, *The Crowd in History: A Study of Popular Disturbances in France and England 1730–1848* (New York: Wiley, 1964)). The most influential study of all was unquestionably: E.P. Thompson, *The Making of the English Working Class* (London: Gollancz, 1963).
7 Sidney Tarrow, *The Language of Contention: Revolutions in Words, 1688–2012* (Cambridge: Cambridge University Press, 2013); Charles Tilly, *Contention and Democracy in Europe, 1650–2000* (Cambridge: Cambridge University Press, 2004); Craig Calhoun, *The Roots of Radicalism: Tradition, the Public Sphere and Early Nineteenth-Century Social Movements* (Chicago, IL: University of Chicago Press, 2012).
8 Alain Tourraine, *The Voice and the Eye: An Analysis of Social Movements* (Cambridge: Cambridge University Press, 1981); Alberto Melucci, *Nomads of the Present: Social Movements and Individual Needs in Contemporary Society* (Philadelphia, PA: Temple University Press, 1989).
9 Charles Tilly and Sidney Tarrow, *Contentious Politics* (2nd rev. edn.) (Oxford: Oxford University Press, 2015); Doug McAdam, John D. McCarthy, and Mayer N. Zald, eds., *Comparative Perspectives on Social Movements: Political Opportunities, Mobilizing Structures, and Cultural Framings* (Cambridge: Cambridge University Press, 1996).
10 Nicole Doerr, 'Memory and Culture in Social Movements,' in *Conceptualizing Culture in Social Movement Research*, eds. Britta Baumgarten, Priska Daphi, and Peter Ullrich (Basingstoke: Palgrave MacMillan, 2014), 206–226.
11 As has been pointed out by several contributions to Antimo L. Farro and Henri Lustiger-Thaler, eds., *Reimagining Social Movements. From Collectives to Individuals* (Avebury: Ashgate, 2014), especially those in Part 1 entitled 'Subjectivity, Memory and Collective Action,' 15–118.
12 Ron Eyerman, 'Social Movements and Memory,' in *Routledge International Handbook of Memory Studies*, eds. Anna Lisa Tota and Trever Hagen (London: Routledge, 2015), 79–83.
13 Lorenzo Zamponi, *Social Movements, Memory and Media: Narrative in Action in the Italian and Spanish Student Movements* (Basingstoke: Palgrave MacMillan, 2019). On the interrelationship between digital media, cultural memory and social movements, see also Samuel Merrill, Emily Keightley and Priska Daphi, eds., *Social Movements,*

Cultural Memory and Digital Media. Mobilising Mediated Remembrance (Basingstoke: Palgrave MacMillan, 2020).
14 Priska Daphi, *Becoming a Movement. Identity, Narrative and Memory in the European Global Justice Movement* (New York: Rowman & Littlefield, 2017).
15 Priska Daphi and Lorenzo Zamponi, eds., *Movements and Memory*, special issue on memory and social movements of *Mobilization* 24, no. 4 (2019): 399–524.
16 Donatella della Porta and Massimiliano Andretta, *Tiago Fernandes, Eduardo Romanos and Markos Vogiatzoglou, Legacies and Memories in Movements: Justice and Democracy in Southern Europe* (Oxford: Oxford University Press, 2018).
17 Lara Leigh Kelland, *Clio's Foot Soldiers: Twentieth-Century US Social Movements and Collective Memory* (Amherst: University of Massachusetts Press, 2018).
18 Luca Manucci, *Populism and Collective Memory: Comparing Fascist Legacies in Western Europe* (London: Routledge, 2020).
19 See online, https://rememberingactivism.eu/ (accessed 19 April 2020). See also Ann Rigney, 'Remembering Hope: Transnational Activism beyond the Traumatic,' *Memory Studies* 11, no. 3 (2018): 368–380.
20 See footnote 1.
21 This is most evident in the work of Alain Touraine, as he emphasizes in: Alain Touraine, 'The Importance of Social Movements,' *Social Movement Studies* 1, no.1 (2002): 89–95, here: 89.
22 Bruno Latour, *Re-assembling the Social. An Introduction to Actor-Network Theory* (Oxford: Oxford University Press, 2005). For examples of its application to social movement studies, see the special issue of *Social Movement Studies* 17, no. 3, 'Reassembling Activism, Activating Assemblages' (2018). For Bourdieu: Neil Fligstein and Doug McAdam, *A Theory of Fields* (New York: Oxford University Press, 2012); John Michael Roberts, 'Expressive Free Speech, the State and the Public Sphere, A Bakhtinian-Deluezian Analysis of 'Public Speech' at Hyde Park,' *Social Movement Studies* 7, no. 2 (2008): 101–119. On Lefebvre's rhythmanalysis, see Samuel Merrill and Simon Lindgreen, 'The Rhythms of Social Movement Memories: The Mobilization of Silvio Meier's Activist Remembrance across Platforms,' *Social Movement Studies* (2018), doi: 10.1080/14742837.2018.1534680.
23 Maurice Halbwachs, *Les cadres sociaux de la mémoire* (Paris: Presses Universitaires de France, 1952), originally published in *Les Travaux de L'Année Sociologique* (Paris: F. Alcan, 1925).
24 For the broader transformation of the discipline, and the increasing hegemony of operationalized social science, based on social surveys, see Andrew Abbott's fascinating history of the *American Journal of Sociology* and the Chicago Sociology Department, *Department and Discipline: Chicago Sociology at One Hundred* (Chicago, IL: University of Chicago Press, 1999), especially 78, 82, 173–175. On the import of the computer to the rise of quantitative approaches in sociology, and especially social movement studies, see: John T. Crist and John D. McCarthy, "If I Had a Hammer': The Changing Methodological Repertoire of Collective Behavior and Social Movements Research,' *Mobilization* 1, no. 1 (1996): 88–92.
25 On grounded theory, see, for example: B.G. Glaser and A.L. Strauss, *The Discovery of Grounded Theory: Strategies for Qualitative Research* (Chicago, IL: Aldine, 1967). Antony Bryant and Kathy Charmaz, eds., *The SAGE Handbook of Grounded Theory* (Los Angeles, CA and London: SAGE, 2007).
26 Paula Hamilton and Lynda Shopes, eds., *Oral History and Public Memories* (Philadelphia, PA: Temple University Press, 2008); see also: Lynn Abrams, *Oral History Theory* (2nd edn) (London: Routledge, 2016).
27 'Opening Statement,' *Social Movement Studies* 1, no. 1 (2002): 5.
28 Note, for example, that of the four 'most read' articles published in *Social Movement Studies*, as assessed in February 2018, were two studies of 'Occupy' (Jenny Pickerill and John Krinsky, 'Why Does Occupy Matter?' *Social Movement Studies* 11, no. 3–4 (2012): 279–287; Sasha Costanza-Chock, 'Mic Check! Media Cultures and the

Occupy Movement,' *Social Movement Studies* 11, no. 3–4 (2012): 375–385); a third a study of alternative lifestyle movements (Ross Haenfler, Brett Johnson, and Ellis Jones, 'Lifestyle Movements: Exploring the Intersection of Lifestyle and Social Movements,' *Social Movment Studies* 11, no. 1 (2012): 1–20); and a fourth a study of 'prefiguration' in social movements that draws upon the alter-globalization movement in Barcelona (Luke Yates, 'Rethinking Prefiguration: Alternatives, Micropolitics, and Goals in Social Movements,' *Social Movement Studies* 14, no. 1 (2015): 1–21).

29 For examples of a shifting of theoretical investment in 'global movements' as successors to 'new social movements', see: Michel Wieviorka, 'After New Social Movements,' *Social Movement Studies* 4, no. 1 (2005): 1–19; Kevin McDonald, *Global Movements: Action and Culture* (Malden, MA and Oxford: Blackwell, 2006).

30 Laurajane Smith's book *Uses of Heritage* (London: Routledge, 2006) has been influential in that regard, distinguishing between authorized and non-authorized articulations of heritage. Heritage activism has also been explored in the context of de-industrialization, see, for example, Ilinca Păun Constantinescu, Dragoş Dascălu, and Cristina Sucală, 'An Activist Perspective on Industrial Heritage in Petrila, a Romanian Mining City,' in *The Public Historian* 39, no. 4 (special issue Deindustrialization, Heritage and Representations of Identity, edited by Christian Wicke, Stefan Berger, and Jana Golombek): 114–141. For recent work directly on activism over cultural heritage, see, for example, Tod Jones (eds.). *Heritage Movements in Asia: Cultural Heritage Activism, Politics, and Identity* (New York: Berghahn: 2019), K. Fouseki and M. Shehade, 'Heritage Activism and Cultural Rights: The Case of the New Acropolis Museum,' in *Heritage in Action*, eds. H. Silverman, E. Waterton, and S. Watson (Cham: Springer, 2017); Sarah De Nardi. 'Everyday Heritage Activism in Swat Valley: Ethnographic Reflections on a Politics of Hope,' *Heritage & Society* 10, no. 3 (2017): 237–258.

31 https://www.memorystudiesassociation.org/madrid-conference-2019-info-program/ [accessed 15 June 2019]

32 Endless variants of Nora's project on France have been published in the meantime and there is hardly a nation left that has not produced its variants of national realms of memory. For a review of the enormous success of the concept of 'realms of memory', see Stefan Berger and Joanna Seiffert, eds., *Erinnerungsorte: Chance, Grenzen und Perspektiven eines Erfolgskonzepts in den Kulturwissenschaften* (Essen: Klartext, 2014).

33 On war see, for example, Paul Fussell, *The Great War and Modern Memory* (Oxford: Oxford University Press, 1975); Jay Winter, *Sites of Memory: Sites of Mourning: The Great War in European Cultural History* (Cambridge: Cambridge University Press, 1995); on genocide compare, for example, Jutta Lindert and Armen T. Maarsobian, eds., *Multidisciplinary Perspectives on Memory and Genocide* (London: Springer, 2018).

34 Christian Wicke and Ben Wellings, 'History Wars in Germany and Australia: National Museums and the Relegitimisation of Nationhood,' in *The Palgrave Handbook of State-Sponsored History after 1945*, eds. Berber Bervernage and Nico Wouters (Basingtoke: Palgrave Macmillan, 2018), 431–445.

35 Jeffrey Alexander, 'Toward a Theory of Cultural Trauma,' in *Cultural Trauma and Collective Identity* (Berkeley: University of California Press, 2004), 1–30. Wulf Kansteiner. 'Genealogy of a Category Mistake: A Critical Intellectual History of the Cultural Trauma Metaphor,' *Rethinking History: The Journal of Theory and Practice* 8, no. 2 (2004): 193–221. See also Jenny Edkins, *Trauma and the Memory of Politics* (Cambridge: Cambridge University Press, 2003). The growing attention to trauma is noted in a recent survey: Kate Darian-Smith and Paula Hamilton, 'Memory and History in Twenty-first Century Australia: A Survey of the Field,' *Memory Studies* 6, no. 3 (2013): 375.

36 The strong affinity of memory studies to traumatic events such as war and genocide has also been noted by Paula Hamilton, 'The Knife Edge: Debates about Memory and History,' in *Memory and History in Twentieth Century Australia*, eds. Kate Darian-Smith and Paula Hamilton (Melbourne: Oxford University Press, 1994), 16.

37 Melissa Nobles, *The Politics of Official Apologies* (Cambridge: Cambridge University Press, 2008).
38 Michel Foucault, *Language, Counter-Memory, Practice: Selected Essays and Interviews* (Ithaca, NY: Cornell University Press, 1977). See also: Jeffrey K. Olick and Joyce Robbins, 'Social Memory Studies: From 'Collective Memory' to the Historical Sociology of Mnemonic Practices,' *Annual Review of Sociology* 24 (1998): 108, 126; James Mark, *The Unfinished Revolution: Making Sense of the Communist Past in Centraleastern Europe* (New Haven, CT: Yale University Press, 2010), xxii.
39 Ernest Renan, *Ou'est-ce qu'une nation? [Lecture at Sorbonne, 11 March 1882] in Discours et Conferences* (Paris: Caiman-Levy, 1887), 277–310; Paul Ricoer, *Memory, History, Forgetting* (Chicago, IL: University of Chicago Press, 2004).
40 Marcel van der Linden, Walking Fish: How Conservative Behaviour Generates and Processes Radical Change (Valedictory Lecture, University of Amsterdam, 27 October 2017. Published in Newsletter International Social History Association 6, no. 1 (2018): 9–14.
41 Kurt Forster, 'Aby Warburg's History of Art: Collective Memory and the Social Mediation of Images,' *Daedalus* 105, no. 1 (1976): 169–176.
42 Andreas Huyssen, *Twilight Memories: Marking Time in a Culture of Amnesia* (London: Routledge, 1995), 2 f.
43 Peter L. Berger and Thomas Luckmann, *The Social Construction of Reality: A Treatise in the Sociology of Knowledge* (New York: Anchor Books, 1966).
44 Jan Assmann, *Cultural Memory and Early Civilization: Writing, Remembrance and Political Imagination* (Cambridge: Cambridge University Press, 2011); Aleida Assmann, *Cultural Memory and Western Civilization: Arts of Memory* (Cambridge: Cambridge University Press, 2011).
45 See, for example, Elizabeth Jelin, *State Repression and the Labor of Memory* (Minneapolis: University of Minnesota Press, 2003); Richard A. Wilson, *The Politics of Truth and Reconciliation in South Africa: Legitimizing the Post-apartheid State* (Cambridge: Cambridge University Press, 2001).
46 Guy Beiner, *Forgetful Remembrance: Social Forgetting and Vernacular Historiography of a Rebellion in Ulster* (Oxford: Oxford University Press, 2018).
47 Janet Polasky, *Revolutions without Borders* (Yale: Yale University Press, 2015), 25–27.
48 Maarten Prak, *Citizens without Nations: Urban Citizenship in Europe and the World, c. 1000–1789* (Cambridge: Cambridge University Press, 2018), 44–45.
49 Joep Leerssen, *National Thought in Europe: A Cultural History* (Amsterdam: Amsterdam University Press, 2006).
50 Robert Gildea, James Mark and Annette Warring, eds., *Europe's 1968: Voices of Revolt* (Oxford: Oxford University Press, 2017); see also Ingo Cornlis and Sarah Waters, eds., *Memories of 1968: International Perspectives* (Bern: Peter Lang, 2010).
51 Renee C. Romano and Leigh Raiford, eds., *The Civil Rights Movement in American Memory* (Athens and Georgia: The University of Georgia Press, 2006).
52 Andrea Hajek, *Negotiating Memory of Protest in Western Europe: The Case of Italy* (Basingstoke: Palgrave MacMillan, 2013). One of the most canonical works in the field of memory studies unpacks the various ways in which the death of an Italian Communist has been remembered: Alessandro Portelli, *The Death of Luigi Trastulli and Other Stories* (Albany: State University of New York Press, 1991).
53 Berber Bevernage, *History, Memory and State-Sponsored Violence. Time and Justice* (London: Routledge, 2012).
54 Astrid Erll and Ann Rigney, eds., *Mediation, Remediation and the Dynamics of Cultural Memories* (Berlin: De Gruyter, 2009).
55 Christian Wicke, Stefan Berger, and Jana Golombek, eds., *Industrial Heritage and Regional Identities* (London: Routledge, 2018).
56 https://petapixel.com/2017/01/21/artist-shames-disrespectful-holocaust-memorial-tourists-using-photoshop/ [accessed 15 June 2019]

57 Richard Vinen, *The Long '68: Radical Protest and Its Enemies* (London: Allen Lane, 2018), quotes on 7 and 11.
58 Charles Tilly, 'Getting it Together in Burgundy, 1675–1975,' *Theory and Society* 4, no. 4 (1977): 479–504.
59 Charles Tilly, *Regimes and Repertoires* (Chicago, IL and London: University of Chicago Press, 2006), 35.
60 Tilly sometimes called it the 'social movement repertoire'. For example, Charles Tilly, *Social Movements, 1768–2004* (Boulder, CO and London: Paradigm Publishers, 2004), 31. His major works on the repertoire include: Charles Tilly, *The Contentious French: Four Centuries of Popular Struggle* (Cambridge, MA: Harvard University Press, 1986); Charles Tilly, *Popular Contention in Great Britain, 1758–1834* (Cambridge, MA: Harvard University Press, 1995); Tilly, *Regimes and Repertoires*; Charles Tilly, *Contentious Performances* (Cambridge and New York: Cambridge University Press, 2008).
61 Tilly, *Contentious Performances*, 45.
62 Sean Scalmer, *Gandhi in the West: The Mahatma and the Rise of Radical Protest* (Cambridge and New York: Cambridge University Press, 2011); Sean Chabot, 'Transnational Diffusion and the African American Reinvention of the Gandhian Repertoire,' *Mobilization* 5, no. 2 (2000): 201–216.
63 Michael Biggs, 'How Repertoires Evolve: The Diffusion of Suicide Protest in the Twentieth Century,' *Mobilization* 18, no. 4 (2013): 407–428.
64 Jeroen Van Laer and Peter Van Aelst, 'Internet and Social Movement Action Repertoires: Opportunities and limitations,' *Information, Communication and Society* 13 (2010): 1146–1171.
65 Graham St John, 'Protestival: Global Days of Action and Carnivalized Politics in the Present,' *Social Movement Studies* 7, no. 2 (2008): 167–190.
66 Daniel J. Sherman, 'Disruption or Convention? A Process-based Explanation of Divergent Repertoires of Contention among Opponents to Low-level Radioactive Waste Disposal Sites,' *Social Movement Studies* 7, no. 3 (2008): 265–280.
67 Theresa Ann Hunt, 'A Movement Divided: SlutWalks, Protest Repertoires and the Privilege of Nudity,' *Social Movement Studies* 17, no. 5 (2018): 541–557.
68 Lee A. Smithey and Michael P. Young, 'Parading Protest: Orange Parades in Northern Ireland and Temperance Parades in Antebellum America,' *Social Movement Studies* 9, no. 4 (2010): 393–410.
69 A point made in Biggs, 'How Repertoires Evolve, 407.
70 See especially: James M. Jasper and Jan Willem Duyvendak, eds., *Players and Arenas: The Interactive Dynamics of Protest* (Amsterdam: Amsterdam University Press, 2015). Jasper notes (approvingly) the move to 'micro' studies in his introductory chapter to that volume, 'Introduction: Playing the Game,' 9–10. The strategic approach has especially been advanced by James Jasper in works such as: 'A Strategic Approach to Collective Action: Looking for Agency in Social-Movement Choices,' *Mobilization* 9 (2004): 1–16 and *Getting Your Way: Strategic Dilemmas in the Real World* (Chicago, IL: University of Chicago Press, 2006).
71 Ruth Cardoso, 'Building Senses of "Community": Social Memory, Popular Movements, and Political Participation,' *Vibrant: Virtual Brazilian Anthropology* 10, no. 1 (2013), https://doi.org/10.1590/S1809-43412013000100006, [accessed 2 June 2020].
72 Raluca Abăseacă, 'Collective Memory and Social Movements in Times of Crisis: The Case of Romania,' *Nationalities Papers* 46, no. 4 (2018): 671–684.
73 Kubal and Becerra, 'Social Movements and Collective Memory,' 865–875.
74 Ann Rigney, 'Plenitude, Scarcity and the Circulation of Cultural Memory,' *Journal of European Studies* 35, no. 1 (2005): 11–28, here: 16.
75 Within the field of 'memory studies' this is most influentially put in Michael Rothberg's emphasis on 'multi-directional memory' and the borrowing of memories and

strategies between groups. See: Michael Rothberg, *Multidirectional Memory: Remembering the Holocaust in the Age of Decolonisation* (Stanford, CA: Stanford University Press, 2009).
76 Charles Tilly, 'Event Catalogs as Theories,' *Sociological Theory* 20, no. 2 (2002): 248–254.
77 See, for example: William H. Sewell, Jr., 'Historical Events as Transformations of Structures: Inventing Revolution at the Bastille,' *Theory and Society* 25 (1996): 841–881; Doug McAdam and William H. Sewell Jr., 'It's About Time: Temporality in the Study of Social Movements and Revolutions,' in *Silence and Voice in the Study of Contentious Politics*, ed. Ronald R. Aminzade, et al. (Cambridge and New York: Cambridge University Press, 2001).
78 Sewell, 'Historical events,' 844.
79 Ibid., 844.
80 Ibid., 861, 871.
81 Ibid., 861, 865, 867–868.
82 Ibid., 859.
83 Ibid., 852–853.
84 This relatively exclusive interest in the 'ongoing interpretation of events' is also evident in the otherwise insightful discussion advanced in McAdam and Sewell, 'It's About Time,' 118.
85 Etkind, *Warped Mourning*, Chapter 9.
86 Anne Fuchs, *After the Dresden Bombing: Pathways of Memory 1945 to the Present* (London: Palgrave Macmillan, 2014), 10.
87 Helmut Schelsky, *Die Skeptische Generation: Soziologie der deutschen Jugend* (Dusseldorf and Cologne: Diederichs, 1957); Dirk Moses, *German Intellectuals and the Nazi Past* (Cambridge: Cambridge University Press, 2009).
88 Christoph H. Schwarz, 'Collective Memory and Intergenerational Transmission in Social Movements: The "Grandparents' Movement" iaioflautas, the indignados Protests, and the Spanish Transition,' *Memory Studies*, published online 19 June 2019, https://doi.org/10.1177/1750698019856058.
89 Kimberly A. Longfellow, 'Social Movements and Memory: Education, Age and the Memories of the Women's Movement,' *Gettysburg Social Sciences Review* 1, no. 1 (2017), https://cupola.gettysburg.edu/gssr/vol1/iss1/3 [accessed 2 June 2020].
90 Hélène le Dantec Lowrie and Ambre Ivol, eds., *Generations of Social Movements: The Left and Historical Memory in the USA and France* (London: Routledge, 2016).
91 Anna Wiemann, 'Making Memory by Disassociating the Past from the Present: Narratives of Movement Intellectuals of the Post-Fukushima Protest Cycle in Japan. Research Note,' *International Quarterly for Asian Studies* 50, no. 1–2 (2019): 157–169.
92 Karl Mannheim, 'The Problem of Generations,' in *Essays on the Sociology of Knowledge: Collected Works* (Volume 5), ed. Paul Kecskemeti (New York: Routledge, 1952), 276–322. Originally published in German in 1928. The quote is on 286 f.
93 Lutz Niethammer, *Kollektive Identität: Heimliche Quellen einer unheimliche Konjunktur* (Reinbek bei Hamburg: Rowohlt, 2000).
94 John R. Gillis, 'Identity and Memory: The History of a Relationship,' Introduction to *Commemorations: The Politics of National Identity* (Princeton, NJ: Princeton University Press, 1994), 3–24; Jan Assmann, 'Kollektives Gedächtnis und kulturelle Identität,' in *Kultur und Gedächtnis*, eds. Jan Assmann and Tonio Hölscher (Frankfurt am Main 1988), 9–19.
95 Sheldon Stryker, Timothy J. Owens, and Robert W. White, eds., *Self, Identity and Social Movements* (Minneapolis: University of Minnesota Press, 2000); David S. Meyer, Nancy Whittier, and Belinda Robnett, eds., *Social Movements: Identity, Culture and the State* (Oxford: Oxford University Press, 2002); Jo Reger, Daniel J. Myers, and Rachel L. Einwohner, eds., *Identity Work in Social Movements* (Minneapolis: University of Minnesota Press, 2008).

96 Christina Flesher Fominaya, 'Collective Identity in Social Movements: Central Concepts and Debates,' *Sociology Compass* 4 (2010): 393–404.
97 Dieter Rucht, Kollektive Identität: Konzeptionelle Überlegungen zum Desiderat in der Bewegungsforschung, *Forschungsjournal NSB* 8, no. 1 (1995): 9–23.
98 Alexander Kluge and Oskar Negt, *The Proletarian Public Sphere as a Historical Counterconcept to the Bourgeois Public Sphere* (London: Verso, 2016).
99 Bart van der Steen and Knut Andreesen, *A European Youth Revolt: European Perspectives on Youth Protest and Social Movements in the 1980s* (Basingtoke: Palgrave, 2016).
100 Elizabeth A. Armstrong and Suzanna M. Crage, 'Movements and Memory: The Making of the Stonewall Myth,' *American Sociological Review* 71, no. 5 (2006): 724–751.
101 Jan Plamper, *The History of Emotions: An Introduction* (Oxford: Oxford University Press, 2015).
102 James Jasper, 'Emotions and Social Movements: Twenty Years of Theory and Research,' *Annual Review of Sociology* 37 (2011): 285–303.
103 For example, Alex Sergeui Oushakine, 'Remembering the Public: On the Affective Management of History,' *Ab Imperio* 1 (2013): 269–302.
104 Ute Frevert, 'Comment: History of Emotions,' in *Debating New Approaches to History*, eds. Tamm and Burke (London and Oxford: Bloomsbury, 2018), 202–208; see also Ute Frevert, *Emotions in History: Lost and Found* (Budapest: Central European University Press, 2001); Ute Frevert, ed., *Emotional Lexicons. Continuity and Change in the Vocabulary of Feeling, 1700 – 2000* (Oxford: Oxford University Press, 2014).
105 William M. Reddy, *The Navigation of Feeling. A Framework for the History of Emotions* (Cambridge: Cambridge University Press, 2001), 144 ff.
106 Deborah B. Gould, *Moving Politics: Emotion and ACT UP's Fight against AIDS* (Chicago, IL: University of Chicago Press, 2009).
107 Randall Collins, 'Social Movements and the Focus of Emotional Attention,' in *Passionate Politics: Emotions and Social Movements*, eds. Jeff Goodwin, James M. Jasper, and Francesca Polletta (Chicago, IL: University of Chicago Press, 2001), Chapter 1.
108 Daniel Reisberg and Paul Hertel, eds., *Memory and Emotion* (Oxford: Oxford University Press, 2004).
109 Tea Sindbæck Anderson and Barbara Törnquist Plewa, eds., *Disputed Memory: Emotions and Memory Politics in Central, Eastern and Southeastern Europe* (Berlin: DeGruyter, 2016).
110 Mihaela Mihai, *Negative Emotions and Transitional Justice* (New York: Columbia University Press, 2016).
111 On human rights and memory compare Daniel Levy and Natan Sznaider, *Human Rights and Memory* (University Park: The Pennsylvania State University Press, 2010).
112 Compare also Red Chidgey, *Feminist Afterlives: Assemblage Memory in Activist Times* (Basingstoke: Palgrave MacMillan, 2018), on how popular feminist memories have travelled through a diversity of media and institutions in the twentieth and twenty-first centuries.
113 See also Ron Eyerman and Andrew Jamison, *Music and Social Movements. Mobilizing Traditions in the Twentieth Century* (Cambridge: Cambridge University Press, 1998).

2

THE ASCENSION OF 'COMFORT WOMEN' IN SOUTH KOREAN COLONIAL MEMORY

Lauren Richardson

Introduction

The former so-called 'comfort women' occupy a preeminent position in South Korean memory of colonialism.[1] Their historical sexual subjugation at the hands of Japanese imperial forces has, in many respects, become emblematic of the brutality that characterized Japan's colonial regime on the Korean peninsula (1910–45). The ascendant status of comfort women in national memory has manifested in manifold ways. Statues commemorating their victimhood stand in symbolic locations around the country, most notably in front of Japan's two diplomatic missions in South Korea. Public discourse has moreover privileged the plight of comfort women over other victims of Japanese colonial policies. And at the level of the state, the matter of redress for these women has dominated Seoul's diplomatic agenda vis-à-vis Tokyo since the turn of the century.

Given that the primary victimization of Korean comfort women occurred in the context of Japan's imperial expansion in the 1930s and 1940s, it may come of some surprise that their ascension in colonial memory has been a relatively recent phenomenon. The comfort women system was only substantially incorporated into South Korean narratives of colonialism in the early 1990s. Up until then, this episode of history was shrouded in silence and the victimhood of the women remained largely unrecognized by the public and officials alike. This prolonged period of non-recognition cannot simply be fathomed in terms of historical amnesia. In the post-liberation milieu of South Korea, many of the comfort women were in fact willfully shunned by their families and communities. Government officials, for their part, were disinclined to bring the issue to light despite their cognizance of the women's fate under colonialism. It can thus be said that the virtual absence of the comfort women in national memory was more a function of suppression than oblivion.

How then were these women ultimately integrated in and able to achieve ascendancy in South Korea's national memory of colonialism? And why did this occur at the late juncture of the 1990s? This chapter argues that central to such outcomes was the development of a comfort women advocacy movement in South Korea and its effective framing of victimhood. While the movement quickly took on international dimensions, it was the efforts of activists in the domestic sphere that played the definitive role in shaping national memory. Leaders of the South Korean movement initially coaxed the reluctant victims forward, framed and politicized their plight, and ultimately transformed public perceptions of their colonial adversity. They also established a repertoire of contention that came to be adopted and adapted by comfort women advocates around the world. The agency of the movement was facilitated by the structural transformation engendered by South Korea's democratic transition in the late 1980s, and a subsequent global normative shift toward the protection of women from violence.

This chapter aims to elucidate how the movement shaped national memory of the comfort women. It draws on fieldwork undertaken in South Korea from 2009 to 2012, including interviews conducted with the victims and movement leaders. The chapter begins by delineating the contours of marginalization of the former comfort women in post-liberated South Korea. It then traces the emergence of the advocacy movement and analyzes its framing strategy. Next, it turns to assessing the impact of this strategy on national memory. Finally, and to further illustrate the centrality of the movement in shaping memory, the chapter examines the counterfactual case of former comfort women in China, where a full-fledged domestic advocacy movement has yet to emerge.

Memory of comfort women in post-liberated South Korea

The colonial ordeal endured by comfort women was largely a non-issue in post-liberated South Korea. This was not so much a consequence of social oblivion of Japan's comfort women system as it was the highly stigmatized nature of it. The defining attributes of this system—the provision of sexual services to Japanese soldiers by young Korean women—served to challenge and contravene an array of Confucian and patriarchal codes. The resultant stigma that marked the women, coupled with the dictates of authoritarian rule, functioned to suppress this historical episode in national memory for a number of decades.

Traditional patriarchal norms of female sexuality in South Korea (and the Korean peninsula more broadly) emphasize chastity and prescribe that women remain virgins until marriage. Those who served as comfort women under Japan's imperial reign in Korea—typically young, unmarried females—were thus considered tainted or promiscuous by their compatriots. Such perceptions encouraged the women to self-censor their colonial adversity after emancipation from Japanese rule. As relayed by one former comfort woman, 'in Korea, it was said that if a woman couldn't protect her chastity, her village would be cursed;

I therefore felt ashamed and didn't want to tell anyone.'[2] In fact, some women did not even venture to return to their communities in the knowledge that they would be unwelcome. This tendency toward concealment was reinforced by the fact that most of the women were at marrying age—in their early 20s—when liberated from the military brothels, and feared that their 'shameful' pasts would preclude them from entering wedlock. While some of the former comfort women succeeded in keeping their colonial experiences buried throughout the course of their lives, those whose identities were revealed were oftentimes renounced by their husbands and parents.[3]

There was furthermore a nationalist facet to Korean patriarchal ideology that served to marginalize the comfort women in national memory. This was centered on a notion that the sexuality of Korean women belonged to Korean men.[4] Given that the comfort women system was masterminded by the Japanese imperial government and primarily catered to Japanese soldiers, in many ways the system symbolized the subservience and disempowerment of Korean men to their (foreign) colonial overlord. Adding a further layer of complexity was that Korean middlemen often facilitated the recruitment of the women, albeit guided by colonial power structure. As Bruce Cumings observes, 'to open an inquiry on this sexual slavery would be to find that many women were mobilized by Korean men. Japan fractured the Korean national psyche, pitting Korean against Korean.'[5] That women and girls had been recruited from their homes, schools, and villages posed an additional challenge to Korean patriarchal culture by calling into question the protective role assigned to males.

The context of decolonization in South Korea was similarly unconducive to public and official recognition of the victimhood of comfort women. As part of the process of reclaiming national identity and negating the colonial experience, Koreans who had migrated to the colonial metropole under Japanese rule and/or had served the colonial government or imperial army in any capacity—regardless of how that eventuated or the power relationship at play—were subject to perceptions and accusations of traitorship and collaboration. This of course applied to the comfort women and it also extended, among others, to the Koreans who were mobilized to carry out labor in Japan's military industrial factories. Female laborers in particular recall being treated with contempt on account of their 'work' under colonialism having contravened the Confucian code of virtue.[6]

Owing to a combination of these factors, the comfort women system was a sensitive subject for the post-colonial, authoritarian South Korean government, and officials were reluctant to draw attention to it. This was evinced in Seoul's negotiations over the normalization of its diplomatic relations with Tokyo, a process which was conducted between 1951 and 1965. A central agenda of these fraught and protracted talks was the issue of compensation for the civilian victims of Japanese colonial policies. Declassified records of these negotiations reveal that, although the two governments deliberated at length about the forced laborers, the comfort women did not receive a mention.[7] This was partially a reflection of the fact that the victimhood of the women had yet to be publicly or officially recognized. Even if the women had mobilized to demand recognition and redress at this juncture, the government presumably would have been unreceptive to their claims. Indeed, then President Park Chung-hee invoked martial law on two occasions to quell civil unrest in relation to the terms of the normalization settlement. Ultimately he forced the treaty bill through Korea's National Assembly and thus finalized all civilian redress claims with Tokyo on his citizenry's behalf.

In short, throughout the post-colonial period, there was little room in national memory for the highly stigmatized comfort women, and likewise for the various other specific categories of victims in Korea. Remembrance was focused, rather, on the colonial victimization and exploitation of the populace at large. Historical episodes with shameful associations served no particular utility for a society and government grappling to restore national integrity and remove the vestiges of colonialism. It would be decades before the socio-political context would become amenable to the integration of comfort women into the terrain of colonial memory.

The emergence of the comfort women redress movement

As South Korea began its democratic transition in the late 1980s, opportunities materialized for activists to shape not only the government agenda, but also national history narratives. A comfort women advocacy movement led by female Korean intellectuals emerged against this backdrop.[8] In its incipient stages this movement was critical in coaxing the women forward and eliciting and compiling their testimonies. These efforts laid the foundation for the public and official recognition of the victimhood of comfort women in South Korea and beyond.

Democratization, provided the structural context for the mobilization of advocacy movements in South Korea, much like the effect of historical events conceived by Sewell.[9] Following years of civil discontent with oppressive governmental policies, a nationwide struggle against the authoritarian leadership unfolded in the late 1970s. This was marked by a decade of violent clashes between the state and society, and characterized by martial law, military coups, widescale protests and tear gas. Ultimately the civil uprising prevailed, ushering in the beginnings of democratic transition in 1987. A corollary of this process was the gradual emergence of a rights-based culture, enabling activists to make claims for recognition vis-à-vis the state. T. A. Jacoby describes the political opportunities that democratization brings to victims as follows:

> In democracies people mobilize politically given greater rights consciousness and higher expectations that the political system will be responsive to their plight. Victims expect their struggles to produce positive results in a democracy [as it] offers avenues for expressions of dissatisfaction and anger through the political process as opposed to against it, providing greater opportunity for reform as opposed to violence and revolution.[10]

Networked advocacy on behalf of comfort women first sprouted in South Korea in the context of this transition to democracy, and amidst a growing national feminist movement. Up until the early 1970s, issues of sexual violence and prostitution had not been a focal point among Korean feminists. With the rise of *kisaeng* sex tourism in 1973, however, a transformation began in feminist consciousness.[11] This form of tourism catered in part to the influx of male Japanese tourists in Korea following diplomatic normalization, and served to trigger protests among Korean Christians and feminist activists.[12] By 1983, a group known as Korea Church Women United published a survey on this 'prostitution tourism,' deeming it 'an affront to humanity' that was effectively 'stripping the human dignity' from Korean women.[13] A series of events that ensued in Korean society at around the same time served to highlight the relationship between power and sexual violence. These included a 1986 court case filed by a female student against the Korean government on charges of sex torture. Two years later, the Korea Church Women United revealed that they had conducted an investigation into the comfort women system and presented the findings of such at an international seminar on women in tourism, which was held in Seoul. A combination of these developments prompted feminists in South Korea to conceive of the historical comfort women system within a framework of sexual violence.

Although none of the former comfort women were willing to identify as such and speak publicly of their ordeal at this time, Korean feminist intellectuals began campaigning on their behalf. Yun Chung-ok, a female professor at South Korea's Ewha Womans University, was instrumental in encouraging public recognition—and, by extension, destigmatization—of the victims. After meeting and exchanging information with a Japanese journalist and fellow feminist, Matsui Yayori,[14] Yun initiated her own research into the comfort women system. She published her findings from this as a series of reports in a Korean newspaper in 1990.[15] In the same year, Yun with the help of a number of feminist activists in South Korea institutionalized their support for former comfort women through the establishment of the Korean Council for the Women Drafted for Military Sexual Slavery (hereafter the Korean Council).[16]

In the context of Seoul's burgeoning economic partnership with Tokyo, garnering official recognition of the victims proved to be a more formidable challenge for their advocates. The South Korean government's initial response to the movement was tepid, and Japanese officials, meanwhile, denied the official involvement of the imperial government in the comfort women system. Spurred by Tokyo's reluctance to admit culpability, one of the former Korean comfort woman, Kim Hak-soon, came forward in August 1991 and relayed her colonial adversity through a widely publicized press conference.[17] This watershed event helped to break the shackles of stigma surrounding the issue and prompted other women to identify and speak out as victims. As one such woman relayed, 'I started to realise that it was not I who should be ashamed but the Korean and Japanese governments.'[18]

In light of the victims' testimonies and increasing media interest in the issue, the society, and government of South Korea were compelled to reckon with the notion that the colonial experience of comfort women entailed unique adversities relative to that of the general populace. This reckoning gave rise to the official recognition of comfort women as victims, a development that served to transpose the issue to the diplomatic realm. Within months of Kim Hak-soon's press conference, the South Korean government had begun to press Japanese officials to conduct fact-finding into the issue and express remorse toward the women. While it is beyond the scope of this chapter to discuss the diplomatic consequences of these developments, suffice it to say that within a few short years, the matter of redress for comfort women was threatening to unravel the two countries' interstate relations.

How the movement shaped colonial memory

Once the predicament of comfort women had been acknowledged in various sectors of South Korean society and government, a gradual shift occurred in national memory of colonialism. This entailed the integration of specific categories of victims into the narrative of the victimization of the general populace. Driving this shift was a growing recognition that these victim categories—which included former comfort women, forced laborers and atomic bomb victims—had borne the brunt of Japanese imperial policies. However, as Jacoby argues, 'being recognized as a victim is a right and even arguably, a privilege, not bestowed equally on all injured people.'[19] Indeed, a hierarchy soon emerged among the various categories of victims, with the former comfort women attracting the greatest sympathy and support and also more media attention. The historical subjugation of these women to Japanese soldiers ultimately evolved to become emblematic of South Korea's colonial domination by Japan. This memory shift can largely be attributed to the framing strategy employed by the comfort women movement, which imbued the issue both with domestic and international resonance.

Frames act as schemata of interpretation of an issue and are thus essential to any advocacy movement. As David Snow et al. describe, they function to help 'attract participants, allies, supporters, and media attention in order to influence political discourse and change.'[20] The victimization of comfort women was framed by the Korean Council at the outset of the movement as a human rights violation. This was evidenced in the parlance of the redress demands that they issued to Tokyo: 'acknowledge the war crime,' 'reveal the truth about… crimes of military sexual slavery,' and 'make legal reparations.'[21] This framing was reinforced at a practical level through the convening of biannual 'human rights camps' at the House of Sharing, a nursing home for former comfort women in South Korea.[22] These five-day/four-night camps have aimed to inspire the younger generation to learn the 'historical facts' of the comfort women system and to transmit them to posterity. Over the course of such camps, participants are familiarized with an onsite museum, introduced to the victims residing at the home, and encouraged to engage in group discourse about the issue.[23]

The narrative accompanying this frame is embodied in the various comfort women statues erected by the movement. The most notable of such statues have taken the form of young girls dressed in traditional Korean garb (*hanbok*), sitting placidly—yet with clenched fists—while staring reproachfully at Japan's diplomatic missions. The narrative portrayed in these statues is one of virgin Korean girls having being robbed of their innocence when compelled to sexually submit to the demands of Japan's imperial soldiers. This poses a challenge to the narratives espoused by right-wing elements in Japan, which commonly depict the former comfort women as prostitutes who offered their services autonomously. The international media attention attracted by the statues has enabled the movement to disseminate its narrative of the comfort women system to an ever-widening audience; it has also had the socio-political effect of conferring shame on the Japanese government. The statues installed by the movement in front of Japan's Embassy and Consulate in South Korea have functioned as a continuous act of resistance to Japanese officials and their reluctance to conform with the movements' redress demands.

The chief factor that informed this framing strategy was the input of South Korean intellectuals, such as retired professor Yun Chung-ok, who were well-versed in the vernacular of human rights. The universality of this concept was useful both in appealing to international justice forums about the plight of comfort women, and in ensuring that the issue would not be conceived of as a mere intra-Asian problem. In effect, the human rights frame also served to recast the predicament of comfort women as a contemporary issue, countering Tokyo's treatment of it as a postwar reparations matter to be dealt with in accordance with the normalization treaty. And finally, as many of the comfort women had been recruited from poor rural families, they were undereducated and lacked the discursive tools to articulate their victimization; the human rights discourse provided a framework for relaying the details of their victimization.

The frame's resonance was enhanced by a global normative shift toward the recognition of women's rights as human rights and the protection of women from violence. This shift was geared toward overturning the conception of sexual violence in conflict as the inevitable collateral damage of war. It was ushered in with the enactment of a number of UN resolutions aimed at the protection of women from human rights abuse, which occurred around the time that the first comfort woman spoke out. These included the Vienna Declaration and Programme of Action (VDPA) and the Declaration on the Elimination of Violence Against Women,[24] both of which came into effect in 1993. Hilary Clinton featured prominently in this 'third wave of feminism,' in her capacity as First Lady of the United States, famously declaring in a 1995 speech at the Fourth World Conference on Women in Beijing: 'let it be that human rights are women's rights and women's rights are human rights, once and for all.'[25] The advocacy movement in South Korea would only benefit from this normative shift to the extent that it was able to align the comfort women issue with such understandings, and to link their victimization with that of other female victims of conflict. Leaders of the movement succeeded in this regard by submitting an appeal to the United Nations Secretary-General and the Sub-Commission on the Promotion and Protection of Human Rights in Geneva, and framing the comfort women issue in human rights terms. This led to two official UN inquiries into the comfort women system, the results of which were published in 1993 and 1996, and the emergence of the issue as a prominent UN agenda.

In the context of these international developments, it became increasingly evident that national consciousness of the plight of former comfort women in South Korea was converging with the movement's framing of the issue, specifically with regard to the violation of the women's human rights by Japan and the attendant claim to state compensation. This was revealed in South Korea's domestic reactions to the Japanese government's first attempt at a resolution of the issue. In response to mounting international pressure to redress to former comfort women, Japanese officials lent tacit support to the establishment of an Asian Women's Fund (AWF) in 1994; this initiative, which entailed substantial civic involvement in Japan, aimed to provide atonement money to victims in South Korea, Taiwan, the Philippines, Indonesia, and the Netherlands. Yet leaders of the Korean Council vehemently rejected the AWF on the grounds that the funds being extended to individual victims were not drawn from government coffers but were constituted of donations from ordinary Japanese citizens. From the perspective of the Korean Council, this was tantamount to an evasion of legal responsibility on the part of Japan, and an inadequate redress measure for victims of a human rights violation. The South Korean public and media vigorously supported the movement's interpretation of the AWF, by and large, criticizing the Fund on similar grounds. The former comfort women, who dared to apply for the Fund against stern warnings from their advocates, were ultimately ostracized by society and branded 'turncoats.'[26] In this way, the issue had become less about the pursuit of redress for individual victims and more about national recompense for Japanese transgressions against (South) Korea. In other words, the victimization of comfort women had become the basis of a collective identity in relation to the colonial past.

This is not to suggest that South Korean society came to uniformly accept and uphold the movement's narrative of the comfort women system. In fact, recent years have witnessed a number of attempts by Korean academics to challenge prevailing accounts of the specifics of this system. However, the movement's narrative has become so deeply entrenched in the social, political, and legal fabric of South Korea that individuals who publicly deny or attempt to significantly nuance any aspect of it have typically been subjected to punitive legal action. The most obvious example of this phenomenon is the litigation battle that has been playing out between Park Yuha, a female history professor at Sejong University in Seoul, and nine of the former comfort women since 2014. Park's controversial book, *Comfort Women of the Empire*, takes the movement's narrative to task, particularly in relation to the methods by and circumstances under which the women were mobilized and recruited.[27] Consequently she was indicted for defamation by the victims and pronounced guilty by the Seoul High Court in October 2017. The court proceedings, which remain ongoing, have drawn considerable international attention: academics from Japan and the United States issued a statement of protest to the South Korean judiciary in 2018, penned by Noam Chomsky, pronouncing the trial 'injust and improper.'[28] In a less publicized case, a professor at South Korea's Sunchon National University was handed a six-month jail sentence for making 'blasphemous' comments about the former comfort women in a 2017 lecture. The professor in question, whose name was withheld by the court, described the recruitment of comfort women as follows: they were 'taken for sexual slavery, or they voluntarily followed [the Japanese soldiers] because they were seductive,' and they 'probably had a clear idea of what they had to do.'[29] More recently, in September 2019, a sociologist at South Korea's prestigious Yonsei University found himself locked out of his lecture theater after drawing certain parallels between former comfort women and modern day prostitutes during an earlier class that was recorded by students.[30] Evidently, academics who willingly challenge the narrative propounded by the comfort women movement in South Korea now do so at great risk to their careers and livelihoods.

It is clear that the movement's achievements have extended well beyond the integration of comfort women in national memory. The narrative of victimization disseminated by the Korean Council, with its roots in the human rights discourse, has been crystallized in the form of comfort women statues and dominates public perceptions of the issue. This narrative has not only become salient in South Korean society today, but has also pervaded the executive and judicial branches of government and the international community more broadly.[31] While the human rights frame has given rise to widespread recognition of and support for the former comfort women, it has also had the adverse effect of imposing uniformity on their diverse colonial experiences and differential conceptions of justice.

The counterfactual case of Chinese comfort women

The central role played by the advocacy movement in transforming national memory in South Korea becomes all the more apparent when considering the counterfactual case of comfort women in China. In contrast to their South Korean counterparts, former Chinese comfort women have struggled to achieve prominence in national memory of Japanese imperial aggression, despite having attained public and official recognition as victims in the late 1990s. Their victimhood has been superseded in memory by the Nanking Massacre (1937–8), a historical episode in which Japanese troops committed mass murder and rape against the residents of the (then capital) city of Nanking. This massacre has become symbolic in China of Japanese imperial violence. The disparity in memory status between the Chinese and South Korean comfort women cannot be simply explained in terms of a significant discrepancy in victim numbers.[32] Rather, a combination of China's relatively closed opportunity structure and the human rights associations of the comfort women issue have mitigated against the rise of an analogous advocacy movement. As a corollary, the plight of the Chinese women has been far less politicized and publicized than their victim counterparts in South Korean.

Similarly to the South Korean case, China's national memory of Japanese imperial expansion after WWII was not focused on the atrocities committed against specific sectors of society. The Chinese government preferred to highlight its resistance to Japanese aggression as a means to establish political legitimacy. As James Reilly describes, 'the Chinese Communist Party's [CCP] nationalist credentials are inextricably intertwined with the Chinese resistance to Japan's invasion,' and 'the CCP exploited this legacy in academic research and public history of the wartime period by emphasizing its leadership of military resistance to Japan.'[33] This resistance narrative was disseminated by the state primarily through party-affiliated history departments and war memorials.[34] Even in the process of normalizing relations with Tokyo in 1972, the CCP remained reluctant to draw attention to the thousands of wartime victims among its nationals. This was despite the fact that during the lead up to the normalization process, a Japanese newspaper published a series on Japan's war crimes in China that included a feature on the Nanking Massacre.[35] Beijing was concerned that raising the sensitive issue of war victims might deter Japanese investment in China, and these same apprehensions prompted Chinese officials to restrict its citizens from joining overseas redress movements and other advocacy efforts against Japan.[36]

It was not until the 1980s that China's wartime history with Japan became politicized in the domestic and bilateral spheres. The context of this was a 1982 Japanese newspaper report on the school textbook screening process in Japan. The Ministry of Education, according to the report, made a request of a Japanese history textbook author that they change a description of Japan's military expansion into Northern China from 'invaded' to 'advanced.' Although the report was later found to be inaccurate, the article ignited protests within both China and South Korea and drew attention to historical revisionism in Japan.[37] This controversy spurred Chinese historians to start documenting Japanese transgressions toward China more earnestly. Throughout the 1980s, various academic publications emerged from these scholarly efforts, and although their primary focus of such studies remained on national resistance to Japanese imperialism, references to the Nanking Massacre also began to emerge. Yet there was still no discourse on the Chinese comfort women at this time.

Again showing resemblance to the South Korean case, the earliest advocacy efforts on behalf of former comfort women in China were instigated by intellectuals. A professor of Chinese history, Su Zhiliang, has been a leading figure by this endeavor. Su began compiling testimonies of former Chinese comfort women upon his return to China from Japan in 1992, where he had witnessed South Koreans protesting about the issue.[38] He also began to arrange trips for Japanese tourists to visit some of the many historical 'comfort women stations' that he identified in his residential city of Shanghai.[39] Following this, in 2016, Su Zhiliang established a Chinese Comfort Women Museum and Research Center at the Shanghai Normal University—his workplace—which provided financial support to the victims among other initiatives. Although Su's activism was supplemented by the efforts of various other individuals in China, including lawyers, intellectuals, volunteers and even a private investigator, their campaign to uncover the facts about the issue and seek redress for the victims never evolved into a full-fledged domestic social movement. This fact is somewhat surprising given that Beijing played host to the aforementioned women's conference in 1995, an event that provided impetus to comfort women movements elsewhere. Essentially, most of the advocacy developments in relation to comfort women in China have been largely concentrated in the Shanghai and Shanxi Province environs. To be sure, Chinese intellectuals have participated in regional and international fora in relation to the comfort women issue, and have strong links with international offshoots of the movement, but their role has been significantly less prominent than that of South Korean activists.

What factors, then, explain the lack of a domestic comfort women movement in China? The reasons are primarily twofold. First, the Chinese political regime is unconducive to the emergence of social movements that are non-aligned with state interests and policies. As has been documented by scholars, the few social movements that have managed to flourish under the CCP's authoritarian leadership have been those in pursuit of causes that support the party line.[40] The inextricable human rights associations of the comfort women issue run counter to the party agenda. Thus, even if activists had the will to develop or participate in a domestic comfort women movement in China, their efforts would likely be met by suppression from state officials. As Reilly argues, activists that are engaged in history problems in China partly derive their power from 'rigid moral adherence to Chinese government rhetoric' on such issues.[41] Given that the human rights frame of the comfort women issue has been firmly established by the South Korean branch of the movement, and this frame has been endorsed by the United Nations and adopted by the movement's various international offshoots, it would be infeasible for activists in China to reframe the issue for their own domestic purposes.

Second, and in connection to this, national memory in China continues to be shaped by a top-down process by which the state privileges historical episodes with political utility. And while history is still utilized by the CCP for the purpose of maintaining legitimacy, the ways in which it serves this end have transformed in recent decades. In the past, as we have seen, narratives of the 'War of resistance against Japan' were mobilized for legitimacy gains. Since the history of Japanese militarism became politicized in the 1980s, however, the CCP's legitimacy has been predicated more on anti-imperialist narratives, and historical episodes that stir up nationalism have had greater utility for the state. These narratives have mostly been based on China's so-called 'century of humiliation' (1840–949), a period encompassing the two Sino-Japanese Wars and various interventions by Western powers. Mobilizing this history has been particularly useful at times when the CCP has sought to deflect attention from contentious domestic issues, or to justify its assertiveness on territorial sovereignty disputes in the region. Since a relatively narrow spectrum of Chinese society was victimized under the comfort women system, this historical episode is not especially useful for inflaming nationalism. The Nanking Massacre, which entailed the mass execution of Chinese soldiers by the Japanese imperial army, as well as random acts of rape and murder, better serves this purpose.

It follows that former Chinese comfort women do not occupy a prominent status in national memory. This is evinced in their relative absence in China's war commemoration landscape. It was as recently as 2016 that the first two comfort women statues were erected in China, both at the Shanghai Normal University on the initiative of Su Zhiliang. A comfort women museum displaying oral testimonies of the victims and other historical evidence was subsequently established on the same premises. These commemorative efforts, however laudable, still pale in comparison to the extensive scope of monuments and events dedicated to the victims of the Nanking Massacre in China. Typically such events attract thousands of Chinese residents every year, and they have entailed the blowing of air sirens on the anniversary of the commencement of the Massacre (December 13); they are also replicated abroad by the Chinese diaspora.[42] The extent of commemoration of comfort women in China also stands in stark contrast to the ever-proliferating comfort women statues in South Korea, which now even appear on buses in Seoul with routes that pass the Japanese Embassy.

The relative obscurity of Chinese comfort women in national memory has been reflected at the diplomatic level. Whereas the matter of redress for South Korean comfort women has tended dominate Seoul's diplomatic dealings with Tokyo throughout the last two decades, Beijing has only tended to raise the issue with Tokyo sporadically. The main points of Sino-Japanese tension have been focused, rather, on territorial sovereignty issues, Japanese history textbooks and prime ministerial visits to the controversial Yasukuni Shrine in Japan. The common thread between these issues is that they pose a challenge to state interests and national history narratives in China. The CCP's stance on the comfort women issue first became clear when Tokyo established the previously mentioned Asian Women's Fund in 1995. Chinese officials dismissed the initiative outright and would not cooperate in establishing an authorization system to determine the victims' eligibility to receive the Fund.[43] A prominent Japanese intellectual who was involved in implementing the Fund, Wada Haruki, explained Beijing's reaction as follows: 'There were lots of victims of the war in China, and I believe it was difficult for the Chinese government just to single out comfort women for help.'[44] Together these anecdotes imply that the CCP's narrative of Japanese imperialism remains centered on the victimization of the Chinese populace at large, which has parallels to the memory landscape of authoritarian South Korea.

In sum, the fact that Chinese comfort women have not been integrated into national memory to the extent of their South Korean counterparts can be explained in large part by the lack of a domestic advocacy movement representing the victims. If China had undergone a democratic transition in recent decades, such a movement presumably would have emerged and a more narrow spectrum of victims would likely have come to the fore—both in national memory and on the diplomatic agenda. In other words, the trajectory of the comfort women issue in China would have aligned more closely with the South Korean case.

Conclusion

The phenomenal ascension of comfort women in South Korean colonial memory can only be understood in relation to the advocacy movement that coalesced around their plight. This movement was able to successfully incorporate the hitherto marginalized women into the contested memory terrain; it also propelled them to preeminence in the domestic hierarchy of colonial victims. Ultimately, the colonial ordeal endured by the former comfort women became symbolic of Japan's annexation of the Korean peninsula. Leaders of the movement achieved such feats primarily through framing the comfort women's victimization in human rights terms; this frame simultaneously mitigated against stigma and intersected with global normative understandings of violence against women. The human rights frame and its attendant historical narrative of the comfort women system became pervasive and entrenched in South Korea, to the extent that there was no longer any room for competing narratives.

While agency was the key variable behind the comfort women's ascent in national memory, the structural context that facilitated the movement's efforts was regime transformation in South Korea. The democratization of politics paved the way for the emergence of a rights-based culture and the rise of advocacy movements. In China, by contrast, the long-standing authoritarian regime has inhibited the development of an analogous movement and, consequently, Chinese comfort women remain relatively marginalized in national memory of Japanese wartime transgressions. Under the CCP's reign, memory continues to be shaped via a top-down process by which officials only privilege those 'history problems' that align with state interests. A corollary of such dynamics is that the matter of redress for Chinese comfort women has not featured prominently on the Sino-Japanese diplomatic agenda.

It is worth noting that the primary intention of the South Korean branch of the movement was not to shape national memory of comfort women per se, but to elicit comprehensive redress—including state compensation—from Tokyo on their behalf. Nevertheless, the success of the movement in the memory domain was essential toward the latter end, as it constituted a necessary condition for diplomatic agenda-setting. The fact that the movement has yet to undermine the Japanese right-wing narrative of the comfort women system has, however, negated its ability to shape the redress policy of Japan's long-ruling conservative party in accordance with the movement's demands.

In sum, the case of South Korean comfort women is illustrative of the power of social movements to transform national memory of historical episodes—under certain political conditions. When such episodes entail the victimization of vulnerable groups, this memory transformation and the recognition it bestows helps to alleviate—albeit it only partially—the plight of victims. The memorialization and commemoration efforts that typically accompany this process help to ensure that the memories of the victims will be transmitted to and preserved by succeeding generations.

Notes

1 The term 'comfort women' is a wartime and colonial-era euphemism denoting the women and girls subjected to sexual slavery by Japanese imperial forces. It is a translation of the Japanese *ianfu*. I employ this label throughout this chapter (hereafter without quotation marks) on account of it being the historical term that was in use under the Japanese Empire.
2 Interview with former comfort woman, November 3, 2009, Seoul.
3 Sue R. Lee, 'Comforting the Comfort Women: Who Can Make Japan Pay?' *University of Pennsylvania Journal of International Economic Law* 24 (2003): 509–547, here: 518.
4 Hyunah Yang, 'Remembering the Korean Military Comfort Women: Nationalism, Sexuality, and Silencing,' in *Dangerous Women: Gender and Korean Nationalism*, eds. Elaine H. Kim and Chungmoo Choi (New York: Routledge, 1998), 123–139, here: 131.
5 Bruce Cumings, *Korea's Place in the Sun: A Modern History* (New York and London: W. W. Norton & Company, 2005), 179.
6 *Kyodo News*, August 12, 1999.
7 A digital archive of the records of negotiations between South Korea and Japan is accessible here (in Korean): http://www.donga.com/news/d_story/politics/K_J_agreement65/data.html.
8 For an overview of the state of the feminist movement at this time, see Miriam Ching and Yoon Louie, 'Minjung Feminism: Korean Women's Movement for Gender and Class Liberation,' *Women's Studies International Forum* 18, no. 4 (1995): 417–430.
9 See the Introduction chapter of this volume. William H. Jr Sewell, 'Historical Events as Transformations of Structures: Inventing Revolution at the Bastille,' *Theory and Society* 25 (1996): 841–881.
10 Tami Amanda Jacoby, 'A Theory of Victimhood: Politics, Conflict and the Construction of Victim-based Identity,' *Millennium: Journal of International Studies* 43, no. 2 (2015): 511–530, here: 520.
11 The term *kisaeng* originally referred to female entertainers who often served as concubines or second wives to the ruling class of dynastic Korea. The term later evolved to refer to Korean women who served as prostitutes to male Japanese tourists and domestic elites.
12 Bang-Soon L. Yoon, 'Imperial Japan's 'Comfort Women' from Korea: History and Politics of Silence Breaking,' *Northeast History Journal* 7 (2010): 5–39, here: 10.
13 Korea Church Women United, 'Kisaeng Tourism, a nationwide survey report on conditions in four areas: Seoul, Pusan, Cheju, Kyongju,' *Research Material Issue No. 3* (Seoul: Korean Church Women United, 1983).
14 Yoshiko Nozaki, 'The 'Comfort Women' Controversy: History and Testimony,' *The Asia-Pacific Journal: Japan Focus* 3, no. 7 (2005). https://apjjf.org/-Yoshiko-Nozaki/2063/article.html
15 Ibid.
16 The Korean Council was established in November, 1990.
17 Yoshiko Nozaki, 'Feminism, Nationalism and the Japanese Textbook Controversy over 'Comfort Women,' in *Feminism and Anti-Racism*, eds. Kathleen. M. Blee, and France Winddance Twine (New York and London: New York University Press, 2001), 170–192, here: 172.
18 Interview with former comfort woman, November 3, 2009, Seoul.
19 Jacoby, 'A Theory of Victimhood,' 517.

20 David A. Snow, et al., 'Frame Alignment Processes, Micromobilization, and Movement Participation,' *American Sociological Review* 51 (1986): 464–481, here: 481.
21 These phrases are featured on a number of pamphlets produced by the Korean Council.
22 'Nanumu no Ie Nihongun 'Ianfu' Rekishikan: Kokusai Heiwa Jinken Sentaa' [The History Museum of Japan's Military 'Comfort Women' at the House of Sharing: International Peace and Human Rights Center], brochure produced by the House of Sharing, 2012.
23 Ibid.
24 These resolutions stipulated 'the urgent need for the universal application to women of the rights and principles with regard to equality, security, liberty, integrity and dignity of all human beings.' They also conveyed the conviction that

> violations of the human rights of women in situations of armed conflict are violations of the fundamental principles of international human rights and humanitarian law. All violations of this kind, including in particular murder, systematic rape, sexual slavery, and forced pregnancy, require a particular effective response.

25 *The New York Times*, September 6, 1995.
26 Chunglee Sarah Soh, *The Comfort Women: Sexual Violence and Post-colonial Memory in Korea and Japan* (Chicago, IL: University of Chicago Press, 2008), 96.
27 For a more in-depth discussion of Park's book, see Yang Li, 'Reflections on Postwar Nationalism: Debates and Challenges in the Japanese Academic Critique of the 'Comfort Women' System,' *Chinese Studies in History* 53, no. 1 (2020): 41–55, here: 50–53.
28 This statement can be read here: https://www.comfortwomenoftheempire.org/2018/09/12/noam-chomsky-defense-park-yuha/
29 *The Korea Herald*, November 15, 2018.
30 *United Press International*, September 26, 2019.
31 Japan is an exception to this statement about the 'international community' as the comfort women issue remains a divisive topic domestically.
32 Peipei Qiu, Su Zhiliang and Chen Lifei, *Chinese Comfort Women: Testimonies from Japan's Imperial Sex Slaves* (Vancouver: University of British Columbia Press, 2013).
33 James Reilly, 'China's History Activists and the War of Resistance against Japan: History in the Making,' *Asian Survey* 19, no. 2 (2004): 276–294, here: 277.
34 Ibid., 277–278.
35 These articles, written by Japanese journalist Honda Katsuichi, appeared in a serialized form under the title 'Chūgoku no Tabi' [Travels in China] in *The Asahi Shimbun* between August and December 1971.
36 Reilly, 'China's History Activists,' 278.
37 Franziska Seraphim, *War Memory and Social Politics in Japan, 1945–2005* (Cambridge, MA: Harvard University Press, 2006), 26. For some examples of the concerns expressed by Chinese intellectuals, see Qiu, Zhiliang, and Lifei, *Chinese Comfort Women*, 166–167.
38 This research was later published as Qiu, Zhiliang, and Lifei, *Chinese Comfort Women*.
39 Reilly, 'China's History Activists,' 276–294.
40 See, for instance, Michael J. Hathaway, 'Global Environmental Encounters in Southwest China: Fleeting Intersections and 'Transnational Work,' *The Journal of Asian Studies* 69, no. 2 (2010): 427–451; Fengshi Wu, 'Environmental Activism in Provincial China,' *Journal of Environmental Policy & Planning* 15, no. 1 (2013): 89–108.
41 Reilly, 'China's History Activists,' 294.
42 Ibid.
43 *BBC News*, April 10, 2007. Su Zhiliang was apparently also consulted by the Asian Women's Fund committee and conveyed the message that the victims did not want to receive it. Qiu, Zhiliang, and Lifei, *Chinese Comfort Women*, 163.
44 *BBC News*, April 10, 2007.

3

THE PAST IN THE PRESENT

Memory and Indian women's politics

Devleena Ghosh and Heather Goodall

Memory and women's politics in India

Political narratives in South Asia in the twentieth century have been shaped by memory: the heroes of the past and the narratives of struggles, historic or mythic, have been invoked to bolster the promises of a modern, democratic, equal future. This uneasy entwining of a future modernist goal and a traditionalist and heroic past has characterized much Indian political rhetoric. Yet historians have been less interested in how memory has crafted this rhetoric than have ethnographers and scholars of literature.

In *The Nation and its Fragments*[1] (2009), Partha Chatterjee presents 'community' and 'women' as two fragments of the nation. At the moment of the birth of two nation states out of one colonial state, the bodies of numberless women were brought under the control of their respective communities in an act of disciplinary power that marked the idea of a community. Like other social and political movements, women's movements in this context faced the challenges of building both alliances and autonomy.[2] This entailed the construction of strong women's movements internally while forging international and transnational relationships with other civil society groups. Gandhi and Shah, for example, describe how the various women's movements in India used diverse strategies, including consciousness raising, pressuring public officials, and boycotting those who committed violence against women, to address a wide range of issues including violence, health, work, and law.[3] Memories were crucial building blocks of community and national identities. How women in these struggles remembered their pasts remade their conceptions of the present and demands from the future.

Many dominant Indian narratives of Independence assume that women became visible through Gandhian movements, such as the Salt March in 1930. Early Indian nationalists like Tilak argued that the traditionally subservient role of women in many Indian cultures had to change if India were to achieve independent modernity.[4] More recent works[5] have highlighted the limitations of such accounts, drawing attention to women's writing from the late nineteenth and early twentieth centuries in, *inter alia*, Tamil, Marathi, and Bengali, in which there was energetic discussion about emancipation and modernity, though the strategies advocated were those of negotiation and conciliation rather than overt challenges to either Indian or British patriarchy.

In India, colonial rule and the freedom struggle marked the beginning of an awakening among women; there were, however, differing views on the role and status of women within the anti-imperialist anti-feudal struggle.[6] The visibility of women in the Gandhian movement from 1930 emerged from an alliance between a network of women activists and the Gandhian movement of *satyagraha*. The impact of this alliance was demonstrated in the Karachi Fundamental Rights Resolution of the Indian National Congress in 1931, which brought together the views expressed by women in their writing (as above) and those of liberal reformers. The Resolution demanded freedom, justice, dignity, and equality for women, seeing these as essential for nation-building. The national constitution of independent India reiterated these principles. Women involved in the Gandhian struggle based their politics on clear memories of previous attempts at changing the status and role of women in India.

The support of women for the Nehruvian socialist government after 1947 was by no means homogeneous nor unconditional. The All India Women's Conference (AIWC) was a broad organization, many of whose members were middle-class and higher-caste Hindu women. The AIWC identified itself substantially with the Gandhian Independence movement and later the Nehruvian government, focusing on 'service' as its strategy for supporting newly independent India.[7] In southern India, the Women's Indian League and the Self-Respect Movement,[8] among other organizations, explored avenues for socio-economic and political mobility against the limitations of a low-income ex-colonial state which promised emancipation but failed to deliver, riven by the conflicts between women's rights and a longstanding patriarchal social hierarchy. Historians like Mazumdar and John argue that the decades after Independence were a loss for women, in contrast to the 1931 Karachi Resolution and the National Constitution in 1950.[9]

In this article, we explore two sites of memory which bring together repertoires of contention in the context of historical events, inter-generational connections, collective identities, and affective links or emotions. As Wydra contends, collective memory has been seen as a product of social frames that enable individuals to remember by means of language, symbols, and spatial-temporal markers. He quotes Pierre Nora as describing generations as communities of remembrance that perpetuate a foundational event, which created a self-conscious generation in the first place.[10] Both of our sites involve the memories and activism involved in the establishment of the National Federation of Indian Women (NFIW) and are excellent examples of these contentions, connections, and conflicts.

An increasing number of women were unhappy with the class and cultural limitations of the AIWC. Many of those had been involved in the Independence movement and their memories of resistance to British rule did not resonate with the 'service' ethos of the AIWC. Within five years of Independence, in 1953, these women met in Delhi to discuss the formation of an alternative national structure, which would include rural and urban female workers and those from different religions and social groups. These women participated in regional meetings in India and the left-wing Women's International Democratic Federation in Copenhagen in October 1953 before establishing the National Federation of Indian Women (NFIW) in Calcutta in August 1954. This meeting called on the memories of women's activism and desires for change in the decades before Independence and evoked the courage of the women who had fought for Independence. These activists' repertoire or frame for the break from the AIWC was the inclusion of all women (such as those in agriculture) rather than only the elite class.[11]

By the 1970s, it became clear that Independence had fulfilled few, if any, of the promises of the Karachi Resolution or the Constitution. In 1975, *Towards Equality*, the Report of the Committee on the Status of Women, showed a deterioration in all indices concerning women since Independence. Across India, disillusioned and disappointed women set about building new organizations, linked to the global rise of women's liberation movements. By the 1980s, there was a new body of vital and activist women's organizations across India, much of it critical of the Eurocentrism of the Northern liberation movements.[12] In this period, memory again became vitally important. One of the many activities which these new women's movements undertook via publishing houses such as Kali for Women, founded in 1984 by Urvashi Butalia, and S.P.A.R.R.O.W., led by C.S. Lakshmi in Mumbai, was the publication of the autobiographies and memoirs of women who had founded the NFIW in 1954 as well as those active in the Independence movement. The repertoire of activism in this period drew heavily on the memories and narratives of older women activists, celebrated in publication and in person as heroes of the Independence and women's emancipation movements.

We therefore analyze, first, the complex and conflicted memories of former struggles which were mobilized in the formation of the NFIW in 1953–4. Second, we consider the ways in which the formation of the NFIW was remembered and how those memories influenced the current activism of the founders. As mentioned above, the NFIW arose from political disagreements within the AIWC and the different ways in which some members remembered their previous activism. We interviewed three veterans of the movement: Sarla Sharma, from Delhi, Primla Loomba, originally from Lahore and resident in Delhi after Partition, and Rajni Kumar, originally from England, who lived first in Shimla and later Delhi. Their memories influenced their later political activism as well as comprising part of a set of collective memories constituting the radical pasts that inspire current women activists.

Many authors have recognized the role of generations as carriers of memorial activity, traveling across spatial and temporal distances in time and space to shape narrative commitments.[13] These generational memories are not ruptures with the past, according to Reinhart Koselleck, but 'thresholds of experience,' or hinges which allow doors to open for the transmissions of stories. Koselleck contends that thresholds mediate and connect across differences in biological age, fractures in historical time, and aspirations to future life and it is this fluidity that accomplishes changes of consciousness.[14] Our research shows that many women were frustrated by the marginalizing of women's rights after Independence. Women, including those in the regions, attempted as early as the 1950s to reset the political agenda and fulfill the promises for economic and political justice of the Independence campaign. These promises were remembered in the contexts of the long histories of women's struggle for their rights before and alongside the nationalist campaigns.

Shaping the regional fields

Raka Ray argues that in the mid- to late twentieth century, the strategies and outcomes of women's movements are best understood by analyzing political power in their regions – that is, by the nature of the 'political field' within which organizations develop. She contrasts the 'dispersed' or 'fragmented' political field of Bombay with the 'concentrated' political field of Calcutta.[15] Beyond such regional differences, however, there were significant tensions within these women's movements between those who fought within the existing social structures and those who challenged them.[16] These tensions, reflecting class, status and cultural or religious affiliation, became apparent in the debates around the formation of the National Federation of Indian Women (NFIW) in 1953–4. In later memories, however, the political fields and regional contexts of women's activism became more prominent. Among the women we interviewed, it was their own personal experiences and contexts that imbued their memories of these events in the early years of the twenty-first century. For example, women's activism in Bombay and Calcutta took different routes. Bombay had been a cosmopolitan city for centuries, with populations from neighboring states as well as from West Asia and North Africa. After 1534, the Portuguese, then the British ruled the city and reshaped its land and society, while the Portuguese remained in Goa until 1961.

Padma Anagol demonstrates that, in Bombay, elite women from Hindu, Parsi, or Christian religions mobilized collectively from the early nineteenth century to achieve greater social and political independence.[17] They drew on European ideas of women's rights but deliberately chose strategies of negotiation and compromise so as to not challenge established power. Anagol's analysis, covering the period till 1920, shows that the female editors of the active women's press in Bombay prioritized assertive political agendas while encouraging negotiation and conciliation. It is no surprise then that the All India Women's Conference was established in Bombay in 1927 as an umbrella organization for women's voices.

Southern India's diverse cultures were connected through common Dravidian roots and shared Buddhist, Hindu, and Islamic religious practices. Women in Madras built collective bonds through the Theosophical Society, which recognized the commonalities of all great religions in order to establish a 'brotherhood of man.' Theosophy was associated with progressive social and artistic modernism and attractive to many who opposed European colonialism, though it became closely aligned to Tamil Brahmin groups, mostly enmeshed in caste privilege. Theosophy's emphasis on the equality of women attracted many adherents in England and Ireland, such as Margaret Cousins, who had been involved in the struggle for Irish Independence. She was a driving force in the 1917 establishment of the Women's Indian Association (WIA) and contributed to its newsletter, *Stri Dharma*, published from 1918.[18]

At the same time, the Self-Respect Movement, formally established in 1921 by E.V. Ramasamy (or Periyar), in Madras and southern India, had enormous support. It called for universal equality, an end to Brahminical domination and the oppression of women and 'untouchables.' This movement's radical critique put it at odds with many northern Indian progressive movements, including the nationalists and Congress (which Periyar left in 1925). It was also out of step with the women's movements composed predominantly of elite Hindu, Parsi, or Theosophist women.[19]

Calcutta, the capital of the Empire under the East India Company and later the Raj till 1911, produced numerous activists prominent in cultural movements. Sarojini Naidu, a poet, was a stalwart opponent of the British regime and became the first woman president of the Indian National Congress in 1926. The Communist Party of India (CPI), led by the Bengali Muslim Muzaffar Ahmed, had a strong anti-caste position but was less focused on gender.[20] Bengali women in the CPI were active in a number of campaigns for civil and women's rights in the interwar decades. They became prominent during World War II when Bengal was threatened by the Japanese invasion of Burma and a severe famine in 1943–4. Several women's self-defense organizations, whose core members were from the CPI, formed the local Mahila Atma Raksha Samiti in 1942 to support neighborhood women against the upheavals caused by these threats.[21] All of this activist work became part of a repertoire of memories that made possible the idea of future political work that would be dynamic and potent, based on recollections of unfulfilled promises as well as transformative interventions.

Women's movements and nationalism

The 1931 Karachi Resolution of Fundamental Rights and Duties, adopted by the Indian National Congress in March, was criticized by some Congress members as an awkward compromise between social conservatives and the left. Many saw it as the blueprint for a future independent India since it called for the removal of all legal, economic, and political discriminations against women, including unequal pay and was remarkable for its explicit inclusion of women in each category of equality.[22] There is a passage in the May 1937 issue of *Stri Dharma* expressing its support for the decision by women's movements to abandon their campaigns for reservations or other preferential treatment.

> Consequent on the magnificent terms of the Declaration of Rights in the Karachi Conference and the promise given by Gandhiji to a deputation of the South Indian women who brought the Madras Memorandum to him that he would secure adult franchise for women even if he failed to get it at once for men, all alternative proposals re franchise were dropped. These Declarations have shown Indian women that equality of citizenship is assured to them in the new Constitution. In such circumstances and having realized and demonstrated their power as nationalist citizens during the past year women have risen above all temptations to write themselves down as needing protection or reservation or preferential treatment.[23]

Gandhi believed that women could indeed be *satyagrahis* – and were in fact particularly suited to this role. His approach was reformist; he argued that Hinduism had an honored role for women who were fundamental to the new nation. Their role, however, was still to be defined by their family – they should become stronger wives and mothers. A subsequent meeting in Bombay of the AIWC agreed that they would campaign only for full Adult Franchise. The 1931 Resolution – backed by Gandhi's personal promise – was seen as a real commitment that women would be recognized as equal citizens in the new nation.

After Independence, the AIWC endorsed the new government. Many prominent members, like Sarojini Naidu and Hansa Mehta, were active in the state or diplomatic bureaucracies set up by the new Prime Minister, Nehru. Most women's rights activists welcomed the departure of the British but only some fully supported the directions of the new Government. In the Indian Constitution, adopted in 1950, the distinction between Fundamental Rights and Directive Principles meant that many goals for achieving women's emancipation remained in the amorphous 'Directive Principles' category rather than actionable 'Fundamental Rights.' The women activists who were unhappy with the passive response of bodies like the AIWC sought organizational models elsewhere, such as the Women's International Democratic Federation (WIDF) conference in 1953.

The AIWC had refused to affiliate with the WIDF when it was established in 1945. Over the following years, Cold War anti-communism found an ambivalent response in India. The CPI was banned from 1948 to 1952, with many members forced to go 'underground' or jailed. India developed strong political and cultural ties with the USSR, which were strengthened through the Non-Aligned Movement and because of the conflict with China in 1962. Yet there remained many elites in India who were reluctant to have connections with international organizations labeled as 'Communist fronts.' The AIWC took this more conservative position, and argued against affiliation with the WIDF because of its association with the USSR. The memory of the AIWF's cautious and negative response to overtly socialist organizations was important in the later foundation of the NFIW.

Forming the NFIW, 1953–4

There were two major meetings attended by the women challenging the marginalizing of their sisters in independent India. Those wishing to participate in the WIDF Copenhagen Conference attended the Planning Meeting in Delhi on 9 May 1953. In addition, the inaugural meeting of the NFIW was held in Calcutta in June 1954.

The Delhi meeting was described by the WIDF as 'A Great Event! The first National Conference of the women of India.' There were meetings across India in the months before this event, including, according to the newsletter compiled by the WIDF from Indian reports, many 'in the working class areas' of Bombay; in Calcutta, meetings were held daily with 'great enthusiasm'; in Delhi, 'more than 30 meetings of Mohammedan and Hindu women' had been held in April alone.[24] There were 315 delegates who attended the Delhi conference, which then elected a group of 30 women to go to Copenhagen. This group represented many different Indian women's organizations and was led by Annie Mascrene, Member of Parliament for Travancore.[25]

There were important discussions at these meetings about common goals among left-wing delegates from regional women's organizations. Hajrah Begum's 1973 summary of the key issues discussed is consistent with the memories of Primla Loomba. Generally, the Delhi participants believed that Independence had not fulfilled its promises and that the AIWC no longer represented their goals of equality and justice for women. Many attendees, like Kapila Khandvala and Sarla Sharma, had been active in the AIWC but were now frustrated about specific issues. They had lost confidence that the AIWC would argue for complete economic independence for women, for example, in night shift work. The majority of the AIWC membership was concerned that night shifts were not 'respectable' and should be banned for the protection of women. Left-wing AIWC members, like Primla Loomba, Sarla Sharma, and Kapila Khandvala, argued that women would lose their jobs and become dependent on their husbands or families and that the AIWC should demand crèches and other amenities to enable women with children to work at night in safety and security. They lost this vote.[26] Sarla, Primla, and Rajni retained strong memories of these debates and their failure to convince the AIWC that family ties and marital status should not define and entrap women. These memories became important triggers for their later break with the AIWC.

Another issue that these women remembered was the exorbitant fees for AIWC membership, which excluded working-class and peasant women. Hajrah Begum said:

> Our slogan was '4 anna membership, mass membership of women.' They could not afford more. We wanted all women to come.[27]

This vote, too, was lost. Only a few AIWC members, like Rameshwari Nehru and Rajkumari Amrit Kaur, supported this fee reduction. Again, this demand recalled past struggles in the campaigns for wider membership and the recognition of working women, which had been crucial to the rural literacy work of many educators in the interwar years.

The third problem was thorny. The AIWC refused to affiliate with the WIDF. Many of the women at the May 1953 Delhi meeting were members of or closely associated with the CPI and reluctant to break with the AIWC. The memories of the contributions they had made to the Independence struggle increased their frustration with the AIWC's decision. Their dilemma was resolved only after the formal inauguration of the NFIW in June 1954.

The delegation of 30 Indian women attended the World Congress of Women in Copenhagen, with an enthusiasm which Anasuya Gyan Chand described with amusement and affection in her recollections in 1973.[28] All the delegates returned with new ideas and the Bombay women's organization with the impetus to establish a separate organization.[29] The inaugural NFIW Congress Report optimistically records a diverse attendance, including women from the industrial working-class and agricultural laborers, although in subsequent decades support came predominantly from lower-middle-class professional women, like teachers. The theme of remembrance was strong in the warm wishes sent to the new organization. Smt Sharadaben Mehta, a patron of the AIWC, wrote:

> I am in full sympathy with the objects of the Congress. Women of India enjoy equal rights with men only on paper. For full seven years, our legislators have failed to give us just laws in respect to marriage, special marriage or divorce. The provision of midwives and nurses in the village is extremely slow... Education of girls in the villages is extremely inefficient... the Government of India has done nothing to minimize prostitution by providing work for all women.[30]

Sarla, Primla, and Rajni, particularly the latter, have vivid memories of their participation in the meetings and the conference and these pasts were seminal to the way in which they conceptualized their future activism and involvement in the young Indian nation.

The past in the present

How do the surviving veterans remember these events, which can be identified from historical research? Memory is more than a floating signifier; rather it is constructed, renovated, and subjectively negotiated; retellings of memory tell us more about those processes of subjective renovation than they necessarily do about the events of the past. Memory is elusive, neither the past not the present. The rich textured ephemeral quality of memory means that, in daily life, it is always being negotiated with the present.[31]

The potent force of memory endures, not because it is ahistorical or apolitical but because it is politically, discursively, and historically constructed.[32]

Memories of the past are constituted of a continuous and dialectical process of the transmission of knowledge, information, beliefs and practices and the trajectory of customs and values proceeding from one generation to another. The memories of activism retold by Sarla Sharma, Primla Loomba, and Rajni Kumar were vulnerably linked to an entire network of personal, national, social, and cultural identifications. Their views of past radical movements were not static, mired in unchanging tradition; rather they resembled the artistic device of *pentimento*, a thinking and re-thinking of historical and contemporary political and social experiences. They were located in an unstable present between a past history of meaningful struggle, their current opposition to the oppression and marginalization of Indian women, and an unpredictable future where the rights they thought they had gained retreated like a mirage. Their present acquired its meaning within these disjointed and conflicted temporalities. Gramsci refers to the 'strangely composite' nature of identity 'which contains prejudices from all past phases of history' and 'deposited in you an infinity of traces without leaving an inventory.'[33] These three activist women were therefore constantly involved in different forms of negotiation, between the memories of past activism and current regressive political discourses, between their families and communities and the Indian state. Their memories mediated the past and present, the local and the national. They were aware that the role and status of Indian women was a specter that haunted the national imaginary as anomaly, threat and the object of uneasy reflections about the nature of tradition and progress.

The women we interviewed each undertook different forms of negotiation between memory and forgetting. They had to travel the spaces opened up by changing notions of tradition and cultural change, the associations and inter-meshings of family, community, and politics and the individual and the ongoing mediations on silence and speaking.[34] The twentieth century promoted the cause of gender justice by internationalizing struggles for the equality of women and other oppressed people. Women's struggles against their subordination were intertwined in varying degrees with ideologies and movements based on the values of freedom, self-determination, equality, democracy, and justice. No longer confined by region or means of communication, these now found expression through movements against imperialism, for national liberation and social transformation. The defeat of fascism and the forced retreat of imperialism around the mid-century paved the way for social advances of which gender relations were a key component, along with the other broad objectives of human rights and the end of iniquitous social orders. The revolutionary changes which followed the two world wars also created fora and structures that promoted debates on women's rights. The International Women's Decade was initiated in 1976 during this period of hope, but by the end of the decade these aspirations were already shaky. By the time we interviewed our narrators, the context in which the international struggle for the advance of women's rights was waged had been transformed.[35]

In this section, we consider the memories of Sarla Sharma, Primla Loomba, and Rajni Kumar about the formation of the organization to which they all belonged, the National Federation of Indian Women (NFIW). These women had been active in progressive movements from the 1930s onwards and they continued to be involved in anti-colonial and left-wing struggles for all their lives. All were in their nineties when we interviewed them, each on several occasions between 2012 and 2015.

Primla was born in 1924, in Lahore in present-day Pakistan, to a well-off Hindu family. Her father was a High Court judge and she spent the academic year at school in Lahore, and summer vacations at the family home in Simla. She gained her BA from Kinnaird College and graduated from Government College, Lahore in 1946. Primla had been active during her undergraduate years in the students' movement in Lahore and its vigorous Independence campaigns had left her strongly committed to public activism. In June of 1947, Primla left her parents' house to visit her sister in Ferozepur in Punjab. In August, partition happened, and Primla never returned home again. She left India in January of 1948 to study for an MA program in political science at Radcliffe College, Harvard University.

Primla married a trade union organizer, Satish Loomba, and both decided to dedicate their lives to the work of rebuilding their new country. They believed in Nehru's idea of India, a nation which would transcend class, caste, religion, and gender, and they were appalled by the violence and hatred unleashed by Partition. Both joined the Communist Party of India, for which Satish worked full-time, and Primla threw herself into organizing the National Federation for Indian Women. She also started teaching full-time at Delhi Public School. In the late 1960s, Primla received a Fulbright Scholarship to teach in Florida for a year, at a time when those schools were de-segregating. Primla became the first (and possibly only) female Indian teacher in the USA who, wearing a sari, held the hands of black children and escorted them into previously white-only classrooms. She sat with the black students through their classes to ensure they weren't mistreated and escorted them back onto the buses that took them home. In her conversations with us, she recounts how these memories of inequality in one of the most powerful and wealthy nations of the world spurred her into her fight against caste and gender oppression in India.

Sarla Sharma was born in 1921 into an enlightened and progressive upper-class family of Theosophists. Her grandfather had been one of the founders of the first girls' school in India, Indraprastha Hindu Kanya Vidyalaya, and had employed an Australian theosophist, Leonora Gmeiner, as its principal. Sarla attended this school and her activism began early. She led a movement among the school's students against singing the British national anthem or saluting the British flag. She was involved from the time she was a schoolgirl in the nationalist struggle in Delhi and was injured in a baton charge by the police at a demonstration. Later, between completing her BA and a degree in Economics, she became a member of the Communist Party of India and was imprisoned for a year for her anti-colonial activities. As a CPI delegate, Sarla visited many countries, including the Soviet

Union, Yemen, Switzerland, Romania, Bulgaria, Czechoslovakia, Mongolia, and China. After a long period of membership of the AIWC, she was one of the founder members of the National Federation of Indian Women.

As women who had grown up in India, Sarla and Primla shared many concerns in common, although the differences in their early lives made their memories of the women's movement distinct in some aspects and similar in others. Rajni Kumar, however, had a different background. Born in 1923, she grew up in a middle-class family in England as Nancie Jones and met Yudhishter Kumar when he was studying in England. In 1944, Yudhishter returned to India to take part in the Independence struggle. Nancie followed him soon after, in circumstances we will discuss below. Committing herself to India, Rajni changed her name and married Yudhishter on Independence Day in 1947. The memories which Rajni recounted about the formation of the NFIW are shaped by her different background, but they explain most clearly of all three narratives the ties that bound these activists together.

Each of these women were from affluent and high-status families, but their political and personal choices shaped their lives. From the late 1940s, each of them faced poverty and some form of social exclusion because of their political affiliation with the Communist Party or with left-wing activism. They saw themselves as aligned with working women – mostly urban women in professions like nursing and teaching rather than rural agricultural labor, and they were committed to the economic and legal independence of all women. Each of these women took an active role in the formation of the NFIW, yet each remembered that process in different ways.

The themes that emerge from their memories are three-fold: first, the issues faced by women in India and how to ameliorate them; second, internationalism and solidarity between the women of the world and how to achieve these aims and third, the affective relationships between the women themselves, where their political differences were subsumed by their personal experiences as comrades in the struggle.

Women's issues in India

Many women from overseas attended the founding meeting of the National Federation of Indian Women in 1954 in Ca-lcutta. Betty Riley, from Australia, and Dora Russell, from the British National Assembly of Women, were two of the speakers. Sarla remembered Dora's visit particularly well. She accompanied Dora on a study trip to rural India after the Calcutta conference, and Dora produced a report which she presented to the WIDF. Sarla herself was a visual artist – she supported her family by selling her paintings when her fellow-Communist husband could not find work – and she went with Dora on this trip as photographer:

> I went along with them with my camera .... not big cameras like you have. Kodak camera costing 5 rupees at that time, that was 1954. I'm only acting as the photographer.

Dora, however, took this project seriously, as Sarla explained:

> She went into the interior of the villages, into the huts of the women. How they were working, what they were doing, their occupations. Because, generally, the women in the countryside, they do not go out for jobs. But whatever they can get near their houses or near their huts, they are all employed and they earn something for the family. So that [was what] Dora Russell studied very hard.

Sarla remembers this incident as instrumental in her later focus on the necessity of eyewitness testimony and serious research for the support of causes through the rest of her activist life.

Primla had been active in the women's movement as an undergraduate in Lahore. Despite Sarla's activism at her secondary school, she spoke less about university students' activism than Primla. Sarla's work as an artist, an actor in the Indian Peoples Theatre Association, and her later election to the Municipal Council in Chandni Chowk in 1954 replaced her student activity. Primla's memories of university activism were stronger but they led her into the Communist Party where the powerful tool of class analysis better illuminated the problems of women. She recalled that her primary interest remained the nationalist movement led by Gandhi. As a resident of Lahore, Primla was fascinated by Gandhi's disagreements with Jinnah. The AIWC, however, wasn't very well known in Lahore and, unlike Sarla, Primla was never a member.

> So, you know, … it wasn't a women's question at that time … we never talked about women, about their oppression, but a little later – when we became closer to the Communist Party, most of us were either working on the cultural front or on the student front … they said that you should really go and meet with the men and organize them and educate them about, you know, women and politics.

Primla's initial memories of the NFIW were related to the issues of Indian working women. She recalled many debates about the form and role the NFIW, including its links with the AIWC. She believed, like those on the left in the AIWC, that the new body should be open to all women, whether political or non-political, who 'put in their energy – in positions and without any positions, if they were only housewives – they all came together and joined the NFIW.'[36]

Primla also remembers the major controversies within the AIWC about women doing shift work at night and high fees for membership, as mentioned above. The general consensus among the AIWC was that women shouldn't be working at night.

> [They said] there's far too much you have to do to keep the safety for women. So they (the AIWC) said, 'Don't employ them.' So we said, 'You

cannot leave them, give them alternatives.' And that was one controversy with the AIWC. They were stopping this night work. And the second one was about the membership. See, we said there should be an open membership and ... the mass of women should be able to come. And we said there should be just a four anna (1/4 of a rupee) membership, you know ... And they said, 'Well, you know, YOU can work for them' and there was a much more sort of welfarist attitude of the AIWC.[37]

Sarla recalled being actively involved with Kapila Khandvala in the struggle for the rights of women nurses and mine workers to night shift work and sick and recreation pay. She explained that the AIWC was reluctant to support these causes as they seemed too political and divisive.

The All India Women's Conference took up this position that they should not be allowed to work for the nightshift ... they were turned out of the [mines]. That was no solution. So we protested against it. So then they [AIWC] said, 'Oh protesting and demanding something, that means political action. We are not going to do politics.' I said, 'That is human action, not political action!'[38]

Primla recalled that another major focus of activism by was the question of dowry, and the property rights of women.

And we wanted to activise women to make these women think about themselves. So the first activity that people indulged in, was the Hindu Code Bill and of course [that] bill never became a reality. They passed only two, different married laws ... But property rights were given, you know, that is the father's self-earned property ... but at the same time, the issue was dowry. And dowry wasn't really initiated by the NFIW. It was an issue taken by the AWC also and women's education, that was there.[39]

Primla found it hard to get a job because her husband was a known Communist and trade union activist. Without the artistic skills which had helped Sarla to support her family, Primla used her tertiary education to teach in a coaching college. There, however, she experienced sexual harassment first-hand and realized that, as well as poverty and economic discrimination, this was another issue that women had to battle.

[I]t was a horrible experience, very horrible. They wouldn't pay and there was so much sexual harassment and I wasn't conscious, can you imagine? ... You know, I mean the fellow, he would sort of go and touch – I used to have a lot of hair, a lot of hair ... and he would ... do this and do that ... you know, we were not conscious that all these things, you see at that time there was no such thing, you know? As a matter of fact, women's issues were mainly that our understanding was, arising out of poverty, you see. And we said that the main discrimination that women face and the oppression, comes from poverty, and it is true also in a way. But there is the other side of this, you know, that harassment.

It is important to emphasize that, for Primla and Sarla, the early memories of their student activism were crucial in the break from the AIWC. They were convinced that being passive and domesticated in the political arena would not advance the cause of women's rights. The remembrances of the failed promises of the Karachi Resolution and the Indian Constitution were essential to the future activism of these women and their commitment to a more dynamic form of politics. Their political ideals contained mnemonics of failure, on shift work, dowry and the property rights of women, which spurred them on in their future activism.

Internationalism and solidarity

Raza, Roy, and Zachariah call the interwar period (1917–39) the 'internationalist moment,' when attempts were made to create platforms, movements, and political networks that transcended state and national boundaries.[40] Then World War II intensified the international connections of many activists, through education overseas or interactions with servicemen from abroad. Such networks continued to be important after the war, particularly for decolonizing independence and women's movements, offering support for emerging socialist countries. The AIWC had been active in making international contacts but baulked at interacting with the socialist world. The Charter of Women's Rights was adopted at the AIWC Congress in January 1946 before being taken to the United Nations by Hajrah Begum that same year. Socialist organizations took part in events in India, including the meeting in February 1948 of the World Federation of Democratic Youth Congress in Calcutta, after which a WIDF team of inquiry traveled through northern India. The All India Peace and Solidarity Congress in Madras in December 1954 had delegates from all over the world. The left-wing members of the AIWC who eventually formed the NFIW fostered international alliances with the socialist and the non-socialist world: its members Malabika Chattopadhyay and Primla Loomba both worked at the WIDF in Berlin in the 1980s.

Sarla considered that international networks were crucial to the formation of the NFIW. She thought, for example, that memories of the Women's Declaration of Rights passed at the World Congress of Women at Copenhagen in June 1953 had inspired the formal establishment of the NFIW. In particular, the remembering of a moving episode at that Congress where a document with 17,000 signatures by Bengali women in support of the declaration was presented to Dora Russell, was inspirational for the founders of the NFIW.

In her speech at the 1954 conference, Dora spoke of the need for women's emancipation and the role of women in preventing further world wars. 'Women's struggle for social rights, for peace, are not a separatist women's movement, nor can it be anti-man.'[41] Sarla remembers that speech well, particularly because she wrote the Hindi language sections of the NFIW newsletters:

> She spoke about that and how women need bread and peace for their children and not wars. That was the main strain of her speech, which was very much liked. And immediately an illiterate woman from the audience got up, got up came to the mike and said, 'Can I say something? ... We are all women, we all love our home and children and all ... We don't want wars. We don't want bombs. We only want bread. Bread for our children so that they can feed.' It was clap – everyone.

Sarla also recalled the other international visitor, Betty Riley from Australia, who spoke eloquently about the horrors of the war and the hydrogen bomb, saying that women throughout the world must unite against them.

> 50% of the world's population are women. For whatever they unite and strive must have far-reaching and effective consequences.[42]

Primla's narration of the inaugural meeting focused more on the Indian founders of the NFIW whom she saw as motivated by world peace. The NFIW was involved in most of the peace conferences held at that time in India and the world.[43] Both Primla and Sarla were in constant contact with the national liberation movements of Palestine, Vietnam, Cambodia, and Laos, the women's committee of the Soviet Union and the CND in England on issues of world peace. Primla later was specifically involved with international protests, like those against the Tomahawk missiles in the UK in the 1980s. After this, Primla spent a year at the WIDF in Berlin in 1986 where she cemented her international contacts. The memories of these international links and actions were instrumental in both Primla and Sarla retaining their sense of being 'citizens of the world,' concerned with injustice wherever it happened. Even at their advanced age, they were frequently called upon to speak at demonstrations in support of global liberation movements.

Affective relationships

It became clear through our interviews that the strongest memories held by these women which influenced their activist work were of the relationships they had built with their fellow activists. They met women from other cultures, with different religious beliefs, ways of life, and political ideologies. The major factors that kept them active in various causes were memories and ties of personal affection. When we asked Primla about Freda Brown, she fondly remembered her personal qualities as well as her activism.

> Oh Freda was really a lovely person ... and she just had a way of making a speech – she appealed to common people, otherwise you know we tend

to talk so much in jargon ... or we feel that those high ideas must go to the common people. But she had such a knack of putting things and she was really a lovely person, lovely person ... She spent an evening here [at Primla's house] and she ate everything. Oh, she loved it ... we had a good evening, you know. But I remember Freda, you know when her first grandchild was born, she would bring all these photos ... and we all felt that we knew her.

One particular case demonstrates these affective ties clearly, that of Rajni Kumar. As Nancie Jones, she had met her Indian husband Yudhishter Kumar in London where he was studying during the war. In 1944, he decided he would return to India, to a turbulent life in the Freedom Movement and later the Communist Party. Nancie's mother and the colonial government discouraged her from following him as she wanted to do.

... when we went up to the ward office to get my permission to go, they also put my mother off and said that, 'How would you know this man is not married with a family? We find so many Indians who come here and when they go back there, we find that they're already married with a family and you knew nothing about him. We know nothing about his family so you're taking a big risk.'

Kumar, however, contracted tuberculosis and wrote to Nancie, telling her not to come as his condition was dire. Nancie continues:

When the letter came and I read it out to my mother, I said, 'Mum, what would you do?' She said, 'You must go, dear. He needs you.' ... They were very supportive, no doubt about it. I think when you're very sick, you have somebody you love by your side. It certainly helps them. It gives you that desire to live, yeah. So I think I did do the right thing and of course I was very much in love with India.

Rajni Kumar became active in working among the left in India. She considers herself as a founding member of the NFIW though she was not able to attend the 1953 Delhi meeting because her only child was gravely ill. He died in the coming months, leaving Rajni devastated. Her fellow activists decided that Rajni should go to the Copenhagen conference in October, even though she was not originally chosen to go, because she urgently needed a change of scene:

I was very, very broken. [He was] just four and a quarter, four years and actually I was out for a few months.... So I was recovering from my shock and the [ladies] said, 'Rajni should join the delegation. It'll be a therapy for her to go.' So normally I think I would not have been added, frankly. They did this for me because I was in a state of suffering and it did help me a lot because I went there and seeing all of that makes you realize other people's sorrows are much more than your own.[44]

Remembering is the means through which individuals bring their past to bear on the present and connect old and new spaces. Rajni's remembering practice co-exists with both the present moment and her memories of affective relationships. The memories of these women demonstrate that people, places, and memories are too expansive for the national borders that attempt to contain them. Rajni's memories are rooted in her body and geography, the physical loss of her son and the geography of exile. They locate similarities among women from a variety of backgrounds, troubling the binary oppositions between the foreign and the familiar, safe and dangerous, acceptable and unacceptable, and home and away. They enact what Zadie Smith calls 'a mockery of that idea, a neutral place'.[45]

For Sarla, Primla, and Rajni, memories of affective and emotional ties were an intrinsic part of their politics. The narratives of their activist lives were filled with remembrances of other activist lives, where the ties of affection mitigated against premises not necessarily held in common. Whether Communist, Congress, Theosophist, or of other political persuasion, these activists could work together on common goals and maintain personal relationships that transcended their differences. These memories were important in shaping their present politics which was about finding common ground on which to work, rather than highlighting differences. The memories of Sarla, Primla, and Rajni are active practices, producing analogies among locations and people and enabling them to move fluidly between the present moment and stories of the past. Our narrators experienced and remembered their activism, in the women's movements, the nationalist struggles, and current battles for female rights, in different ways and sought to remain both attuned to those divergences and communicate across them. For them memory is inclusive, not because every member of their communities remembers their activist experiences in the same ways, but rather because each is engaged in the practice of active remembering, which creates new spaces that incorporate disparate backgrounds and histories without flattening differences.[46]

Notes

1 Partha Chatterjee, *The Nation and Its Fragments* (Princeton, NJ: Princeton University Press, 2009).
2 Amrita Basu, *Women's Movements in the Global Era: The Power of Local Feminisms* (Boulder, CO: Westview Press, 2010), 3.
3 Nandita Gandhi and Nandita Shah, *The Issues at Stake: Theory and Practice in the Contemporary Women's Movement in India* (New Delhi: Kali for Women, 1992).
4 Geraldine Forbes, *Women in Modern India* (New York: Cambridge University Press, 1996); Sanjay Seth, *Postcolonial Theory and International Relations (Interventions)* (London: Routledge, 2013).
5 Gail Pearson, 'Women in Public Life in Bombay City with Special Reference to the Civil Disobedience Movement' (PhD diss., JNU, New Delhi, 1979); Gail Pearson,

'Reserved Seats: Women and the Vote in Bombay,' *Indian Economic and Social History Review* 20, no. 1 (1983); Padma Anagol, 'Agency, Periodisation and Change in the Gender and Women's History of Colonial India,' *Gender and History* 20, no. 3 (2008): 603–627; Padma Anagol, 'Feminist Inheritances and Foremothers: The Beginnings of Feminism in Modern India,' *Women's History Review* 19, no. 4 (2010): 523–546; Annie Devenish, *Debating Women's Citizenship in India, 1930–1960* (New Delhi and London: Bloomsbury, 2019).
6 Kumkum Sangari and Sudesh Vaid, eds., *Recasting Women* (New Delhi: Kali for Women, 1989).
7 Devenish, *Debating Women's Citizenship.*
8 Michelle E. Tusan, 'Writing Stri Dharma: International Feminism, Nationalist Politics, and Women's Press Advocacy in Late Colonial India,' *Women's History Review* 12, no. 4 (2003): 623–649; V. Geetha and S. V. Rajadurai, *Towards a Non-Brahmin Millennium: From Iyothee Thas to Periyar* (Kolkata: Samya, 1998).
9 Vina Mazumdar, *Role of Rural Women in Development* (University of Sussex, Institute of Development Studies; Bombay: Allied Publishers, 1978); Mary E. John, 'Feminism, Poverty and the Emergent Social Order', in *Social Movements in India: Poverty, Power and Politics*, eds. Raka Ray and Mary Fainsod Katzenstein (Lanham, MD: Rowman & Littlefield, 2005), 107–134, here: 109.
10 Harald Wydra, 'Generations of Memory: Elements of a Conceptual Framework,' *Comparative Studies in Society and History* 60, no. 1 (2018): 5–34. doi: 10.1017/S0010417517000391.
11 Renu Chakravartty, *Communists in Indian Women's Movement 1940–1950* (Delhi: People's Publishing House, 1980); Gargi Chakravartty and Supriya Chotani, *Charting a New Path: Early Years of National Federation of Indian Women* (New Delhi: People's Publishing House, 2018).
12 Vina Mazumdar, *Women's Participation in Political Life* (UNESCO, 1983), Geneva, 10; John, 'Feminism,' 109–110.
13 Wydra, 'Generations of Memory.'
14 Reinhart Koselleck, *Zeitschichten* (Frankfurt/Main: Suhrkamp. 2003) quoted in Wydra, 'Generations of Memory,' 6.
15 Raka Ray, *Fields of Protest: Women's Movements in India* (Minneapolis: University of Minnesota Press., 1999), 11.
16 Hajrah Begum, *Recalling Old Days: How the NFIW Was Formed* (NFIW Twenty Year Anniversary Special ed.) (Primla Loomba, 1973), 4–5; Geraldine Forbes, 'The Politics of Respectability: Indian Women and the National Congress,' in *The Indian National Congress: Centenary Highlights*, ed. D.A. Low (Bombay: Oxford University Press, 1988), 54–97.
17 Padma Anagol, *The Emergence of Feminism in India, 1850–1920* (Aldershot: Ashgate, 2005).
18 Sarah K. Broome, 'Stri-Dharma: Voice of the Indian Women's Rights Movement, 1928–1936' (MA thesis, Georgia State University, 2012).
19 Uma Ganesan, 'Gender and Caste: Self-Respect Movement in the Madras Presidency, 1925–1950' (PhD diss. University of Cincinnati, 2011); Geetha and Rajadurai, *Towards a Non-Brahmin Millennium*; V. Geetha, 'Periyar, Women and an Ethic of Citizenship,' in *Gender and Caste*, ed. Anupama Rao (London: Zed Books, 2005).
20 Suchetana Chattopadhyay, *An Early Communist – Muzaffar Ahmad in Calcutta. 1913–1929* (Calcutta: Tulika Books, 2017).
21 Chakravartty and Chotani, *Charting a New Path*; Manikuntala Sen, *In Search of Freedom: An Unfinished Journey* (Kolkata: Stree, 2001).
22 Kama Maclean, 'The Fundamental Rights Resolution: Nationalism, Internationalism, and Cosmopolitanism in an Interwar Moment,' *Comparative Studies of South Asia, Africa and the Middle East* 37, no. 2 (2017): 213–219. doi 10.1215/1089201x-4132833.
23 *Stri Dharma*, May 1937, 286.
24 *WIDF Bulletin*, 1953 #10.

25 Begum, *Recalling Old Days*, 4.
26 Primla Loomba, interviewed by Devleena Ghosh and Heather Goodall, Delhi, January 2014.
27 Hajrah Begum, NMML Oral History interview by S.L. Manchanda, 1994. NMML, 9 September 1994, quoted in Chakravartty and Chotani, *Charting a New Path*, 42.
28 Primla Loomba, ed., *NFIW Twenty Year Anniversary Special*. (1973), 5.
29 Begum, *Recalling Old Days*, 4–5.
30 NFIW Congress Report (Calcutta: Sarla Sharma Personal Copy, 1954), 12–13.
31 Alessandro Portelli. *The Death of Luigi Trastulli and Other Stories. Form and Meaning in Oral History* (Albany: SUNY, 1991).
32 Akhil Gupta and James Ferguson, eds., *Culture, Power, Place: Explorations in Critical Anthropology* (Durham, NC: Duke University Press, 1997).
33 Quoted in David Forgacs, *A Gramsci Reader* (London: Lawrence and Wishart, 1988), 326.
34 Sharon Crozier-De Rosa and Vera Mackie, *Remembering Women's Activism* (London and New York: Routledge, 2018).
35 Indu Agnihotri and Mazumdar Vina, 'Changing Terms of Political Discourse: Women's Movement in India, 1970s–1990s,' *Economic and Political Weekly* 30, no. 29 (1995): 1869–1878.
36 Sarla Sharma, interviewed by Devleena Ghosh and Heather Goodall, Delhi, 28 November 2012; 14 February 2013; 18 January 2014.
37 Primla Loomba, interviewed by Devleena Ghosh and Heather Goodall, Delhi, January 2014.
38 Sarla Sharma, interviewed Devleena Ghosh and Heather Goodall, Delhi, 28 November 2012.
39 Primla Loomba, interviewed by Devleena Ghosh and Heather Goodall, Delhi, January 2014.
40 Ali Raza, Roy Franziska and Benjamin Zachariah, eds., *The Internationalist Moment: South Asia, Worlds, and World Views, 1917–39* (New Delhi, Thousand Oaks, CA; London, Singapore: Sage, 2015).
41 NFIW Newsletter II (7) 1954: 4–5, (Women's News, on Madras Peace Conference.), 4.
42 NFIW Congress Report (Calcutta. Sarla Sharma Personal Copy, 1954), 4.
43 NFIW Newsletter II (7) 1954: 4–5, (Women's News, on Madras Peace Conference), 4–5.
44 Rajni Kumar, interviewed by Devleena Ghosh, 20 January, 2013.
45 Zadie Smith, *White Teeth* (London: Penguin, 2001), 464.
46 Katie Logan, 'Re-membering Displacement: Miral al-Tahawy's Brooklyn Heights and the Politics of Memory,' *Signs: Journal of Women in Culture and Society* 43, no. 3 (2018): 617–639.

4

HISTORY AS STRATEGY

Imagining universal feminism in the women's movement

Sophie van den Elzen and Berteke Waaldijk

Introduction

Anna Julia Cooper was one of six African American women invited to speak at the World Congress of Representative Women, which gathered over 2,000 women at the Chicago World's Fair of 1893.[1] In her speech, she gave a short history of the progress of African American women since the abolition of slavery in the US in 1865, which linked their enforced silence under slavery to their continued absence from historical narratives of women's emancipation:

> [A]ll through the darkest period of the colored women's oppression in this country her yet unwritten history is full of heroic struggle, a struggle against fearful and overwhelming odds [...] The painful, patient, and silent toil of mothers to gain a free simple title to the bodies of their daughters, the despairing fight, as of an entrapped tigress, to keep hallowed their own persons, would furnish material for epics. That more went down under the flood than stemmed the current is not extraordinary. The majority of our women are not heroines but I do not know that a majority of any race of women are heroines. [...] The white woman could at least plead for her own emancipation; the black woman, doubly enslaved, could but suffer and struggle and be silent.[2]

Cooper, a scholar and activist who would obtain her PhD in history from the Sorbonne in 1925, was one of the early theorists of Black feminism. Her comments beautifully introduce several questions which our chapter seeks to explore: how do emancipation movements remember 'their' histories? Who are remembered as hero(in)es, and whose histories remain 'unwritten'? How are 'movement histories' connected to political debates? Who are included, and in what ways can historical silences and exclusions be remedied? With our opening we pay tribute to bell hooks who, 90 years later, quoted Cooper's words at the beginning of her now classic work *Ain't I a Woman*, in which she celebrates Black women's feminist voices and criticizes the exclusion of black women's perspectives from feminism and women's movements.[3]

Historical references are omnipresent in social and political movements, taking the shape of popular celebrations of anniversaries, honorific naming, veneration of a 'pantheon' of selected movement leaders, and the reverent preservation of material objects, as the introduction points out.[4] Scholarly historiographical work about the origins of a movement and struggles from the past plays a role in this collective remembrance. Across social movements, scholarly or well-researched histories, whether book-length studies or shorter articles, facilitate activists' imagined relation to the past and help them to decide what is worthy of being remembered.[5] Historical perspectives legitimize causes and courses of action, construct historical continuities, and enable identification with and affection for those identified as significant historical actors, within the movement or from other contexts.

Within cultural memory studies, forms of popular remembrance often attract more attention than the production and reception of historiographical works. The relative paucity of scholarly analysis of the memory dynamics of historical writing might be the result of a perceived opposition between history and memory: where memory is considered personal, history is imagined to be more objective; where memory is democratic and accessible, history is more institutional and hierarchical; memories seem to make the voices of victims heard, where histories are supposedly written by the victors. There has been an increasing recognition, both within academic history and within cultural memory studies, that this opposition is artificial, as the rise of oral history and new historicism within literary studies indicate.[6] With this chapter we want to contribute to such efforts to strengthen links between historiographical research and cultural memory studies.

In their introduction, the editors have rightly emphasized the need for more historical perspectives on social movements. In our contribution, we hope to show that attention to historical perspectives of activists deepens the understanding of social movements. Our chapter considers the roles that the production of historical knowledge plays in a key debate of women's organized contention: the debate about whom women's movements represent. We focus on a main question in this debate: that of the possibility of a 'universal' women's movement spanning the globe. As we will show, this universalism was a dream which motivated a substantial body of feminist 'movement histories' at the turn of the nineteenth century.[7] However, through this 'universalism' these actors also produced exclusions which were continued for decades. At the turn of the twentieth century, feminist scholars deployed a range of approaches in their historiographical work to unsettle the universal and make space for the excluded. We will conclude that strategies to include what is excluded in historical and political narratives blur the traditional boundaries between grass roots and academy, and scholarly and vulgar knowledge, and ultimately allow us to rethink the opposition between memory and history.

As the example of hooks' citation shows, references to the past continued to play a role in political debates about the character of women's movements in the twentieth century. hooks uses Cooper's words to address the silencing of Black women in women's movements in the late twentieth century. Because we cannot give a complete overview of the role of historical narratives in women's movements and feminist activism since its beginnings, we have decided on a focus on historical writings that address the possibility of a universal, global, or 'all-inclusive' feminism. Imagining this possibility, in response to the central claim that gender plays a role everywhere, has been a crucial element of feminism as a social movement.

We contrast six histories from the international campaign for suffrage in 1880–914, a period later historically interpreted the 'First Wave' of feminism, with a diverse range of recent (1980–present) well-known historiographical interventions that address racial exclusion within feminist movements. We study these texts from a memory perspective; we approach how they operated in their social lives, reflecting on and intervening in political debates of their times, by asking what 'strategies' their authors employed.[8] From this perspective, self-historicization in books and articles emerges as a 'mnemonic practice' of social movements, that operates with distinct dynamics of authorization, exclusion, and power, in complex conjunction with others, like the erection of monuments or the singing of songs.[9]

In our analysis, we ask what strategies authors who wrote as experts and as activists employed to imagine, affirm, criticize, or deconstruct the idea of a 'universal' women's movement that would include all women, all over the world. These strategies encompass choices for particular forms and media; narrative structures, authorization strategies; and research designs. In the first-wave movement histories we distinguish two 'origin stories' of feminist agitation which accomplish the imagination of a 'universal' feminism that transcends national boundaries by excluding non-Western, underprivileged perspectives; a gesture of inclusion at the price of exclusion. They are the 'European' narrative of the role of middle-class women in charity and philanthropy, and the 'American' narrative of white women's 'betrayal' by abolitionists. In the post-1980 texts that reject these exclusions and develop alternative modes of engaging with history, we distinguish three trends. One is the effort for full and diverse transnational overviews, and another includes works that suggest that the inclusion of excluded voices not only completes the historical picture, but actually changes what can be considered feminism. The final strategies we identify are in some ways 'beyond history'; even though many contemporary inclusive arguments about feminism and women's movements do still refer to the past and continue to employ historical narratives, they transgress boundaries between 'history' and 'memory' by proposing alternative relations to the 'archive,' time and representations of the past.

1880–914: creating the history of a 'global' women's movement

The tendency of women agitators to conceptualize their activities as part of a large transnational, or even global, movement significantly increased around the turn of the century (1880–914). Following the first international women's congress in Paris in 1878, members of organizations like the International Council of Women (1888) and the International Alliance of Women (1904; originally International Woman Suffrage Association) created and promoted a 'feminist internationalist' collective consciousness.[10] One, perhaps surprising, vehicle for this was their self-historicization.

During this period, a wave of movement histories appeared, which took the shape of transnational overviews and were interconnected through citations and the authors' personal networks. In the following, we survey six; three reference works, which claimed scientific validity; and three more programmatic, partisan suffragist histories. We discuss these in their respective ideological contexts, but ultimately show that they promoted the idea of a unified transnational women's movement through similar exclusions of stories from non-white and underprivileged women. Moreover, both types of histories employed two central narratives which were instrumental to this exclusion.

Reference works

Theodore Stanton's *The Woman Question in Europe* (1884), Helene Lange and Gertrud Bäumer's *Geschichte der Frauen in den Kulturländern* (1901) and Käthe Schirmacher's *Féminisme aux États-Unis, en France, dans la Grande Bretagne, en Suède et en Russie* (1898) were presented as reliable reference works which could serve as information sources for readers who were, as Lange and Bäumer worried, too busy to study their movement's history individually.[11] A closer look, however, reveals the underlying operations of exclusion by which they achieved semblances of transnational coherence. The ideas of transnational coherence these volumes presented were legitimated and authorized by various formal and compositional strategies: their contributors were authoritative scholarly or veteran voices, they presented statistical information, and/or they directed readers to further readings.

Theodore Stanton, famous American feminist Elizabeth Cady Stanton's son, published *The Woman Question in Europe* in 1884. Mainly intended for American audiences,[12] it contains a collection of contributions on the history of the women's movement in various European countries, written by prominent movement actors such as Millicent Garrett Fawcett, and accompanied by an introduction by well-known Anglo-Irish reformist author Frances Power Cobbe. The eminent activist standing of all the contributors within the women's movement is emphasized not only in the introduction, but also in a lengthy biographical note opening each chapter.

The Woman Question in Europe shows a tension between the desire to conceptualize the women's movement as transnational and multi-vocal, and the suffrage-organizational need to keep tight control over the definition of women's progress, defined as an outgrowth of Western liberal progress. In her introduction, Frances Cobbe suggests that women's political awakening should be seen on a global scale, characterizing it as a 'uniform impetus' which 'has taken place within living memory among the women of almost every race on the globe [and] has stirred an entire sex, even half the human race.' She posits that political franchise is the single 'crown and completion of the progress,' discerning the same shape in the mobilization of each national context.[13] Cobbe's narrowing of the impulse to think globally to a specific white Western narrative is especially apparent when she suggests that feminists should not ally themselves with what she considers 'experiments fraught with difficulty and danger;' the extension of suffrage to men of 'alien races,' supposedly untrained in civil liberty.[14]

This reterritorialization can be observed throughout the collection. Stanton groups his chapters in an 'ethnological order,'[15] beginning with England and ending with a single chapter on the 'Orient.' This last chapter is itself again 'hierarchically' divided; Athens-educated, fiercely Greek-nationalist contributor Kalliope Kehaya distinguishes between Greek women in Greece, Christian Greek women under a 'foreign yoke,' and 'Oriental' women, including Ottomans and Jews.[16] Whereas Europe is presented as increasingly rich in liberal women activists, Oriental women are presented as not just irrelevant to this history, but to history in general: 'I shall say but little concerning these latter races, for their women are in a state of lamentable inactivity which offers almost nothing worthy of record.'[17] *The Woman Question in Europe* claims to describe a universal movement that 'unites' all women. However, it does so by using imperialistic and racialized categories of civic, political, and economic progress as emanating from Europe. Its ambition to make the women's movement universal was based on the exclusion of women's experiences that did not conform to this model.

Helene Lange and Gertrud Bäumer's *Geschichte der Frauen in den Kulturländern* was published in 1901, as the first part of a four-volume *Handbuch der Frauenbewegung*.

The editors collected contributions detailing the history of the movement in 15 European countries, as well as Russia and the US. They professed the hope that, by providing a handbook, they could unite women's individual efforts into a larger movement:

> So many work industriously on little tasks, without connecting these to the grand goal, which they too help achieve, and some stand at the rudder without having a compass, exploring opportunities for development, where they haven't learned, from the history of the movement, its developmental laws.[18]

They explain that they privileged coherence over detail since they wanted their readers to grasp the broader developmental narrative: 'The expanded propaganda is more prone to lead one astray, than to orient her.'[19] This coherent narrative aimed to demonstrate that the women's movement was not a simple side-effect of economic progress, but originated in women's rising awareness, which the editors, with a Whiggish perception of history, deemed inevitable.[20] The political context the authors imagined for their book becomes clear from remarks about the hope they feel that their arguments will support moderate, but persistent work toward making all women aware of their position, over 'noisy agitation.'[21] Lange and Bäumer belonged to the more moderate women's movement in Germany and were in their writing and publishing keenly aware of the socialist and radical competition.[22]

Käthe Schirmacher's comparative study, *Féminisme aux États-Unis, en France [etc.]* (1898) sought to portray the women's movement as a phenomenon that could be sociologically explained. Schirmacher argued that different degrees of feminist mobilization could be explained by societal difference, looking at population, economic strengths, and political differences. Her introduction stressed the importance of factual and statistical accuracy, as well as detailed contextualization, over reading pleasure.[23]

Though making the universalist argument that 'feminism is an international movement which is [...] born from the same intellectual, moral and economic causes,'[24] Schirmacher stressed the diversity of the feminist impulse in each European country by ending her chapters with a note on the specific praiseworthy characteristics of women's mobilization in that country. This way, she conceptualized national differences as a source of inspiration for a unified cause.[25] However, this generous view of difference is limited to Western middle-class traditions. Schirmacher is not interested in working classes, contending that, with the exception of France, no socialist feminism exists.[26] Nor do non-Western contexts pique her interest; she presents Russia as a victim of 'certain Oriental influences' to explain its supposed developmental lag.[27]

Schirmacher had visited the Chicago World's Fair in 1893, at which various 'congresses' and 'parliaments' gathered representatives and visitors from all over the world.[28] She had spoken at the World's Congress of Representative Women, at which Anna Cooper also spoke. Yet aside from a statistic on African American women's literacy rates,[29] her analysis does not mention Black or Asian women, and her explanatory schemes are not interested in non-Western contexts. It is apparent that these 'reference works' of international feminism, which ostensibly aimed to facilitate, for their readers, a more objective and scholarly engagement with the past, encouraged major blindnesses.

Partisan views of the past

We now turn to some examples of shorter and more provocative historiographical interventions, which explicitly allied themselves with the political campaign for female suffrage.

Käthe Schirmacher wrote her *Die Moderne Frauenbewegung: ein geschichtlicher Überblick* (1905) after her conversion to German nationalism.[30] It quickly became a quasi-official handbook of the International Woman Suffrage Alliance (IWSA), together with Alice Zimmern's work, discussed below. It was endorsed by IWSA President Carrie Chapman Catt, reprinted in 1909,[31] and translated into English in 1912.[32]

Die Moderne Frauenbewegung presents a grand narrative of embattled Western enlightened values. Schirmacher describes the oppression of women as a universal phenomenon: 'In the greater part of the world, woman is a pack animal or slave [...] even in a large number of countries that have European civilization, woman remains mute and unfree.'[33] The resistance against this oppression, however, is a Western prerogative, which is only spread through education.

Like Stanton, Schirmacher orders her chapters into ethnic groupings, beginning with an 86-page section on 'Germanic' countries, which include her favored example of the US as well as the UK, and concluding with the 'Orient and Outer Orient,' a section taking up only nine pages. Schirmacher explains that the women's movement has been most successful in 'Germanic' countries in part because of the superior values of their Protestant heritage. The women's movement in Slavic countries, discussed in the second to last section, however, have had little success as these countries 'lack an old and deep Western European culture. Everywhere have oriental conceptions of women's character left persistent traces.'[34]

About the Orient, she writes:

> Here woman, nearly without exception, is a mere toy or pack animal, to the extent that it viscerally affects us Europeans. Of course analogies may be found with us, and these unfortunate backslides into barbary cannot be reprimanded and despised enough.[35]

She further attributes women's rights activity outside Europe to individual praiseworthy Western initiatives.[36] Too brief to provide any real insights, the last section merely casts the Orient as Europe's timeless and menacing Other.[37] Schirmacher rouses her Western readers by encouraging pride in their exceptional shared modernity, supposedly derived from their Protestant culture which encouraged 'a stronger education for self-sufficiency and responsibility,' and provides them with the image of a barbaric enemy at the gates.[38]

Alice Zimmern's booklet *Women's Suffrage in Many Lands...* appeared in 1909, in time for the fourth congress of the International Woman Suffrage Alliance in London. It received a second edition within a year. The work starts with the US and ends with chapters on South Africa and 'Australia and New Zealand.' Zimmern explains that she had to confine herself to only those countries where there was sufficient organized effort, which meant her selection 'are for the most part members of the [IWSA].'[39]

Zimmern's account was also meant to extend to readers outside the women's movement. In her foreword, Chapman Catt writes that after a long period of quiet suffrage efforts, 'now all the world is talking of it, and is asking questions concerning its past, its present, and its future aims. This little book will answer those questions.'[40] Considering Zimmern's account as an extension of the IWSA's propaganda efforts explains its insistence throughout on the vote as feminism's ultimate goal, with suffrage activities and internationalization rounding out most chapters. Catt's foreword makes this conformity explicit: 'The history, with change of scene and personality of advocates, is practically the same in all lands; a struggle against similar customs and traditions which have held women in universal tutelage.'[41] Like Schirmacher's 1905 account, which was a main source for the book,[42] Catt casts backwardness and tradition as the main adversaries of women's emancipation. Zimmern's chapters orchestrate national histories in such a way that the achievement of suffrage and international organizing appear as the highest stadium of feminist development.

In her popular *Wegbereidsters* [Pathbreakers] (1909), Johanna Naber described the lives of four English reformers, Elizabeth Fry, Florence Nightingale, Josephine Butler, and Priscilla Bright McLaren. According to Naber, a prolific Dutch historian and prominent women's rights advocate, these four cases all illustrated a universal principle of women's agitation; through philanthropic work, women awakened to their social and political limitations, and these individual awakenings were followed by a period of association.[43] Naber ultimately suggests that female suffrage is the 'lever' by which more philanthropy can be achieved, and explains that she selected these British cases as the most pronounced examples of a universal development: 'This process is international. It is how matters developed here, and how they developed elsewhere.'[44]

In her attempt to articulate universal characteristics of the women's movement, Naber's account of powerful female reformers prunes the possibilities of female agitation down to a very specific shape, leaving no space for alternative trajectories of political awakening. Protagonists such as Josephine Butler and Elizabeth Fry famously improved the lot of other women, in brothels and prisons. These women in need, however, formed the terrain, the passive background, on which the English middle- and upper-class women worked. Only the philanthropists could be heroines and feminists; they united and formed the associations, and they were the vanguard of the movement that educated and lifted others.[45]

Two origin stories

Both the reference works and the partisan histories sought to contribute to a feminism that looked across borders, and supply it with a sense of historical continuity. However, all works ultimately mobilized the colonial and imperialist view of the world as divided in modern enlightened nations and 'Oriental,' backward or undeveloped countries. They promoted as the vanguard of a global women's movement, a fundamentally Western organized suffragism, which started in the US and was understood as based on European Enlightenment ideals of equality. Across the corpus, two recurrent origin stories of feminism can be identified which were used to underwrite this conception. One, more Europe-oriented, storyline positions women's involvement in philanthropy and charity as a starting point; the other 'American' historical narrative focuses on white women's involvement in abolitionism.

The European account almost ritualistically narrates how suffrage activism developed among philanthropic 'heroines.' Bäumer and Lange's collection is full of philanthropic efforts, such as Anna Pappritz's account of the Versailles conference.[46] Johanna Naber's pantheon of philanthropic suffragists connected women's political activation fundamentally to their social work. Theodore Stanton's decision to have philanthropist Frances Cobbe, who suggested that woman suffrage would bring about the 'happiest Peace the world has ever seen,'[47] introduce his volume, was crucial to create a sense of an overarching 'European' perspective. This philanthropic genealogy of feminism was useful in the broader imagining of a 'custodial citizenship' in which traditionally feminine virtues were valorized while addressing middle- and upper-class women at the same time in their professional positions, as teachers, social workers, doctors, and lawyers.[48]

This historical narrative, inspiring as it was to middle-class female philanthropists and the first women in professions around 1900, was based on an exclusionary perspective that silenced and marginalized the many for the benefit of select actors. Organized charity and philanthropy was represented as a white middle-class activity, ignoring voluntary association by working-class women and women of color, whose stories of civil activism were not integrated and hence became marginal in construction of universal feminism. This process was based on decisions about what to hear, what to repeat, and what not to hear and exclude.[49]

The 'American' storyline about the origin of feminism in women's participation in the abolitionist movement was central to all accounts of American feminism. The authors wrote sympathetically about white women's outrage at their 'betrayals' by male abolitionists: first when female delegates were barred from participating in the World Anti-Slavery Convention in London in 1840; again when the abolitionists supported the 15th Amendment, which gave Black men the right to vote but withheld the vote from women. This origin story located the beginnings of feminism in white women's outrage at these exclusions, and their perception of an analogy between their own position and that of slaves. Schirmacher's comment is representative of the tone with which this narrative is rendered: 'Heavily and deeply the American women felt it, that in the eyes of their lawmakers a member of a lowly race, just for being a man, was valued over any woman, no matter how well educated.'[50]

This narrative was reproduced from the highly influential American *History of Woman Suffrage* by Elizabeth Cady Stanton, Susan B. Anthony and Matilda Gage (1881–922). It offered several rhetorical advantages to European feminists; it legitimated feminists' contentious action, as it suggested that, like in the US, European women's philanthropy would not yield suffrage without agitation. Moreover, it was an opportunity to further consolidate the opposition between the interests of white women and non-white men, rousing the fears of non-white threats to white women's emancipation on which arguments like those of Cobbe and Schirmacher depended.

The histories leaned on these American and European narratives about the history of the women's movement for their constructions of a coherent 'universal' feminism. As this discussion has shown, these constructions had a price. The centralization of white middle-class perspectives depended on the exclusion of other women's perspectives.

1980–2018: new strategies for inclusions

After 1920, transnational and national feminist contention became less visible. Suffrage having been granted in many countries, many within and outside the movements believed gradual improvement in the position of women could be expected. With new forms of feminist activism in the 1960s, feminists identified their activism as a 'second' wave. While recalling the late nineteenth-century struggle for the right to vote and to get an education, they also began to make more radical demands regarding their bodily autonomy, women's health care, changing sexual norms, and full and equal access to the labor market. In doing so they discovered radical predecessors.

Second-wave feminists forged a relationship between their demands and those of the nineteenth-century suffrage activists. An example of this self-conscious establishment of historical connection is the 1970s Dutch group, the 'Dolle Mina's' (Wild Mina's), who named themselves after the Dutch radical first-wave feminist Wilhelmina Drucker. Writing 'women's history' and histories of feminism was again an important aspect of second wave agitation, as feminist publishing collectives and journals focused on women's history, and feminist historians followed the adage 'to restore women to history and restore our history to women.'[51]

Just as texts written by first-wave feminists, these texts had a social life and connected research and activism. However, there was an important difference: these studies could now also become institutional, when they were produced within academic contexts, conferences, and scholarly journals. In the late nineteenth century, women were nearly invariably excluded from practicing academic history. Despite the efforts to legitimize their work that we discussed above, those women writing histories in the nineteenth century operated in the margins of the professional field. Gender historians have explored how women writing history in the nineteenth century changed the character of historical writing, by exploring historical fiction and including more social and 'personal' themes in their writing.[52] While most first-wave movement histories were written by 'amateurs,' women who were not part of the academic culture of historical writing, now, in the last decades of the twentieth century, there were feminist activists who were trained and socialized as academic historians.

The historiographical interventions that we identify as addressing the (im) possibility of a global, universal feminist movement from 1980 onwards are in dialog with a different present and past than their ancestors. A globalized public sphere had come into being and academic scholarly work was no longer the prerogative of white upper-class men.[53] In the years between 1880 and 1920 the women's movement had competed for attention with socialist and labor movements, and with nationalism in different forms. The struggle for the right to vote increasingly came to unite the movement. In the last decades of the twentieth century, however, feminist movements shared public attention with civil rights movements, sexuality-focused movements, environmental activism, and post- and decolonial anti-globalization activism. The demands of feminists in the twentieth and twenty-first century were often formulated at the intersections with these other social movements and became more diverse.

In this second part of our chapter, we focus on feminist authors who, in the decades around 2000, intervened in the memory and mnemonic practices of feminism by subverting the century-long heritage of racial exclusion and colonial thinking that the canonization of first-wave history writing reinforced. Inclusive histories of feminism and women's movements had by no means become the norm. There are many examples of women's histories that are in fact histories of white Western women, repeating patterns of exclusion and marginalization that are eerily similar to those of the expansive monographs of the early period. Examples like the 'Gender and Race' chapter of 1977s *Becoming Visible* wrote only about non-Western women from the perspective of the white protagonists.[54] However, these now suffered a sustained challenge and critique from both activists and academic scholars, categories that could now overlap.

This section considers some influential examples of works which re-tilled the grounds for any possibility of a global feminism by centralizing in their analyses those images of enslaved, colonized and racialized 'Other' women which were produced in the pursuit of a unified concept of women's emancipation. Different strategies can be distinguished through which these contestations sought to achieve more inclusive histories to serve as the basis of a conception of global feminism. The first two that we describe share a belief in the possibility and relevance of historical knowledge as part of political engagement; the third approach problematizes historiographical activity altogether and might be called an alternative for writing histories.

Restoring women of color to the history of feminism

From the 1970s on there have been authors who want to make marginalized voices heard within histories of feminism. These authors do more than just add women of color to the narrative. Their historical interventions contribute to the debates about what it means to be part of a feminist movement that, in the words of bell hooks, 'has as its fundamental goal the liberation of all people.'[55]

In her *Ain't I a Woman* (1981), titled after Black feminist Sojourner Truth's famous speech for the Akron women's Convention in 1851, bell hooks explores Black women's experiences by examining, as the cover indicates, 'the impact of sexism on the black woman during slavery, the devaluation of black womanhood, black male sexism, racism with the recent feminist movement, and the black woman's involvement with feminism.' hooks re-examines 'forgotten' feminists and points to historical connections between the struggle against slavery and the struggle against the oppression of women, and between sexism in slavery and contemporary sexism. Instead of the established narrative of white women joining white men in pursuit of abolitionism and coming to understand their own position through observing slavery, she foregrounds how black women experienced and theorized the connection between the two systems of oppression.

What makes hooks' text remarkable is the constant shift between sexism and racism in present and in past, and her systematic attention to historical work, especially when produced by Black women such as Anna Cooper and twentieth-century Black radical thinker Angela Davis. hooks also debunked the notion of solidarity between white and Black women, referring to an early article by Rosalyn Terborg-Penn, which showed that many white suffragists did not accept Black women as their equal in struggles.[56] Her political intervention cannot be imagined without the rich tapestry of historical references; references, we might add, that do not follow the pattern of enlightenment-inspired 'awareness' of oppression that dominated so many earlier histories of feminism. On the contrary, the historical references address the experiences of being enslaved, Black women's experiences with sexual violence, and the disregard for their love for partners and children. hooks describes the feminism of Sojourner Truth surviving and emerging triumphant from persecution, abuse, torture, and rape.[57] In contrast to the nineteenth-century conception, she suggests that nineteenth-century Black American women were more aware of sexist oppression 'than any other group.'[58]

The strategy of recuperating alternative historical facts is also very clear in one of the most frequently quoted critiques of Western feminist myopia and prejudice: Chandra Mohanty's 'Under Western Eyes' (1988). We do not want to repeat or summarize her extensive argument here, but think it is important to point out that in Mohanty's argument, attention to history and respect for historical specificity are crucial elements. While hooks focuses on Black American women, Mohanty's frame of reference is the colonial division between women in the Western world and 'Third World women.'

Mohanty addresses descriptions of women outside the West that conceive of them as a homogenous group of victims of both imperialist colonialism and 'traditional' religions, cultures, and practices such as Islam and Purdah. These histories, she argues, do not problematize the difference between Woman as an ideological concept and women as different, living, historical beings. This distinction, so fruitfully applied by feminists who discuss the position of women in the West, suddenly disappears when women in Africa, Asia, or other non-Western parts of the world are described.[59] This results, as Mohanty contends, in an unproductive return to the notion of biological features as uniting all women's experience.

Mohanty's essay takes the form of a critical description of histories of 'Third World women,' published by authors who seek to include non-Western women by portraying them as powerless victims. Many of these studies start from a universal definition of gender, which presumes that women are oppressed by men. For Third World women, this male oppression is supposedly sometimes aggravated, sometimes slightly relieved by colonial interventions, but the bottom line remains that all women suffer from the same male oppression. The authors of these histories, many of them Western themselves, tend to ignore different histories, different ways of organizing society.

For Mohanty, attention to the 'contradictions inherent in women's location' is crucial to understanding political action. She proposes historically precise narratives as an antidote to 'methodological universalism' that postulates women's oppression as key to understanding women outside the West. Women's resistance and agency are much more diverse; women are not only victims, but also agents that transform the structures that assign meaning to their lives and acts. With her call for other forms of understanding global feminism, Mohanty criticizes 'rescue-narratives' about non-Western women. Although she does not explicitly refer to first-wave narratives about feminism, she offers an alternative for Schirmacher's descriptions of women as 'pack animals'; she proposes to consider all women as agents and subjects who have a past, and have historical agency.

Mohanty and hooks' arguments are contributions to feminist debates; they are about the political future of feminism as a social movement.[60] They point out that historical marginalization is not only about the past, but also characterizes the contemporary women's movement and its continuing patterns of exclusion. It is instructive to read these texts not only as historical revisions, but also as texts that played a crucial role in expanding the cultural memory of feminism and women's movements. Like the examples from the turn of the century, they had a 'social life' far beyond academic discussions. They are quoted, referenced, and canonized in a wide range of discussions, even years after they were published. Mohanty captured this powerful potential of texts when she mused in 2003 that her essay has 'been widely cited, sometimes seriously engaged with, sometimes misread, and sometimes used as an enabling framework for cross-cultural feminist projects.'[61] A recent example of this enabling function is the use of hooks' and Mohanty's ideas in publications supporting the American activist group *Black Lives Matter*.[62]

Arguments such as those of hooks and Mohanty also impacted historical studies, as they inspired feminist historians to formulate new research questions. Unpublished or forgotten texts by Black women were recovered, published, read, and discussed. Scholars rewrote histories of feminism, paying attention to racism and colonial condescension. These instances were no longer excused as regrettable mistakes, as behavior that could be explained and in a way accepted. New analyses instead pointed out that the image of the autonomous enlightened Western feminists was predicated on the othering of those of another race, class, or culture.

This approach required new, non-heroic narratives about feminism. A pioneer of this revision of feminism was Antoinette Burton (1994). She described how British feminists were inspired by imperialism: Victorian feminists' admiration for empire and their identification with its racial and cultural ideals shaped a nineteenth-century women's movement with recognizably imperial concerns and sympathies. In other countries, similar revised histories of women's movements revealed the deeply colonial or fascist standpoints of feminist authors. Ann Stoler, another scholar of gender and colonialism, critically expanded the ways in which the 'colonial archive' is investigated, arguing for a move from 'archive-as-source to archive-as-subject.'[63] Maria Grever and Berteke Waaldijk's *Transforming the Public Sphere* analyzed the interaction of the colonial and the philanthropic impulses in the Dutch women's movement.[64] This rejection of heroism was a strategy to come to terms with the heritage of exclusion of the nineteenth-century women's movement. With these new histories, the tradition of heroic histories celebrating victories and hoping for the gradual arrival of a better future was replaced with movement histories that tried to be more sophisticated, both scholarly and politically.

The social life of this critical work went beyond re-imagining historical research. Knowledge about exclusion became part of popular knowledge about feminism. When, in January 2017, a Woman's March was planned in Washington, newspapers and social media reported widespread skeptical reactions. 'Decades of exclusion leave black women sceptical,' read one article, which made detailed references to statements by Susan B. Antony to illustrate the story.[65] When in 2016, the main actors of the film *Suffragette* partook in a promotional photo shoot wearing T-shirts with the print 'I'd rather be a rebel than a slave,' angry responses online were historically informed by knowledge of the complicated history of racism in the American suffrage movement.[66]

Another example of the way historical knowledge about those forgotten in feminist narratives of white middle-class heroines has entered the public and popular domain of online newspaper discussions is the discussion that followed Nancy Fraser's gloomy analysis of second-wave feminism in *The Guardian*, 'How feminism became capitalism's handmaiden—and how to reclaim it,' in 2013.[67] Although her analysis was part of a body of criticism that addressed the white middle-class bias of large parts of twentieth-century women's movements, her interpretation also received critical response. Brenda Bhandar and Denise Ferreira da Silva, in their critical reply, argued that feminism as a social movement is not limited to the history of liberal women's emancipation, defined as the struggle for equal rights within the public and private spheres of capitalist world.[68] They contended that not all feminism has been co-opted by neoliberalism in the first place. Black feminism, and the struggles of women of color against racism, sexism, and capitalism have been as important for the development of contemporary feminism as the struggle of white middle-class women to join the capitalist labor market. The authors point out, for example, how some feminist claims that did *not* accept the logic of the capitalist labor market, such as 'wages for household work,' were substantially developed by Black feminists.

What we find particularly interesting in this public exchange at the crossroads of academic and activist discourse are the competing historical invocations. Fraser proposes to revise the image of second-wave feminism, pointing out that it was much more aligned with neoliberal ideas than commonly believed. Bhandar and Ferreira da Silva criticize this with a reference to the movement that claimed wages for household work, and by discussing the role black women played in developing feminist strategies. They write: 'Following [Angela] Davis, we note that White feminists need to recognize when they engage political strategies that Black and Third World feminists have already been theorising and practising for a long time.'[69] By situating themselves, via Davis, in an alternative canon of women's resistance and opposition, they actively contribute to enunciating the different genealogy for which they argue.

These historiographical interventions, within and outside academic historical research, make a double move; by revisiting highly iconized historical narratives, and researching and retelling them from decentered positions, they not only intervene historically, but also re-open the discussion on what it means to be a feminist. These forms of dealing with the colonial past of modern feminism articulate alternative canons, as new names and events are remembered and celebrated, and they also yield new theoretical horizons.[70] They open the channels for historical arguments like Sojourner Truth's and Anna Cooper's about the intersectionality of their experiences of oppression, to contribute to new interpretations of feminism.

The development of intersectional approaches has made more space for scholarship that addresses exclusion, both in activist and in academic circles.[71] Nevertheless, it should be noted that to speak about feminist activism as a single social movement is problematic, as the political diversity of those claiming to speak on behalf of women is enormous. It ranges from progressive and radical anti-racist and anti-capitalist activists to conservative femo-nationalists who believe that the struggle for women's rights is a Western invention, and that non-Western cultures and religions would endanger the results of this struggle.[72]

Completing overviews of global feminism

The second strategy is less explicitly political, and has as its stated aim to further expand scholarly knowledge about a mosaic vision of global feminism. Formally, it resembles first-wave historiographical practices of providing transnational overviews of women's movements in the form of collected volumes. It also recalls the practice of using reference books to support international cooperation. These works are often the products of commissions or institutionalized academic collectives, and as part of women's or gender history, they explore histories of feminism in connection with histories of women. Nevertheless, even though they resemble the first-wave representations of global feminism in these respects, it is important to note that these histories appeared after interventions made by scholars like hooks and Mohanty, and in many ways were responses to political critiques of the historical imagination. Rather than adding to the pantheons of national or local accounts, they contextualize them in a broader global picture that is not Western-centric. Broadening the history of women, these volumes focus not only on feminism, but also on experiences that reflect the interaction of race, class, and gender. Hence, they 'provincialize' European genealogies by moving their gaze and adjusting their analytical toolkit accordingly.[73] Their focus is on providing references and background knowledge, and expanding the historical horizon of histories of gender and feminism.

Feminism and Nationalism in the Third World in the 19th and early 20th Centuries (1986), by Kumari Jayawardena, was first published in 1982 by the Institute of Social Studies in the Netherlands, and recovers historical data about feminist movements in non-Western countries.[74] *Expanding the Boundaries of Women's History* (1992) resulted from a project funded by the Organization of American Historians. The editors hardly problematize exclusion as a political issue, stating that 'Third World women (…) are *sometimes* separated by class, culture, ethnicity, ideology, national origin, religion, and "race" or color' (x, our italics).[75] Ruth Roach Pierson and Nupur Chaudhuri's volume *Nation, Empire, Colony: Historicizing Gender and Race* was result of the 1995 conference of the International Federation for Research in Women's History, which was dedicated to 'Women, Colonialisms, Imperialisms, and Nationalisms through the Ages.'[76] It focuses on histories that do not follow the pattern of Western women's emancipation, such as those of women in Iran, the Punjab, and of 'comfort women' exploited by Japanese army during WWII. The collection of essays sets as its explicit goal to change the histories of colonialism and imperialism that have paid too little attention to gender, and to women's roles in imperialism and resistance movements.

Bonnie Smith's edited three-volume series *Women's History in Global Perspective* (2004) is one of many collections that go beyond an overview of women in different geographical locations, to offer historical studies of gender as an analytical category in global history. It addresses women and gender in transnational connections and migration, and in transnational cultures, organizations, and institutions. The volume's contributions were commissioned by the American Historical Association's Committee of Women Historians. This fact in itself indicates that discussions about history of women and feminism became fit for academically recognized research. While the books we discussed in the first part of our chapter were produced and circulated by women's suffrage groups, these books show how feminism as a social movement and the women participating in it were no longer excluded from academia. For some, this increasing overlap implied a deplorable loss of pure activism, while for others it constituted the chance to finally theorize with the experiences of those whose lives had never been considered worthy of scholarly research before.

The strategies of these works from the period since 1980 have in common a somewhat Whiggish hope that historical understanding can be improved, and that better, more inclusive views of women's activism in the past might contribute to better, more inclusive feminism. They share with their predecessors from 1880 to

1914 the conviction that historical research, producing more and more sophisticated knowledge, can make a substantive positive contribution to public political debate. Yet writing the history of the women's movement is not the prerogative of historians; other disciplines also refer to the past. We close our discussion of historiographical interventions with a look at approaches that seem to move 'beyond history.' They are linked to historical research, but are at the same time skeptical about the idea that history as a discipline will provide the last word.

Beyond history

Close attention to the role of historiography in social movements blurs the traditional boundaries between grass roots and academy, between scholarly and vulgar knowledge, and ultimately between memory and history. This is reflected in the elements of skepticism about the value of historical interpretations in Mohanty's essay, when she suggests that the homogenized description of 'Third World Women' might 'tie into the larger economic and ideological praxis of "disinterested" scientific inquiry and pluralism, which are the surface manifestations of a latent economic and cultural colonization of "non-Western" world.'[77] Moreover, in 'Postmodern Blackness' (1990), bell hooks concludes that uncanonized popular cultures, Black pop music, films and their reception, constitute a better subject of inquiry to write about Black feminism.[78] Implicitly, hooks argues against research that locates Black feminists in history, suggesting that agency and subject positions are to be found in cultural practices, not historical narratives.

Another pioneer of the explicit refusal of history as the master narrative about feminist connections was postcolonial scholar Gayatri Spivak, whose 'Can the Subaltern Speak' (1985) suggested that literary scholars are better equipped to hear and analyze voices that have no place in the grand narratives about colonial oppression, resistance, and revolution. Like Mohanty, Spivak invokes Marx' description of petty landowning peasants in France as a class without 'class awareness,' whose members 'cannot represent themselves' in *The Eighteenth Brumaire* (1869).[79] By showing how Marx' historical analysis declared the disconnect between some subjects and their representation as unbridgeable, Spivak demonstrates the 'epistemic violence' inherent in the historiographical approach of so-called emancipation and liberation movements. For Spivak, then, the solution cannot be more historical research.

For this type of engagement with past women's agency, the traditional historical methods, of collecting primary printed and textual sources from archival institutions and letting them speak to the present, are not enough. The innovations within historical writing, such as oral history and attention to material culture, and the linguistic, cultural, and affective turns, bring scholars beyond the boundaries of the historical discipline. They cross the boundaries between scholarly history and artistic, popular and mediatized representations. History from below, histories of marginalization, and oral histories dealing with the experiences and memories of the 'losers' of history find their way into research, education, and popular awareness. The idea that 'history' as a disciplined narrative is about winners and hope, while other fields, such as literary scholarship and cultural memory take care of trauma, loss, and exclusion no longer holds. What started as alternatives for writing history now turn into scholarly and political cooperation.

In this process, new forms of understanding archives are proposed. In Amsterdam, one of the founders of 'Black Archives,' Jessica de Abreu, shows how books and papers collected by people from African descent outside official archives can change the perception of history.[80] Gloria Wekker, working with Edward Said's concept of a 'cultural archive,' coined the concept of 'colonial archive' in order to analyze the set of symbols and attitudes that characterize Dutch postcolonial culture.[81] These examples all reject the opposition between history and memory, pointing out that representation of the past is not limited to academic historiography but requires other forms of sharing, showing, and celebrating.

With this we come back to our claim that writing history is one of the mnemonic practices of social movements. The work of the Black Archives, just like the intervention by Wekker, can be considered as historiographical interventions. The same goes for Fraser and Bhandar and Denise Ferreira da Silva, who correct accepted images of respectively liberal feminism and of Black feminism. Again, references to a forgotten past become a tool in constructing new political positions, and history is used as a strategy. However, unlike the authors of movement histories of a century earlier, these activists not only refer to the past to make their political points; they also subvert the opposition between history and memory.

Let us return to Anna Cooper, who spoke in 1893 about the 'yet unwritten histories' of Black women under slavery. In a way, she already drew attention to the social dynamics and social life of historiography. She did not say that it was impossible to write such histories, but drew attention to the fact that Black women's 'painful, patient, and silent toil' had thus far been forgotten, and reminded her audience of these women:

> The white woman could at least plead for her own emancipation; the black woman, doubly enslaved, could but suffer and struggle and be silent.

Projects that think beyond the distinction between memory and history might do more justice to the forgotten suffering and struggles, and to the silences of history. They are also innovative mnemonic practices that help social activists to understand what binds them, and to invent new forms of representing their past as well as their future.[82]

Notes

1 May Wright Sewall, ed., *The World's Congress of Representative Women : A Historical Résumé for Popular Circulation of the World's Congress of Representative Women, Convened in Chicago on May 15, and Adjourned on May 22, 1893, under the Auspices of the Women's Branch of the World*, Internet Archive (Chicago, IL: Rond, McNally, 1894), https://archive.org/details/worldscongressof00worluoft/page/n6/mode/2up.

2 Wright Sewall, 'World's Congress,' 711–712.
3 That the American author and researcher Gloria Watkins uses the name 'bell hooks' for her publications is itself an act of remembering that crosses public history and personal memories. With it she refers to her great-grandmother who was known for 'talking back.' The lower case indicates her commitment to showing the message is not hers alone.
4 For 'pantheon,' see Maria Grever, 'The Pantheon of Feminist Culture: Women's Movements and the Organization of Memory,' *Gender & History* 9, no. 2 (August 16, 1997): 364–374.
5 David S. Meyer and Deana A. Rohlinger, 'Big Books and Social Movements,' *Social Problems* 59, no. 1 (February 1, 2012): 136–153.
6 Christina Crosby, *The Ends of History: Victorians and 'the Woman Question'* (London: Routledge, 1991); Harold Aram Veeser, ed., *The New Historicism* (New York: Routledge, 1989); Marianne Hirsch and Valerie Smith, 'Feminism and Cultural Memory: An Introduction,' *Signs: Journal of Women in Culture and Society* 28, no. 1 (2002): 1–19; Selma Leydesdorff, Luisa Passerini, and Paul Thompson, eds., *Gender & Memory* (New Brunswick, NJ and London: Transaction Publishers, 2009); Ann Rigney, 'Remembering Hope: Transnational Activism beyond the Traumatic,' *Memory Studies* 11, no. 3 (July 7, 2018): 368–380.
7 Leila J. Rupp, *Worlds of Women : The Making of an International Women's Movement* (Princeton, NJ: Princeton University Press, 1997); Nitza Berkovitch, 'The Emergence and Transformation of the International Women's Movement,' in *Constructing World Culture: International Non-Governmental Organizations Since 1875*, ed. George Thomas John Boli (Stanford, CA: Stanford University Press, 1999), 100–126.
8 Kiene Brillenburg Wurth and Ann Rigney, *The Life of Texts : An Introduction to Literary Studies* (Amsterdam: Amsterdam University Press, 2019).
9 Jeffrey K. Olick and Joyce Robbins, 'Social Memory Studies: From 'Collective Memory' to the Historical Sociology of Mnemonic Practices,' *Annual Review of Sociology* 24, no. 1 (August 28, 1998): 105–140, https://doi.org/10.1146/annurev.soc.24.1.105; see also Nicole Doerr, 'Memory and Culture in Social Movements,' in *Conceptualizing Culture in Social Movement Research*, ed. Priska Daphi, Peter Ullrich, and Britta Baumgarten (Houndmills, Basingstoke: Palgrave Macmillan, 2014), 206–226.
10 Rupp, *Worlds of Women*; Leila J. Rupp and Verta Taylor, 'Forging Feminist Identity in an International Movement: A Collective Identity Approach to Twentieth-Century Feminism,' *Signs* 24, no. 2 (December 22, 1999): 362–386, https://doi.org/10.1086/495344; Berkovitch, 'The Emergence and Transformation of the International Women's Movement'; Mineke Bosch and Annemarie Kloosterman, *Politics and Friendship : Letters from the International Woman Suffrage Alliance, 1902–1942* (Columbus: Ohio State University Press, 1990).
11 Theodore Stanton, ed., *The Woman Question in Europe : A Series of Original Essays* (London: Low, Marston, Searle, and Rivington, 1884), Internet Archive, https://archive.org/details/womanquestionine00stanrich/page/n4/mode/2up; Käthe Schirmacher, *Le Feminisme Aux États-Unis, En France, Dans La Grande-Bretagne, En Suède et En Russie* (Paris: A. Colin & cie, 1898), Internet Archive, http://archive.org/details/lefeminismeauxt00schigoog; Helene Lange and Gertrud Bäumer, ed., *Handbuch Der Frauenbewegung* (Berlin: Omnia-Mikrofilm-Technik, 1901), Internet Archive, https://archive.org/details/handbuchderfrau00bugoog/page/n10/mode/2up/search/vorwort.
12 Mineke Bosch, 'The Woman Question in Europe' in European History Contribution to the Web-Feature European History – Gender History, Themenportal Europäische Geschichte, 2009, https://www.europa.clio-online.de/essay/id/fdae-1509.
13 Frances Power Cobbe, 'Introduction,' in *The Woman Question in Europe : A Series of Original Essays*, ed. Theodore Stanton (London: S. Low, Marston, Searle, and Rivington, 1884), xiii–xviii, xiii–xiv, xiv, xv, http://archive.org/details/womanquestionine00stanrich.

14 Cobbe, 'Introduction,' xv.
15 Stanton, 'The Woman Question in Europe,' 6; see also Bosch, '"The Woman Question in Europe" in European History Contribution to the Web-Feature European History – Gender History.'
16 Kalliope Kehaya, 'The Orient,' in *The Woman Question in Europe : A Series of Original Essays*, ed. Theodore Stanton (London: S. Low, Marston, Searle, and Rivington, 1884), 457–472, 458, https://archive.org/details/womanquestionine00stanrich/page/n17/mode/2up.
17 Kehaya, 'The Orient,' 458.
18 Helene Lange and Gertrud Bäumer, 'Vorwort,' in *Handbuch Der Frauenbewegung* (Berlin: Omnia-Mikrofilm-Technik, 1901), v–x, iv, https://archive.org/details/handbuchderfrau00bugoog/page/n10/mode/2up/search/vorwort.
19 Lange and Bäumer, 'Vorwort,' vii.
20 Ibid., ix.
21 Ibid., ix.
22 Their biographer Angelika Schaser points out how they used their definition power in journals as well: Angelika Schaser, *Helene Lange Und Gertrud Bäumer : Eine Politische Lebensgemeinschaft* (Köln: Böhlau, 2000).
23 Schirmacher, 'Le Feminisme Aux États-Unis,' 2.
24 Ibid., 70.
25 Ibid., 73.
26 Ibid., 72.
27 Ibid., 60.
28 For instance, the Parliament of the World's Religions gathered representatives of major religions to attempt to create a global conversation between faiths in September 1893.
29 Schirmacher, 'Le Feminisme Aux États-Unis,' 15.
30 Johanna Gehmacher et al., *Käthe Schirmacher : Agitation Und Autobiografische Praxis Zwischen Radikaler Frauenbewegung Und Völkischer Politik* (Wien, Köln, Weimar: Böhlau Verlag GmbH & Co, 2018); Karen Offen, 'Kaethe Schirmacher, Investigative Reporter & Activist Journalist: The Paris Writings, 1895–1910,' *The Western Society for French History* 39 (2011), http://hdl.handle.net/2027/spo.0642292.0039.019.
31 Elisa Heinrich, 'Netzwerke, Beziehungen, Praktiken,' in *Käthe Schirmacher : Agitation Und Autobiografische Praxis Zwischen Radikaler Frauenbewegung Und Völkischer Politik*, ed. Johanna Gehmacher et al. (Wien, Köln, Weimar: Böhlau Verlag GmbH & Co, 2018), 159–282, 208.
32 Käthe Schirmacher, *The Modern Woman's Rights Movement; a Historical Survey* (trans. Carl Conrad Eckhardt) (New York: The Macmillan company, 1912), Internet Archive, https://archive.org/details/modernwomansrigh00schi/page/n4/mode/2up.
33 Schirmacher, *Modern Woman*, 129, 130.
34 Ibid., 108.
35 Ibid., 120.
36 Ibid., 129.
37 Edward W. Said, *Orientalism* (London: Penguin Books, 2006).
38 Schirmacher, *Modern Woman*, 1.
39 Alice Zimmern, *Women's Suffrage in Many Lands* (London: Francis & Co., The Athenaeum Press, 1909), Internet Archive, https://archive.org/details/womenssuffrageinalic/page/n9/mode/2up.
40 Carrie Chapman Catt, 'Foreword,' in *Women's Suffrage in Many Lands*, ed. Alice Zimmern (London: Francis & Co., The Athenaeum Press, 1909), i–ii, https://archive.org/details/womenssuffrageinalic/page/n7/mode/2up.
41 Chapman Catt, 'Foreword,' i.
42 Ibid., ii.
43 In a much later second edition (1928), Naber referred to her own original work as propaganda.

44 Johanna W. A. Naber, *Wegbereidsters* (Utrecht: Erven J. Bijleveld, 1928), 7, 8.
45 On the Naber's vanguardism, see Maria (Maria Christina Rosalia) Grever, *Strijd Tegen de Stilte : Johanna Naber (1859–1941) En de Vrouwenstem in Geschiedenis* (Hilversum: Uitgeverij Verloren, 1994).
46 Anna Pappritz, 'Die Geschichte Der Frauenbewegung in Frankreich,' in *Handbuch Der Frauenbewegung*, ed. Helene Lange and Gertrud Bäumer (Berlin: Omnia-Mikrofilm-Technik, 1901), 361–398, https://archive.org/details/handbuchderfrau00bugoog/page/n380/mode/2up/search/vorwort.
47 Cobbe, 'Introduction,' xviii.
48 Berteke Waaldijk, 'Subjects and Citizens: Gender and Racial Discrimination in Dutch Colonialism at the End of the 19th Century,' in *Racial Discrimination and Ethnicity in European History*, ed. Guðmundur Hálfdanarson (Pisa: PLUS, Università di Pisa, 2003), 101–118.
49 Anne Firor Scott, 'Most Invisible of All: Black Women's Voluntary Associations,' *The Journal of Southern History* 56, no. 1 (February 1990): 3–22; Maria Tamboukou, *Sewing, Fighting and Writing : Radical Practices in Work, Politics and Culture* (London: Rowman International, 2015).
50 Schirmacher, *Modern Woman*, 6.
51 Joan Kelly-Gadol, 'The Social Relation of the Sexes: Methodological Implications of Women's History,' *Signs* 1, no. 4 (1976): 809–823.
52 Bonnie G. Smith, 'The Contribution of Women to Modern Historiography in Great Britain, France, and the United States, 1750–1940,' *The American Historical Review* 89, no. 3 (June 1, 1984): 709–732; Maxine Berg, 'The First Women Economic Historians,' *The Economic History Review* 45, no. 2 (May 1, 1992): 308–329; Natalie Zemon Davis, 'History's Two Bodies,' *The American Historical Review* 93, no. 1 (February 1, 1988): 1–30; Grever, *Strijd Tegen de Stilte*; Billie Melman, 'Gender, History and Memory: The Invention of Women's Past in the Nineteenth and Early Twentieth Centuries,' *History and Memory* 5, no. 1 (1993): 5–41; Bonnie G. Smith, *The Gender of History : Men, Women, and Historical Practice* (Cambridge, MA: Harvard University Press, 1998); Isabelle Ernot, 'L'histoire Des Femmes et Ses Premières Historiennes (Xixe-Début Xxe Siècle),' *Revue d'Histoire Des Sciences Humaines* 16, no. 1 (2007): 165–194.
53 Main developments to this globalized public sphere were the founding of the UN, the increasing efficacy of NGOs and the advent of globally consumed media channels.
54 Renate Bridenthal, Claudia Koonz, and Susan Mosher Stuard, ed., *Becoming Visible : Women in European History*, 2nd compl. (Boston, MA etc.: Houghton Mifflin, 1987).
55 bell hooks, *Ain't I a Woman : Black Women and Feminism* (Boston, MA: South End Press, 1981), 13.
56 Rosalyn Terborg-Penn, 'Discrimination against Afro-American Women in the Woman's Movement 1830–1920,' in *The Afro-American Woman*, ed. Sharon Harley and Rosalyn Terborg-Penn (New York: Kennikat Press, 1978), 17–27.
57 hooks, *Ain't I a Woman : Black Women and Feminism*, 160.
58 Ibid., 161.
59 Joan W. Scott, 'Gender: A Useful Category of Historical Analysis,' *The American Historical Review* 91, no. 5 (December 1, 1986): 1053–1075; Rosi Braidotti, *Nomadic Subjects: Embodiment and Sexual Difference in Contemporary Feminist Theory* (New York: Columbia University Press, 1994).
60 Mohanty is quoted in Donna Haraway, 'A Cyborg Manifesto: Science, Technology, and Socialist-Feminism in the Late 20th Century,' in *The International Handbook of Virtual Learning Environments* (Dordrecht: Springer, [1991] 2006), 117–158; Braidotti, 'Nomadic Subjects'; Nina Wallerstein and Bonnie Duran, 'Community-Based Participatory Research Contributions to Intervention Research: The Intersection of Science and Practice to Improve Health Equity,' *American Journal of Public Health* 100, no. Suppl. 1 (April 1, 2010): 40–46; Sara R. Farris, *In the Name of Women's Rights : The Rise of Femonationalism* (Durham, NC and London: Duke University Press, 2017).

61 In 2003, Mohanty writes in Signs: 'Under Western Eyes' has enjoyed a remarkable life, being reprinted almost every year since 1986 when it first appeared in the left journal Boundary 2 (1986). The essay has been translated into German, Dutch, Chinese, Russian, Italian, Swedish, French, and Spanish. It has appeared in feminist, postcolonial, 'Third World', and cultural studies journals and anthologies and maintains a presence in women's studies, cultural studies, anthropology, ethnic studies, political science, education, and sociology curricula. It has been widely cited, sometimes seriously engaged with, sometimes misread, and sometimes used as an enabling framework for cross-cultural feminist projects.
62 Kia M. Q. Hall, 'A Transnational Black Feminist Framework: Rooting in Feminist Scholarship, Framing Contemporary Black Activism,' *Meridians* 15, no. 1 (December 1, 2016): 86–105, https://doi.org/10.2979/meridians.15.1.06.
63 Ann Laura Stoler, *Along the Archival Grain : Epistemic Anxieties and Colonial Common Sense* (Princeton, NJ: Princeton University Press, 2009).
64 Maria Grever and Berteke Waaldijk, *Transforming the Public Sphere : The Dutch National Exhibition of Women's Labor in 1898* (Durham, NC and London: Duke University Press, 2004).
65 Sherri Williams, 'Historic Exclusion From Feminist Spaces Leaves Black Women Skeptical of March,' *NBC News*, January 21, 2017, https://www.nbcnews.com/news/nbcblk/decades-exclusion-leave-black-women-skeptical-womens-march-n710216.
66 Mahita Gajanan, 'Meryl Streep and Co-Stars Attract Backlash over Suffragette T-Shirt Slogan,' *The Guardian*, October 5, 2015, https://www.theguardian.com/film/2015/oct/05/meryl-streep-backlash-suffragette-t-shirt-slogan.
67 Nancy Fraser, 'How Feminism Became Capitalism's Handmaiden – and How to Reclaim It,' *The Guardian*, October 14, 2013, https://www.theguardian.com/commentisfree/2013/oct/14/feminism-capitalist-handmaiden-neoliberal.
68 Brenna Bhandar and Denise Ferreira da Silva, 'White Feminist Fatigue Syndrome,' *Critical Legal Thinking – Law and the Political*, October 21, 2013, https://criticallegalthinking.com/2013/10/21/white-feminist-fatigue-syndrome/.
69 Silva, n.p.
70 Grever, 'The Pantheon of Feminist Culture.'
71 Kimberle Crenshaw, 'Mapping the Margins: Intersectionality, Identity Politics, and Violence against Women of Color,' *Stanford Law Review* 43, no. 6 (July 1991): 1241–1299, https://www.jstor.org/stable/1229039
72 Farris, *In the Name of Women's Rights*.
73 Dipesh Chakrabarty, *Provincializing Europe : Postcolonial Thought and Historical Difference* (Princeton, NJ and Oxford: Princeton University Press, 2000).
74 Kumari Jayawardena, *Feminism and Nationalism in the Third World* (London and New Delhi: Zed Books, 1986).
75 Cheryl Johnson-Odim, and Margaret Strobel, *Expanding the Boundaries of Women's History : Essays on Women in the Third World* (Bloomington: Indiana University Press, 1992).
76 Ruth Roach Pierson, Nupur Chaudhuri, and Beth McAuley, *Nation, Empire, Colony : Historicizing Gender and Race* (Bloomington: Indiana University Press, 1998).
77 Chandra Talpade Mohanty, 'Under Western Eyes: Feminist Scholarship and Colonial Discourses,' *Feminist Review* 30, no. 1 (November 1, 1988): 353–354.
78 bell hooks, 'Postmodern Blackness,' *Postmodern Culture* 1, no. 1 (1990), https://muse.jhu.edu/article/27283.
79 Karl Marx, *Der Achtzehnte Brumaire Des Louis Bonaparte* (Berlin: Dietz Verlag, 1972), 117. Marx phrase, 'they cannot represent themselves, they must be represented' was also the motto of Said's *Orientalism*.
80 Krystel Singh, 'The Black Archives: Een Interview Met Jessica de Abreu,' *Stichting Democratie En Media*, last updated November 13, 2018, https://www.stdem.org/2018/11/13/the-black-archives-een-interview-met-jessica-de-abreu/.

81 Gloria Wekker, *White Innocence: Paradoxes of Colonialism and Race* (Durham, NC: Duke University Press, 2016).
82 We thank Maria Grever and Ann Rigney for crucial comments on a first draft, the editors for their helpful feedback and Anita Prša, MA, for her valuable assistance in the last phase. Our jobs at Utrecht University in Gender Studies and Literary Studies are funded publicly.

5

'THE MEMORY OF HISTORY AS A *LEITMOTIF* FOR NONVIOLENT RESISTANCE' – PEACEFUL PROTESTS AGAINST NUCLEAR MISSILES IN MUTLANGEN, 1983–7

Richard Rohrmoser

On 12 December 1979, the 'NATO Double-Track Decision' offered the Warsaw Pact a mutual limitation of medium- and intermediate-range nuclear missiles in combination with the threat that in case of discord, the Western defence alliance would deploy a large amount of new atomic missiles in Europe, especially in the Federal Republic of Germany. Since the talks about nuclear disarmament remained without conclusion in the following years, the German parliament eventually agreed to the stationing of intermediate-range nuclear missiles (with a reach of 500–5,500 kilometres) in the autumn of 1983. At that time, the German peace movement staged a series of peaceful protests and mass demonstrations, but could not avert a further twist in the conflict spirals of the Cold War.[1] In late 1983, NATO initiated the deployment of a total number of 108 Pershing-II and 464 Cruise Missiles in four locations in the south of Germany.

One of the stationing sites was the Swabian municipality Mutlangen, which is about 60 kilometres east of Stuttgart. Although there were minor protests at the three other Pershing-II and Cruise Missiles storage locations (Heilbronn, Neu-Ulm, and Hasselbach), Mutlangen turned into an epicentre for the German peace movement and a symbolic site for nonviolent resistance against the nuclear arms race.[2] In a broader sense, the Swabian location also became emblematic for the 'normalization' of (peaceful) protest – as a legitimate form of political participation.

From 1983 until 1987, when the United States and the Soviet Union eventually reached an agreement on the elimination of their shorter-range and intermediate-range missiles, there were continuously various kinds of nonviolent protest and civil disobedience against the Pershing-II in Mutlangen. The peace activists considered themselves to be acting in a tradition marked out by their role models in the realm of civil disobedience: Henry David Thoreau, Mahatma Gandhi, and Martin Luther King.[3] The most common form of action was the peaceful blockade, involving a group of protesters assembling in front of the missile storage site and blocking the gate of the depot via sit-down demonstrations. Since the US Army was not legally entitled to intervene in such situations, the German police had to carry away the blockers after the enunciation of three verbal warnings. In the years from 1983 until 1987, the police arrested almost 3,000 protesters as a consequence of such peaceful blockades; about 2,000 peace demonstrators were controversially convicted for *Nötigung*[4] (coercion) according to the *Strafgesetzbuch* (German Criminal Code) in the nearby city Schwäbisch Gmünd.[5]

By virtue of the controversial jurisprudence and subsequent constitutional complaints, Germany's Federal Constitutional Court was eventually to decide, whether the nonviolent blockades were illegitimate or not. However, due to a stalemate between the councils' members the court could not reach a unanimous decision in its first verdict in the autumn of 1986. Therefore, the equally divided vote within Germany's federal supreme court upheld the convictions for the time being, which resulted in a continuing academic and popular scientific discourse about the jurisdiction. Eventually, the Federal Constitutional Court was to decide again in 1995. This time, the court superseded the former verdict, declared it as unlawful, and revoked the sentences of the peace protesters retroactively. This verdict has been regarded as one of the most controversial decisions in the history of Germany's federal supreme court. One article in the liberal-conservative *Frankfurter Allgemeine Zeitung* referred in this context to the aspirations of the student movement of 1968 and declared that

> [it is] now totally obvious that the [movement's] 'march through the institutions' has completely penetrated the Federal Constitutional Court. The politicization of this previously highly respected court resulted in further concessions to the so-called spirit of the age and thereby promoted the undermining of the [judicial] power.[6]

Likewise, Major General Ernst-Ulrich Hantel concluded in the *Frankfurter Allgemeine Zeitung* that the Federal Constitutional Court's decision of 1995 could be considered as 'Dutschke's revenge.'[7]

Leitmotifs for the protest against nuclear missiles

Until the Federal Constitutional Court's decision in 1995, there were several hundreds of trials, in which the protesters sought to justify their nonviolent blockades against nuclear missiles through some specific recurrent themes. A vast number of defendants articulated their ethical and moral opposition towards the existence of nuclear weapons, as their use could lead to a genocide of the civilian population worldwide. It was the peace movement's stance that nations are on no account justified to use nuclear missiles – not even in the case of self-defence. And since nuclear missiles must on no account be used, nations are therefore not justified in threatening others with this sort of weaponry.[8] Linked to this fundamental criticism of the existence of nuclear weapons, further protesters in court categorically denounced the excessive costs for nuclear technologies and of the arms race between NATO and the Warsaw Pact. Some defendants meticulously calculated the worldwide expenses for armament and contrasted the figure with alternative fields of potential investment such as aid to developing countries. Particularly those protesters with strong religious beliefs declared that the enormous discrepancy between the expenses for armament and development assistance was a fundamental contradiction to Christian ethics and values.[9] In contrast to these positions, the dominant narrative in the German parliament in 1983 was that the experience of National Socialism was an absolutely blatant reason that the Soviet totalitarianism would have to be repressed.

Furthermore, the peace movement claimed that the deployment of Pershing-II and Cruise Missiles constituted an infringement of (international) law. According to their reasoning, the stationing of these nuclear intermediate-range missiles inter alia violated article 2, Section 2 of the *Grundgesetz* (the Basic Law of the Federal Republic of Germany), which states: 'Every person shall have the right to life and physical integrity. Freedom of the person shall be inviolable. These rights may be interfered with only pursuant to a law.'[10] Likewise, the peace movement criticized the deployment of Pershing-II and Cruise Missiles from the standpoint of international law, as the Soviet Union, the United Kingdom, and the United States as the three depositary states as well as over 40 others had signed the Treaty on the Non-Proliferation of Nuclear Weapons (NPT) in 1968, which entered into force in 1970.[11] The objective of this treaty has been 'to prevent the spread of nuclear weapons and weapons technology, to promote cooperation in the peaceful uses of nuclear energy and to further the goal of achieving nuclear disarmament and general and complete disarmament.'[12]

Next to these leitmotifs of the peace protesters against nuclear missiles, two of the dominant topoi were the aspects 'history' and 'memory.' Frequently, defendants tied unfolding events to their memory of Nazi Germany, which began on a small scale and had not been fully challenged. Drawing on this version of the history of Nazism, protestors argued that it was imperative to resist preparations for a new war from the outset. In the case of 'Mutlangen,' it is striking that the protestors' reasoning with the National Socialist Period eventually caused scores of victims of the totalitarian Nazi regime to become politically active against the nuclear arms race. Moved by their memory of the Second World War, plenty of senior peace protestors participated in several blockades of the missile storage site in Mutlangen in order to demonstrate against the threat of a nuclear clash between the two superpowers in the East and West.[13] Therefore, 'Mutlangen' is a prime example that the production of 'social,' 'collective,' or 'cultural' memory has been inextricably intertwined with the history of social movements as well as their activism and the construction of their collective identity. Furthermore, this case represents that social movements do not only have the capacity to use and shape the official memory but that memory itself can function as the key motivation for the formation of social movements.

The 'seniors' blockade' on 8–10 May 1986

The epitome of the protest by senior citizens was the so-called 'seniors' blockade' from 8 to 10 May 1986. The organizer of this unconventional form of protest was the 65-year-old retired teacher Luise Olsen from Oldenburg, a city in the north-west of Germany. She developed the idea of the 'seniors' blockade' due to her son's strong commitment to the peace movement in Mutlangen. After the deployment of the first Pershing-II in Germany in late 1983, Hinrich Olsen had resigned from his job as a waiter and moved to the Swabian municipality in order to constantly demonstrate against the stationing of intermediate-range nuclear missiles. Henceforth, he lived there with about 15 further peace protesters from all over West Germany in a decrepit shelter in close proximity to the missile storage site and participated in regular pickets and sit-in demonstrations.

Initially, Luise Olsen was not particularly approving of her son's decision to terminate his employment and to become a full-time peace activist in the Swabian province. However, because of his commitment, the former teacher for the first time started to concern herself with subjects such as armament policies, the controversy about the NATO Double-Track Decision, and the deployment of nuclear Pershing-II and Cruise Missiles in Germany and Western Europe. Furthermore, Luise Olsen was extremely outraged by her son's first conviction by the local court in Schwäbisch Gmünd resulting from his participation in peaceful blockades in front of Mutlangen's US-American military base. Following the trial, she was furiously opposed to the strict legal-positivist stance of the court's judges.[14]

As a consequence, Luise Olsen became a peace activist herself. In an interview with the politically left-leaning newspaper *Die Tageszeitung* in 1988, she declared that these events had been an enlightening experience for her. Therefore, she became involved in political issues herself and her main explanation was that as a devoted mother of four sons and as a dedicated teacher for French, English, and German, she did not have sufficient time for political activism.[15]

In retrospect, Luise Olsen said that she was extremely ashamed of having awoken so late from her political lethargy. She explained that during the National Socialist Period, she studied together with Hans and Sophie Scholl in Munich and that she has always admired the siblings for their enormous courage and their resistance against Nazi Germany. However, it never came to Luise Olsen's mind to follow suit. Nevertheless, she did not only regret her silence during the National Socialist Period, but also during the era of the first Chancellor of the Federal Republic of Germany, Konrad Adenauer (Christian Democratic Union of Germany, CDU), who enforced the nation's remilitarization, the establishment of the *Bundeswehr* (the Armed Forces of Germany), and its armament with nuclear weapons in the late 1950s.[16]

Eventually, after several visits to her son in Mutlangen, Luise Olsen decided to participate in demonstrations against the deployment of intermediate-range nuclear missiles. It was in the course of a several-day-long event in respect of the 40th anniversaries of the Hiroshima and Nagasaki bombings that she protested in front of Mutlangen's missile storage site for the first time. There, Luise Olsen discerned that the German police arrested a vast number of young peace protesters, whereas the senior demonstrators were mostly neglected and not persecuted any further. Due to this discriminating experience, she decided to plan a three-day-long blockade explicitly carried out by senior peace protestors. Shortly thereafter, Luise Olsen set the beginning of the 'seniors' blockade' on 8 May 1986, which was the 41st anniversary of the end of the Second World War.[17]

In the call for this event, Luise Olsen claimed that especially Germany's senior citizens would know about the atrocities of war, which is the reason why she assumed that the public would probably pay special attention to this form of protest. Furthermore, she reasoned that especially the elder generation – in contrast to younger people, who are more occupied with their jobs and families – would have time to reflect on the Cold War, to have conversations and discussions about the arms race, and to participate in peaceful protests. In general, the call for the 'seniors' blockade' was also a plea towards the peace movement for not getting seized by the feeling of powerlessness against the government and the military blocs in East and West.[18]

Several hundred people from the peace movement followed the call for this unconventional form of protest. All of them were witnesses of the atrocities of the Second World War and insofar were often war victims, widow(er)s, or orphans. Coming from all over Germany, the senior protesters assembled from 8 until 10 May 1986 in order to demonstrate their resistance against armament and nuclear power, celebrate church services, establish contacts among the peace movement, and to disturb the military duties via peaceful sit-ins.[19] The entire event was extremely emotional. This was especially the case on the second day of the 'seniors' blockade,' when a few military trucks with five Pershing-II-missiles returned from an exercise unit. Since the senior protesters performed an insistent blockade on the access road to the missile storage site, the German police carried away several of them in a ruthless manner, whereupon some senior citizens broke into tears due to consternation, desperation, and rage. However, some of the police forces were similarly bewildered and torn between the performance of their duty and respect towards the demonstrators' age. Eventually, the German police arrested a total number of 76 people in the course of the three-day event and brought them to the police department in Schwäbisch Gmünd for personal identification.[20]

(Controversial) recurrent topics

Most of the peace protesters justified the 'seniors' blockade' with references to the National Socialist Period, the Second World War, and the Holocaust. 'Never again' advanced to the central statement of the protest action. One attendant from Munich, for instance, declared towards the large number of reporters from several different national as well as international press institutions:

> Before the Second World War, our generation failed. That is the reason why I still have feelings of guilt. We must not let this happen a second time.

> Today, the risk is even greater than in those days. Then, the consequences were severe; today's consequences of a nuclear war are just unthinkable. That is the reason why we are here.[21]

It evolved into a legitimatory leitmotif of the 'seniors' blockade' that the participants sided with the younger generation and tried to provide at least some sense to the pointless mass extinction of both world wars by warning with those atrocities against the threat of another war.[22] Insofar, the peace movement considered this form of peaceful protest as a reference to the danger of a nuclear clash between the two superpowers on both sides of the Iron Curtain. Concerning this matter, one of the 'seniors' blockade' demonstrators remarked:

> It is not that important for us anymore, but for our descendants! Among other things, that is a very important argument for me. […] My siblings and I, we often confronted our father with discussions such as: 'How could you let this happen? How could you contribute to it? Why didn't you refuse to? Why didn't you join [resistance] forces?' Well, I really don't want that my children will one day say those same things to me. Instead, I want to be able to say: 'I have tried everything in my feeble power.' Well, that is a very important argument for me.[23]

However, in the context of the 'seniors' blockade' were also some controversial references to subjects such as the National Socialist Period, the Second World War, and the Holocaust. For instance, one member from the peace initiative *Ohne Rüstung Leben* (*Living without Armament*) flanked the peaceful blockade with a contentious banner reading the slogan 'PERSHING MACHT FREI' ('Pershing will set you free'), which was a clear allusion to the infamous words 'Arbeit macht frei' ('work will set you free') at the gate entrance to Auschwitz.[24] Another controversial reference came from a one-legged senior protestor, who wore a sign around his neck, reading 'war victim against war armament.' He insulted the police forces, who were clearing the road from peaceful blockers, by exclaiming the words: 'Just like in Auschwitz! There were executors, too!'[25] Furthermore, one participant of the 'seniors' blockade' wrote a detailed report of this peaceful protest action and described that – due to the barbed wire, the watchtowers, and the several floodlights of Mutlangen's US-American military base – there was an atmosphere like in a concentration camp.[26]

Such controversial references to the National Socialist Period, the Second World War, and the Holocaust were not restricted to the conflict in Mutlangen. It was, in fact, an integral component of the West German discourse on nuclear armament in general. For instance, the theologian Dorothee Sölle called the Pershing-II 'fliegende Verbrennungsöfen' ('on-board incinerators').[27] Furthermore, in the course of a writers' blockade in front of the missile storage site in Heilbronn in December 1983, Sölle wrote the word 'Auschwitz' on a US-military warning sign, which stated that firearms might be used in case of trespassing.[28] At the same sit-in demonstration, the German writer and SPD-politician Dieter Lattmann actually called the US-depot a concentration camp; German Nobel Prize laureate for literature, Günter Grass, did not contradict this statement, but added further that this time, the victims would be outside of the purported concentration camp.[29] According to these remarks, the NATO Double-Track was in general often compared to Hitler's *Ermächtigungsgesetz* (*Enabling Act*) of 1933, which constituted the fundament in order to transform the National Socialist government into a legal dictatorship.[30] With such controversial analogies, references, and statements, some senior peace protestors suggested that they tried to compensate their non-resistance against a dictatorship with a belated resistance against a non-dictatorship. Particularly the conservative press criticized this behaviour as a clever mechanism of the senior peace protestors in order to deflect their own inactivity during the National Socialist Period.

In front of the court

Following the arrests in the course of the 'seniors' blockade,' the senior peace protestors had to stand in front of the court due to the charge of coercion (*Nötigung*) according to Section 240 of the German Criminal Code (*Strafgesetzbuch*). In their defence speeches, the personal experiences of the Second World War became a recurrent theme. For example, one of the defendants' narratives was that they were completely indifferent towards politics in earlier days. Therefore, they ignored the developments during the National Socialist Period and declared that they were utterly inactive during the Second World War and the Holocaust. Due to this apathy towards Nazi Germany and its atrocities several protestors declared that they became extremely alert towards the state's activities. For some of the peace movement, the events in Mutlangen were, in fact, the final trigger for a turning point to become politically active. One telling example for this kind of reasoning was Luise Olsen's defence speech in court on 4 March 1986. Therein, she elaborated:

> As a young person, I was not interested in politics. When I realize today, how carelessly I witnessed the rise of the National Socialism, the Second World War and the time after it, the Holocaust, the execution of Hans and Sophie Scholl, Hiroshima and Nagasaki, the remilitarization of our nation, and how I throve in my private life, in my education and temporarily in my career, and later in my family with my husband and my sons, then I am deeply shocked and pushed by guilt, and I realize, that as an adult person, I have to bear responsibilities for our young democracy, which still carries a strong legacy of the Prussian authority-based-thinking. After two devastating and incredible crimes against humanity, neither can I trust the government blindly, nor can I demand that the government alone is able to take care of our common welfare.[31]

Despite this elaborated pleading, Dr. Werner Offenloch – the best-known and most controversial trial judge from the local court in Schwäbisch Gmünd – sentenced Luise Olsen to a financial penalty in the amount of 600 Deutsche Mark, which she refused to pay. When the recalcitrant senior peace protestor was about to go to jail in January 1988, the prosecution declared that the sentence would be suspended for the time being. The entire case and the strict law enforcement, which was broadly discussed in the German press, was too embarrassing for the prosecution.[32]

Another revealing example of senior peace protestors is the one of Inge Aicher-Scholl, the eldest sister of the nonviolent resistance fighters Hans and Sophie Scholl.[33] Born in 1917, she also focussed in her defence speech on 10 February 1986 on her historical experiences. In front of the local court in Schwäbisch Gmünd, the founder of an adult education centre in Ulm explained in detail the reasons for her activism in the German peace movement and her participation at its most spectacular protest actions such as the human 'peace chain' from Stuttgart to Neu-Ulm on 22 October 1983, or several peaceful blockades in front of the Pershing-II storage site in Mutlangen. According to her statements, Inge Aicher-Scholl was deeply touched by one certain formulation from one of her siblings' leaflets, for which they eventually lost their lives on the scaffold on 22 February 1943: 'Cast off the cloak of indifference you have wrapped around you. Make the decision before it's too late' reads the fifth leaflet 'Aufruf an alle Deutsche' ('A Plea to All Germans') of the nonviolent, intellectual resistance group the White Rose.[34]

In front of the local court in Schwäbisch Gmünd, Inge Aicher-Scholl explicitly stressed the political topicality of this citation; especially the words 'too late' would have a very final character in today's context – if humankind was not determined to embark on radical disarmament actions in due time. She explained further that after previous wars, there was always a new start. This was even the case after the devastating Second World War. However, she warned that this time, the 'mass extinction of people, animals and lovely trees and plants would be irrevocable [translation R.R.].'[35] Insofar, Inge Aicher-Scholl considered the participation in a peaceful blockade in front of a Pershing-II storage site as a form of societal self-defence, as the nuclear arms race threatened the world peace.

Therefore, Inge Aicher-Scholl was shocked that the German justice regarded such kind of 'existential activism for peace' as a form of criminal coercion and sanctioned it accordingly. She claimed that the fathers of the German Constitution had certainly envisioned a different kind of constitutional state, when they conceptualized the German Basic Law. Nevertheless, Inge Aicher-Scholl did not consider a criminal conviction in this context as a disgrace – just as little as when she was arrested by Nazi Germany's *Gestapo* for kin liability because of her siblings' leading roles in the White Rose.[36] This example illustrates that the peace movement's fear of an imminent nuclear war was so distinct that some peace protestors drew an analogy between the years 1933 and 1983 and regarded themselves as resistance fighters of some kind.

Concerning this issue, Inge Aicher-Scholl declared that for a long time, she considered analogies between the National Socialist Period and NATO's Double-Track Decision – especially in terms of law enforcement – as incorrect, since such analogies could potentially trivialize Nazi Germany and its victims. In this context, she explained that, for instance, the university professor and *White Rose* resistance fighter Kurt Huber was also sentenced to death by guillotine in July 1943, after he had severely criticized legal positivism in front of Nazi Germany's People Court in his defence speech.[37] However, Inge Aicher-Scholl also remarked that every democratic state is prone to 'signs of a power-political recidivism' and she registered some similarities between the National Socialist Period and the West German society at one certain point: 'The tendency, to raise silent subjects and followers, who retreat in their private lives as deep as possible in order to risk no conflicts or statements [translation by R.R.].'[38] For this reason, Inge Aicher-Scholl finally declared that decent citizens would owe it to democratic states to not remain silent – especially since those provide a great deal of freedom to them.[39] As with Luise Olsen, Inge Aicher-Scholl was also sentenced to a financial fine of 600 Deutsche Mark.

Epilogue

'Mutlangen' not only stands for peaceful protests against the deployment of intermediate-range nuclear missiles in the years from 1983 until 1987. Indeed, the Swabian municipality turned into an epicentre for the German peace movement and a focal point for the nonviolent resistance against the nuclear arms race in general.[40] Of course, the peace movement could not reach its prime objective – that is, the prevention of the deployment of intermediate-range nuclear missiles on German and European territory. However, it still contributed to the resolving of the East-West conflict to a certain extent. Due to its continuous peaceful protests such as in Mutlangen even after the deployment of the intermediate-range nuclear missiles, the peace movement also signalled towards the Soviet Union that a substantial part of West German and West European societies resisted developments that could eventually lead towards war. In turn, this influenced the willingness of Soviet leader Mikhail Gorbachev to pursue reforms.[41]

Furthermore, the peace movement was an essential corrective for the democratic constitutiveness of the West German state. One key element of its regulative function was the controversy over the discursive power over Germany's history and the official memory. The prevailing narrative in the German parliament in 1983 was that the experience with the national-socialist dictatorship was a striking evidence that the Soviet totalitarianism would have to be contained.[42] This was one reason for the deployment of the Pershing-II and Cruise Missiles in West Germany and (Western) Europe. However, the peace movement – especially the senior citizens – reinforced the construction of a 'counter-memory' on an 'individual,' 'communicative,' and 'cultural' basis,[43] according to which Germany's responsibility for the outbreak of the Second World War should function as a warning sign against the deployment of intermediate-range nuclear missiles in West Germany and (Central) Europe, since these weapons could either challenge the Soviet Union to a preventive first strike or encourage the United States in the view that a nuclear war could be winnable. Eventually, from a larger historical and cultural context, not only the debate over NATO's Double-Track Decision but also the dispute over the discursive power over the German history led to a substantial extent to a societal understanding in Germany in terms of security politics, peace politics, and decision-making.

Notes

1 For further contextual information concerning the NATO Double Track Decision, the Cold War in the 1980s, and the (German) peace movement, see: Christoph Becker-Schaum, Philipp Gassert, Martin Klimke, Wilfried Mausbach, and Marianne Zepp (eds.), *The Nuclear Crisis: The Arms Race, Cold War Anxiety and the German Peace Movement of the 1980s* (New York and Oxford: Berghahn Books, 2016). See also: Philipp Gassert, Tim Geiger and Hermann Wentker, eds., *Zweiter Kalter Krieg und Friedensbewegung: Der NATO-Doppelbeschluss in deutsch-deutscher und internationaler Perspektive* (Munich: De Gruyter Oldenbourg, 2011).
2 For a general overview of the peaceful protests in Mutlangen from 1983 until 1987, see: Reinhold Weber, 'Mutlangen – mit zivilem Ungehorsam gegen Atomraketen,' in *Aufbruch, Protest und Provokation: Die bewegten 70er und 80er-Jahre in Baden-Württemberg*, ed. Reinhold Weber (Stuttgart: Theiss, 2013), 141–146.
3 For a general overview of key figures and texts of the protest form 'civil disobedience,' see: Andreas Braune, ed., *Ziviler Ungehorsam. Texte von Thoreau bis Occupy* (Stuttgart: Reclam, 2017). See also: Sean Scalmer, *Gandhi in the West: The Mahatma and the Rise of Radical Protest* (New York: Cambridge University Press, 2011).
4 There is no corresponding provision in American, English, or French law for the criminal offence of *Nötigung*. The regarding Section (§ 240) of the German Criminal Code states:

> Whosoever unlawfully with force or threat of serious harm causes a person to commit, suffer or omit an act shall be liable to imprisonment not exceeding three years or a fine. (2) The act shall be unlawful if the use of force or the threat of harm is deemed inappropriate for the purpose of achieving the desired outcome […].

See: *The German Criminal Code: A Modern English Translation* (translated by Michael Bohlander) (Oxford, Portland and Oregon: Hart Publishing, 2008), 159.
5 See: Manfred Laduch, Heino Schütte, and Reinhard Wagenblast, eds., *Mutlanger Heide: Ein Ort macht Geschichte* (Schwäbisch Gmünd: Remsdruckerei Sigg, Härtel & Co, 1990).
6 Peter E. Quint, *Civil Disobedience and the German Courts: The Pershing Missile Protests in Comparative Perspectives* (London and New York: Taylor & Francis, 2008), 204.
7 Ibid.
8 For this kind of reasoning, see: Martin Singe, 'Entschieden gegen alle Massenvernichtungswaffen!', in *Mutlangen – unser Mut wird langen: Vor den Richtern in Schwäbisch Gmünd: Elf Verteidigungsreden wegen Nötigung*, eds. Hanne Vack and Klaus Vack (Sensbachtal: Eigenverlag des Komitees für Grundrechte und Demokratie, 1986), 35–42.
9 For this kind of reasoning, see: Günter Fuchs, 'Hier muss ich mich einmischen,' in *Mutlangen – unser Mut wird langen: Vor den Richtern in Schwäbisch Gmünd: Elf Verteidigungsreden wegen Nötigung*, eds. Hanne Vack and Klaus Vack (Sensbachtal: Eigenverlag des Komitees für Grundrechte und Demokratie, 1986), 43–46.
10 Trevor C. Hartley, *European Union Law in a Global Context: Text, Cases and Materials* (Cambridge: Cambridge University Press, 2004), 274.

11 For this kind of reasoning, see: *Inge Radau's defense speech in front of the local court of Schwäbisch Gmünd on 14 May 1987*, in: Archiv Aktiv (Hamburg): GMA – Marianne Gmelz – Juristisches.
12 *Treaty on the Non-Proliferation of Nuclear Weapons*, https://www.un.org/disarmament/wmd/nuclear/npt/ [accessed 1 May 2020].
13 See: Volker Nick, Volker Scheub and Christoph Then, *Mutlangen 1983–1987: Die Stationierung der Pershing II und die Kampagne Ziviler Ungehorsam bis zur Abrüstung* (Mutlangen and Tübingen: Eigenverlag, 1993), 132–149.
14 The information of the genesis of the 'senior's blockade' is mainly based on an oral history interview with the long-time peace activist Holger-Isabelle Jänicke, conducted in Hamburg on 16 November 2016.
15 See: Vera Gasserow, 'Ich bin beschämend spät aufgewacht', *Die Tageszeitung* (12 January 1988).
16 Ibid.
17 See: Luise Olsen, '*Aufruf zur Seniorenblockade*,' in Archiv Aktiv (Hamburg): GMA KZU I Kampagne Regionalgruppe GD II Golfkrieg – Info + Aktionen.
18 See: Ibid.
19 Luise Olsen, 'Die Medien schweigen – wir nicht,' in *Mutlangen 1983–1987: Die Stationierung der Pershing II und die Kampagne Ziviler Ungehorsam bis zur Abrüstung*, eds. Volker Nick, Volker Scheub and Christoph Then, (Mutlangen and Tübingen: Eigenverlag, 1993), 140.
20 Ibid.
21 Janni Werner, 'Grüne Uniformen gegen graue Haare,' *Die Tageszeitung* (12 May 1986), translated by Richard Rohrmoser.
22 Luise Olsen, 'Vorwort', in *Wir treten in den Un-Ruhestand: Dokumentation der 1. Seniorenblockade Mutlangen 8. bis 10. Mai 1986*, in: Archiv Aktiv (Hamburg): GMA HGL Disziplinarische Vorermittlungen Sonstiges.
23 See Karin Hoffmann's documentary, 'Wer Recht zu Unrecht macht... Seniorenblockade nach Tschernobyl,' https://www.youtube.com/watch?v=ywuvzlBGfgc. For the quotation, see 17:38 – 18:12 [accessed 1 May 2020], translated by Richard Rohrmoser.
24 For this and further controversial references to the National Socialist Period by the peace movement, see: Eckart Conze, 'Missiles Bases as Concentration Camps: The Role of National Socialism, the Second World War, and the Holocaust in the West German Discourse on Nuclear Armament,' in *Nuclear Threats, Nuclear Fear and the Cold War of the 1980s*, eds. Eckart Conze, Martin Klimke, and Jeremy Varon (New York: Cambridge University Press, 2017), 96.
25 See Karin Hoffmann's documentary, '*Wer Recht zu Unrecht macht... Seniorenblockade nach Tschernobyl*', https://www.youtube.com/watch?v=ywuvzlBGfgc. For the described scene see 13:20 – 13:35 [accessed 1 May 2020].
26 Renate Eisenberg, 'Mitglieder der Friedensgruppe Stiftberg, Herford, beteiligten sich am 8. und 10. Mai an Blockaden des Atomwaffendepots in Mutlangen,' in *Wir treten in den Un-Ruhestand – Dokumentation der 1. Seniorenblockade Mutlangen 8. bis 10. Mai 1986*, ed. Hinrich Olsen, in Archiv Aktiv (Hamburg): GMA HGL Disziplinarische Vorermittlungen Sonstiges, 37.
27 See: Dietmar Süß and Meik Woyke, 'Schimanskis Jahrzehnt? Die 1980er Jahre in historischer Perspektive,' in *Archiv für Sozialgeschichte 52. Wandel des Politischen: Die Bundesrepublik Deutschland während der 1980er*, eds. Beatrix Bouvier, Dieter Dowe, Anja Kruke et al. (Bonn: Dietz, 2012), 18.
28 Wulf Reimer, 'Frösteln und eisiges Schweigen,' *Süddeutsche Zeitung* (19 December 1983).
29 Tim Warneke, 'Aktionsformen und Politikverständnis der Friedensbewegung: Radikaler Humanismus und die Pathosformel des Menschlichen,' in *Das Alternative Milieu: Antibürgerlicher Lebensstil und linke Politik in der Bundesrepublik Deutschland und Europa, 1968–1983*, eds. Sven Reichardt and Detlef Siegfried (Göttingen: Wallstein, 2010), 463.

30 Werner Balsen and Karl Rössel, *Hoch die internationale Solidarität: Zur Geschichte der Dritte Welt-Bewegung in der Bundesrepublik* (Cologne: Kölner Volksblatt, 1986), 59.
31 Luise Olsen, 'Mein Entschluß hat lange reifen müssen,' in Mutlangen – unser Mut wird langen: Vor den Richtern in Schwäbisch Gmünd: Elf Verteidigungsreden wegen Nötigung, eds. Hanne Vack and Klaus Vack (Sensbachtal: Eigenverlag des Komitees für Grundrechte und Demokratie, 1986), 15 f. (translated by Richard Rohrmoser).
32 See: Gasserow, 'Ich bin beschämend spät aufgewacht.'
33 The siblings Hans and Sophie Scholl were members of the nonviolent, intellectual resistance group *Weiße Rose* (*The White Rose*) against the National Socialist dictatorship and the Second World War. The Munich-based circle of friends distributed leaflets and conducted a graffiti campaign that appealed to active opposition to Hitler's regime. On 18 February 1943, the core group was arrested by the *Gestapo* and seven members of the White Rose were subsequently sentenced to death and executed by the National Socialist judiciary. In post-war Germany, Hans and Sophie Scholl have been considered as the central protagonists of the Christian German resistance against the totalitarian Nazi regime. For more information, see: Detlef Bald, *Die Weiße Rose* (Berlin: Aufbau Verlag, 2003).
34 See: Harald Steffahn, *Die Weiße Rose* (7th edn.) (Hamburg: Rowohlt, 2005), 142, translated by Richard Rohrmoser.
35 Inge Aicher-Scholl, 'Zerreißt den Mantel der Gleichgültigkeit,' in Mutlangen – unser Mut wird langen: Vor den Richtern in Schwäbisch Gmünd: Elf Verteidigungsreden wegen Nötigung, eds. Hanne Vack and Klaus Vack (Sensbachtal: Eigenverlag des Komitees für Grundrechte und Demokratie, 1986), 68.
36 Ibid., 70.
37 Ibid., 72.
38 Ibid.
39 Ibid.
40 Furthermore, 'Mutlangen' also epitomizes some macrosocial developments in West Germany in the 1980s. First of all, it can be considered a touchstone for the state's democratic constitutiveness in terms of its culture of participation and protest; second, the peaceful conflict in the Swabian province exemplifies the normalization of protest and its incorporation into the democratic system; third, the continuous peaceful protests (re)activated the discourse over a long-time not substantially critiqued security policies and also launched alternative security concepts.
41 For this explanatory pattern concerning the end of the Cold War, see: Warneke, 'Aktionsformen und Politikverständnis der Friedensbewegung,' in *Das Alternative Milieu*, 451.
42 See: Freimut Duve, *Die Nachrüstungsdebatte im Deutschen Bundestag: Protokoll einer historischen Entscheidung* (Hamburg: Rowohlt, 1984).
43 Jan Assmann, *Cultural Memory and Early Civilization: Writing, Remembrance and Political Imagination* (Cambridge: Cambridge University Press, 2011); Aleida Assmann, *Cultural Memory and Western Civilization: Arts of Memory* (Cambridge: Cambridge University Press, 2011).

6

ATOMIC TESTING IN AUSTRALIA

Memories, mobilizations and mistrust

David Lowe

This chapter focusses on the remembered legacies of British-Australian joint atomic testing in Australia in the 1950s and early 1960s. Between 1952 and 1963 the British carried out 12 major weapons tests in the centre and off the north-western coast of Australia, and also conducted around 300 minor trials. The Australian Government welcomed the testing and was involved in all aspects. The joint testing stands out as an extraordinary episode in at least three ways: first, for its strategic significance in Australians' thinking about their role in the Cold War; second, for the atomic utopian future that Australians briefly embraced, as they discovered huge reserves of uranium in South Australia and the Northern Territory in the late 1940s and early 1950s, and imagined unlimited industrial uses, irrigation of the desert and also access to atomic weapons. And, especially since the 1970s, it has become infamous for the mounting human toll for those involved in or proximate to the tests – made known by the uncovering of aspects previously kept secret and the remembering of more contested and traumatic aspects of Australia's atomic testing legacies through anti-nuclear and other organized protests. In all three cases the mixture of scientific excitement, nuclear potential and dread, and Australian-British relations complicated by the Cold War and colonial legacies loom large.

While historians continue to explore the first two aspects of Australia's nuclear testing,[1] this chapter focusses on the third, the remembering of contest and human suffering since the 1970s, in the context of the anti-nuclear movement more broadly. Shared remembering of the tests has grown in significance since the 1980s and has been strengthened recently by an anniversary. The year 2017 marked the 60th anniversary of the commencement of atomic weapons testing at the main site in the South Australian desert, called Maralinga (an Aboriginal word meaning 'thunder'), prompting a number of media events, the publication of new books by enterprising historians, and a travelling Art Exhibition, all of which contribute to what follows in this chapter. As a case study of intertwining social movements and memory, the following offers thoughts about the creative uses of State and non-State cultural resources and constructed memories as the means of mobilization. It suggests that a consensus memory around the atomic tests relies heavily on an official government report joined with manifestations of Australian nationalism, remediated in artistic, educational and popular forms. Those who protested, and those who subsequently constituted themselves as an anti-nuclear movement, protesting nuclear testing and later uranium mining, French nuclear tests in the Pacific and visits to Australia by nuclear-capable ships have been able to draw on memories of the earlier testing to powerful effect. In this sense, they have drawn on available repertoires in ways similar to how repertoires have been explored by Charles Tilly in his studies of contentious politics and regimes. He defines repertoire as 'the limited, familiar, historically created arrays of claim-making performances that under most circumstances greatly circumscribe the means by which people engage in contentious politics'.[2] Others, including Kubal and Becerra, have found repertoires helpful in analysing varied remembering of social movements according to different cohorts subjected to particular cultural representations of these movements.[3] This case study also seeks to test the explanatory virtues of this interpretive approach.

Remembering nuclear testing in Australia has been examined by Dieter Michel for its contests and its straddling official memory (authorized, by government or institution) and popular memory (collective memory that is strongly communal and easily invoked).[4] Michel points to the shared interest between British and Australian governments in maintaining an official version of events minimizing the possibility of any potential harm to human life or any long-term consequences. He points to the fracturing of this joint story in the 1980s, when surging Australian nationalism and the rise of popular memories forced official narratives in Canberra and London to diverge.[5] This chapter extends Michel's interpretation with closer consideration for the different media forms involved in what he calls popular memory, and for the agency of remembering. It also highlights the importance of late twentieth-century Australian popular nationalism, and it elevates as a theme capable of binding together past atomic testing and more recent anti-nuclear protest the ongoing injustices perpetrated on Indigenous people.

In the context of current scholarly interest in exposing transnational connectedness and internationalist impulses among protest movements,[6] this case study presents some distinctive characteristics, stemming from available repertoire, pragmatism and timing. In the organized remembering of the tests, and their opponents, the power of colonialism as a meta-narrative against which activists built and still build stories of opposition is notable. So too, is the persistence of nationalism as a response to British colonialism in Australia. Testing atom bombs in the Australian desert has become the last great play of colonialism at the height of modernity – 'nuclear colonialism' in the words of one author writing recently about Maralinga.[7]

In short summary, the broad lines of the 'nuclear colonialism' story are these: the nefarious British cavalierly disregarded the long-term consequences of nuclear experimentation for their former settler colonies in Australia, and then both Australians and British shamefully showed scant regard for Aboriginal groups living near or down-wind from the testing areas, as they were not going to stop this particular advance in scientific progress and Cold War preparedness. This interpretation is especially directed at the conservative government led by Robert Menzies, 1949–66 tapping into Menzies' reputation as an anglophile who bemoaned the passing of empire. The Menzies government's disregard for Aboriginal groups was linked to other forms of short-sightedness: it was partly a case of being unquestioningly loyal to the British in the Cold War, it was partly being duped by the duplicitous British who did not pass on the fullest details of tests and risks, and partly being over-excited by the likely benefits of atomic energy that saw the government basically hand over thousands of square kilometres for testing without rudimentary safeguards or guarantee of a return in Australia's interests.[8]

This colonialist-nationalist lens, I suggest, sits importantly alongside more transnational perspectives derived from peace and environmentalist movements. It also enables productive exchanges with the greater prominence of Aboriginal mistreatment in the best-known narratives and images that recur in popular remembering of the nuclear tests. Thus, the anti-nuclear social movement in Australia has drawn regularly on the past injustices of colonial acts, especially those that have impacted on Aboriginal welfare. The hurt to Indigenous Australians has proven to be one of the most effective sources of continuity and bookends for anti-nuclear protest movements – Indigenous groups suffered at the start and they still suffer now. In addition, I suggest that protesters have drawn on memories of robust, oversimplified nationalism – the repertoire that has been made easily available to them – as a source of mobilization, and as a smoothing agent, evening out potted histories of Australia's anti-nuclear movement. My related observation is that these two features stand out all the more on account of their capacity for recirculation and remediation in different media forms.

Nationalism, anti-colonialism and nuclear weapons

To recall some basic details about the atomic testing, of the 12 bomb tests between 1952 and 1957, three of these were on or near the Monte Bello Islands off the coast of Western Australia, two at a South Australian desert location called Emu Field and seven at Maralinga also in the South Australian desert. Australian newspapers reported the tests with a mixture of excitement, speculation and the types of inaccuracies inevitable due to the tight secrecy surrounding the details of testing.[9] After a test in the Monte Bello Islands in the middle of 1956, The (Melbourne) *Age* newspaper speculated that the radioactive cloud resulting had drifted inland, contrary to expectations, forcing a denial from the Minister responsible, Howard Beale,[10] but, in general, journalists had difficulty in gaining any access to reliable information and were forced to remain in speculative mode, about both 'success' and potential dangers arising.

Not surprisingly, some of the strongest protest at the time came from the Communist Party of Australia (CPA). By the mid-1950s, however, the party was haemorrhaging from a combination of external attacks and internal divisions, compounded by its penetration by members of Australia's Security Intelligence Organisation (ASIO). From a membership of more than 20,000 at the end of the Second World War, its numbers had slipped to less than 6,000 by the end of 1955.[11] While communists occupied prominent roles in some trade unions, including in mining and waterfront industries, their influence also caused divisions among the Left in Australia, contributing to a major split in the Australian Labor Party (ALP) in the middle of the decade. As one account puts it, the CPA's stuttering fortunes shaped an awkward mix of responses to the nuclear tests but also, partly on account of splits within and from the party, spawned a less ideological and more socialist humanist approach that drew inspiration from the Campaign for Nuclear Disarmament in Britain.[12] The CPA's *Tribune* newspaper railed against the tests, emphasizing their potential to increase the risk of nuclear war and their extreme health hazards to soldiers and civilians involved and to any Aborigines in the vicinity.[13] The Australians involved were guinea pigs for imperialist preparations for another war, *Tribune* said, at a time when the West should have been exploring options for peace and disarmament with the Soviet Union.[14] Also forced to guess test details (often wrongly) the *Tribune* drew recurringly on photo stock and stories emanating from the atomic bombs dropped on Hiroshima and Nagasaki in August 1945.[15]

In addition to the big bomb tests, there were 25 minor (but significant) tests through to 1963. Some of the last of these, at Maralinga, involved the detonation of simulated warheads containing plutonium. These tests were the least well known by Australian authorities, and the least well cleaned up afterwards by the British. The debris left by the minor tests proved the trigger for a Royal Commission investigating the legacies of the testing in the early 1980s after Geiger counters had been sent crazy in a routine check of the area. The Royal Commission into British Nuclear Tests in Australia heard evidence during 1984–5 and reported towards the end of 1985. (The Commission was also known as the McClelland Royal Commission, as it was headed by former Labor Senator James McClelland, a colourful figure who had publicly questioned the role of the Queen as Australia's Head of State in the controversial dismissal of Australian Prime Minister Gough Whitlam in 1975.)

The Royal Commission's hearings were held in open session, and included 210 written statements and appearance by 311 witnesses. In its 615 pages and 201 conclusions, the McClelland Royal Commission report of 1985 used terms such as 'grovelling' to describe the conservative Menzies Government's enthusiastic response to the British request that they test atomic weapons in Australia. When the Commission travelled to London in 1985 McClelland publicly slammed

British bureaucracy for obfuscation and hindering his enquiry. The Commission Report took the form of annotated literature and evidence compilation, so its recirculation of witness statements, news reports, official cables and previously published work is striking. Another important quality is its identification of villains: especially Australian Prime Minister Robert Menzies, who, according to the report, was slavishly wedded to Britain as the moral force for good in the world, and Professor Ernest Titterton, English-born nuclear scientist who came to work at the Australian National University before the tests. Titterton assumed responsibility for safety during the tests on behalf of Australian Government but, in the eyes of the Commission, was acting primarily in the interests of British scientists and defence chiefs who were dismissive of Australians safety concerns.[16] Some excerpts illustrate this very short summary:

> In taking it upon himself to embrace British interests as being synonymous with those of Australia, and to expose his country and people to the risk of radioactive contamination, Menzies was merely acting according to his well-exposed Anglophilian sentiments.[17]
>
> It is inconceivable, especially in the light of Titterton's cavalier treatment of the truth throughout his testimony ... that he did not know that he had been planted on Menzies ... Titterton can hardly be considered to have been at arms' length from the British.[18]
>
> ... Aboriginal people were placed at risk by official ignorance, incompetence, cynicism and, in the face of repeated warnings, preference for a 'need to not know'.[19]
>
> 'Hypocrisy and Lies'[20]
>
> Titterton played a political as well as a safety role in the testing programme ... He was prepared to conceal information from the Australian Government and his fellow Committee members if he believed to do so would suit the interests of the UK Government and the testing programme.[21]
>
> The Royal Commission believes that Aboriginal people experienced radioactive fallout from Totem 1 in the form of a black mist or cloud at and near Wallantinna.[22]

The Commission Report is easily found online.[23] It tends to be extensively quoted by anyone writing about atomic testing in Australia, given its powerful narrative and striking language. It also translates readily to other media forms and has entered popular culture to reverberate in education materials, song, art, theatre. The Commission heard evidence at the height of a surging wave of popular nationalism in the lead up to Australia's bicentennial celebrations in 1988, and fuelled by the rise of the Australian film industry. It reported four years after Australians watched the dastardly British send Australian troops to their futile slaughter in the 1981 film, *Gallipoli*, depicting Australian involvement in the disastrous British campaign to seize the Dardanelles in 1915. And it was only one year after Australians changed their national anthem from *God Save the Queen* to

Advance Australia Fair, that they heard of the British contempt for Australian interests in the findings of the Royal Commission.[24] They also read exposé-styled books written by journalists eager to ride the wave of interest generated from 1978 by the first investigative journalist to uncover the inadequacies of clean-ups, Brian Toohey,[25] and then the great interest stirred by the Royal Commission. Joan Smith's *Clouds of Deceit* and *Fields of Thunder* by Denys Blakeway and Sue Lloyd-Roberts in 1985; and Robert Milliken's *No Conceivable Injury* in 1986 are good examples.[26]

Those protest groups willing to take up or resume campaigning for the anti-nuclear cause in the 1980s thus had an easily accessed memory of nuclear colonialism to draw on. Some probably saw another piece of Australian film-making from 1981 – a documentary called *Backs to the Blast*, about the atomic testing in Australia, shown first on Channel 7, a commercial station, in Australia and then on Channel 4 in Britain – making an impact in both places. *Backs to the Blast* positioned its excursion into the past against the likelihood in the early 1980s of expansion in uranium mining in Australia. It featured interviews with Aboriginal people and white servicemen (Australian and British) and families who had suffered illnesses in the aftermath of the tests; and it also gave the villain, Ernest Titterton prominence in his interview comments. Dressed formally and sounding imperious and vaguely condescending, the clipped Titterton was the perfect foil for the very working class accents of those who were later affected.[27] At 50 minutes running time and including a press kit, and interviews, *Backs to the Blast* was, and remains, very useable in school classrooms. Six years after it screened, in 1987 an Australian-made conspiracy drama movie followed: *Ground Zero*[28] centred on a cinematographer uncovering connections between his father's death and his filming of the atomic testing decades earlier.

The early to mid-1980s marked the re-emergence of the Australian peace movement harnessed to a burgeoning anti-nuclear movement, and later joined with the environmental movement. It might have been stirred to action by the ready export of uranium by the conservative Liberal coalition governments of the late 1970s and early 1980s, but the change to Labor in 1983 did not end uranium mining. Thereafter, anti-uranium mining merged with anxieties about French nuclear testing in the Pacific (where there were 69 tests between 1980 and 1985) and new nuclear missile deployments across Europe amidst deepening tensions between East and West; but telling the story of how protest in Australia swelled and spilled into other battles is contested and messy. One historian's account of the anti-nuclear movement in the 1980s might be summarized broadly as a tale of vibrant but uneven and uncoordinated development. The movement grew rapidly but argued over how closely or otherwise to work with the ALP; it was weakened by differences at State-level organizations, and it struggled to control special interest groups such as students, and doctors and lawyers against nuclear energy.[29] The new Nuclear Disarmament Party gained a Senate seat in 1984, at the height of its influence. But, after around a quarter of a million protesters were drawn onto the streets in this year, it fractured, with the Socialist Workers

Party trying to drag radicals towards unilateral disarmament, leaving the remaining leaders isolated. The ALP weathered the blows from the disaffected and remained resolved in its limited uranium mining and exporting policy.[30]

The protest group featuring in the documentary film *Backs to the Blast,* Friends of the Earth, was established nationally in Australia in 1974, as a grass-roots environmental movement at the time of Australia's toying with greater investment in nuclear energy, and its early campaigns were focussed mostly on opposition to nuclear energy and protesting French nuclear testing at Mururoa Atoll in the Pacific. Indigenous rights quickly emerged as another strand in its burgeoning activism, especially as nearly all the uranium mines were on Aboriginal land. And, as Cold War tensions mounted in Europe, increasing attention in Australia turned to the role of American electronic surveillance/communication bases in Australia, such as Pine Gap and North West Cape, which might logically become targets in the event of a nuclear exchange. Australia's Nuclear Disarmament Party was established in 1984 as news spread of radioactive contamination at Maralinga, and the Royal Commission commenced its hearings.[31] In the same year, the New Zealand decision in to ban any US ship that did not declare its non-nuclear credentials caused a crisis in the Australian-NZ-US alliance and emboldened the left, as did a humiliating back-down by PM Bob Hawke who had earlier given a green light to the testing of US nuclear-capable missiles off the east coast of Australia.[32]

The mid-1980s serves as a logical mnemonic focal point then, partly on account of international events – especially French nuclear testing in the Pacific and the escalation of medium-range missiles deployment in Europe – but also on account of its leveraging a strident form of thwarted nationalism in multiple media. No more US bases, prominent also in Friends of the Earth (FOE) campaigns and pop culture, and perhaps best expressed in the lyrics of Australian rock-band Midnight Oil, sat neatly alongside narratives of earlier colonial appropriation of land through nuclear testing. Midnight Oil's hugely successful album of 1982 titled, *10, 9, 8, 7, 6, 5, 4, 3, 2, 1,* featured hits such as 'US Forces', 'Short Memory' and 'Maralinga'. And Paul Kelly, famous balladist, referenced the Royal Commission text when he sang, 'Maralinga' in 1986. While Kelly is not an Indigenous Australian the song was written from an Indigenous perspective.

Among the protest badges and car stickers that spread rapidly through Australian cities were some emphasizing the nexus between Aboriginal injustice and planned mining: 'Land Rights: Not Uranium' in the red, yellow and black colours of the Indigenous flag was one of the most popular.[33] After the special moment of the mid-1980s, the incumbent ALP Government, having been scared at the rush by younger voters towards green and peace causes at the expense of the party's vote, adjusted to better be able to co-opt these movements.

Clearly the timing of the Royal Commission and its report was critical to the ways in which a repertoire of historically familiar claim-making memories of the atomic tests could be drawn on in the mid-1980s, and also beyond. Three other aspects of the tests contributed to their enduring presence in subsequent protest consciousness. One was the extreme secrecy with which the media had complied, thereby guaranteeing that any subsequent revelations would always be regarded as the tip of the iceberg. All those involved were sworn to secrecy under Official Secrets legislation and the D-notice system and so could not protest to any line of authority other than that conducting the tests if they had concerns. The second was the desperate, repeated claims for compensation for those whose health was impacted by the tests. This applied, and still applies both to Aboriginal groups and Australian and British ex-servicemen and civilians. Aboriginal groups both in the region of the testing and affected by wind-borne radioactive materials were not compensated – in fact, while stories told of great sicknesses and deaths in several locations, such was the lack of census data in some cases, and lack of care in others, that there remain many unknowns about the full impact on the Indigenous population. One of the best-known accounts, told at the Royal Commission in 1985, was of a black mist blanketing the sky north of the Emu Field testing area in 1953, followed by illnesses and deaths of Aborigines. These claims have not been recognized. As historian Heather Goodall has suggested, it is possible that the deadly measles epidemics at the Aboriginal settlement of Ernabella in 1948 and 1957 were merged in remembering with later memories of nearby nuclear tests. The Yankunytjatjara Anangu people from the Ernabella and Wallantinna settlements provided evidence in 1984–5 about deaths and ill-health resulting from colonialism, but the leading testing-related questioning conducted by the Royal Commission over-determined the shape of Yankuntjatjara Anangu answers.[34]

Successive governments in Britain and Australia have failed to recognize cancers contracted by ex-servicemen involved in the tests (including many national servicemen), decades later, and have effectively stalled while claimants have died off, there being very few remaining today. And the third feature was the poor quality and incompleteness of several attempts to clean up the affected area of desert. Among the Royal Commission's recommendations were for proper remediation of the land, paid for by the British, compensation for victims whose health suffered in the wake of the test (though that group was very small), and full return of land to Aboriginal owners of the affected lands, after their clean-up, with suitable compensation for their use in testing.[35]

Peace movements, Aboriginal welfare

The first anti-testing protests in Australia grew at the same time that new media were revealing more of the Australian desert to the majority populace concentrated in cities. The earliest protests were on behalf of Aborigines and through the Australian peace movement. Initially, concern for the welfare of Aborigines arose when their land was being blasted from earlier testing of long-range (non-nuclear) missiles at Woomera, in another part of the South Australian desert from the late 1940s. Anti-weapons campaigners emerged as early as the mid-1940s when rumours of long-range rocket testing began circulating. Church groups, including Quakers, joined with trade unions and an Aborigines' Friends Society and the Socialist League in an early coalition which would grow in size but with broadly the same type of partners in alliance.[36]

Concern for Aboriginal welfare merged more often and more structurally with the peace movement with the formation of the Australian Peace Council at the end of the 1940s. There is now considerable research on both Australian Indigenous transnationalism and some of the strongest sinews joining campaigns for Aboriginal welfare with the CPA in Australia.[37] Any perusal of *Tribune* for the 1950s and 1960s is a reminder of how important the CPA was in pointing to injustices and mounting campaigns for Aboriginal rights, and also a reminder of the diversity of the coalition of like-minded groups, including the Aboriginal Advancement League and the Women's International League for Peace and Freedom.[38] This is also evident in groups' surveillance by ASIO, which focussed not only on communists but also on those they called communist stooges, the YWCA, the League of Women's Voters, the Women's Christian Temperance Union, trades unions, doctors, scientists, authors and artists and others, making for a diverse surveillance story.[39] Up to the late 1960s, when a greater sense of Indigenous agency and empowerment encouraged Aboriginal activists to form their own organizations, the CPA and allied organizations maintained a steady stream of support for Aboriginal rights, including redress from the effects of the atomic tests.

The Australian peace movement grew in parallel. There was a succession of peace congresses held throughout the 1950s. Some, like the massive Melbourne Peace Congress in April 1950, and Australian participation in the Warsaw Peace Congress in November 1950, were organized by the communist-dominated Australian Peace Council; others, such as the Australian Convention on Peace and War in September 1953, were instigated purely by the clergy.[40] In 1959, the same year that Hollywood's 'nuclear-end-of-the-world' movie *On the Beach* was being filmed in Australia, the most ecumenical peace congress occurred. The Australian and New Zealand Congress for International Co-operation and Disarmament, held in Melbourne in November, was broad ranging in support but marked by public controversy after ASIO persuaded some high-profile sponsors to withdraw their endorsement. The Campaign for International Co-operation and Disarmament (CICD), born in 1958, continued throughout the 1960s to organize peace activities and coordinate the anti-nuclear movement.[41]

Arguably, the Cuban Missile crisis of 1962 provided a substantial vindication of the CICD position that all nuclear bases be dismantled by the two superpowers, and that the United Nations play a more central role to ease international tensions. The Partial Test Ban Treaty signed by the Soviet Union and the United States (underground testing was still permitted) in the summer of 1963 dented the *raison d'être* of the CICD. It staged its final Easter march, modelled on the famous Aldermaston marches in England, in 1965 and increasingly turned its attention to opposing the Vietnam War.[42] Although French atmospheric tests at Mururoa in 1966–7 aroused the ire of nuclear pacifists, the Nuclear Non-Proliferation

Treaty of 1968 and the first Strategic Arms Limitation Treaty of 1972 meant that the early momentum of the CICD was lost.

In his analysis of memories of nuclear testing in Australia, Michel was right to point to the importance of heroes and villains in ensuring their popular interest. In suggesting that we need also to give greater consideration to the media in which such heroes and villains appeared, I am mindful of some early examples that would re-circulate later. The case of William Grayden's activism is one example. In the mid-1950s, an agitated Western Australian politician William Grayden had initiated a parliamentary committee report into native welfare, focussed on and around the Warburton mission, which was close to continuing Anglo-Australian long-range (non-nuclear) missile testing. The report found many problems, including health, malnutrition, lack of food, lack of education opportunities and so on. And it prompted public debate, a counter-report from a young Rupert Murdoch (*Adelaide News*) who undertook his own whirl-wind tour, finding that conditions were not bad at all, and, with different newspapers now invested in the issue, a new tour by Grayden and a Victorian Aboriginal activist Doug Nicholls to the remote central desert area to report on the conditions of Aborigines, some of whom had been relocated to make way for the testing.[43]

In brief terms, they were shocked by what they saw and made the most of their abilities to tell others. Grayden took a 16 mm camera and produced a silent film called *Their Darkest Hour*, in which the camera lingered on the physical effects of disease, malnutrition, a decomposing body, a dying baby and other images of degradation in and around the Warburton Ranges area. The film had some town hall and church showings in 1957 before it was picked up by a commercial TV station, Channel 9, and screened to a bigger, shocked audience (only one year after television's introduction in Australia). In his public advocacy for better treatment of Aborigines, Grayden conflated long-range missile testing with the atomic testing then occurring 800 kilometres away at Maralinga. So accelerated an important phase of activism on behalf of Aborigines according to most who have studied these events. It was assisted by an international climate in which there was a growing sensitivity to race, especially in the UN and increasingly in relation to South Africa and the US civil rights movement, important deliberations by the International Labour Organisation, including its 1957 Convention on Indigenes and Tribal Populations, and the slow growth of human rights consciousness.[44]

Grayden also wrote a short polemical book, *Adam and Atoms* (1957)[45] that circulated well among the left and the burgeoning peace movement. It also continued to circulate later. An extract relating to Grayden's conversations with Aborigines in the Warburton area featured in the 1985 Royal Commission Report:

> ... most of the natives questioned by our party were under the impression that some foreign country was going to drop a bomb somewhere in their territory. It was apparently beyond their comprehension that the Government of this country would drop a bomb on its own territory.[46]

Images, texts

Grayden's film contained images that have since recurred in public remembering as a mobilizing source of information for social activists and an important remediation of popular memory. The nexus between the moving image and popular memory in Australia has been the subject of increasing scholarly attention.[47] Some mnemonic benefits of the medium of film are general, namely the rise since the 1950s in access and attraction to moving images, which can also be easily reproduced, tailored and interspersed among other sources. Other remembering weight grows from the particular circumstances of mobilizing around a cause in remote desert regions, not easily accessed, and not readily appreciated by Australia's highly urbanized population. In contrast to some of the successful British peace marches from the 1960s through the 1980s, it is too difficult to march on foot as a group from any township to a cattle or weather station in support of Aboriginal welfare. One of the more successfully remembered events of the 1980s was an exception to the formidable distances often involved, the women's two-week camp at the Australian-US Joint Defence Space Research Facility at Pine Gap in the Northern Territory in November 1983. Aboriginal women were able to lead a march of around 700 activists to the site as Pine Gap is 18 kilometres south of the town of Alice Springs.[48]

Aboriginal welfare activism has thus joined with anti-nuclear peace protests, and each has continued to inform the other in how the events of the 1950s–60s are remembered. Australians heard much about another anniversary, the 40th anniversary in 2017 of the 1967 referendum recognizing Australian Aborigines in census data and enabling the Commonwealth to create laws for them; and the lead up to this also prompted film-making in which images from Grayden's *Their Darkest Hour* reappeared. Two well-known examples are the latest documentary on nuclear testing, through the eyes of veterans and Aboriginal elders, Katherine Aigner's *Australian Atomic Confessions* (2009)[49] and Rachael Perkins' series on Indigenous Peoples, *The First Australians* (2008).[50] And at the level of more popular movie-making there runs a strong thread of nuclear-related or post-apocalyptic film in the Australian desert, from the late 1950s, with *On the Beach*, through the Mad Max genre to recent years.[51]

In popular, easily accessed forms, Aboriginal rights have bookended the story of anti-nuclear protests, being very much to fore at the outset, and looming large in the cultural memory. Recent research has uncovered new features of Australian-based anti-nuclear activism, including the transnational impetus behind protesting French testing in the Pacific in the 1960s through the 1980s peak of activities.[52] Equally, it has proven hard to show neat lines of continuity between the events of the 1950s and early 1960s and the resurgence of the anti-nuclear movement in Australia in the 1970s to the mid-1980s. There were more than 350 peace groups in Australia in 19585, and their diversity was reflected in class, age, ideological and geographical ways – with many either in the ALP or focussed primarily on pressuring the ALP to halt its creep back towards uranium mining and its enthusiasm for US bases.[53]

106 David Lowe

The media of remembering, song, visual, audio-visual, play an important role in how easily Aboriginal colonial injustices are drawn on and joined up with a range of anti-nuclear protest moments. Australian secondary school teachers have ready access to the film resources discussed above and to resource kits such as 'What are the mysteries of Maralinga?',[54] a package of materials that starts students with the joint tests and moves with them through a narrative of Cold War conditions to contemporary legacies of atomic testing in Australia. Australian photographer-activists such as Jessie Boylan have worked determinedly to make the invisible horror of atomic testing (radiation and other legacies) visible and have taken pride in seeing their work incorporated in educational materials.[55]

It seems reasonable to assume too, that a generation of teachers who entered the education system in the 1980s was highly sensitive to the dangers of nuclear weapons, and was likely to be drawn to pedagogic materials that contained this message. This was certainly the view of a number of witnesses who appeared at an Australian Parliamentary Inquiry in 2006. The House of Representatives Standing Committee considering greenhouse-friendly fuels, including nuclear energy, attracted exasperated submissions from Australia's Nuclear Science and Technology Organisation and the Australian Nuclear Forum whose representatives bemoaned 'evidence of children being taught very anti-nuclear and anti-uranium views in school', and recounted episodes of sending nuclear-industry literature to schools, only to have it posted back, torn in half.[56] Australia's longest-running uranium producers, Energy Resources, Australia, suggested 'public perceptions of uranium mining in Australia were due to its perceived connection with "British and French nuclear testing at Maralinga and in the South Pacific"', reinforcing negative attitudes towards uranium mining.[57]

A recent (2017–18) touring art exhibition *Black Mist, Burnt Country* (blackmistburntcountry.com.au)[58] takes its name from that mist that Aboriginal people at Wallantinna station claimed afflicted them after a test at Emu Field in 1953. That no conclusive links between health problems and black mist have been proven is not important because the black mist has, through repeated remembering, acquired metaphorical status. It represents the ongoing lack of openness shown by Australian and British governments. Teachers' materials linked to the site include inviting students to send 1,000 folded paper cranes to place in the exhibition, following the well-known story of Sadako and the Thousand Paper Cranes that became a historical novel set in the aftermath of the bomb dropped on Hiroshima. Analysis of the materials, and pedagogical recommendations around their use, have featured in History teachers' association journals in Victoria and New South Wales.[59]

The resource package moves students through the atomic age as well as the events in Australia:

   Timeline of Nuclear Testing in Australia
   The Development of the A-Bomb
   The Bombing of Hiroshima

British Tests in Australia
Maralinga: Ground Zero
Indigenous Culture and Land Rights
Impact on Country and Environment
The Clean Up
Victims and Survivors
'Ban the Bomb': The Australian Anti-Nuclear Movement
Australia's Nuclear Future?[60]

In 2009, some 3,000 square kilometres around Maralinga was handed back to traditional owners, Pitjantjatjara, having finally been cleaned, and their access was completely unrestricted from 2014. Today, with permission of Pitjantjatjara People, there are guided tours for intrepid tourists.[61]

Repertoire recirculation

The use of multiple media forms, especially those such as film, visual art and popular music, has enhanced the ease with which memories of nuclear testing are drawn on and linked to contemporary causes, anti-nuclear and Indigenous rights. As is clear from the *Black Mist, Burnt Rain* educational resources, Australia's experience is remembered in anti-colonial and internationalist forms simultaneously. In another example, protest marches in Australia in March 2013 and 2014 marking the second and third anniversaries of the 2011 Fukushima reactor disaster in Japan featured placards joining Hiroshima, Fukushima and Maralinga. In the words of historian-observer Vera Mackie, 'These events have built on a pre-existing repertoire of practices and symbols, while also creating new practices and new ways of performing and representing feelings of empathy, solidarity and connectedness'.[62]

The memory of atomic testing has also been stirred in recent years by protests against proposals by Federal and State (South Australian) governments for the building of nuclear waste facilities in the South Australian desert.[63] Since the mid-1990s, the internet has been an excellent means of remediating the mix of personal testimony and striking visual reminders of previous tests. In 1998, when the Kunga Tjuta people in the north of South Australia campaigned against one such iteration of the nuclear waste proposal, they reached insistently for connections between the 'black mist' produced by earlier British testing and the modern dangers of radioactive waste. According to Eve Vincent who wrote of her time with the campaign, 'the remembering and re-telling of "bomb testimonies" became a priority of campaign work, and individual stories were made publicly available on the campaign website'.[64]

Both Australian governments and uranium mining companies have a long history of ignoring or misleading Aboriginal groups, and the banners and rallying calls of 'Land Rights, Not Uranium' work effectively to tap into one of the longest running sores in unfulfilled social justice in Australia. The same memories of injustice continue to energize social movements engaging in contentious politics. This case study therefore adds weight to recent calls for greater attention to the connections between memory and activism. As Kubal and Becerra argue, 'Success in eliciting cultural change is dependent upon the ability to use words and symbolic tactics that resonate with the public. By tapping into the repertoire, movements signal a cultural understanding about when and why people mobilize'.[65] In this study, ready access to a repertoire of cultural resources relating to British-Australian atomic testing of the 1950s and 1960s has been enabling for Australian anti-nuclear activists. The resources range from repeated narratives, including in official documentation, to songs, audio-visual materials, artistic symbols and teachers' resources kits. A repertoire embedded within overarching narratives of banal nationalism and injustice for Indigenous Australians comes with the limitations of these narratives' boundaries, but the repertoire has also allowed activists to skip over the disruptions and messiness in the longer history of anti-nuclear protests. Activists have also moved easily between anti-colonialist and internationalist frames, such is the national/transnational mnemonic repertoire available and the ease with which it lends shape to the more inchoate histories of the anti-nuclear movement.

A recent episode serves by way of a postscript and testifies to the continued importance of the repertoire of atomic test memories in Australia. Following another Royal Commission, there emerged, in 2016, a proposal by the South Australian Government to set up a nuclear waste processing plant. The proposal was rejected after widespread citizen consultation, including online forums in which Maralinga was a recurring reference.[66] Aboriginal activists were among leaders of the opposition, maintaining that they didn't want 'the outback poisoned again', and deploying all available arguments about lack of respect for sacred country, desecration of Dreamtime stories and ancient trading routes amounting to 'cultural genocide'.[67] Whether mobilizing against the storage of nuclear waste, nuclear power or weaponry, the memories of past struggles relating to atomic testing more than 50 years ago continue to provide legitimacy and consensual simplicity.

Notes

'With permission, this chapter draws upon an earlier publication: David Lowe, 'Australia's Atomic Past: Memories, Mistrust and Policy Legacies', Journal of Applied History, 2 (1-2), 2020: 98–111.'

1 On the strategic aspect of atomic testing, see Wayne Reynolds, 'Atomic War, Empire Strategic Dispersal and the Origins of the Snowy Mountains Scheme,' *War & Society* 14 (1996): 121–144; J. L. Symonds, *A History of the British Atomic Tests in Australia* (Canberra: Australian Government Publishing Service, 1985); Lorna Arnold, *A Very Special Relationship: British Atomic Weapons Trials in Australia* (London: HMSO, 1987); Lorna Arnold and Mark Smith, *Britain, Australia and the Bomb: The Nuclear Tests and Their Aftermath* (2nd edn) (Basingstoke: Palgrave Macmillan, 2006); Wayne Reynolds, *Australia's Bid for the Atomic Bomb* (Melbourne: Melbourne University Press, Melbourne, 2000); Jim Walsh, 'Surprise Down under: The Secret History

of Australia's Nuclear Ambitions,' *The Nonproliferation Review* 5 (1997): 1–20; David Lowe, *Menzies and 'the Great World Struggle: Australia's Cold War, 1948–54* (Sydney: UNSW Press, 1999), 128–143; Jacques Hymans, 'Isotopes and Identity: Australia and the Nuclear Weapons Option,' *The Nonproliferation Review* 7, no. 1 (2008): 1–23; On the utopian and scientific dimensions, see Alice Cawte, *Atomic Australia, 1944–1990* (Sydney: UNSW Press, 1992); Anna-Eugenia Binnie, 'From Atomic Energy to Nuclear Science: A History of the Australian Atomic Energy Commission' (PhD diss., Macquarie University, 2003); Lowe, *Menzies and 'the Great World Struggle,'* 128–143.
2 Charles Tilly, *Regimes and Repertoires* (Chicago, IL: University of Chicago Press, 2006), vii.
3 Timothy Kubal and Rene Becerra, 'Social Movements and Collective Memory,' *Sociology Compass* 8, no. 6 (2014): 865–873. The approach taken herein is influenced especially by Kubal and Becerra's work, and also the work of Ann Rigney in 'Plenitude, Scarcity and the Circulation of Cultural Memory', *Journal of European Studies* 35, no. 1 (2005): 11–28.
4 These concepts are discussed in detail in Aleida Assmann, 'Memory, Individual and Collective,' in *The Oxford Handbook of Contextual Political Analysis*, eds. Robert E. Goodin and Charles Tilly (Oxford: Oxford University Press, 2006), 210–224; and Jeffrey Olick, 'What Does it Mean to Normalize the Past? Official Memory in German Politics since 1989,' *Social Science History* 22, no. 4 (1998): 547–571.
5 Dieter Michel, 'Villains, Victims and Heroes: Contested Memory and the British Nuclear Tests in Australia,' *Journal of Australian Studies* 27, no. 80 (2003): 221–228.
6 For discussion see, Christopher Bayly et al., 'AHR Conversation: On Transnational History,' *American Historical Review* 111, no. 5 (2006): 1440–1464. On the subject of transnational anti-nuclear protest, see, Astrid Mignon Kirchhof, 'Spanning the Globe: West-German Support for the Australian Anti-Nuclear Movement,' *Historical Social Research* 39, no. 1 (2014): 254–273; and Astrid Mignon Kirchhof and Jan Henrik Meyer, 'Global Protest against Nuclear Power: Transfer and Transnational Exchange in the 1970s and 1980s,' *Historical Social Research* 39, no. 1 (2014): 165–190; and focussed on the Pacific, Lawrence Wittner, 'Nuclear Disarmament Activism in Asia and the Pacific, 1971–1996,' *The Asia-Pacific Journal* 25, no. 5 (2009): 1–10; and Nic MacLellan, 'Grappling with the Bomb: Opposition to Pacific Nuclear Testing in the 1950s,' in *Proceedings of the 14th Biennial Labour History Conference*, eds. Phillip Deery and Julie Kimber (Melbourne: Australian Society for the Study of Labour History, 2015), 21–38.
7 Elizabeth Tynan, *Atomic Thunder: The Maralinga Story* (Sydney: New South, 2016), 3.
8 A number of journalists' and participants' publications hinge on this overarching interpretation. For example, see, Robert Milliken, *No Conceivable Injury* (Ringwood: Penguin, 1986); Joan Smith, *Clouds of Deceit: the Deadly of Legacy of Britain's Bomb Tests* (London: Faber and Faber, 1985); and Frank Walker, *Maralinga: The Chilling Exposé of Our Secret Shame and Betrayal of Our Troops and Country* (Sydney: Hachette, 2014). These were made possible by the material produced for the Royal Commission into British Nuclear Tests in Australia, *Report and Conclusions* and *Recommendations* (Canberra: Australian Government Publishing Service, 1985).
9 For examples, see *The Advertiser* (Adelaide), 16 October 1953, 8; *The Sun* (Melb), 17 May, 1956, 1; *The Age* (Melb), 18 May 1956, 1.
10 *The Age*, 21 June 1956, 1.
11 Phillip Deery, 'Australian Communism in Crisis,' in *The Far Left in Australia since 1945*, eds. Evan Smith, John Piccini and Matthew Worley (Abingdon: Routledge, 2018), 28.
12 Kyle Harvey, 'How Far Left? Negotiating Radicalism in Australian Anti-nuclear Politics in the 1960s,' in *The Far Left in Australia since 1945*, eds. Evan Smith, John Piccini and Matthew Worley (Abingdon: Routledge, 2018), 118–133.
13 *Tribune*, 16 April 1952, 8; Ibid., 7 October 1953, 1.
14 Ibid., 11 January. 1956, 2.

15 Ibid., 22 October 1952, 7; Ibid., 14 October 1953, 5; Ibid., 14 August 1957, 2.
16 Frank Bongiorno, *The Eighties: The Decade That Transformed Australia* (Melbourne: Black Inc, 2015), 117; Royal Commission into British Nuclear Tests in Australia, *Report and Conclusions and Recommendations* (Canberra: Australian Government Publishing Service, 1985).
17 Royal Commission into British Nuclear Tests in Australia, *Report and Conclusions and Recommendations* (Canberra: Australian Government Publishing Service, 1985), vol. 1, 11.
18 Royal Commission into British Nuclear Tests in Australia, *Report and Conclusions and Recommendations* (Canberra: Australian Government Publishing Service, 1985), vol. 1, 17.
19 Royal Commission into British Nuclear Tests in Australia, *Report and Conclusions and Recommendations* (Canberra: Australian Government Publishing Service, 1985), vol. 1, 368.
20 Royal Commission into British Nuclear Tests in Australia, *Report and Conclusions and Recommendations* (Canberra: Australian Government Publishing Service, 1985), subheading, vol. 1, 369.
21 Royal Commission into British Nuclear Tests in Australia, *Report and Conclusions and Recommendations* (Canberra: Australian Government Publishing Service, 1985), vol. 2, 526.
22 Royal Commission into British Nuclear Tests in Australia, *Report and Conclusions and Recommendations* (Canberra: Australian Government Publishing Service, 1985), 17.
23 The full report is available via the Australian Commonwealth Parliament website: https://parlinfo.aph.gov.au/parlInfo/search/display/display.w3p;query=Id:%22publications/tabledpapers/HPP032016010928%22;src1=sm1 [accessed 3 July 2018].
24 Bongiorno, *The Eighties*, 227–262 and passim.
25 On Toohey's influential exposés of 1978 and the role of journalists more generally, see Elizabeth Tynan, 'Maralinga and the Journalists: Covering the Bomb Tests over Generations,' *Linq* 38 (2011): 131–145.
26 Smith, *Clouds of Deceit*, 1985; Denys Blakeway and Sue Lloyd-Roberts, *Fields of Thunder: Testing Britain's Bomb* (London: Faber and Faber, 1985); Milliken, *No Conceivable Injury*.
27 *Backs to the Blast: An Australian Nuclear Story* (Australia: Ronin Films, 1981).
28 Directed by Bruce Myles and Michael Pattinson (Australia: Burrowes Film Group, 1987).
29 Jonathan Strauss, 'The Australian Nuclear Disarmament Movement in the 1980s', in *Proceedings of the 14th Biennial Labour History Conference*, eds. Phillip Deery and Julie Kimber (Melbourne: Australian Society for the Study of Labour History, 2015), 39–50.
30 See, Ibid.; Bongiorno, *The Eighties*, 88–94, 113; James Walter, *What Were They Thinking: The Politics of Ideas in Australia* (Sydney: UNSW, 2010), 276–277.
31 *Canberra Times*, 18 June 1984, 3.
32 Bongiorno, *The Eighties*, 113–118.
33 P. Nistor, 'Nuclear Disarmament Protest Badges in Museums Victoria Collections,' 2016, https://collections.museumvictoria.com.au/articles/15183 [accessed 3 July 2018].
34 Heather Goodall, 'Colonialism and Catastrophe: Contested Memories of Nuclear Testing and Measles Epidemics at Ernabella,' in *Memory and History in Twentieth Century Australia*, eds. Kate Darian-Smith and Paula Hamilton (Melbourne: Oxford University Press, 1994), 55–73.
35 Tynan, *Atomic Thunder*, 200–311.
36 Bob Boughton, 'The Communist Party of Australia's Involvement in the Struggle for Aboriginal and Torres Strait Islander Peoples' Rights, 1920–1970,' in *Labour and Community: Historical Essays*, ed. Raymond Markey (Wollongong: University of Wollongong Press, 2001), 263–294.

37 Ravi de Costa, *A Higher Authority: Indigenous Transnationalism and Australia* (Sydney: UNSW Press, 2006); Jon Piccini, "'People Treated Me with Equality': Indigenous Australians Visiting the Soviet Bloc during the Cold War,' *Labour History* 111 (2016): 45–57; Boughton, 'The Communist Party of Australia's Involvement in the Struggle for Aboriginal and Torres Strait Islander Peoples' Rights,' 263–294; Jennifer Clark, *Aborigines and Activism: Race and the Coming of the Sixties to Australia* (Crawley: University of Western Australia Publishing, 2008); Tracey Banivanua Mar, *Decolonisation and the Pacific: Indigenous Globalisation and the Ends of Empire* (Cambridge: Cambridge University Press, 2016).
38 *Tribune*, 23 January 1957, 2; ibid., 15 February 1956, 10; ibid., 12 April 1961, 8; ibid., 28 June 1961, 1; ibid., 24 February 1965, 1; ibid., 17 July 1968, 1; and Bain Attwood, *Rights for Aborigines* (Sydney: Allen & Unwin, 2003), 149–150.
39 See works by Phillip Deery, 'ASIO and the 1951 Berlin Youth Carnival,' *Overland* 168 (2002): 84–87; Deery, 'The Dove Flies East: Whitehall, Warsaw and the 1950 World Peace Congress,' *Australian Journal of Politics and History* 48, no. 4 (2002): 436–457; Deery, 'War on Peace: Menzies, the Cold War and the 1953 Convention on Peace and War,' *Australian Historical Studies* 34, no. 122 (2003): 248–269. And the history of ASIO, David McKinght, *Australia's Spies and Their Secrets* (Sydney: Allen & Unwin, 1994).
40 Deery, 'ASIO and the 1951 Berlin Youth Carnival,' 84–87; Deery, 'The Dove Flies East,' 436–457; Deery, 'War on Peace,' 248–269. And the history of ASIO, McKinght, *Australia's Spies and Their Secrets*.
41 Bill Gollan, *Bond or Free. The Peace and Disarmament Movement and an Independent Australian Foreign Policy for Peace and Security* (Sydney: NSW Teachers' Federation, 1987), 49–65; Norman Rothfield, *Many Paths to Peace* (Melbourne: Yarraford Publications 1997), 51–66. The University of Melbourne Archives holds the records of the CICD.
42 Malcolm Saunders and Raph Summy, *The Australian Peace Movement: A Short History* (Canberra: Peace Research Centre, Australia National University, 1986), 35.
43 Pamela Faye McGrath and David Brooks, '"Their Darkest Hour": The Films and Photographs of William Grayden and the History of the "Warburton Range Controversy" of 1957', *Aboriginal History* 34 (2010): 115–141.
44 Ibid.; Clark, *Aborigines and Activism*, 76–77.
45 Daniels, *Perth*, 1957.
46 Quoted in *Royal Commission into British Nuclear Tests* 1 (1985), 377.
47 On the significance of television, see Kate Darian-Smith and Sue Turnbull, eds., *Remembering Television: Histories, Technologies, Memories* (Newcastle: Cambridge Scholars Publishing, 2012).
48 Alison Bartlett, 'Feminist Protest and Cultural Production at the Pine Gap Women's Peace Camp, Australia, 1983,' *Women: A Cultural Review* 24, no. 2–3 (2013): 179–195. The Jessie Street National Women's Library in Sydney curated an exhibition of *Remembering Pine Gap* in 2009: Alison Bartlett, 'Sites of Feminist Activism: Remembering Pine Gap,' *Continuum: Journal of Media and Cultural Studies* 13, no. 3 (2016): 307–315. The material dimensions of the protest – banners, t-shirts, photographs, wire, earrings and so on – have since been elevated in its exhibited remembering.
49 Galloping Films, 2009.
50 Blackfella Films, 2008; McGrath and Brooks, 'Their Darkest Hour,' 134–135.
51 See Mick Broderick, '"There Is Still Time … Brother": Antipodean Cinema and Nuclearism in the Mid-to-Late Cold War,' *Historical Journal of Film, Radio and Television* 36, no. 1 (2016): 53–67.
52 Kyle Harvey, 'Nuclear Migrants, Radical Protest, and the Transnational Movement against French Nuclear Testing in the 1960s: The 1967 Voyage of the "Trident",' *Labour History* 111 (2016): 79–98; Kirchhof, 'Spanning the Globe,' 254–273.
53 Strauss, 'The Australian Nuclear Disarmament Movement,' 1–43.
54 https://www.australianhistorymysteries.info/casestudies/mysteries-of-maralinga/ [accessed 2 July 2018].

55 Jessie Boylan, 'Atomic Amnesia: Photographs and Nuclear Memory,' *Global Change, Peace & Security* 28, no. 1 (2016): 67–72.
56 Australian House of Representatives Standing Committee on Industry and Resources Report, *Greenhouse-friendly fuel for an Energy-hungry world* (2006), 608–609.
57 Ibid., 610.
58 https://www.blackmistburntcoutnry.com.au [accessed 3 June 2017].
59 J. D. Mittmann, 'Testing the Bomb: Maralinga and Australian Art,' *Journal of the History Teachers' Association of NSW* (March 2017): 52–54; Jo Clyne, 'Black Mist, Burnt Country: Testing the Bomb: Maralinga and Australian Art. An Educational Resource for Years 9–12,' Praktikos, *Agora*, 63–66. The exhibition includes photographs by Jessie Boylan.
60 https://www.blackmistburntcoutnry.com.au [accessed 3 June 2017].
61 See Maralinga Tours: https://maralingatours.com.au/ [accessed 2 June 2018].
62 Vera Mackie, 'Fukushima, Hiroshima, Nagasaki, Maralinga ....,' *Asia-Pacific Journal: Japan Focus* 13, no. 7 (2015): 29 and 25–31.
63 Jim Green, 'The Ugly Face of Australia's Nuclear Racism,' *Chain Reaction* 115 (2012): 34–35.
64 Eve Vincent, 'Nuclear Colonialism in the South Australian Desert,' *Local-Global*, 105 and 103–112.
65 Kubal and Becerra, 'Social Movements and Collective Memory,' 871.
66 See Citizen Jury reports, as well as the Royal Commission report, links to online discussion boards, and other aspects of the decision-making process at the website dedicated to the process: https://nuclear.yoursay.sa.gov.au/the-program/citizens-jury [accessed 5 May 2019].
67 *Nuclear Waste News* 6, 3 June 2016, 9.

7

'THE FBI STOLE MY FIDDLE'

Song and memory in US radical environmentalism, 1980–95

Iain McIntyre

From the 1980s onwards the radical environmental network Earth First! (EF!) provided new challenges to existing land use regimes and paradigms. Responding to the pro-development policies of the Reagan government, and perceived failures of existing mainstream organisations, EF! raised maximalist demands encapsulated by the slogan, 'No Compromise in Defence of Mother Earth.' The network began in the US and by 1985 had 40 local groups in the US and a journal with a readership of more than 10,000. By 1990, alongside chapters around the world, there were around 100 US groups carrying out local and national campaigns. During this time EF! had gained a high national profile and much media coverage, largely due to controversy regarding its confrontational tactics. These were primarily aimed at preserving undeveloped, biodiverse places and included blockading extractive work, spiking trees and sabotaging logging and mining equipment.[1]

Music is one of the oldest and most enduring forms of social movement culture. The performance of songs, communally and through individual performance, was particularly prevalent in the American EF! network, and has often been identified as one of its core characteristics. US members organised hundreds of concerts and associated musicians released dozens of recordings from 1980 to the mid-1990s, with both forming a key part of fundraising and promotional activities. Music was employed to a degree rarely seen elsewhere at the time and members typically performed and collectively sang at demonstrations, occupations, gatherings and during time spent in jail. As a result a canon of songs was generated which included original compositions, as well as a smaller number of reinterpretations specific to the movement.[2]

Although a number of academic works regarding music and politics exist, analysis of how social movements reconstruct their pasts and link themselves to others' via music has been relatively limited. Where it has been undertaken it has mainly been in relation to folk music and communism, the US civil rights movement and various forms of folk and rock music during the 1960s. There has also been little examination of how musicians and audiences construct accounts that memorialise recent events and figures.[3]

The chapter will pay particular attention to the connection of social movement memory to 'tradition.' Within social movements, as elsewhere, traditions both express and influence collective memory. In their work regarding social movements and music Eyerman and Jamison define traditions as 'beliefs and practices that are passed on from one generation to the next' in a 'conscious process of diffusion' that involves 'collective remembrance' and the 'coexistence of past and present.'[4] Their ability to shape current forms of action is rooted in understandings of historical events and ways of life which, despite being typically portrayed as fixed and timeless, are continuously contested and constructed in both deliberate and unconscious ways.

Differing EF! members drew on and shaped understandings of a diverse mix of memories and traditions through musical performance. This chapter canvases and analyses examples associated with radical syndicalism, US civil rights struggles, non-Christian spirituality, environmental philosophy, British revolts, patriotic symbology, Native American resistance and cowboy mythology as well as dramatic events within the network's own history. As will be seen the diverse nature of the EF! network and its rich musical culture make it a particularly useful case study for exploring how understandings of music, tradition and memory interact in social movements.

The rise of Earth First!

EF! was founded on a camping trip in 1980 by five activists whose experiences had led them to reject the culture and praxis of mainstream environmental preservation. Having in some cases worked for mainstream environmental groups they believed that the movement had become ineffective and was unable to deal with the incoming Reagan administration's plans to remove regulatory protections and aggressively exploit publicly owned lands. Beginning with a name, slogan and newsletter they soon attracted like-minded individuals and within two years were in a position to launch their own campaigns.[5]

EF! was a diverse movement, but included common and defining characteristics such as its 'No compromise' position regarding preservation. This combined a demand for maximum protection of forests, rivers and other biodiverse areas premised on concepts of 'biocentrism' and 'deep ecology,' central to which was the idea that all 'life on Earth has an intrinsic value and that human behaviour should and must change drastically.'[6] This challenge to the development based ethos of US society and its economy was combined with a confrontational attitude towards those who threatened lightly or undeveloped places. Through this approach EF!'s founders hoped to match the increasingly aggressive tactics of their opponents, who included mining, logging and other companies based in extractive and polluting industries and, despite attempts by some EF! members to build coalitions, often the workers employed by them. During the 1980s and 1990s companies and communities reliant on extractive industries organised anti-environmentalist counter movements and politicians at various levels of government spoke out and legislated against radical tactics and demands.[7] EF!'s positions and methods were also deliberately designed to allow the movement to act as a 'radical flank' which would make the moderate demands of other environmentalists seem more palatable.[8]

Major environmental organisations in the US at this time were mainly hierarchically structured around professional activists who drew on largely passive memberships to raise money for the lobbying of politicians. In contrast EF! encouraged a grassroots, direct action approach.[9] Its decentralised form of organisation involved local, autonomous chapters who were linked by regional and national gatherings, which involved camping out rather than formal meetings and conferences. Further coordination came via travelling activists and musicians, the *Earth First! Journal* (EFJ), and other publications.[10]

EF!'s outlook and organisational form made for an inventive political culture. Its founders explicitly encouraged members to apply and innovate a range of tactics and strategies previously eschewed by preservationists. Members engaged in unconventional protest action that was often aimed at directly disrupting environmental destruction rather than gaining protection via legislation or litigation, although in practice both strategies often dovetailed. EF!'s direct action practice manifested in two main ways. The first of these, dubbed 'monkeywrenching,' involved the sabotage of opponents' equipment and property via clandestine individual and small group actions. The second, and most popular form, was comprised of collective and public actions. EF! members initiated and supported forms of blockading with bodies and objects that sought to directly prevent logging, mining, clearing and other extractive and development activities from occurring. They also engaged in disruptive group actions in urban settings such as occupying and picketing corporate and regulatory offices and meetings.[11]

Music and EF!

Theorists have identified a number of functions that music plays within social movements, including aiding in recruitment, mobilisation, education and debate. Along with other cultural elements it serves a role in affirming beliefs, ridiculing opponents, creating and reinforcing collective identities, and defining boundaries. It also provides emotional sustenance during stressful periods of repression, confrontation and imprisonment.[12]

Flack and Rosenthal argue that academic analysis of music tends to overly focus on lyrics, with these being seen as the primary, if not only, carrier of content, with audiences' passively receiving the meanings transmitted via them. While lyrics clearly play an important role in conveying messages, and thus inculcating and influencing communicative and collective memory, the pair contends that meaning is also conveyed in other ways. Further to this the interpretation of meaning is an interactive process influenced by a variety of emotional, physical, intellectual and contextual factors. These include the way in which lyrics are sung and the music to which they are set in terms of melodies, harmonies, structure, beat, pace, volume, instruments and rhythm. Genres and other musical conventions that connect with learned musical and social codes help indicate whether music is nostalgic, sad, angry, disposable, ironic, etc. Certain genres can become associated with ideas, politics, periods and memories even if the lyrics do not explicitly address them. The way performers are dressed, how they move, how they relate to their audience, whether they perform together around a microphone or separately, the equipment they use, their reputation, relationship to music industry and what they say in between songs and in interviews also contribute to meaning.[13]

As such lyrics and other elements under the control of performers are only part of the process by which meanings are constructed since listeners interpret them in 'ways compatible with audience member's interests and personal experiences, including ways that have nothing to do with the artist's intent at all.'[14] In this chapter the role of musical genres, the stories that accompanied performance, the dress and attitude of different subcultures, and the very use of music itself will be shown to have had importance alongside lyrics in contributing to collective memory and interpretations of tradition. This sum of musical expression will be shown to have operated in combination with other forms of expression, including speeches, articles and naming. In doing so, EF! will be used as a case study to highlight the function of song and memory in reinforcing and challenging beliefs, preferences and emotions tied to collective identities, repertoires of contention and events.

From its inception EF! identified music as a core part of its ethos. Its initial activities included performances by co-founder Bart Koehler, aka 'Johnny Sagebrush.' By 1982 he had been joined by Cecelia Ostrow at gatherings and on promotional tours and the number of musicians associated with EF! steadily increased thereafter.[15] Sagebrush produced the movement's first Li'l Green Songbook in 1981. Its fifth, and largest, edition was released five years later and featured a foreword from EF!'s then leading spokesperson and EFJ editor David Foreman stating,

> I don't need to tell you how important music is to our cause…The singers in this book help me keep fighting…In a two-minute song, Johnny Sagebrush can capture more magic, passion and meaning that I can in an hour-long harangue.[16]

Although one musician, Dana Lyons, would go on to enjoy wider popularity with the comic song 'Cows With Guns,'[17] EF!-associated music mainly had an insider focus and was mostly aimed at, distributed among and performed to, with and by other environmentalists. While some performers came to be primarily known for their musical contribution to the movement, or intersected with it as part of their overall careers, the majority also took part in other aspects of protesting and campaigning. Although some hoped to have a broader influence, much of the role their music played was in regards to communicative memory within the network.[18]

During the 1980s and 1990s hundreds of songs with political and environmental themes were composed by artists connected to EF! Albums were mostly self-released and while the EFJ sold releases via mail-order, and helped facilitate and promote tours, these aspects were controlled by the musicians themselves rather than entrepreneurs or record labels.[19]

Although activists listened to music at home or in groups via recordings, it was primarily experienced live. As in other communities music played a major role in providing entertainment and facilitating bonding at concerts, fundraisers and gatherings such as the movement's annual Round River Rendezvous.[20] Another key site of performance were 'Roadshows,' promotional tours that combined musical performance, speeches, slide shows and film screenings. These visited up to 40 towns and cities at a time and were a primary means of recruiting and promotion during the network's early years. Many EF! events employed a lively style which Koehler states was intended to be 'like going to the circus' and 'poke fun at ourselves and the opposition' in order to avoid the 'dangerous path of self-importance' and the 'doom and gloom' associated with other environmental events.[21]

William Roy's work on American social movements, folk music and race in the US draws a major distinction regarding performer to audience relationships. In the first, exemplified by communist folk musicians of the 1930s and 1940s, these are characterised as top-down, with musicians performing for audiences and attempting to transmit messages to them. The second is more collective with musicians acting as song-leaders for group singalongs in which audience and performer merge.[22] In practice these are points along a spectrum and within EF! there was music making that at times was in concert mode, but also much collective singing, as well as a mix of the two.[23]

EF!, movement memory and tradition

Alongside other roles music played an important function in shaping and framing historical memory and tradition within EF! Eyerman and Jamison postulate that the importance of tradition stems from a 'deep-rooted anthropological level at which reality is interpreted and experienced… providing bridges between movements and generations… and forming part of a collective memory which carries ways of seeing and doing between past and present and between individuals and generations…'[24] Flacks and Rosenthal similarly argue that one way music encourages allegiance

> is to tie a group or movement to a tradition that people feel is theirs… Music helps us to create a form of collective memory, a shared vision of the past, and thus perhaps a shared view of the future.[25]

Music fosters a sense of the collective and shapes and affirms identity via emotion. As a ritual, communal singing and taking part in other's performances can engender feelings of connection to existing political movements as well as a bond with those of the past. Tradition in this sense is not a re-enactment of the past, even when it is framed as being so, but a creative remembrance.[26]

Unlike political movements that position themselves as a decisive break with those who have preceded them, many EF! activists, writers and musicians placed themselves squarely within existing radical traditions and rejected mainstream organisations as betraying the beliefs of those who had founded the American conservation movement. This practice reflected a conscious attempt to use what was seen as effective, enjoyable and normatively appropriate within tradition, but also to claim a legacy.[27]

EF!'s musical link to tradition can first be seen in the encouragement by founding members to make song a core part of movement culture. This was not just because they enjoyed playing it and, based on historical precedence, intellectually calculated that music could be effective in achieving goals. It was also because there was an emotional and intuitive sense, based on collective memory, that this was something that successful and healthy political movements had always done.[28]

The musical genres which members and composers employed belonged primarily to the American political folk tradition that had developed from the early twentieth century onwards. Following the convention of the 'truth telling' of bard poets this at times journalistic style of music had come to be associated with left-wing politics and been repopularised via waves of interest from the 1930s onwards.[29] Although songs from the era were not commonly played, many EF! members had either participated in the movements of the 1960s or grown up with the music of singer-songwriters associated with the counterculture. Given the movement was primarily Anglo-American and based around outdoors activity it is unsurprising that members gravitated towards acoustic folk and country styles that had long been performed around campfires.[30]

Playing and reinterpreting certain music from other times and places, such as Australian protest songs and Woody Guthrie's 'This Land Is Your Land,'[31] gave members a general sense of ties to other movements and traditions as well as being part of a greater whole.[32] As is common in other parts of life, the music associated with members' activity, regardless of lyrical content, has since come to evoke personal and shared memories of the recent past, in this case intensified by its association with the camaraderie, bonding and risk associated with shared political action.[33]

EF!, the Industrial Workers of the World and 'Freedom Summer'

As in other social movements EF! members' conscious and unconscious work of taking on and re-contextualising traditions shaped and reflected certain memories and accounts of earlier movements and traditions, and forgot, ignored and marginalised others. Beyond a general sense of following in the American political song tradition some EF! musicians made conscious attempts to align with specific historical movements. Foremost among these in EF!'s formative period was the Industrial Workers of the World (IWW).

A syndicalist union dedicated to the 'abolition of the wage system,' the IWW played a leading role in American radical activity from 1905 onwards. It established itself as a force within timber and agriculture industries, reaching a peak membership of more than 100,000 in the mid-1920s, and forming overseas chapters. Following concerted employer and government repression, the demonisation of its anti-war position and use of sabotage, and internal disputes, the IWW was reduced to a small national network of activists by the 1930s.[34]

American social movement memory has long lauded and romanticised the IWW, particularly in the form of songwriter and 'labour martyr' Joe Hill. As a diverse and often fractious movement the union's history has provided a wide range of events, repertoires of contention and aspects of collective identity for members and others to draw upon in constructing memories regarding it. A major part of the union's enduring status, and memory associated with it, has derived from its lively use of music, as evidenced by the popularity of its Little Red Songbook, which has gone through 38 editions since 1909. Drawing on musical practices from American and European popular and left-wing culture, IWW members produced hundreds of songs, some of which became staples of labour movements or later enjoyed high record sales, such as 'Solidarity Forever' and 'Hallelujah I'm A Bum.'[35] Much of this success was drawn from Hill and others' setting of witty and topical lyrics to religious and well-known tunes, a practice which they popularised and which has since become a staple of political music.[36]

Although the majority of the network would never be concerned with labour issues, key EF! founders and leading figures admired, and wished to emulate, the IWW's militancy, non-hierarchical organisation, and predilection for sardonic humour. EF! writer, theorist and spokesperson Dave Foreman stated in a 1989 debate that at the time of EF!'s formation, 'we consciously tried to learn from the strategy and tactics of left social movements. The Wobblies [IWW] were certainly one group we were drawn to.' An early issue of the network's newsletter described EF! as 'the Wobblies of the environmental movement.'[37] In 1988 EF! activist Roger Featherstone told IWW member and historian Franklin Rosemont, 'We admire the IWW spirit, sense of humor, art and music; its direct action tactics; its unwillingness to buy into the political scene; its no-compromise attitude and, most-importantly, its guts.'[38]

IWW terminology and iconography, such as calling stickers bearing slogans 'silent agitators,' using the motto 'No compromise,' and employing images of the syndicalist black cat, were adapted by EF! and the sabotage manual *Ecodefense* was issued under the name of the union's early leader Bill Haywood.[39] Organisationally the group also cited IWW principles with Foreman writing, 'We have not sought any grants or funding with strings attached. Nor do we plan to have paid staff, although we hope to have field organizers receiving expenses in the tradition of the Wobblies.'[40]

Culturally the use of song, and the way in which it was employed, played a major role in creating further connections to the IWW's historical legacy, and memory of it. The IWW's attitude, as expressed in its bitingly satirical songs and cartoons, directly influenced EF!'s use of music and its disrespectful approach to itself and its opponents. Chief among EF!'s early musicians and satirists was Koehler, whose stage name was adopted to lampoon both 'Johnny Horizon,' the mascot of the Bureau of Land Management, and the 'Sagebrush Rebellion' by 13 Western states who sought to enable ranchers, extractive industries and others to access and exploit publicly owned and Federally controlled lands.[41]

Foreman and Koehler chose to name the EF! Li'l Green Songbook after the IWW's publication. Initial editions contained a number of the Koehler's compositions before expanding out to include others' songs.[42] In further keeping with the IWW model, as carried forward by later radical folksingers who fashioned themselves upon the union's traditions, Koehler matched religious, popular and traditional themes and songs to satirical lyrics. These included 'Amazing Waste' (to the tune of 'Amazing Grace'), 'They'll Be Tearing Down The Mountain' ('She'll Be Coming Round The Mountain'), 'Justifiable Rivercide' ('Down By The Riverside'), and 'It's Time To Fight' ('I Saw The Light').[43] Religious themes and songs would also be drawn upon and parodied by other EF! musicians, most notably in Daryl Cherney's 'This Monkeywrench of Mine' ('This Little Light of Mine'), 'You Can't Clearcut Your Way To Heaven' and 'Spike A Tree For Jesus.'[44]

As detailed below, Cherney would come to join the union in the late 1980s, but IWW members and musicians, such as Utah Phillips and Walkin Jim Stoltz, had been a part of EF! during its formative years. These regularly performed IWW songs to its members, with Stoltz reworking Joe Hill's 'There Is Power In A Union' into 'There is Power In The Earth.'[45] However, underlining the selectivity of memory, during this early period the movement's portrayal of the IWW and adoption of elements of its historical legacy was largely based on the IWW's radicalism and preference for direct action rather than its ideology. As such it did not initially extend to the IWW's class-based outlook and worker-focussed syndicalism.[46]

A more tangible link to the IWW came during the late 1980s and early 1990s. During this period Northern Californian EF! activists reached out to timber workers in the hope of fostering joint action regarding corporate takeovers which had led to job losses, workplace restructures and a marked increase in the 'liquidation' of forest assets. The vehicle they chose for this project was a new chapter of the IWW. In part this was because of the independence of the union from existing labour organisations, but also because activists hoped to renew and draw legitimacy from radical labour traditions in a region where the IWW had been active and enjoyed support in the first decades of the twentieth century. EF! activist and musician Judi Bari, who had a background in labour organising, initiated much of this activity and would become most closely associated with it.[47]

Explicitly drawing on IWW traditions regarding social justice and syndicalism, Bari and other Northern Californian EF! members called for an alliance between environmentalists and workers against lumber corporations. In the build up to the IWW chapter's formation a 1988 California EF! rendezvous featured a workshop on IWW history and musicians Daryl Cherney and Dakota Sid performed a set of IWW songs including 'The Preacher and the Slave' and '50,000 Lumberjacks.' The latter song was written in 1917 and provided commentary on a strike led that same year by the IWW against appalling living and working conditions in the timber industry. The closing line of its chorus warned employers that 'The more you try to buck them now the more they organise.'[48]

By performing such songs and focussing on the past radicalism of timber workers in a union whose history was already viewed favourably within the EF! milieu, activists sought to break down the perception that workers had always, and would always, identify with their employers. These aspects of memory were also deployed to highlight the unique industrial power that workers could wield against EF!'s opponents. They were also used to counter arguments within the contemporary IWW that rejected a renewed focus on the timber industry.[49]

In the interests of alliance building, as well as due to ethical concerns and a desire to diffuse community tensions, Bari and other Northern Californian activists publicly denounced tree spiking and sought to distance their EF! chapter from forms of sabotage which potentially put workers in harm's way. This, the alignment with workers and a related commitment to social justice issues caused a serious rift within EF! which led Foreman and other key members to leave the network. The dispute did not include contention over whom was truly carrying on the IWW's legacy, as would periodically occur within the IWW itself. Nevertheless it demonstrates how sections of social movements can selectively draw on understandings and memory of the same organisation in differing ways and to different ends. Foreman, and other members of what became dubbed as the 'Old Guard' faction had emphasised the early IWW's radicalism and humour and used narratives about it to justify and promote the use of direct action tactics and decentralised power structures. Bari, and members of the 'social justice' faction, subsequently went beyond the union's broad tradition of rebelliousness to remind EF! members that this style and attitude was specifically rooted in syndicalist tactics and strategies. By going deeper into the union's history they were able to draw on memory to argue for the use of a different repertoire of contention, one based on the belief that the IWW, and workers in general, had a contemporary relevance to radical environmentalism.[50]

The IWW-EF! initiative among timber workers was stymied by various factors. Occurring in a period of increasing unemployment, largely caused by mechanisation, corporate restructuring and overseas competition, environmentalists were successfully made a target of blame by business, union and government forces.[51] Militant imagery and songs written by Cherney and others prior to the renunciation of tree spiking, which light heartedly and satirically extolled the practice and monkeywrenching in general, were used to smear EF!-IWW activists as 'ecoterrorists.'[52] Most importantly and tragically, the bombing of a car containing Bari and Cherney injured the pair, the former critically, bringing a temporary halt to their organising work. Since the survivors were initially charged with transporting the bomb, the attack further allowed their opponents to portray them as dangerous. The activists were later exonerated and subsequently received $4.4 million in compensation from the FBI and Oakland City Council. No one has yet been charged with the crime.[53]

The bombing came in the run up to a summer of protest which, drawing on another powerful component of American social movement memory, was initially dubbed 'Mississippi Summer in the Redwoods,' but became better known as 'Redwood Summer.' As protest participant and environmental journalist Dean Kuipers later recalled it was 'modelled after the call to Freedom Riders to come to Mississippi to register African Americans to vote in 1964.'[54] Promotional materials and the campaign's title explicitly established a link with the iconic US civil rights campaign 'Mississippi Summer Project' or 'Freedom Summer.' As with the civil rights activists of the 1960s the Northern Californians believed that a sustained, intensive campaign would make their issue a national one, expand the concept of 'rights' (in this case to nature), and expose and counter the harassment and repression local activists were suffering.[55]

In drawing upon memories of the 1964 event they not only hoped to recruit participants, but also to emphasise that Redwood Summer would be based on a repertoire of contention adhering to strict non-violent principles. Within EF! the memory and impact of the civil rights campaign was used to justify arguments in favour of employing mass, open, peaceful yet confrontational protest over covert, more individualised tactics such as tree-spiking which carried risks of physical harm to opponents. Externally and internally it was also used in an attempt to overcome EF!'s association with the latter and to turn away and repudiate anyone intending to commit sabotage during the campaign.[56]

Musical performances meshed with other forms of expression. They made up a major part of publicity events and civil rights songs were sung during the campaign itself. The connection between the events of 1964 and 1990, and the lessons to be learnt from the former, was further promoted in compositions such as Cherney's 'The Ghosts of Mississippi.' In chronicling the story of Redwood Summer its lyrics recalled how the name and concept for the protest came out of an encounter Bari had with Fred Moore, also known as 'Walking Rainbow,' who 'came to her and said the time is yours, He said freedom riders for the forest come, Just like in Mississippi it was done.'[57]

Luddites, philosophers, pagans and outlaws

As noted previously, early EF! activists' repudiation of mainstream environmentalism was partially rooted in what they saw as a betrayal of the beliefs that originally inspired American preservationism. Most central to this was EF!'s restatement of the value of nature as a thing in itself rather than as a resource, combined with a rejection of modernity and the idea of industrial progress. Pioneering American environmental preservationists and philosophers John Muir, Aldo Leopold, Ralph Waldo Emerson and Henry David Thoreau were regularly cited as a core influence upon these views with founder Mike Roselle stating in 1985 that 'they are the old-time religion for us.'[58]

Songs such as 'Muir Power To You' and 'Green Fire' celebrated and incorporated these thinkers' ideas and hailed radical environmentalists as their modern-day equivalent. They also referenced and reinforced earlier forms of memory activism which depicted industrialisation and resource exploitation as negative rather than positive historical practices and processes.[59]

'Muir Power To You' was composed by Bill Oliver, a Texan musician who was associated with the Austin chapter of EF! during the 1980s. Much concerned with musical and cultural tradition Oliver's first songs in the 1970s had been inspired by 'Chuck Berry and campfire music' which he found 'mixed well with the Mark Twain I was reading.'[60]

'Muir Power To You' was originally written for an EF! rally on the Tuolumne River, an area which had greatly inspired Muir's writing and whose damming he had opposed. One of three songs Oliver wrote and regularly performed about the philosopher during the 1980s, it is a typical example of how singer-songwriters associated with EF! sought to shape movement memory. First, it commemorated Muir's life in a celebratory manner. Second, it highlighted specific aspects of his story to remind listeners that his well-known love of nature was intrinsically tied to his efforts to preserve it. Third, it intellectually and emotionally drew direct continuities between the past and present activism via lyrics such as, 'The same river's flowing through you and me, It's living in the steps we take' and a statement that Muir would have been proud of modern activists.[61]

EF! also initially modelled itself consciously on the attitude, politics and repertoires of contention embodied in Edward Abbey's 1976 book *The Monkeywrench Gang*. This novel, in turn, drew ideas from a century of American philosophy regarding deserts and nature and West Coast versus East Coast traditions in American literature, culture, activism and thought.[62]

Further to this, the network discussed and celebrated the English Diggers and Luddites in their writings and through other means which educated members and emphasised continuities. The Diggers had led a peasant revolt in 1649 premised on the interconnection of humans and land and the need to abolish private ownership of it. The Luddites had destroyed textile machinery in the 1810s which was eradicating their crafts and jobs. Selectively emphasising the direct action and anti-industrial aspects of these movements a section in the EFJ regarding sabotage was entitled 'Dear Ned Ludd' and the network's main publishing house was named Ned Ludd books.[63]

Connections between the radical past and present were also expressed through the performance and collective singing of songs such as the traditional 'General Ludd' and Koehler's composition 'For Ned Ludd.' A transcription of the latter was accompanied by a note in the Lil' Green Songbook about the history of the Luddites. Its lyrics warned modern-day strip miners, loggers and oil drillers that their equipment too was under threat from Ludd's descendants.[64]

As a pluralistic movement rather than an organisation, EF! drew in people from a variety of social and cultural backgrounds. These embodied and expressed differing cultural identities, many of them rooted in specific traditions. One initial pole within the network, influenced heavily by Abbey and his interpretation of the memory and traditions of Western states within the US, was around those characterised as 'buckaroos' or 'cowboys.'[65] Not surprisingly these same members were fans of country music, particularly of the 'outlaw' variety. The 'outlaw country' genre had emerged in the early 1970s and was associated with mainstream musicians such as Willie Nelson, Kris Kristofferson and Waylon Jennings whose songs, as performed by themselves and others, had sold tens of millions of records. The genre's innovative aspects showed the influence of the 1960s counterculture in that performers were long haired and casually dressed with some openly using marijuana. Musically they introduced elements of modern rock, but also embraced tradition, and claimed legitimacy, by embracing a less produced and slick style of 'roots' performance and recording that harked back to pre-Second World War country-music.[66]

The adoption of an image normally associated with conservative rural working-class Americans, many of whom were employed in environmentally destructive industries, was partially tongue in cheek and partially authentic. Some EF! members' tastes were already in this mode, but the embrace of the 'outlaw country' lifestyle also expressed a rejection of the polite liberalism of mainstream environmentalism during the late 1970s and a desire to culturally connect with opponents and potential supporters.[67] Roselle quotes Foreman as stating at the network's first national gathering, 'We are getting killed out here in the western states because we are seen as weak, effete and wimpy.'[68]

For these activists avoiding such a reputation meant playfully, yet seriously, adapting elements of national collective memory, largely shaped in songs, movies and novels, about nineteenth- and early twentieth-century 'cowboy' traditions and 'outlaw' behaviour. The fusion between these and contemporary environmentalism was expressed by Koehler and other EF! musicians through the performance of country music influenced songs whose lyrics praised forms of activism which exemplified and sentimentalised 'cowboy' traits in terms of being confrontational, rowdy, loyal and tough. As in country music more generally, embodiment of this attitude and tradition was also consciously and unconsciously expressed through EF! performers and activists wearing modern versions of 'Western' grab, such as press-stud shirts, large belt buckles, boots and 'cowboy hats,' singing with particular accents and holding their instruments and moving in specific ways.[69]

Some EF! members selective embrace of mainstream American tradition and memory extended to using patriotic imagery. The national anthem was sung, and US flags flown, by these activists during protests and other events. Influential early members, including Foreman, believed that such customs and symbols could be used to mobilise a love of country that also included love of its environment. This, and the 'buckaroo' outlook in general, drew criticisms of sexism and nationalism from members who cited ideas and traditions of a feminist and internationalist bent. These deployed radical movement memory in highlighting the negatives associated with American colonialism and imperialism and by identifying—via anti-patriotic songs, letters, articles and acts such as burning the

US flag—with historical and continuing resistance from Native American, leftist and other communities.[70]

Given EF!'s link to forests and other undeveloped biodiverse places it was not surprising that some activists and musicians within the movement were involved in alternative spiritual movements. Even those who did not specifically associate themselves with earth-based religion often spoke of a personal and almost mystical link to nature. The need to protect biodiverse places was generally cast in redemptive terms, expressing the need for humans to connect with their 'wild' selves. These understandings of 'wildness' were primarily based on selective memory regarding pre-industrial traditions and ways of living and being. Contact with and respect for undeveloped, biodiverse places was thus portrayed as a way to directly connect with older traditions and non-human perspectives, which ideally, if not inevitably, would lead to a more harmonious relationship with nature.[71]

Songs such as Koehler's 'Thinking Like A Mountain,' Walkin' Jim Stoltz's 'Listen To The Earth' and Joanne Rand's Never Alone' expressed sentiments that drew on these concepts of innate and ancient 'wildness' and reconnection.[72] Singing such songs was not only a means of disseminating ideas but, along with communal music making in general, seen by musicians as a tool to arouse affective and emotional collective memories and experiences of nature that they believed industrial society was erasing.[73]

Clifford's 'Green Fire' explicitly combined these themes with a concept pioneered by environmental philosopher Aldo Leopold. In the author's posthumously published 1949 memoir A Sand County Almanac he recalled, during the early years of the twentieth century, seeing a 'green fire' in the eyes of a wolf he and other foresters had killed. This experience awakened in him a connection with nature and a realisation of the need to view the world from a broader perspective as 'there was something new to me in those eyes, something known only to her [the wolf] and the mountain.'[74] From this flowed the conviction that an action was only 'right when it tends to preserve the integrity, stability and beauty of the biotic community' and 'wrong when it tends otherwise.'[75]

Much aired within EF!, Leopold's concept of 'green fire' was expressed in articles and also provided the name for a column, a newsletter and a bookshop. According to various accounts, Foreman regularly closed his roadshow addresses with the story, 'exhorting the assembly members to rediscover their own wild animal selves, believing that were they to do so, they would defend the wildlands with passion and commitment.'[76] Beyond its title, Clifford's lyrics also expressed such sentiments in lyrics such as: 'Mankind's just a shadow of what they used to be, Forgotten how to be themselves, Set their spirit free...'[77] The musician also used the term as the title for an album in 1991 as well as a series of roadshow tours he carried out from 1989 onwards with Roger Featherstone.[78] Collectively the use of the story, term and concept commemorated Leopold and his life and shaped understandings of environmentalism's roots and history. It also connected radicals to the philosopher and to particular historical interpretations of pre-industrial lifestyles and beliefs, positing them as 'timeless' traditions innate to human nature.

Those EF! members with an overtly neo-pagan, shamanistic or 'New Age' outlook performed songs that explicitly referenced religious beliefs situating old-growth forests and other biodiverse places as sites of pre-Christian wisdom and magic. As with the other examples discussed in this article, the memories and understandings of people, places and beliefs were expressed through songs that were shaped and supported by identification with specific traditions. The cultural impact of such spiritual affinities is seen less in musical styles, as there is little of the traditional Celtic or Indian influence usually associated with such milieux. However Wiccan songs from earlier times celebrating nature and commemorating European witchcraft and pre-Christian goddesses were sung (and sometimes parodied by EF! members of a less spiritual bent).[79] Lyrical portrayals of ancient ways and spirituality, as perceived and selected by their composers, were also common in the lyrics of some songwriters within EF!, particularly women. Depictions of nature, and by extension its worshippers and defenders, as embodying traditional knowledge and spirituality were extant in songs such as Cecelia Ostrow's 'You Were There For Me' and Alice DiMicele's 'The God In You' and 'New Moon.'[80]

Some EF! members also claimed an affinity with Native American traditions. Although only a few Native Americans were actively involved in the network, members worked on campaigns with Indigenous communities around the world. During the 1980s and 1990s EF! members carried out blockades with or in support of Native American communities at sites such as Mt Graham in Arizona, Enola Hill in Oregon, and Cahto Peak in California.[81] One of the first actions of the newly formed network was to erect a memorial in New Mexico to Victorio, an Apache chief who, their inscription claimed, 'strove to protect these mountains from mining and other destructive activities of the white race.'[82] The network's Round River Rendezvous was named in tribute to events formerly held by both Native Americans and the 'mountain men of the Old West.'[83] In some cases songs directly addressed the effects of colonialism, such as Koehler's 'The Buffalo Are Gone,' while others, like Cherney's 'Big Mountain Will Not Fall' and DiMicele's 'Song For Leonard Peltier' discussed, depicted and sought to shape the memory of recent events and contemporary figures.[84]

Some Indigenous people, supporters and academics have argued that the concept of 'wilderness' implies that biodiverse places spared industrial development lack any influence from human culture. This idea of wilderness, as well of Indigenous people as living in total harmony with nature, is said to continue the repression of First Nations' concepts of land, territory and sovereignty that occurred from initial invasion onwards. During the 1980s conflict over whether biodiverse places should be understood as the home and cultural hearth of First Nations or as closed ecological networks devoid of culture and human interference was particularly strong in Canada. In some cases non-Indigenous Canadian environmentalists came to embrace First Nations' sovereignty and understandings of place, but in others major divisions occurred, even where both groups shared ecological goals, such as preventing the clear felling of forests. While such conflict involved current understandings of biodiverse places, and indeed of settler nations in their entirety, it was also a struggle over how they and their past were to be remembered.[85]

As previously discussed, various songs written by EF! musicians expressed and drew links between Native American struggles and environmentalism, but the depiction and valorisation of 'wilderness,' and the romanticisation of Indigenous cultures, meant such compositions portrayed the present and past in ways subject to the critiques outlined above. While these issues were raised in other settler nations during the period covered by this chapter they do not appear to have been major areas of contention in the US until after the mid-1990s.[86] More commonly the employment and adaption of Indigenous words, rituals, instruments and practices by musicians and others was challenged either due to inappropriate use or as a form of cultural appropriation.[87]

EF! memorialisation of recent events through song

This chapter has so far focussed upon songs which referenced events, beliefs, traditions and movements prior to the 1980s. It will now briefly consider the role of those that employed the topical folksinger mode of delivery to specifically memorialise and shape understandings of key events and overall trends within EF!'s own history. Competition to define the past, particularly by those who believe they have been unfairly portrayed, if not vilified, by the mainstream media and internal and external opponents, regularly motivates activists to take action in relation to their legacy.[88] With music such a key part of movement culture it is not surprising that it was used within EF! to such ends.

Songs which explicitly addressed recent movement history included Cecilia Ostrow's 'Blockade Song' and Darl Cherney's 'Give 'Em Hell, Sally Bell,' both of which chronicled aspects of Oregon and Californian forest campaigns.[89] Dana Lyons' composition 'Rod Cornoado' paid tribute to the imprisoned Native American animal rights activist and eco-saboteur and Bill Oliver's 'Bugis and The Bulldozer' detailed the first time an EF! member locked themselves to logging equipment to successfully delay clearing at Four Notch, Texas in 1986.[90]

Beyond celebrating certain figures and events in order to educate, entertain and inspire audiences, commemorative songs were also used to address trauma, relieve tension and impart warnings. Daryl Cherney and Mike Roselle's song 'He Looked A Whole Lot Like Jesus' satirised traditional religious music and sentiments in the process of detailing the infiltration and entrapment of EF! members in Arizona by an undercover FBI agent.[91]

A series of compositions memorialised the events surrounding the 1990 bombing of Bari and Cherney. Songs by Cherney, such as 'The Ghosts of Mississippi' and 'Who Bombed Judi Bari?' harrowingly depicted the violent effects of the attack and challenged official narratives that had portrayed the victims as responsible for the explosion.[92] Their lyrics also named specific pro-logging activists, religious conservatives, corporate executives and law enforcement officials and highlighted their role in fomenting anti-environmentalist feeling and making, or ignoring, threats against activists in the lead up to the attack. In doing so, these songs sometimes employed sombre modes that drew on traditions and sentiments regarding sacrifice and martyrdom.[93] Others, once again in the IWW and folk song mode, were humorous. 'The FBI Stole My Fiddle,' written by Cherney and Bari, for instance sardonically addressed law enforcement's treatment of the victims with lyrics such as: 'They blamed me for the bomb, That almost took my life, But there's one more thing that they did, One last twist of the knife, The FBI stole my fiddle…'[94] All, as well as a 1997 CD release combining songs with recordings of talks given by Bari, lyrically expressed continuities with the legal and physical repression of earlier generations of radicals and civil rights activists.[95]

EF! members and others have continued to campaign for a full account of the bombing as well as to commemorate it. In 2002, six years after the activist's death from cancer, the Oakland City Council responded to lobbying and designated May 24, the date of the bombing, Judi Bari Day.[96] Various documentary films addressing the incident have been released with the most recent, produced by Cherney, making extensive use of EF! music in the soundtrack to aid its historical narrative.[97]

Conclusion

Processes of selective interpretation and adaption enable social movements, and groups within them, to position themselves in differing ways in regard to the past. All overtly connect themselves to their earlier counterparts through repudiation, endorsement and (re)enactment of elements of historical practice, belief and culture. As this case study concerning Earth First! has demonstrated, music can play a major role in the internal construction, re-contextualisation and expression of social movement memory and tradition. It can be deliberately used to internally and externally challenge or bolster dominant narratives as a form of memory activism or shape communicative and collective memory in more subtle, unconscious ways. Music does not do this alone, but in combination with other forms of expression. Nevertheless it has specific affective properties that can engender emotions regarding social movement events, traditions and memory in ways that other forms do not.

The composition and performance of songs drawn from or about past events and movements can celebrate, downgrade or incorporate contemporary and historical beliefs and ways of being and acting. Although lyrics are important, other factors, such as the use of particular musical genres and the cultural accoutrements and performance styles associated with them, play a major role. As various examples in this chapter have shown the legitimacy obtained from association with, and interpretation of, past movements and traditions through music can have a major impact on movement direction and unity. This can extend from debates regarding particular repertoires of contention and the definition of potential allies and opponents through to the role of music itself.

The example of EF! also demonstrates that music, as part of broader processes of memory, has an impact at differing levels of social movements. Particular styles, interpretations and traditions may resonate or be contested broadly while others will primarily be associated with a particular group or faction. Disputes and divisions may be linked to differing interpretations of specific events and memories. They may also, as in the case of the IWW and EF!, accrue from whether an association is made with the broad nature of past movements or with specific tactics and ideologies within them.

Notes

1 Judi Bari, *Timber Wars* (Monroe, MO: Common Courage Press, 1994), 264–285.
2 Jesse Wolf Hardin, 'Deep Echology: A Quarter Century of Earth Minstrelry,' *Humboldt Journal of Social Relations* 21, no. 1: 102–106; 'Music,' *Earth First!* 14, no. 5 (1994): 38; Rik Scarce, *Eco-Warriors: Understanding the Radical Environmental Movement* (Chicago, IL: Noble Press, 1990), 249; Mikal Jakubal Interview, 27 August, 2018.
3 Two key works that have addressed these areas are Rob Rosenthal and Richard Flacks, *Playing for Change: Music and Musicians in the Service of Social Movements* (Boulder, CO: Paradigm, 2012); Ron Eyerman and Andrew Jamison, *Music and Social Movements: Mobilizing Traditions in the Twentieth Century* (Cambridge: Cambridge University Press, 1998).
4 *Music and Social Movements*, 27.
5 Mike Roselle, *Tree Spiker: From Earth First! To Lowbagging, My Struggles in Radical Environmental Action* (New York: St Martins Press, 2009), 43–55; Anthony Silvaggio, 'The Forest Defense Movement, 1980–2005: Resistance at the Point of Extraction, Consumption and Production' (PhD, University of Oregon, 2005), 51–63.
6 Arne Naess, 'A Defence of the Deep Ecology Movement,' *Environmental Ethics* 6, no. 3 (1984): 265.
7 Susan Zakin, *Coyotes and Town Dogs: Earth First! And the Radical Environmental Movement* (New York: Viking, 1993), 364–372.
8 Scarce, *Eco-Warriors*, 58–59.
9 Douglas Bevington, *The Rebirth of Environmentalism: Grassroots Activism from the Spotted Owl to the Polar Bear* (Washington, DC: Island Press, 2009), 17–27.
10 Dave Foreman, 'Earth First!,' *Earth First!* 2, no. 3 (1982): 4–5; Martha F. Lee, *Earth First!: Environmental Apocalypse* (Syracuse, NY: Syracuse University Press, 1995), 78–80.
11 Silvaggio, 'The Forest Defense Movement, 1980–2005,' 57–70.
12 Christophe Traïni and Johanna Siméant, *Bodies in Protest: Hunger Strikes and Angry Music* (Amsterdam: Amsterdam University Press, 2016), 111–138.
13 Rosenthal and Flacks, *Playing for Change*, 41–65.
14 Ibid., 24.
15 Bart Koehler and Pete Dustrud, 'RRR Tells Getty Where to Go,' *Earth First! Newsletter* 2, no. 7 (1982): 1, 4.
16 Johnny Sagebrush and friends, *The Earth First! Li'l Green Songbook* (Tucson, AZ: Ned Ludd Books, 1986), 1.
17 Dana Lyons, 'Cows with Guns,' track 1 on *Cows with Guns*, Reigning Records, 1996, CD.
18 Bill Oliver Interview, 22 July, 2018; Joanne Rand, 26 July Interview, 2018; Scarce, *Eco-Warriors*, 251–253.
19 Oliver Interview; Rand Interview.
20 Jakubal Interview.
21 Bart Koehler Interview, 16 September, 2018.

22 William Roy, *Reds, Whites and Blues: Social Movements, Folk Music and Race in the United States* (Princeton, NJ: Princeton University Press, 2010), 5–7.
23 Valeri Wade Interview, 18 May, 2016; Rand Interview; Oliver Interview.
24 Eyerman and Jamison, *Music and Social Movements*, 47.
25 Rosenthal and Flacks, *Playing for Change*, 160.
26 Eyerman and Jamison, *Music and Social Movements*, 35–36.
27 Steve Chase, ed. *Defending the Earth: A Dialogue between Murray Bookchin and Dave Foreman* (Woods Hole, MA: South End Press, 1991), 50–51; Christopher Manes, *Green Rage: Radical Environmentalism and the Unmaking of Civilization* (Boston, MA: Little Brown, 1990), 56–76.
28 Oliver Interview; Foreman, 'Earth First!,' 4–5; Hardin, 'Deep Echology,' 100–107.
29 Rosenthal and Flacks, *Playing for Change*, 112.
30 Jakubal Interview; Rand Interview.
31 Woody Guthrie, 'This Land Is Your Land,' track 5 on *This Land is Your Land*, Folkways Records, 1967, LP.
32 'Were You There When We Cracked Glen Canyon Damn?,' *Earth First! Newsletter* 1, no. 4 (1981): 2; Oliver Interview, Rand Interview, Wade Interview.
33 Jakubal Interview.
34 Fred Thompson, 'They Didn't Suppress the Wobblies,' *Radical America* 1, no. 2 (1967): 3–7.
35 Ralph Chaplin, 'Solidarity Forever,' lines 1–27; —Unknown, 'Hallelujah I'm a Bum,' lines 1–24.
36 Franklin Rosemont, *Joe Hill: The IWW & the Making of a Revolutionary Workingclass Counterculture* (Chicago, IL: Charles H. Kerr, 2003), 53–62; David Carter, 'The Industrial Workers of the World and the Rhetoric of Song,' *Quarterly Journal of Speech* 66, no. 4 (1980): 365–374.
37 Chase, *Defending the Earth*, 50–51; 'Fourth of July Round River Rendezvous in Moab, Utah,' *Earth First! Newsletter* 1, no. 4 (1981): 4.
38 Quoted in Steve Ongerth, 'Redwood Uprising, Chapter 10: Fellow Workers, Meet Earth First!,' http://ecology.iww.org/texts/SteveOngerth/RedwoodUprising/6.
39 Paul Lindholdt, *Explorations in Ecocriticism: Advocacy, Bioregionalism, and Visual Design* (Lanham, MD: Lexington Books, 2015), 78–81; 'Silent Agitators!,' *Earth First! Newsletter* 2, no. 4 (1982): 11; Dave Foreman and Bill Haywood, eds., *Ecodefense: A Field Guide to Monkeywrenching* (Tucson, AZ: Ned Ludd Books, 1987).
40 Foreman, 'Earth First!,' 5; Lee, *Earth First!*, 120–121.
41 Johnny Sagebrush and friends, *The Earth First! Li'l Green Songbook*, 3; Robert Antonio and Robert Brulle, 'The Unbearable Lightness of Politics: Climate Change Denial and Political Polarization,' *The Sociological Quarterly* 52, no. 2 (2011): 196–197; Scarce, *Eco-Warriors*, 249.
42 'Get Your Goods Now!,' *Earth First! Newsletter* 1, no. 8 (1981): 8; Johnny Sagebrush and friends, *The Earth First! Li'l Green Songbook*, 1–3.
43 Koehler Interview.
44 Darryl Cherney, 'This Monkeywrench of Mine,' track B8 on *They Sure Don't Make Hippies Like They Used To*, Self Released, 1989, Cassette; 'You Can't Clearcut Your Way to Heaven,' track A5 on *They Sure Don't Make Hippies Like They Used To*, Self Released, 1989, Cassette; 'Spike a Tree for Jesus,' track B7 on *They Sure Don't Make Hippies Like They Used To*, Self Released, 1989, Cassette.
45 'Earth First! Music Festival,' *Earth First!* 3, no. 7 (1983): 23; Joe Hill, 'There Is Power in a Union,' lines 1–26; Walkin' Jim Stoltz, 'There Is Power in the Earth,', track 8 on *Vision*, Self Released, 2000, CD.
46 Steve Ongerth, 'Redwood Uprising. Chapter 5: No Compromise in Defense of Mother Earth!,' https://www.judibari.info/book/5.
47 Bari, *Timber Wars*, 11–18; Jeffrey Shantz and Barry Adam, 'Ecology and Class: The Green Syndicalism of IWW/Earth First Local 1,' *Journal of Sociology and Social Policy* 19, no. 7/8 (1999): 52–56.
48 Anonymous, '50,000 Lumberjacks,' lines 1–28; Joe Hill, 'The Preacher and the Slave,' lines 1–28.

49 Bari, *Timber Wars*, 17–18; Steve Ongerth, 'Redwood Uprising, Chapter 11: I Knew Nothin' Till I Met Judi,' http://ecology.iww.org/texts/SteveOngerth/RedwoodUprising/11.
50 'Tree Spiking Renounced Behind Redwood Curtain,' *Earth First! Journal* 10, no. 5 (1990): 12; Zakin, *Coyotes and Town Dogs*, 396–415; Ongerth, 'Redwood Uprising, Chapter 10: Fellow Workers, Meet Earth First!'.
51 Bari, *Timber Wars*, 13–14; Shantz and Adam, 'Ecology and Class,' 60–66.
52 David Harris, *The Last Stand* (New York: Times Books, 1996), 304–305; 'Gun-Toting Photo a Joke, Friends Claim,' *Ukiah Daily Journal*, 12 June 1990, 1.
53 Roselle, *Tree Spiker*, 127–133; Mike Geniella, 'Bari Juror Explains Verdicts, Marathon Deliberations,' *Press Democrat*, 14 June 2002, A1.
54 Dean Kuipers, *The Deer Camp: A Memoir of a Father, a Family, and the Land That Healed Them* (New York: Bloomsbury, 2019).
55 Harris, *The Last Stand*, 286–297; Jay Matthews, 'Environmentalists Attempt to Revive '60s Activism in Redwood Summer,' *Washington Post*, 8 July 1990, A3.
56 Steve Ongerth, 'Redwood Uprising. Chapter 30: She Called for Redwood Summer,' https://www.judibari.info/book/30.
57 Darryl Cherney, 'The Ghosts of Mississippi,' track 3 on *Real American*, Churn It up Records, CD.
58 Manes, *Green Rage*, 72; Foreman, 'Earth First!,' 4.
59 Bill Oliver, 'Muir Power to You,' track 16 on *Better Things to Do*, Self Released, 1987, Cassette; Dakota Sid Clifford, 'Green Fire,' track 11 on *Green Fire*, Self Released, 1991, Cassette.
60 Oliver Interview.
61 'Muir Power to You.'
62 Edward Abbey, *The Monkey Wrench Gang* (Philadelphia, PA: Lippincott, 1975), 275–278; Zakin, *Coyotes and Town Dogs*, 137–138, 275–278, 303–304.
63 'Ludd Readers,' *Earth First! Newsletter* 2, no. 5 (1982): 11; 'Dear Ned Ludd,' *Earth First! Newsletter* 2, no. 8 (1982): 6; Bron Taylor, 'Diggers, Wolves, Ents, Elves and Expanding Universes: Global Bricolage and the Question of Violence within the Subcultures of Radical Environmentalism,' in *The Cultic Milieu: Oppositional Subcultures in an Age of Globalization*, ed. Jeffrey Kaplan and Heléne Lööw (Walnut Creek, CA: AltaMira Press, 2002), 50–52.
64 Johnny Sagebrush and friends, *The Earth First! Li'l Green Songbook*, 99; Bart Koehler, 'For Ned Ludd,' lines 1—14.
65 'Fourth of July Round River Rendezvous in Moab, Utah,' 4.
66 Charles Hughes, *Country Soul: Making Music and Making Race in the American South* (Chapel Hill: University of North Carolina Press), 159.
67 Zakin, *Coyotes and Town Dogs*, 116–146; Roselle, *Tree Spiker*, 39–53.
68 Ibid., 54.
69 Karen Coulter Interview, 24 July, 2016.
70 Ibid.; Koehler Interview; Scarce, *Eco-Warriors*, 87–91; Taylor, 'Diggers, Wolves, Ents, Elves and Expanding Universes,' 38–39.
71 Ibid., 32–43.
72 Bart Koehler, 'Thinking Like a Mountain,' (1980s); Walkin' Jim Stoltz, 'Listen to the Earth,' (1980s).
73 Taylor, 'Diggers, Wolves, Ents, Elves and Expanding Universes,' 39–40; Hardin, 'Deep Echology,' 104–108.
74 Aldo Leopold, *A Sand County Almanac, and Sketches Here and There* (Oxford: Oxford University Press, 1989), 130.
75 Ibid., 224.
76 Taylor, 'Diggers, Wolves, Ents, Elves and Expanding Universes,' 34, 69; Zakin, *Coyotes and Town Dogs*, 194–197.
77 Clifford, 'Green Fire.'
78 Roger Featherstone, 'Green Fire Sweeps Country,' *Earth First!* 10, no. 2 (1989): 15.

79 Rand Interview; Jakubal Interview; Taylor, 'Diggers, Wolves, Ents, Elves and Expanding Universes,' 41–46.
80 Cecelia Ostrow, 'You Were There for Me,' track B5 on *All Life is Equal*, Self Released, 1983, Casette; Alice DiMicele, 'The God in You,' track 5 on *It's a Miracle*, Alice Otter Music, 1989, CD; Alice DiMicele, 'New Moon,' track 8 on *Too Controversial*, Alice Otter Music, 1990, CD.
81 Jean Eisenhower, 'Red Squirrels and Sacred Runners: Earth First! And the Fight to Save Mount Graham,' *Earth First! Journal* November-December (2000): 44–45; Darryl Cherney, 'Triple Victory in Three Day Revolution,' *Earth First Journal* 9, no. 2 (1988): 1–6; Jakubal Interview.
82 Quoted in Zakin, *Coyotes and Town Dogs*, 146.
83 Scarce, *Eco-Warriors*, 62.
84 Bart Koehler, 'The Buffalo Are Gone,' lines 1–10; Darryl Cherney, 'Big Mountain Will Not Fall,' track 11 on *I Had to be Born This Century*, Self Released, 1986, Cassette; Alice DiMicele, 'Song for Leonard Peltier,' track 8 on *Make a Change*, Alice Otter Music, 1988, CD.
85 Mary Laronde Interview, 20 September, 2017; Bruce Willems-Braun, 'Colonial Vestiges: Representing Forest Landscapes on Canada's West Coast,' in *Troubles in the Rainforest* ed. Trevor Barnes and Roger Hayter (Victoria: Western Geographical Press, 1997), 112–119; Ian Gill, *All That We Say Is Ours* (Vancouver: Douglas & McIntyre, 2009), 102–120.
86 Rand Interview; Jakubal Interview. In 1994 and 1995 American academics Baird Callicott and William Cronon published articles questioning the usefulness of the concept of 'wilderness' to environmentalism and critiquing it as overly dualistic with its nature/society dichotomy rooted in colonialist concepts such as the 'frontier' and 'primitive' which removed Indigenous, indeed all, people from nature. These critiques were discussed in academic and environmentalist publications subsequently and appear to be the first time in the US that such questions were debated in depth. William Cronon, 'The Trouble with Wilderness: Or, Getting Back to the Wrong Nature,' *Environmental History* 1, no. 1 (1996): 7–28; Baird Callicott, 'A Critique of and an Alternative to the Wilderness Idea,' *Wild Earth* 4, no. 4 (1994): 54–59.
87 Rand Interview; Taylor, 'Diggers, Wolves, Ents, Elves and Expanding Universes,' 44.
88 Timothy Kubal and Rene Becerra, "Social Movements and Collective Memory," *Social Movements and Collective Memory* 8, no. 6 (2014): 868–869.
89 Cecelia Ostrow, 'Blockade Song,' musical performance, Berkley Earth Day, April 24 1989, video recording, 19:53, https://www.facebook.com/17340225058/posts/here-is-a-video-of-cecelia-ostrow-george-shook-that-i-videotaped-april-24-1989-a/112297278788875/; Darryl Cherney, 'Give 'Em Hell, Sally Bell,' track 9 on *I Had to be Born This Century*, Self Released, 1986, Cassette.
90 Dana Lyons, 'Song for Rod Coronado,' track 5 on *Cows with Guns*, Reigning Records, 1996, CD; Oliver Interview.
91 Darryl Cherney and Mike Roselle, 'He Looked a Whole Lot Like Jesus,' track 9 on *Timber!*, Self Released, 1990, CD.
92 Darryl Cherney, 'The Ghosts of Mississippi,'; Daryl Cherney, 'Who Bombed Judi Bari?,' track 28 on *Who Bombed Judi Bari?*, Alternative Tentacles, 1997, CD.
93 Lindholdt, *Explorations in Ecocriticism*, 81.
94 Darryl Cherney and Judi Bari, 'The FBI Stole My Fiddle,' track 12 on *Who Bombed Judi Bari?*, Alternative Tentacles, 1997, CD.
95 'Judi Bari,' https://alternativetentacles.com/artists/judi-bari/.
96 Josh Richman, 'Judi Bari Day Celebrated in Oakland,' *Oakland Tribune*, 24 May 2004, 1.
97 Mary Liz Thomson, 'Who Bombed Judi Bari?,' (2012).

8
MEMORY 'WITHIN', 'OF' AND 'BY' URBAN MOVEMENTS

Christian Wicke

Introduction

In the narration of the 'long', 'red' and 'global' 1970s, many cities of the industrialized West experienced a concentrated though uneven development marked by economic and ideological changes. In this transformative context, there was a widespread perception of an urban crisis in industrial, deindustrializing and non-industrial cities.[1] In engaging with this crisis so-called new social movements developed diverse kinds of relationships with and within the 'old' institutions of the labour movement.[2] Against the growing interest in the history of new social movements and the 1970s in general it is remarkable that historians have somewhat overlooked the particularly *urban* movements that have sought to gain control over the transformation of their cities and neighborhoods, and offered platforms for such entanglements between old and new social movement cultures.[3] This chapter discusses two almost parallel urban movements within their very particular settings during the 1970s: the initiatives for the preservation and against the privatization of historic workers settlements in the deindustrializing German Ruhr (often called *Arbeiterintiativen*, in English 'workers initiatives'), and the more than 40 campaigns of the so-called 'Green Bans' operating predominantly between 1971 and 1975 during the construction boom in Sydney, Australia. A good number of suburbs, as well as parks, and most famously Sydney's old town, were preserved by the Green Bans who caused major disruptions to Australian politics and capital investment. When the Green Bans movement declined in Sydney in the mid-1970s, the workers settlement movement in the Ruhr, counting 33 initiatives in 1976, kept on expanding until the early 1980s to probably over 50 initiatives.[4] Not all of them were successful but both movements blocked extensive developments that would have changed the faces of their cities. Both cases selected for this comparison represent not only different kinds of positions of workers within the urban movement, but also strong conservationist ambitions. Their engagement with a changing heritage discourse opened new opportunities for cross-class alliances.[5]

The movements' labels were designed to suggest that the former stood in the tradition of the old labour movement, whereas the latter was part of the then growing (new) environmental movement. They did not conceptualize themselves primarily as urban movements. Today the public memory of the *Arbeiterinitiativen*, a name chosen for distinction from the widespread *Bürgerinitiativen* (*Bürger* in German can mean both citizen as well as bourgeois), has been firmly integrated in the institutionalized and to a great extent de-politicized industrial-heritage landscape of the Ruhr which has been central to its regional identity under conditions of deindustrialization.[6] The fast-growing public memory of Green Bans has taken a more diversified form, in which also ideas of the labour movement and the environmental movement continue to operate, along with an extensive public recognition of the Green Bans' agency in Sydney's heritage preservation. Recently the memory of the Green Bans has been used to provide new urban movement actions in Sydney with historical legitimacy. The Green Bans themselves, that is, their actions and leadership, have become urban heritage.

In this comparison, I will suggest three different perspectives on the relations between collective memory and social movements: first, I shall look critically at the role of memory *within* the two movements. Memory can inform collective identities, which some scholars in the field view as important for the existence of social movements.[7] Memory, moreover, can be used by social movements to instigate and legitimate political action. Second, I will discuss how social movements are publicly remembered today. The memory *of* social movements can be highly political, and be subject to contestation as well as banalization over time. Third, I shall discuss the relations between memory *within* and memory *of* the movements in order to gain insights of how historical cultures have been shaped *by* the two movements, and confront social movements' agency with their intentionality. I will finally argue that the memory *within* the two movements discussed here, *of* the movements and *by* the movements have been fundamentally elite driven and cannot be seen as disconnected from each other. After the demise of the movements, movement elites, that is, the informal, intellectual and cultural leadership of the movements, continued to play important roles in the shaping of historical cultures, even if neoliberal urbanism has ultimately proved more powerful than the sensitive structures of movement memory in its capacity to install alternative futures.

History, memory and social movements over the city

Urban movement action and studies have become very apparent in recent years, as urbanization and the neoliberalization of cities is advancing.[8] Their theoretical frameworks in many ways have been derived from the long 1970s, even if the memory of the actual urban movements during that period is surprisingly absent among activists today. The slogan of 'the right to the city' as disseminated with Henri Lefebvre's and David Harvey's work has become a common reference point among recent groups fighting gentrification.[9] These social scientists, interestingly, had their own historical reference points. Most prominently, the Paris Commune of 1871 was represented as some kind of archetype of an urban movement.[10] Historians today are paying increasing attention to the history of social movements, trying to transcend the more presentist perspectives of social scientists, who have dominated social movement studies, and drawing connections to the strong tradition of labour historiography.[11] However, while historians are actively shaping the memory of social movements, historical studies of urban movements still remain comparably rare.[12]

Urban movements differ from other social movements organizing themselves within cities: the city as such is their primary object of contestation. Nevertheless, there is no agreement on the conceptual spectrum that defines what an urban movement actually is, as on the one side urban movements might be acting under the umbrella of much wider political movements and, on the other, might take the form of extremely localized NIMBY actions. Further, cities as objects of contestation do not only comprise changing material structures but also comprise changing and disputed structures of meaning and memory attached to the built environment. Movements primarily concerned with urban memoryscapes could thus also be conceptualized as urban movements. Memory, as embodied in the built environment, often takes the form of 'banal memory', which is repetitively consumed by the masses without active reflection.[13] Activists, seeking to prevent or produce changes, may turn such banal memory into 'hot memory'. Memory activism, for example, over monuments, museums, or street names in cities can thus be studied from an urban movement perspective.[14] Similarly, actions for the construction or changes in urban heritage when claimed by civil-society groups can be viewed from such a perspective.

In the long 1970s, alternative ideas of history, memory and heritage grew stronger. Self-congratulatory narratives of nations' past were increasingly confronted by more self-critical assessments that sought to make visible the dark sides of history. On top of that, and in correspondence with widespread calls for democratization processes in Western societies as well as the popularization and reformation of Marxist ideology, historians decided to write history also 'from below' in attaching greater agency to the working classes; history became more social.[15] Left-wing intellectuals became fascinated by the life-world of the working classes, sought to forge revolutionary alliances with them, and industrial heritage was discovered. This could be interpreted as a widespread quest for authenticity in aesthetics and lifestyle, but also had to do with the growing appeal of left-wing ideology.[16] Urban movement action then often went beyond, for example, efforts for rent control and the improvement housing conditions, to prevent the construction of a highway or to reduce costs for public transport, but particularly for the preservation of working-class milieus or 'communities'. Evocations of working-class pasts could now serve as a common ground for sections of the *old* labour movement as well as *new* social movement activists in the formation urban movements.[17] New ideas for a post-Fordist city ultimately corresponded with new conservationist practices and forms of public memory.[18]

Two cities of urban movement action: Sydney and the Ruhr

Urban structures, political cultures and historical cultures correspond, to some degree: place matters. But the local cannot be sufficiently analysed without taking into account the transnational and transurban transfer of ideas, people and capital. Local, regional and federal governments in Germany, Australia and many other countries around 1970 sought to encourage comprehensive urban renewal measures. Many Western cities in the long 1970s have witnessed local variants of deindustrialization and economic transitions to tertiary sector jobs.[19] The labour movement was faced with the challenges of what has been historicized as a structural break with the postwar boom.[20] At the same time, they experienced a clash between Fordist city planning and neoliberal visions with the visions of a then growing section of people that believed in a post-capitalist future, based on equality and diversity.[21] Intellectuals and activists such as Jane Jacobs in the United States or Alexander Mitscherlich in West Germany then called for an urban aesthetics where citizen solidarity rather than capital speculation should be the primary focus of future developments. Their demands would become popular among citizen initiatives trying to gain greater control over their transforming urban environment.[22] Thus, it was not only ideas of the past that were pulling apart during this highly politicized period, but also ideas of the future.[23]

As an extremely suburban country with comparably low levels of social inequality, with a relatively small population at the periphery of the world's economic system, and with a relatively derivative intellectual culture, the former British settler colony down-under was internationally certainly not regarded as a hub of radical social-movement action in the long 1970s. But the Green Bans movement with its charismatic leader, Jack Mundey, attracted international attention.[24] Like many other cities of the deindustrializing West, Sydney faced large-scale re-development plans, which threatened the existence of heritage, green spaces and traditional neighborhoods. The city had been the economic heartland of the Australian nation-state. The inner suburbs and the old town, which have been built along the foreshores of the Sydney Harbour and the mouth of Parramatta river, were about to lose their face. During Sydney's building boom, radical labour unions, supported and to some extent controlled by the local Communist Party, which followed an unorthodox Eurocommunist ideology, offered a powerful organizational structure to residents asking them for help. The local citizen initiatives then emerging across the city, the Coalition of Citizen Action Groups (CRAG) and local residents appealed to the union leadership. This comprehensive support over several years represented a new understanding of 'workers control' in shifting the focus of action beyond the workplace into the city. The unions active in Sydney's urban movement were most prominently the NSW Builders Labourers Federation (NSWBLF), but also, for example, the Federated *Engine Drivers*' and Firemen's Association (FEDFA), the Building Workers Industrial Union (BWIU), and the Seamen's Union of Australia (SUA). Despite the importance of the institutionalized labour movement, which was absent in the example of the Ruhr, however, it has not dominated the representation and memory of the urban movement, as I shall argue in more detail further below. The union leadership connected new social movements and expressed solidarity, for example, with indigenous, environmental, anti-nuclear movement, feminist, gay and lesbian and other 'new' social movements, and of course heritage activists. Such cross-movement alliances did indeed also play a role in the Ruhr. Apart from the strong affinity with the industrial-heritage scene in the Ruhr, there were also connections with, for example, the environmental, anti-nuclear, squatters, and youth centre movement as I have argued previously.[25]

The Ruhr, despite its large size, has neither been associated as a hub of (new) social movement action or great intellectual and cultural vibrancy. The Ruhr has developed in an even more polycentric structure than Sydney; the industrial infrastructure that has determined the organization of districts and settlements has been referred to as 'Ruhrbanity'. This peculiar urban structure, following the industrial logic of the coal and steel industries that have given birth to the region, had direct effect on the way urban movement action has been articulated: the initiatives were extremely decentralized as the major umbrella organization that was founded by a working group (*Arbeitsgemeinschaft der Arbeitersiedlungsinitiativen im Ruhrgebiet*) at the Eisenheim settlement in Oberhausen in the early seventies lacked the strong instructional structure that the labour unions in Sydney were able to offer. It presented itself as the working-class version of the citizen initiatives that mushroomed in the Federal Republic in the early 1970s. The Eisenheim group organized the *Ruhr-Volksblatt*, a paper that sought to connect the local initiatives and provide information among them as well as to the outside world. There were also more local organizations in the cities of the Ruhr, which sought to promote solidarity among the individual initiatives across the region. In the Ruhr, the unions with the mining union (*Industriegewerkschaft Bergbau und Energie*) as the most powerful representative, as well as the Social Democratic Party, which became very strong in the Ruhr after the Second World War, were largely opposed to the 'workers intiatives', as they had a strong interest in the valorisation of the properties and a re-development of the Ruhr, which had been dominated by the declining coal and steel industries. The Ruhr's regional identity became strongly dependent on a slowly emerging industrial-heritage movement in which leaders of the 'workers initiatives' sought to embed the urban movement. This connection would become important also for the memory of the urban movement, which I will show below. New Left ideology mattered for the leadership of the initiatives, but not so much for the local residents who gained support from intellectuals, such as academics, artists, architects, Protestant priests and alternative local newspapers, as well as a tenant movement fighting exorbitant rents, and an emerging squatters movement. Such mixed group constellations were important both in the Ruhr as well as Sydney.

Memory within the movements

Different and often overlapping sets of heritage were operating in the historical cultures of the two movements discussed here, that is, the way they articulated their visions of the past: working-class and labour-movement heritage, particular urban and national heritages, as well as environmental heritage. Both movements were representative of a new international heritage discourse employed by the left with a focus on urban conservationism with a social orientation (*sozialorientierte Stadterhaltung*), with communist-led Bologna as a captivating example for many activists and planners.[26] Heritage, like history in general, can be highly political, as social groups with unequal means and agency negotiate the meaning, construction and maintenance of the past in the future. Their memory activism often aims at the institutionalization of heritage in the official historical culture of places, which fluid identities are thus subject to manipulation from below and above. During this process, heritage as originally articulated by social-movement organizations might become alienated from its original meaning and possibly de-politicized and de-historicized. Nevertheless, the original aims and historical perspectives of former activists can later be re-invoked through the construction of memory by future protest generations that seek retrospective alliances as I shall show further below in this chapter.

The urban movement in the Ruhr evoked liberal rights such as 'citizen participation', used social democratic solutions such as the well-established model of housing co-ops that had gained in popularity over the previous 100 years in Germany, and presented itself as part of a transnational tenant movement against exorbitant rents and for social housing. The movement also drew on more radical social movement practices such as hunger strike.[27] More importantly, like in the case of Sydney, urban movement action in the 1970s Ruhr was often presented as a continuation of workers struggles over the production site. It was seen in the tradition of the labour movement and workers' emancipation in transcending the focus to the urban environment.[28] The major 'workers party' in the Ruhr, the Social Democrats, however, were supported by the vast majority of the inhabitants of the workers settlements, including movement leader Roland Günter who had been a member of the SPD's left wing, only very hesitantly provided assistance to the initiatives.[29] And the German unions were indifferent or hostile to the initiatives. Nevertheless both urban movement networks in Sydney and the Ruhr could draw on a repertoire of cultural and political practices derived from labour movement traditions. But there were important similarities and differences between the two.

Since the movement in Sydney was much more institutionalized, labour unions were able to transfer their action repertoire from the workplace to the city more directly. Strike action was directed not primarily to protect rights and welfare of the workers involved but on behalf of the wider community and interest groups beyond the common worker. In the Ruhr, however, the movement could not draw directly on the institutional repertoire of memory offered by the labour unions, simply because the unions in Germany were opposed to its claims. But the cultural repertoire of memory offered by the labour movement, which especially the older generations of tenants in the Ruhr's workers settlements could communicate during the urban protests in the 1970s, was certainly important to the historical culture of the movement in Germany's industrial west. This was beautifully demonstrated by the music of Frank Baier, one of the movement leaders in Duisburg, who collected historic workers songs from the Ruhr.[30] Baier also rewrote well-known German songs as local movement songs,[31] and I will get back to his long-term agency in movement memory later in this chapter.

In the Ruhr, movement leaders predominantly presented working-class heritage embodied by the local communities and architecture of the workers settlements as greatly endangered. In the 1970s, intellectual sympathizers of the movement began to work towards greater public recognition of the architectural, social and cultural values embodied in the history of the workers' settlements.[32] The Ruhr-Volksblatt (RVB) regularly included sections on the particular histories of various workers settlements and the way they had been constructed.[33] Immaterial heritage mattered significantly. The working-class traditions movement leaders sought to preserve also included 'values' of cohabitation, forms of communication and the social life in general, which could not be maintained outside of the settlements. The movement paid, for example, great attention to the preservation of the working-class dialect of the region, which it saw mispresented in the public, or the working-class tradition of pigeon breeding,[34] and rabbit breeding.[35] The regional history of the Ruhr, that is, predominantly its labour history, provided a major memory framework for the urban movement, ranging from catastrophic mining accidents[36] to celebrations of the labour movement, such as 1 May.[37] The RVB also published the personal histories, for example, in the form of autobiographical abstracts on lives that were presented as typical for the Ruhr or in the form of interviews with older dwellers.[38] Legislative history, such as the evolution of tenant rights in the early twentieth century,[39] or 1919 law for the protection of allotment gardens, was used to legitimize protest against privatization. As the RVB editors found, 'after the revolution in 1919 a good number of good laws was produced'.[40] The RVB remembered the November revolution 60 years before also to draw parallels with their own struggles.[41] Again, this is an important aspect of the memory structures within the movement of the Ruhr: while it was highly critical of the role of the trade unions – who acted as agents in the commodification of urban spaces and homes and, thus, were antagonistic to the protests against demolition and privatization – the urban movement activists in the Ruhr still solidarized with labour unions' history and actions. Despite the antagonism, the RVB published chronicles of the 1970s strikes in the local steel sector.[42] At the end of the day, it presented itself as the most authentic relic of the degrading movement in the region. Remarkably, next to the repertoire of memory and practices offered by social movements, religious memory also placed a role in the urban movement of the Ruhr. Clerics engaged with the workers-settlement movement, the tenant movement as well as the emerging industrial heritage movement in the region. Many tenants of the workers settlements were members of the Church and protestant priests involved in the movement presented movement actions as a struggle for the New Jerusalem.[43]

The heritage movement around the world, and conceptions of the past and present, were undergoing great changes in the red 1970s. The urban movement engaged with discussions around the 'European heritage year' of 1975 in seeking to expand the common understanding of heritage. The life and architecture of the workers settlements, thus, began to enjoy greater recognition among conservators and architects also outside the region.[44] 'What does heritage mean for workers', a RVB article asked, informing the readers about movement leaders' participation in the final congress of the heritage year organized by the European Council in Amsterdam. 'This heritage is different to the one of the middle classes', it argued, and demanded the preservation of workers' quarters instead of ignoring the legitimacy of such heritage.[45] While the particularity of working-class heritage was emphasized, the movement leadership understood that writing the history of the settlements provided the protests with wider recognition and legitimacy beyond the workers' needs; it was relevant for society in general.[46] In Sydney, as we shall see, the discourse was similar.

In the context of the European heritage year, RVB readers were recommended a new book entitled *Keine Zukunft für unsere Vergangenheit?* [No future for our past?], which was co-authored by the most prominent urban movement leader of the Ruhr, Roland Günter, complaining about the absence of social history in the official heritage discourse.[47] The volume suggested taking the social structures of urban heritage seriously and made comparative references to urban movement actions, for example, for the preservation of old towns that were threatened by development plans in Germany and elsewhere. It pled for the preservation also of *industrial* heritage. The workers settlements were 'monuments of social history' (p. 118ff). I will get back to the importance of Günter for the memory *of* and *by* the movement below. It is worth noting here, however, that his wife Janne Günter with whom he had moved into the Eisenheim settlement, was part of the movement too and led a research project to investigate the typical life of the workers in their settlement, perhaps indeed an exotic place to the middle-class 'migrants' who sought to integrate while leading the movement.[48] Such outsiders, nevertheless, would watch the development of state heritage legislation very carefully, and would become influential in the recognition of industrial heritage and the institutionalization of the industrial-heritage movement.[49]

While histories of other urban movements mattered little – though movement leader Roland Günter wrote on the history of squatting in Amsterdam –[50] over the years, the workers-settlement movement in the Ruhr also wrote its own history, for example, by providing chronicles of the short history of the protest initiatives to the RVB readership.[51] And, as the workers settlements remained subject to speculation in the early 1980s, the editors reminded readers of the origins of the movement.[52] Important movement events, such as the hunger strike for the protection of the Rheinpreußen settlement, perhaps the most radical protest of the movement, were subsequently remembered in the publications of the movement.[53] Also activists who passed away were remembered.[54] Thus, as is typical for the social movements discussed in this volume, the workers-settlement movement developed its own historical culture, in borrowing strongly from labour and other movements as well as in constructing endogenic memory. Resembling some dynamics in the urban movement of the Ruhr, Sydney's activists also began, shortly after the emergence of the movement, to work on and formalize their own movement memory, for example, in the form of anniversary celebrations of local action groups.[55]

In Sydney, the urban movement articulated heritage in different and in a somewhat wider form, ranging from national to environmental heritage, than in the Ruhr, where the main focus was on working-class heritage as strongly associated with the typical culture of the region. Resident groups and individuals asked radical unions for assistance to prevent the construction of expressways for cars, high-rise building complexes, the demolishing of parks and innercity bushland and so forth. The strong alliance between middle-class and working-class citizens, including neighbourhood action groups, creatives and professionals, and very left-wing unions proved powerful and remains an important episode in the global history and memory of urban movements. BLF leader Jack Mundey presented the extraparliamentary actions as workers simply 'doing their job' on behalf of 'the working people'. To him this was the 'social responsibility' of unions in the 1970s which should get involved in politics beyond the workplace. This responsibility also involved 'history'. In 1972, he prophesied: 'If architects, engineers and building workers combine to preserve a little of our history people in the future will be grateful for our belated action'.[56] While the movement leadership followed ideological and historical motifs, it is doubtful to what extent citizens who sought to protect their home as well as the average construction worker involved in the actions had similar ambitions. It is more likely that, like in the Ruhr, also in Sydney the urban movement participants' motivations varied within a spectrum ranging from NIMBY attitudes to revolutionary visions.[57]

Laurajane Smith pointed out that the Green Bans were installed at a time when there was, like in Europe, also a widespread movement for a comprehensive heritage legislation in Australia.[58] While embedded in transnational developments in ideology and historical culture, the Green Bans movement articulated its heritage activism strongly within a national framework of memory, rather than within the particular, urban framework of the city of Sydney or the one of working-class memory – as it had been the case in the Ruhr. This becomes especially evident in the protests over the preservation of Sydney's oldtown: 'Australia has one heritage, one past, one birthplace: The Rocks' a poster from 1973 to 1974 claimed inviting the public to a meeting at Millers Point chaired by CRAG leader Neil Runcie who sought to prevent urban changes for profit motives.[59] Activists sought to bring greater public attention to the history of Sydney Harbour and the residential settlements in the area, with the Rocks being described as 'the cradle of a nation'. Very localized heritage was associated with a 'discovery' of Australian history and heritage which enjoyed greater public attention than it had before; urban movement action against re-development plans by the government could thus be presented as patriotic.[60] Like in the Ruhr, the action groups in Sydney formed to prevent urban neoliberalization (without using the term, yet) and evictions of low-income earners focussed strongly on the threat to the 'community' as well as material heritage, and 'history' in the widest sense. But 'community' did not necessarily mean only residents in the district concerned, but could also comprise all citizens of Sydney, or even the nation in general.

This is a variation in comparison to the movement in the Ruhr, where representatives of the academic, political and cultural elite still continue to take common efforts for greater national recognition of its workers' heritage. Both movements protested against high-rise buildings for ensuring good living standards for low-income households as well as for aesthetic and historic reasons, and in both cases movement elites strongly drew on the changing heritage discourse. But only in Sydney, during the important campaign for the preservation of Sydney's oldtown, The Rocks, did the unions draw heavily on a rhetoric of *national* heritage. This was perhaps for tactical reasons. Left-wing nationalism has certainly been more acceptable in Australia than in Germany since 1945, and Australia's search for its own glorious past during the emancipation from the British motherland has remained an ongoing process. During this campaign, industrial and working-class history of The Rocks gained public attention in the Australian media.[61] At the same time, The Rocks became increasingly touristic over the 1960s and 1970s, even its former Mining Museum attracted greater number of visitors until the closure in the early 1980s.[62] It is noteworthy that in Sydney, like in the Ruhr, local groups just wanting to stay in their homes, were headed by architects and planners who had different visions than their colleagues working for the state. The committee for the alternative 'People's Plan for the Rocks', indeed, was chaired by the famous architect Neville Gruzman. And also the role of artists was important.[63] Artists then sought to mobilize the public to prevent the closure of the Argyle Arts Centre in a restored wool store of the formerly industrial area in Sydney Harbour.[64] The unions, on the other hand, were careful in not being presented as predominantly ideologically motivated and sought to emphasize the general will of local residents who were simply caring for their environment, and the unions' assistance in making them heard through the development of the alternative 'People's Plan'.[65]

Memory of the movements

Not only social movements overlap, but also the sets of memory attached to particular movements, and their leadership, matter not only within a social movement but also in the memory thereof. Sydney's Green Bans, are enjoying a greater prominence in public memory than the *Arbeiterintiativen* in the Ruhr. The memory of the Green Bans – as a labour and environmental movement as well as a very special form citizen action – is comparably vibrant in the political and historical culture of Sydney and Australia in general, even if by far not every Sydneysider knows about this great episode in their urban history. The memory of the workers-settlement movement, on the other hand, plays a more peripheral role in the German Ruhr, though it is currently developing thanks to efforts from above and below. In Sydney in particular, more than in the Ruhr, the memory urban movement of the 1970s has enjoyed increasing representation in the form of memorial sites including plaques, murals, places and walks. Just to mention a few examples: at Kelly's Bush, a memorial stone was set to celebrate the 25th anniversary of the 1971 Green Ban, stating that this was the place where the 'world's first Green Ban' took place.[66] In the 1990s, the Green Bans park was developed by residents in the inner suburb of Erskineville, displaying a great number of explanatory memorial plaques.[67] I cannot draw a comprehensive picture of the material memoryscape of Sydney's Green Bans here, but to me the murals of Woolloomooloo are its most impressive feature. As suggested above, the memory of urban movements may start shortly after their commencement, often from within the movement. The vast murals of Woolloomooloo, glorifying the social movement, the unions and the leadership, were created already a few years after the decline of the movement in Sydney. The project by the two activist artists Merilyn Fairskye and Michiel Dolk with the Residents Action Group of the district began in the late 1970s and ended in the mid-1980s. The murals were restored by Sydney Artefacts Conservation and Artcare between 2009 and 2013.[68] This innercity suburb until today has maintained relatively large sections of social housing. Poverty is quite visible at the doorstep of the homes of new millionaires who possibly find the grungier sections of their neighbourhood somewhat cool and enjoy the centrality as well as accessibility to the Botanic Garden and the foreshores. More importantly, from the murals it is only a few-minutes walk to the Juanita Nielsen Community Centre opened by the City of Sydney in 1984. This must not be missed when exploring the Green Bans' material memoryscape.[69] Nielsen, who had been associated with the Green Ban and urban conservation movement is widely believed to have been murdered in 1975. Artist Zaggy Begg has just made a film about Nielsen's story, where memory takes a highly aestheticized form.[70] However, it is impossible to draw a complete picture here.

Interestingly, and perhaps more strongly than in the Ruhr, the superhuman side of Sydney's Green-Ban memory is very dominant in correspondence with the leadership of the past. Powerful individuals, especially of the Green Bans, but to a great degree also of the workers initiatives in the Ruhr, stick out in the memoryscapes of both cities and remain living legends. Public memory is strongly of leaders rather than of the social movements in general. The BLF and Jack Mundey, one of the charismatic movement leaders, have been presented most prominently in the public memory of the movement in Sydney and elsewhere in the country. From the early 1980s, the national media promoted mainstream memory of Mundey's persona and movement leadership.[71] In the new millennium, Mundey gained the status of a national hero with representations ranging, for example, from a photo purchased in the National Portrait Gallery,[72] via a film documentary by the National Film and Sound Archive,[73] to a very recent biography that has been widely discussed.[74] Mundey, has been acknowledged not only for his union work, but also for his subsequent work as a heritage conservator in Sydney, New South Wales and Australia. In 2007, a place of The Rocks has been named 'Jack Mundey Place'. He has the official status of a 'living national treasure' in Australia. Thus, like in the memory by the movement, also the memory of the movement has been shaped by a certain degree of Australian nationalism.

The memory of the Green Bans is growing fast, in Sydney and outside. I am myself contributing to the memory of the Green Bans, not only in the course of publishing this work, but also, for example, in teachings on the history of civil society at Utrecht University, where students have to watch Pat Fiske's documentary *Rocking the Foundations* from 1985 about the history of Sydney's BLF with a focus on the Green Bans. And I am certainly not the only academic who works on the memory of this exciting movement. I also understand that I am contributing to the more slowly developing memory of the *Arbeiterinitiativen* in the Ruhr by engaging with the history to which I will come back in a moment. Academics, indeed, play an important role in the memory of social movements. Meredith and Verity Burgmann's standard work from 1998 on the history of the Green Bans, for example, had been out of print for many years, until in 2017 a new edition was sold in the bookshops across the country.[75] As the archival memory of the two urban movements discussed here is vast, it would be surprising if historians would not do further work on them.[76] Last but not least, the internet is becoming an increasingly powerful place of official as well as more informal memory, especially of the Green Bans.[77] There, for example, local initiatives operating today portray the history of the Green Bans,[78] and the City of Sydney serves with wonderful online data from an oral history project including the personal memory of Jack Mundey.[79] But most readers will be able to master the art of googling, so there is little reason why I should preempt any encompassing review here.

The workers initiatives in the Ruhr are presented online only to a very limited extent, and I have experienced calls among academics of the industrial-heritage community in the region as well as local history workshops to commence with a more complete history of this movement. An exceptional example is an extensive master's thesis on the struggles over the Floez Dickebank settlement in Gelsenkirchen, which has been submitted in 2013 to the University of Cologne.[80]

Previously the focus has been predominantly on the material structures and the history of the settlements from an urban planning and heritage perspective.[81] Nineteen of the hundreds of workers' settlements are part of the Route der *Industriekultur* (Route of Industrial Heritage), but the movement struggles play a very marginal role in the representation of the settlements' past.[82] There are a number of possible reasons for this. First, in comparison to Sydney the urban movement of the Ruhr was smaller. The Green Bans were part of a strike wave that went beyond the traditional practices of Australian Labor politics, caused major disruptions for investments into urban developments, and thus caused so much furore in local, regional as well as national politics that also the memory of the movement enjoyed a greater kind of predisposition to prominence than the protests in the Ruhr did. Second, the deindustrializing and politically fragmentized Ruhr has not been seen as a metropolitan centre of urban Germany, whereas Sydney is the urban centre of Australia. Third, the urban crisis of the economically and demographically declining Ruhr has played out very differently Sydney, which has experienced an ongoing influx of population and capital investment.

It is only very recently that the industrial heritage of the Ruhr in general began to be studied from a social movement perspective, which has been largely thanks to the stimulus of the Institute for Social Movements in Bochum, which is located in the House for the History of the Ruhr and is part of the Ruhr University's history department, with Stefan Berger becoming Director in 2011.[83] This is having an effect on the regional museum sector. In 2018, an exhibition in Dortmund by Jana Flieshart and Jana Golombek, who is taking her PhD with Berger, engaged with protagonists of the *Arbeiterinitiativen*.[84] As part of the exhibition, four historical films by Klaus Helle about the movement struggles were shown in parts or at full length.[85] The archiving of such films, as much as other material for the preservation of movement memory, has been largely thanks to private initiative. It is worth noting that these films that have been held in Paul Hofmann's *Kinemathek des Ruhrgebiets* in Essen, which has received financial support by the state government and will soon be transferred to the Ruhr Museum at the Zollverein world-heritage site, where also the regional photo archive is located. It will be interesting to see what such efforts will do to the general memory of the workers-settlement initiatives, which remain part of a de-politicized industrial-heritage network that has become strongly institutionalized and to a great degree commodified and tailored for the wider public, as it is perceived as the most important and distinctive characteristic of the deindustrializing region vis-à-vis others.[86]

The above-mentioned Eisenheim settlement, probably the oldest in the Ruhr and the first one where urban movement action was successful in the early 1970s when being put under protection, has enjoyed disproportionate representation in public memory and is part and parcel of the official representation of the Ruhr's industrial-heritage landscape. Since the 1990s, Eisenheim has a museum focussing on the history of everyday life in the workers quarter.[87] In the late 2000s, a TV programme on a working-class family in the settlement brought further public attention to Eisenheim and could possibly be accused of a certain middle-class voyeurism and banalization of memory.[88] But, Eisenheim is also the most important place in the memory of the movement for the protection of the Ruhr's workers' settlements. This has been partly due to the memory work and leadership of Roland Guenter in Eisenheim, who in some ways perhaps could be seen as the Ruhr's equivalent to Mundey, as I shall further explain below, though Mundey's status as a national hero in Australia cannot be matched by Guenter in Germany.

Memory by the movements

I have already shown, to some extent, how the public memory *of* movement movements has been shaped *by* urban movements themselves. Lifting the level of abstraction further above, one can also see that both cities, Sydney and the Ruhr, would have developed differently without the urban movement actions discussed here. If the built environments of cities are containers of memory, successful urban movement action automatically involves somewhat invisible memories of the movement, which can be made visible by telling urban histories. Needless to say, the heritage landscapes of both the Ruhr and Sydney have been strongly shaped by both movements. My chapter and this volume also show that social movements create memory of themselves and among themselves. Further, social movements, in this comparative history especially the Green Bans, can become important parts of the urban heritage itself. In this last section I focus on the influence of movement leaders on the way the memory of social movements is presented in historical culture.

The reason why the New South Wales branch of the BLF was de-registered and called off many Green Bans already in 1974 was in many ways due to some internal competition with the Federal BLF leadership located in Melbourne and the related Victorian branch under the leadership of Norm Gallagher who would be arrested for corruption. This competition was, to some extent, also shaped by ideological differences within the Australian Left with opposing Maoist and Eurocommunist tendencies. Interestingly, this competition also had repercussions in a conflict over the memory of the Green Bans, with the Melbournians trying to gain public recognition for being the first ones in developing this form of action and trying to downplay the role of the Sydneysiders. This little memory war was very visible in the 'Green Bans Gallery', which opened in 1974 at Melbourne's Trades Hall.[89] This small episode should remind us that we perhaps need to be cautious when writing the history of memory *of* urban movements, and pay attention to the ways it can be shaped *by* the movements.

The ideological battles among the Left of the 1970s, however, seem to matter little today. Civil society is becoming increasingly sensitive to the massive housing problem in Sydney, which recently has been rated the second most expensive city in the world (behind Hong Kong).[90] The Green Bans therefore continue to serve as mobilizing political memory for contemporary urban movement actions in Sydney, which opens perspectives on how the memories *of* movements and *by* movements have been intertwined. In July 2016, I met Jack Mundey and his wife Judy at Millers Point, the old district just next to the Rocks. It was as history would repeat itself. Low income earners were being forced out of their houses. We took a walk along the foreshore at Sydney Harbour and passed by the iconic Sirius building next to Sydney Harbour Bridge that has been threatened to be demolished. Mundey, today himself part of Sydney's heritage, engaged with the protests.[91] Mundey has also supported the Community Action for Windsor Bridge (CAWB) in recent years.[92] He has become a heroic figure of social movement action, a living legend whose charisma remains an important asset in the seemingly hopeless struggles against neoliberal urbanism. The memory of the Green Bans, thus, gains in currency, as in recent years global capital investment into cities has become increasingly attractive. The surviving unions are called upon to revive their heritage, as the Green Ban over the art deco pavilion at Bondi beach demonstrated a few years ago.[93] And the remaining super-union, the Construction, Forestry, Mining and Energy Union (CFMEU) has celebrated the anniversaries of this movement heritage and recently revived it by putting the Sirius building and Bondi Pavilion under a Green Ban.

If we historicize the urban movement as a continuous, singular object over time, it becomes pivotal for our understanding of this object to investigate what its continuity exists of. The repertoire of memory, people and practices of the past, seem to assist a movement in an environment of political competition. In the Ruhr, we also witness such continuities at leadership level of the region's urban movement. The singer Frank Baier, who I mentioned above, has established a private archive on the struggles over his settlements and other social movement action, and he has remained active as a singer in articulating historical consciousness in the region, including the history of its urban movement.[94] Roland Günter of Eisenheim, like Mundey, has remained very active in the official heritage sector ever since his urban movement actions in the early 1970s. Günter has recently been vociferous, for example, in the poor north of the shrinking city of Duisburg, protesting against the demolition of a whole art nouveau quarter and a Max Taut settlement. As chair of the North-Rhine Westphalian Werkbund and most remembered urban movement activist in the Ruhr, he engaged with the local citizens, joined protests and published a new book where he described contemporary urban politics as 'city massacre and social crime'.[95] In 2017, a group around director Mathias Coers produced a film about urban movement initiatives in the Ruhr that has been shown internationally. At the premiere of the film, Günter was present. He had been waiting for a long time for this film, he applauded.[96] It is worth noting, however, that the film is taking almost exclusively presentist perspectives without making historical references. The presence of Günter does demonstrate that historical references are welcome to underpin current initiatives with some prominence, but it remains doubtful how existential they are for the subjective identity of urban movements. They are perhaps more important for the objective identity of urban movements as narrated by historians.

Concluding reflections

I have offered a rough typology of intertwined memory motives *within*, *of* and *by* urban movements, which are idealized and in practice overlap, and which can hopefully be further developed. Memory *within* urban movements is part of the historical culture of the movement participants, for example, alternative ideas of heritage as well as the adaptation of ritual practices from movements in the past and celebrations of the own movement's origins. Memory

FIGURE 8.1 Juanita Nielsen Community Centre (Wicke, 2016).

FIGURE 8.2 Kelly's Bush, Green Bans memorial plaque (Wicke, 2016).

of urban movements is the movements' place in historical culture, that is, the way society has articulated the past of the movements, for example, in the built environment of cities as well as more widely in, for example, artworks, exhibitions, academic and non-academic literature, film and (online) media. The memory *by* the movements, then, constitutes the convergence of memory *within* and *of* the movement, emphasizing the agency of leading movement members in historical cultures and especially in the way their movements are remembered. Urban movement leaders, and I have only been able to address a representative few in this chapter, might engage with memory battles over their place in history. Moreover, urban movement leaders of the past often become active again when new protest occurs and evoke the memory *of* movement to legitimize contemporary action. And last but not least, once urban movement action has successfully manipulated or prevented urban development, the reflexive memory as formed *by* the movement becomes inbuilt into the city.

The impact of urban movements in the long 1970s on city planning has been largely overlooked. We often take our everyday urban environment for granted and observe the changes predominantly through the prism of limited personal experiences. It will require comprehensive efforts for urban, public, hypothetical and perhaps digital histories to show how cities would have developed if

FIGURE 8.3 1979 Mural by activist artists Merilyn Fairskye and Michiel Dolk and the Woolloomooloo Residents Action Group, 'to celebrate the history of the local community and their battle to save the area from high-rise development'. (https://www.cityartsydney.com.au/wooloomooloo-murals) (Wicke, 2016).

FIGURE 8.4 Jack Mundey at Miller's Point (Wicke, 2016).

citizens, during such highly politicized period – when the future of 'the past' was subject to effective struggles – had not practised strong claims for urban democracy and cross-class solidarity. In other words, the memory *of* urban movements still has the capacity to change radically. Much of the material that could be used to write more comprehensive histories of urban movements is still held in private hands; we need to climb into the attics of former activists and rummage through boxes to move this memory and perhaps relativize leadership agency (Figures 8.1–8.4).

Notes

1 Martin Baumeister, Bruno Bonomo and Dieter Schott, eds., *Cities Contested: Urban Politics, Heritage and Social Movements in Italy and Germany in the 1970s* (Frankfurt: Campus, 2017).
2 Christian Wicke, 'Arbeiterbewegung und urbane Bewegung in den 1970er Jahren – Das Ruhrgebiet und Sydney im Vergleich,' *Arbeit – Bewegung – Geschichte. Zeitschrift für historische Studien* 17, no. 3 (2018): 57–73.
3 Hans Pruijt, 'Urban Movements,' in *Blackwell Encyclopedia of Sociology*, ed. George Ritzer (Malden, MA: Blackwell 2007), 5115–5119; cf. Stefan Berger and Holger Nehring, eds., *The History of Social Movements in Global Perspective: A Survey* (Basingstoke: Palgrave, 2017).
4 Jörg Boström and Roland Günter, *Arbeiterinitiativen im Ruhrgebiet* (Westberlin: VSA, 1976).
5 Kurt Iveson, 'Building a City for "The People": The Politics of Alliance-Building in the Sydney Green Ban Movement,' *Antipode* 46 (2014): 992–1013.
6 Stefan Berger, Christian Wicke and Jana Golombek, 'Burdens of Eternity: Heritage, Identity and the "Great Transition" in the Ruhr,' *The Public Historian* 39, no. 4 (2017): 21–43.
7 For a recent study on the importance of identity in the history of social movements, see, for example, Priska Daphi, *Becoming a Movement: Identity, Narrative and Memory in the European Global Justice Movement* (Lanham, MD: Rowman & Littlefield, 2017).
8 Mayer on neoliberal urbanism, Margit Mayer, 'The Career of Urban Social Movements in West Germany,' in *Mobilizing the Community*, eds. Robert Fisher and Joseph Kling (Newbury Park, CA: Sage, 1993), 149–170.

9 Henri Lefebvre, *Le droit à la ville* (Paris: Éditions Anthropos, 1968); David Harvey, 'The Right to the City,' *New Left Review* 53 (2008): 23–40.
10 See also Manuel Castells, *The City and the Grassroots: A Cross-Cultural Theory or Urban Movements* (Berkeley: University of California Press, 1983), 15–26.
11 See, for example, the series: *Palgrave Studies in the History of Social Movements*, edited by Stefan Berger and Holger Nehring.
12 Cf., for example, Philipp Reick, 'Gentrification 1.0: Urban Transformations in Late-19th-century Berlin', *Urban Studies* 55, no. 1 (2018): 2542–2558; Nina Schierstaedt, *Kampf um den staedtischen Raum: Die Madrider Nachbarschaftsbewegungen im Spaetfranquismus und Demokratisierungsprozess* (Essen: Klartext, 2017); Baumeister, Bonomo, and Schott, *Cities Contested*; Mathias Heigl, *Rom im Aufruhr: Soziale Bewegungen im Italien der 1970er Jahre* (Bielefeld: Transcript, 2015); especially on the history of squatting, see, for example, Alexander Vasudevan, *The Autonomous City: A History of Urban Squatting* (London: Verso: 2017); Freia Anders and Alexander Sedlmaier, eds., *Public Goods versus Economic Interests: Global Perspectives on the History of Squatting* (London: Routledge: 2016); Bart van der Steen, Ask Katzeff, and Leendert van Hoogenhuijze, eds., *The City Is Ours: Squatting and Autonomous Movements in Europe from the 1970s to the Present* (Oakland, CA: PM Press, 2014).
13 Michael Billig, *Banal Nationalism* (Thousand Oaks, CA: Sage, 1995).
14 On Memory activism see Jenny Wuestenberg in this volume.
15 E. Thompson, 'History from Below', *The Times Literary Supplement*, 7 April 1966.
16 David Ley, *The New Middle Class and the Remaking of the Central City* (Oxford: Oxford University Press, 1996), cf. Sven Reichardt, *Authenzitaet und Gemeinschaft: Linksalternatives Leben in den siebziger und fruehen achtziger Jahren* (Berlin: Suhrkamp, 2014).
17 Wicke, 'Arbeiterbewegung und urbane Bewegung in den 1970er-Jahren, 57–73.
18 See, for example, Rudy Koshar, *Germany's Transient Past: Preservation and National Memory in the 20th Century, 1998* (Berkeley: University of California Press, 1998).
19 I have previously argued, however, that strong urban movement action also took place in cities that were at the peak of their industrialization, as, for example, Turin in the 1970s. Christian Wicke, 'Urban Movements in the Global 1970s,' Lecture at the German Historical Institute in Rome, 9 May 2018.
20 Doering Manteuffel and Lutz Raphael, eds., *Nach dem Boom: Perspektiven auf die Zeitgeschichte seit 1970* (Goettingen: Vendenhoek & Ruprecht, 2008).
21 Ash Amin, ed., *Postfordism: A Reader* (Oxford: Blackwell, 1994).
22 Jane Jacobs, *Death and Life of Great American Cities* (New York: Random House, 1961), Alexander Mischerlich, *Unwirtlichkeit unserer Staedte: Anstiftung zum Unfrieden* (Frankfurt: Suhrkamp, 1965).
23 Matthew Connelly, 'Future Shock. The End of the World as They Knew It,' in *The Shock of the Global. The 1970s in Perspective*, eds. Niall Ferguson, Charles S. Maier, Erez Manela, and Daniel J. Sargent (Cambridge, MA: Belknap Press, 2010), 337–350.
24 See, for example, interview with Jack Mundey, 'Die "green ban"-Bewegung in Australien,' in *Stadtkrise und soziale Bewegungen: Texte zur internationalen Entwicklung*, eds. Margit Mayer, Roland Roth, and Volkhard Brandes (Cologne: EVA, 1978), 247–253. I am grateful to Jack and Judy Mundey for the time they have spent with me and our correspondences.
25 Wicke, 'Arbeiterbewegung und urbane Bewegung in den 1970er Jahren.'
26 See, for example, Adalbert Evers and Juan Rodriguez-Lores, *Sozialorientierte Stadterhaltung als politischer Prozess: Praxisberichte aus Bologna und ausgewählten Städten* (Cologne: Kohlhammer, 1976).
27 See the *Ruhr-Volksblatt* [RVB] 30, no. 4 (1978). Please note that the style of numeration of this newspaper has been inconsistent over time.
28 Thomas Rommelspacher, *"Wenn wir richtig zusammenhalten ensteht eine Macht" – Zechenhausinitiativen im Ruhrgebiet 1974–-1981: Struktur und Perspektiven in einem regionalen Mieterkampf* (Bochum: Germinal, 1984), 4.
29 See also Koshar, *Germany's Transient Past*, 311.

30 See, for example, Frank Baier, *Arbeiterlieder aus dem Ruhrgebiet: Texte, Noten und Begleit-Akkorde* (Frankfurt: Fischer, 1985)
31 See, for example, the EP album and booklet, *Als die Mieter frech geworden: Lieder aus der Rheinpreußen-Siedlung* (Verlag Pläne/Wohnungsgenossenschaft Rheinpreußen, 1989).
32 See, for example, Franzika Bollerey and Christina Hartmann, *Wohnen im Revier: 99 Beispiele aus Dortmund* (Munich: Heinz Moss, 1975).
33 See, for example, 'Bilderbogen aus Lohberg,' *RVB* 3 (December–January 1975/76): 6; 'Bilderbogen aus der Sachsenkolonie in Dorsten,' *RVB* 5 (February 1976): 8.
34 See, for example, 'Hochdeutsch-Arbeitersprache oder "Gemangert",' *RVB* 4 (October–November 1975): 1, and 'Tiere halten ist schön', *RVB* 4 (October–November 1975): 4.
35 'Kaninchenzucht: Auch damit was Ordentliches im Pott is,' *RVB* 3 (December–January 1975/76): 3.
36 See, for example, 'Ein Stueck Bergbaugeschichte,' *RVB* 53 (April/May 1983): 350 'Maenner starben,' *RVB* 53 (April/May 1983): 12–14.
37 See, for example, 'Heini-Wettig-Haus: Der 1. Mai – nur noch ein bezahlter Feiertag?,' *RVB* 54 (June/July/August 1983): 10.
38 See, for example, 'Geschichte in Geschichten,' *RVB* 7, 8, and 9 (1976); 'Wir waren moderne Sklaven,' *RVB* 30 (1980): 5.
39 'Was bringt uns die Mietrechtsaenderung?,' *RVB* (April/May 1982): 2–3.
40 *RVB* 43, no. 5 (December/January 1978/79?): 1.
41 See, for example, 'Vor 60 Jahren: Novemberrevolution,' *RVB* 33, no. 4 (December/January 1978/79): 7.
42 'Bilderbogen vom Stahlstreik,' RVB 34, no. 5 (1979): 6.
43 See, for example, Strukturausschuß der Vereinigten Kirchenkreise Dortmund und Lünen, *Brennpunkte in unserer Stadt* (Dortmund: n.d., [1977?]). I am very grateful for the support by the members of the History Workshop of Dortmund-Eving, which holds useful archival material.
44 See, for example, a thematic issue on the Ruhr's workers settlements in *Stadtbauwelt* 46 (27 June 1975).
45 'Keine Zukunft für unsere Vergangenheit?' *RVB* 3 (December–January 1975/76): 5.
46 'Geschichte der Arbeitersiedlungen: "Wie alles angefangen hat mit unseren Siedlungen",' *RVB* 52 (November/December/January 1982/83): 11–14.
47 'Habt ihr was gemerkt davon: 1975 war das Jahr des Denkmalschutzes,' *RVB* 5 (February 1976): 8; Heinrich Klotz, Roland Günter, and Gottfried Kiesow, eds., *Keine Zukunft für unsere Vergangenheit? Denkmalschutz und Stadtzerstörung* (Giessen: Wilhelm Schmitz, 1975).
48 Janne Guenter, *Leben in Eisenheim: Arbeit, Kommunikation und Sozialisation in einer Arbeitersiedlung* (Weinheim/Basel: Beltz, 1980).
49 Berger, Wicke, and Golombek, 'Burdens of Eternity.'
50 'Amsterdamer Hausbesetzungen,' *RVB* 50 (September/October 1982): 10.
51 See, for example, '4 Jahre Floez Dickebank und Umgebung,' *RVB* 29, no. 4 (1978): 2; 'Chronik von Eisenheim,' *RVB* 33, no. 4 (December/January 1978/79): 7; '10 Jahre Eisenheim,' *RVB* (April/May 1982): 3–9.
52 Arbeitsgemeinschaft der Arbeitersiedlungsinitiativen im Ruhrgebiet/Mahnwachen gegen die GSB,' *RVB* 50 (September/October 1982): 6.
53 'Hungerstreik vor einem Jahr,' *RVB* 44 (1980): 3.
54 'Heini Rotthoff ist tot,' *RVB* (September/October 1982): 32.
55 '2nd Anniversary of W.R.A.G.' *NOW* 122 (8 October 1974).
56 Jack Mundey, 'Building Workers and Their Job,' *Sydney Morning Herald*, 1 February 1972.
57 Rommelspacher, 'Wenn wir richtig zusammenhalten…'.
58 Smith, *Uses of Heritage* (London: Routledge, 2006), 24–27.
59 Poster at Noel Butlin Archives Centre [NBAC] – Z235 I.
60 'Hanging on History,' *The Paddington Paper* 2, no. 3 (3 March 1973).

61 See, for example, 'The Rocks in 1901 – Exclusive,' *The Sun*, 11 September 1974.
62 See, for example, http://www.shfa.nsw.gov.au/sydney-About_us-Heritage_role-Heritage_and_Conservation_Register.htm&objectid=80http://www.shfa.nsw.gov.au/sydney-About_us-Heritage_role-Heritage_and_Conservation_Register.htm&objectid=80 [accessed 30 July 2019].
63 For the role of artists in urban change, see, for example, Richard Florida, *The Rise of the Creative Class: and How It's Transforming Work, Leisure, Community, and Everyday Life* (New York: Basic Books, 2002). … and also, for example, David Ley, 'Artists, Aestheticisation and the Field of Gentrification,' *Urban Studies* 40, no. 12 (2003): 2527–2544.
64 'Stand Firm Promise by Artists,' *Sydney Morning Herald*, 2 October 1974.
65 See, for example, letter from John Cambourn, FEDFA Secretary, to John Benson, Secretary of the Seaman's Union, 27 February 1947, NBAC – Z235 I.
66 I am grateful to Paul Ashton for showing me this wonderful place.
67 https://www.cityartsydney.com.au/artwork/green-bans-park-friezes/ [accessed 30 July 2019].
68 https://www.cityartsydney.com.au/wooloomooloo-murals/ [accessed 30 July 2019].
69 https://www.cityofsydney.nsw.gov.au/explore/community-centres/juanita-nielsen-community-centre [accessed 30 July 2019].
70 Natassia Chrysantos, 'Sydney Mystery Revived in the Neighbourhood Juanita Nielsen Disappeared,' *Sydney Morning Herald*, <U>https://www.smh.com.au/entertainment/art-and-design/sydney-mystery-revived-in-the-neighbourhood-juanita-nielsen-disappeared-20181218-p50n1m.html </U>[accessed 30 July 2019]. I am grateful to Zaggy Begg for sending me some of her work.
71 Jack Mundey, The BLF and 'Green Bans', *ABC*, http://education.abc.net.au/home#!/media/521067/?id=521067 [accessed 30 July 2019].
72 Lewis Morley, Portrait of Jack Mundey, at National Portrait Gallery, https://www.portrait.gov.au/portraits/2007.44/jack-mundey [accessed 30 July 2019].
73 National Film and Sound Archive, 'Australian Biography: Jack Mundey,' 2002.
74 James Colman, *The House That Jack Built – Jack Mundey: Green Bans Hero* (Sydney: NewSouth Books, 2016).
75 Meredith and Verity Burgmann, *Green Bans, Red Union: The Saving of a City* (Sydney: NewSouth Books, 2017). I am grateful to Meredith and Verity for their personal support during my research project.
76 The most important archive on the Sydney Green Bans is the Noel Butlin Archives Centre in Canberra and the State Archive of New South Wales on the related local branch of the Communist Party in Australia. In the Ruhr local history workshops hold precious material on the workers initiatives, the Archiv fur alternatives Schrifttum in Duisburg holds a good number of alternative local newspapers that symphathised with the movement, and most importantly the Ruhr-Volksblatt has been digitized (for enquiries, my email is c.wicke@uu.nl).
77 For a comprehensive website on the Green Bans, see http://greenbans.net.au/ [accessed 30 July 2019].
78 See, for example, Community Action for Windsor Bridge, http://www.cawb.com.au/history-of-green-bans.html [accessed 30 July 2018].
79 City of Sydney's Oral History Collection, https://www.sydneyoralhistories.com.au/jack-mundey/ [accessed 30 July 2019].
80 Johanna Lutgenbrune, 'Strukturwandel im Ruhrbergbau – Der Protest gegen den Abriss von Arbeitersiedlungen im Ruhrgebiet am Beispiel der Initiative "Flöz Dickebank" in Gelsenkirchen in den siebziger Jahren,' (Magister Atrium, University of Cologne, 2013).
81 See, for example, Hans-Werner Wehling, 'Wer arbeitet, muss auch wohnen: Werkssiedlungen und Kolonien,' in *Atlas der Metropole Ruhr*, eds. Achim Prossek et al. (Cologne: Emons, 2009), 52–55; Karl-Heinz Cox and Christa Reicher, 'Wohnkultur und Siedlungsstruktur gestalten: soziale und baukulturelle Aufgaben,' in

Raumstrategien Ruhr 2035+: Konzepte zur Entwicklung der Agglomeration Ruhr, eds. Jan Polivka, Christa Reicher, and Christoph Zöpel (Dortmund: Kettler, 2017), 59–90. I am grateful to Hans-Werner Wehling for the support and correspondence.
82 Route der Industriekultur, http://www.route-industriekultur.ruhr/themenrouten/19-arbeitersiedlungen/bergarbeiter-wohnmuseum.html?L=0 [accessed 30 July 2019].
83 Berger, Wicke, Golombek, 'Burdens of Eternity: Heritage, Identity and the "Great Transition" in the Ruhr.'
84 'RevierGestalten – Von Orten und Menschen' exhibition, LWL-Industriemuseum Zeche Zollern in Dortmund, 24 February-28 October 2018, see Jana Flieshart and Jana Golombek, eds., *RevierGestalten: Von Orten und Menschen – Ausstellungskatalog* (Essen: Klartext Verlag, 2018).
85 Recht auf die Auguststraße (1981), Gegen Spekulanten (1976) and Flöz Dickebank: Wir sind mittlerweile wachgeworden (1975).
86 Berger, Wicke, Golombek 'Burdens of Eternity: Heritage, Identity and the "Great Transition" in the Ruhr.'
87 For the website, see https://industriemuseum.lvr.de/de/die_museen/st__antony/museum_eisenheim_1/museum_eisenheim_2.html [accessed 30 July 2019].
88 Per Schnell and Werner Kubny, *Helden von Eisenheim* (Cologne: Westdeutscher Rundfunk, 2005).
89 Burgmann and Burgmann, *Green Bans, Red Union: The Saving of a City,* 49–51.
90 Kelsey Munro, 'Sydney More Expensive to Live in Than London and New York, Study Finds,' *The Guardian*, 15 March 2018, https://www.theguardian.com/australia-news/2018/mar/15/sydney-more-expensive-to-live-in-than-london-and-new-york-study-finds [accessed 30 July 2019].
91 Louis Nowra, 'Jack Mundey Still Fighting Sydney's Development in Sydney's Rocks,' *The Australian* (14 October 2016), https://www.theaustralian.com.au/arts/review/jack-mundey-still-fighting-development-in-sydneys-rocks/news-story/15807fa8c66ea9ecf8b514524a1a506e [accessed 30 July 2019].
92 Tony Bosworth, 'Windsor Bridge Battle Begins,' *Hawkesbury Gazette*, 6 June 2012, https://www.hawkesburygazette.com.au/story/273991/windsor-bridge-battle-begins/
93 Jon Piccini, 'Bondi Pavilion "Green Ban": Why Revive an Old Union Heritage Protection Tactic?' (1 June 2016), http://theconversation.com/bondi-pavilion-green-ban-why-revive-an-old-union-heritage-protection-tactic-60200 [accessed 30 July 2019].
94 For the website of Frank Baier, see <U>http://www.frank-baier.de </U>[accessed 30 July 2019], I am grateful for the conversation we had at his home in 2015, the ongoing correspondences and the material Frank has provided me for this project.
95 Roland Guenter, *Stadtmassaker und Sozialverbrechen: Studie zur Kommunalpolitik am Fallbei(l)spiel Stadtzerstoerung und Stadtentwicklung in Duisburg* (Essen: Klartext, 2013).
96 http://gegenteilgrau.de/2017/03/29/lange-auf-einen-solchen-film-gewartet/ [accessed 30 July 2019].

9

MEMORY AS A STRATEGY? – DEALING WITH THE PAST IN POLITICAL PROCEEDINGS AGAINST COMMUNISTS IN 1950/60S WEST GERMANY

Sarah Langwald

After World War II, in the beginning of the 1950s, the division of Germany was further solidified. In 1949, the Western allies had established a parliamentary democracy in West Germany, the Federal Republic of Germany (FRG), while in the Eastern zone the German Democratic Republic (GDR), a communist state, was founded under Soviet dominion. From the start, in the FRG the situation for the West German Communist Party (KPD) was not simple, because of the hostility between the two states, and the KPD's own role during Cold War 'as the western face of the East German SED.'[1] While the threat posed by communism (and thus also by the KPD) was rated as high in the FRG, the communists on each side of the Iron Curtain felt endangered by an alleged 'refascistization' of the West German state and society.[2] Because many former NS civil servants and jurists were back in the civil service as well as judges and prosecutors were back in the courts. This issue was also part of broad propaganda campaigns by the KPD (and by the Socialist Unity Party (SED)), which aimed at elucidating West German society, at delegitimizing the FRG, at showing the GDR as the better German state, and at trying to win the masses for the idea of a revolution against the West German government.[3]

In this context, the government of the FRG feared that communism would spread from the Eastern bloc.[4] Because the government wanted to defend itself and the state institutions of the FRG against this alleged danger, in 1951, it introduced the 1. Strafrechtsänderungsgesetz (a law for the protection of the democratic state) to the penal code. In addition to the reintroduced articles on high treason and national treason, which the allies had removed from the penal code after World War II, the new law also included 'a package'[5] of new elements of an offense, such as endangering the state (which 'was defined as the attempt to bring the state "under foreign dominion"').[6] In fact, these elements of an offense were valid for everybody but they were mainly used for the prosecution of (assumed) communists. Between 1951 and 1968, approximately 125,000 preliminary proceedings were mainly initiated against them. Because of the fear of communist subversion, in the FRG political justice 'had become a weapon against the extreme left.'[7] In this context, it seems to be no coincidence that the proposal for banning the KPD fell into the same year as the adoption of the 1. Strafrechtsänderungsgesetz. Even if only between 6,000 and 7,000 people were convicted by reason of this law, critics saw it as a loss of proportionality in political justice.[8] Besides communists, unionists, opponents of the West German rearmament or Western integration, and anti-fascists were suspected of belonging to the communist movement and thus being enemies of the state. In this way, the anti-fascist memory in general and the memory of many communists in particular were also suppressed and played no role in memory culture of the FRG for a long time.

While the subject of political justice against communists has long been neglected in German historiography, that has changed since the last two decades.[9] Interestingly, one of the first recent studies which also deals, among others, with this subject was published in the UK.[10] The studies that have been published on this topic in Germany during the last few years have mainly concentrated on state or justice authorities.[11] Research on activists and lawyers is extremely rare in this context.[12] Memory studies largely played no role in these works.[13] This article is intended to be a first step in helping to close this research gap.

Thereby, my thesis is that different groups of activists used the memories of the communist movement as a strategy in the court proceedings, and later in reports and articles on such trials while pursuing different interests. While communist activists used memory as an argument not only to fight the anti-communist judiciary, but the state in general, later the defenders, who were also organized as activists in alliances, tried to act against the political judiciary by cooperating with the state. Thereby, they did not longer use the memories of communists as a part of their strategy to confront judges but shifted their discussions of the Nazi past (of communist persecutees and former NS judges and prosecutors) to press publications in order to reach a larger public. Because this happened in the context of the Cold War, it should be shown that the attempts to delegitimize the rival German state also played a role for the communist activists until the defenders (who were also organized as activists) tried to mediate between the different positions of the communist movement and justice. Perhaps these groups – both the communist activists and the activist alliances of defenders – could be defined as a part of an early social movement, because they were collective stakeholders of 'contentious politics' (Charles Tilly and Sidney Tarrow), too. Even if the term 'social movements' has mainly been used since the 1960s, these protagonists acted in a similar way, for example, when they framed their memory-political arguments against state decisions and court decisions in trials, at meetings, and in interviews in order to reach a wider public.[14] As an interesting point, it should be mentioned here that some of the non-communist activists themselves were employed in the civil service. The typical front line between state actors, on the one hand, and activists, on the other hand, which is used in most research on social movements, cannot be maintained here.

The following chapter focuses on three groups which all tried to use memory as a strategy in cases launched against (alleged) communists respectively in their reports on these trials and political justice. It shows how the players and arenas changed over time: from communist activists using the court room as their political arena for their strategy to use memory as an argument to fight their enemies (the judges and prosecutors as well as the state in general), to the defenders who tried to take the arguments of their communist clients seriously but also tried to cooperate with their colleagues on the other side of the dock. And who acted as activists (not in their role as defenders), especially in other arenas, outside the court.[15] Thereby, selected legal proceedings against communists (such as one of the first high treason trials in 1954, and the KPD banning trial) as well as conference reports and articles by activists about such legal proceedings and political justice in general are taken as a basis. First, the chapter will examine how communist activists and the defendants themselves reacted to the circumstance of a possible confrontation with the judges and prosecutors who had maybe also been responsible for the jurisdiction during the NS years. Second, it will investigate the role of the judges and prosecutors who usually used the argument of subversion in trials by accusing the defendants of being directed by the GDR up front and urged the defendants to prevent any kind of (memory-)political argumentation in the trials. Third, it will analyze how the defense lawyers of (alleged) communists tried to mediate between these different positions primarily in order to reform political justice – but the chapter will also show how they tried helping communist memory to find a place in prevailing remembrance for an alternative narrative in a pragmatic way and how media supported this development.

Communist activists and defendants and the politicization of trials

In September 1951, one month after the 1. Strafrechtsänderungsgesetz was introduced in the FRG, the *Zentralrat zum Schutze demokratischer Rechte* (Central Council for the Protection of Democratic Rights) was founded in Stuttgart. Until the mid-1950s, the *Zentralrat* was *the* organization which (assumed) communists addressed when they needed help. It organized financial and legal assistance for the affected persons and coordinated alliances, which were engaged in similar tasks at a local or regional level. For the trials in court, the *Zentralrat* provided lawyers for the defendants who were usually communists. In the first line, non-communist persons represented the organization to create the impression of political independence. But in fact, the *Zentralrat* was dominated by communists and did not act independently.[16] Through the West Commission, which was part of the National Front, an alliance of political parties and mass organizations in the GDR, the *Zentralrat* was funded by the East German Socialist Unity Party (SED). The SED coordinated its engagement and propaganda campaigns in West

Germany via these organizations.[17] The *Zentralrat* also received its instructions from the GDR and forwarded them to the defendants and their defenders by providing them with guidelines. These guidelines included a 'political argumentation in court' and suggested an 'aggressive defensive strategy' to them. Through these guidelines they tried to organize collective action against justice in the FRG.

Alice Stertzenbach was responsible for the coordination and organization of legal assistance in these cases and for preparing and sending the 'aggressive defensive strategy' to the defense lawyers and the defendants. This strategy was developed by the members of the *Zentralrat* to politicize the trials. In this way, courts should become a place of political struggle. By using this kind of 'political argumentation,' it was not only the aim to criticize the anti-communist jurisdiction of the West German courts but also to make clear that a large number of former NS civil servants were working in similar positions as in the NS years again. The defendants often followed these guidelines because they feared a revival of fascism.[18] But at the same time, they also adhered to the party's requirements and agitated for the GDR which was the better German state for them, where any form of fascism was overcome. The revival of fascism in the FRG that was expected by the communists should therefore be mentioned in every context that argued with daily politics of the West German government to discredit the state in general.[19]

But apart from these attacks by the communists on daily politics, with reference to NS continuities such concerns were not unreasonable on the left, they were also shared by leading SPD members. 'The fear that Western integration came at the price of clear memory of and timely justice for Nazi crimes contributed to an enduring fissure between right and left in West German politics.'[20] Crimes of the Nazis were less and less persecuted. Instead, 'anti-communism began to assume priority over denazification.'[21] After the West German authorities – in line with the Western allies – had searched for political reliable administrative and judiciary staff in order to consolidate the state in the immediate post-war period, that changed since 1949/50. In the early post-war years, in the FRG often conservative civil servants who had been either politically active against the NS system or at least had not been politically active in the Nazi party, took up leading positions in administration and justice. But that changed since the beginning of the 1950s, when former NS personnel received responsible positions in the state institutions. Covered by law and government-issued amnesties,[22] they were primarily integrated to fight communism, and not because they seemed to be particularly reliable.[23] Extensive research has already shown that between 1933 and the 1960s there were hardly any breaks in the careers of these political and judicial functionary elites.[24]

But there were also exceptions that had been instated in civil service or justice during this period and remained active there. Such as the Jewish prosecutor Fritz Bauer who had been detained in a concentration camp as a member of the Social Democratic Party (SPD) and of the *Reichsbanner Schwarz-Rot-Gold*, a defense league for the protection of democracy in the Weimar Republic, himself in 1933 and who could no longer work in his profession after his release. Finally, he went into Swedish and Danish exile to save his life. When he came back to Germany in 1949, he became attorney general in Brunswick a year later.[25] In 1952, one of his first lawsuits there he conducted against a former major general of the Wehrmacht, now leading member of a right-wing extremist party, who had vilified members of the military resistance against Hitler as traitors. This classification of resistance was no exception at that time, especially in the judiciary. When Bauer decided to focus solely on military resistance in trial, the reason was that the West German government had started to honor it.[26] As he has written in an essay in this context in 1955, he was concerned with 'the memory of all men and woman who had died for the preservation of human rights.'[27] But Bauer, who had been considered an 'integration figure'[28] for social democrats and communists during his exile, also had to be careful when trying to gradually recognize the resistance by judiciary. So in the trial against the general major in 1952, Bauer asked a joint plaintiff and member of the so called 'Red Orchestra,' which was a name for various resistance groups against the Nazi regime that had been defamed as a communist espionage group since the NS years, to withdraw their criminal complaint against the accused. If he had included their resistance in the court proceedings, he would also have made West German anti-communism the subject of the trial.[29] For a long time, in the FRG, the broad public classified the resistance against the NS regime as a hostile act to the state. In the context of the Cold War, particularly communist resistance was excluded from public memory because it was assumed that in the past, former communist resistance fighters only wanted to replace the NS system by the communist one. For them and for communist victims of the NS regime, this also meant that they were legally exempted from restitution (Wiedergutmachung) and did not get compensation payments.[30]

Contrary to most of the people who had leading positions in justice, among those defendants and activists who helped communists in proceedings such personal experiences like Bauer's were not uncommon. This had also been an impulse for Alice Stertzenbach's commitment to the *Zentralrat*. The activist was born in Dortmund in 1909 as Alice David. As a young student she was persecuted by the Nazis because she was Jewish and a member of the KPD since 1930. She could not finish her academic studies because she was arrested in 1933. After her release, she went into exile in the Netherlands. When the war was over, she returned to Germany and married the communist journalist Werner Stertzenbach. First, she worked for the KPD, then at the party's disposition she founded the *Zentralrat* with Karl Hartmann, another KPD member.[31] With the help of the 'political argumentation' of this organization, the defendants and defenders should also point out their personal experiences from the Nazi period in court and they should also refer to the existing continuities in justice and government. The members of the *Zentralrat* as well as the defendants not only wanted to gain individual benefits in the context of the upcoming convictions in this way. It was also their goal to show the continued and hardened structures in justice and to clarify their anxieties for authoritarian ruling, which they feared due to the many reinstated former NS civil servants in justice and government. Therefore, an important point in their confrontation strategy was to show that justice made common cause with the government:

> Behind the prosecution due to subversion and high treason, that's where the goals of the government are hidden, which are opposed to any form of peace. This is also the reason for the prosecutions and reprimands.[32]

In their eyes, justice and government wanted to prepare war again. Specifically, that means that the *Zentralrat* wanted to criticize the anti-communist jurisdiction of the West German courts and to brand it as a 'persecution of the freedom of opinion.' Even the trials in the FRG should be compared with the ones in the Nazi past where many opponents were persecuted as 'public enemies' and the fundamental rights were suspended.[33]

> We have to raise our voices against the so-called 'blitz law' [= the 1. Strafrechtsänderungsgesetz, S.L.]. The law seems to have created a legal basis for all undemocratic measures by the state institutions. [...] History has taught us that free democratic rights are always broken where violence and war are prepared.[34]

On the one hand, this was propaganda, because the guidelines of the *Zentralrat* were similar in their objectives to the programmatic orientation of the KPD: accordingly, the party wanted to overcome the 'bourgeois state' and the 'burgeoning militarism' in the FRG in order to create a 'real' democracy there.[35] When they referred to the lessons learnt from history, this was connected with criticizing the West German state, which the party argued was in line with the National Socialist state – in contrast to the anti-fascist GDR. On the other hand this repeatedly made clear the enormous insecurity and fear of the defendants and their allies. In the addition to the effort to discredit the West German state, it must be pointed out that the equation of the NS system and the FRG was also shaped by the biographical experiences of many communist defendants.[36]

Even if they were supposed to use the 'aggressive defensive strategy' in court, the defenders who cooperated with the *Zentralrat* hardly followed this invitation. The guidelines were not necessarily followed by their addressees (that means that the defenders often refrained from this method). But the communist defendants whose cases were conducted before court in 1954 did so – as accused persons and in their additional role as functionaries of the KPD. Using this strategy in trial was no exception: in the proceedings against the functionaries Horst Reichel and Herbert Beyer in May 1954, and also in the trial against the chairman of the Free German Youth (FDJ), Josef Angenfort, and his comrade Wolfgang Seiffert in June 1955, the activists and defendants tried to use political arguments in court and compared their situation in the presence with the persecution under the NS regime.[37]

In the trial against Neumann and his comrades in 1954, the accused persons put their anti-fascist commitment at the center of their argumentation and also referred to the repressive measures which were done to them and their families during the NS years – especially the arrests by the Gestapo, their time in concentration camps, or in exile. It was one of the first trials due to high treason which took place in the Federal Court of Justice of the FRG (the Bundesgerichtshof, BGH). The defendants were leading members of an organization which had fought against the remilitarization of the West German forces. But the accused persons were also communist functionaries and because of this their organization had been suspected of being a secret section of the KPD, and of getting financial support from the GDR. As we know today that was not wrong. But back then, there was insufficient evidence to convict them for these reasons. None of the defendants were sentenced for high treason but for other reasons. They were convicted among others for having formed a criminal organization and for having committed national treason. They were supposed to go to prison for three years but fled to the GDR and did not accept their sentences.[38]

In the trial, they had described in detail how they had established contact with communists during World War II or already in the time before. Oskar Neumann, for example, came into contact with communists in the resistance and also later as a prisoner of a concentration camp. In court, he declared his motivation for becoming a KPD member himself.

> We did not ask for the ideology or the alignment with the party. […, S.L.] We risked our heads because we had made the experience that the communists had recognized the danger of fascism for us and our people most clearly.[39]

Even if emphasizing their anti-fascist activities was central in their argumentation in the court proceedings, that was also based on individual experiences they had made in their pasts. They did not only use it as a kind of self-victimization, as it is often shown for simplification.[40] It should be considered that approximately half of the 350,000 members of the KPD in 1932 'did not return to the party's ranks after 1945, either because they were dead or had been permanently depoliticized by Nazi persecution.'[41] Because many of these members had indeed been confronted with NS justice, they revealed how often judges and prosecutors who were responsible in their cases now had also been the offenders during the NS years. The communist defendants, however, took this chance to offend these jurists. In this way, the defendant Neumann in 1954 pointed out, 'that 80 to 90 percent of the West German judges had been fascists.'[42] For him they seemed to be prejudiced. In general, this information about the German judiciary was exaggerated. But these numbers were not pure propaganda, they exceeded the correct figures by around 10% relating to the BGH,[43] which was the central judicial instance in political proceedings against communists.[44] After all, many of the communist defendants had been in opposition to the

NS regime. For the defendants, their accusation by the prosecutors seemed mainly been based by political purposes by the state. They assumed that the state wanted to fight communism and anti-fascism at the same time and saw themselves and the West German state in danger.[45] At the same time, they were able to use such figures in the context of the KPD's campaigns, which were supported by the *Zentralrat*.[46]

First, it was their personal interest to substantiate their own threats of persecution in court: as victims of the Nazi regime they referred to the continuities in justice by taking their own cases as an example. Second, they wished to generate public interest for their proceedings and to elucidate the West German society in this way. For the judges and prosecutors this was not only a threat for the stability of the young FRG but also a danger for themselves, because the defendants used this opportunity to describe their personal experiences during the NS period in court. By reference of their own biography and the biographies of possibly involved judges and prosecutors, their strategy was also to draw parallels and to show continuities between justice in the NS years and in the present time. In doing so, the communist defendants Neumann and comrades accused justice of implementing repressive measures as under the Nazi regime. They charged the courts of preparing war again and of making common cause with the government in this case. That also agreed with the guidelines of the *Zentralrat*. By trying to show continuities between the FRG and the NS state they orientated themselves to the fascism theory which was central in the GDR and in its campaigns against West Germany. According to this theory, the legacy of National Socialism lay solely in the FRG. In following an anti-fascist narrative, the GDR saw itself freed from this heritage.[47] Thereby, it helped that the FRG considered itself as a successor state of the German Reich (including the NS years).[48]

For the defendants (who became also accusers in this way), an indication for their assumption was the rearmament of the West German forces. They did not just follow a strategy; from their perspective, many opponents of this development were silenced by being put into prison. Meanwhile, the East German SED wanted to transfer the disputes to the courts in West Germany. To a large extent, the politicization of the trials had been motivated by such communist orientated organizations, such as the *Zentralrat*. But even some non-communists used a similar argumentation because some of their main arguments seemed to reflect parts of the truth in their minds.[49] Ernst Müller-Meiningen jr., a journalist from Munich who published his articles in the *Süddeutsche Zeitung*, a popular left-liberal newspaper, reported regularly about these proceedings and other trials against (alleged) communists and in a similar way the accused persons did. He designated such proceedings as a 'witch hunt' and he also remarked that the

> Federal's Prosecutor's office and BGH effectuated that practically every German court agreed to be bound by the determination that everybody who was linked to the KPD or SED, whether in a political, personal or financial relation was classified as a high traitor.[50]

It is probable that it was also one of the interests of the defendants to generate a broader public for their proceedings by using their politicization to create a memory-political area for their own experiences. The trials could be a first step for them to construct their memorization as an alternative to the hegemonic one. By the articles of those court reporters it not only seemed to be possible to inform the public about their pasts but also to help finding an own place for remembrance because the (alleged) communists were more or less isolated with their commemoration.[51] Another strategy of the *Zentralrat* was to influence such trials not only in the court room but also from the outside: solidarity letters, protesting letters, and petitions were sent to the judges, the prosecutors, and to politicians. In these documents, comparisons were made between NS justice and the current justice, too. A woman, who was on trial for a testimony in the proceedings against Neumann and comrades complained to Friedrich Wilhelm Geier, the president of the criminal division of the BGH that she had been insulted as a 'gunwoman' in the rooms of the court house, and that she should be 'transported to Siberia' with the help of the court. Thereby she felt reminded of the 'Third Reich.' As a result, she stressed that this was not honorable for the court and wished for a better future in which she could trust justice again, 'unlike under the Hitlerite injustice regime.'[52] The fact that such anti-communist statements against this woman not only refer to an anti-Soviet enemy image, but could also be made in the court rooms without consequences, raised doubts as to whether the West German constitutional state also existed for communists and their allies. The fact that the woman expressed her fears that an unjust regime could arise in the Federal Republic, such as under the Nazi regime, can be read as a request to the court to intervene in similar cases in future. Unlike this writing, other letters which already characterized the FRG an unjust state, were sent from the GDR.[53] Therefore, the judges and prosecutors suspected that the trials should be exploited from there.[54] Today we know, that this largely corresponded to reality, at least as far as the activists and the accused were concerned. However, the defense lawyers mostly did not follow the KPD(SED)-influenced guidelines of the *Zentralrat*.[55]

Judges and prosecutors and the juridification of trials

On these grounds, the judges and prosecutors used the argument of subversion in trials by accusing the defendants of being directed by the GDR. They often used this argument upfront, before the beginning of the trial. It was already part of the indictment, even though it could hardly be proven. In the court proceedings, the judges and prosecutors urged the defendants not to use the 'political argumentation' (according to the guidelines of the *Zentralrat*) in the trials. For example, in the trial in 1954, the judge called on the accused persons to discuss their cases with less passion, but they hardly followed this invitation.[56] Because the defendants often took this chance for using the 'aggressive defensive strategy' to offend the judges and prosecutors and to draw parallels with the NS system, it was easy for them to forbid these accusations as 'political demonstrations.' The trials were not considered to be political by the judges and prosecutors. Therefore, the judges tried to prevent political argumentations. They knew that the accused persons used this kind of argument not only to defend themselves but also to exploit the courtroom as an advertising platform for GDR propaganda. Because thereby, the defendants tried not only to delegitimize the politics of the government of the FRG in general, but also the entire West German judiciary, the judges saw the 'political argumentation' as a danger to the rule of law. But besides propaganda, this kind of argumentation by the defendants was also linked with their wish for clarification relating to the pasts of their accusers. By preventing this confrontation, the judges and prosecutors tried to divert from their own pasts. There was a competition between the GDR and the FRG over which state would be 'the better Germany.' Because thereby, the memory of Nazism was central, the West German judges and prosecutors also used the juridification of the trials in the presence for equating the political justice in the GDR with NS justice. In this way they tried to keep the political arguments of the defendants out of the trials. They just wanted to deal with the law.[57] But in this way, it was also possible for them to fend off the Nazi period as a subject in the court proceedings. They also tried to keep their memories and their potential involvement to the NS system a secret.

In 1954, for example, the proceedings against Neumann and his comrades were led by judge Geier, the president of the first BGH criminal division. Geier himself worked as a judge for the Wehrmacht (name of the German armed forces from 1935 to 1945) during the NS years.[58] The Federal Public Prosecutor Walter Wagner and, for example, one of the other judges of the criminal division, Paulheinz Baldus, had been active in justice during the NS years, too. Wagner had been a senior prosecutor for the Attorney General in Poznan (in NS occupied Poland),[59] Baldus had been, among others, a staff member in the department for penal law in the Reich Ministry of Justice (Reichsjustizministerium).[60] Finally, he had worked in the 'Führer Chancellery.'[61] While, on the one hand, former NS jurists could be judges and prosecutors in political justice in the FRG, on the other hand, many communists who had been persecuted by the Nazis in political cases, were brought to court, again. This was communicated at least by communists (in the proceedings or via publications), even if the defense lawyers refused to tolerate such allegations.[62]

Nevertheless, in Neumann's case, he and his comrades attacked the judges and prosecutors on this assumption and challenged their impartiality. In their bias petitions the accused tried to refuse all judges at once because they supposed that 80% to 90% of the West German judges had been fascists, as Neumann also stated at another point of the proceedings. In this context, it was not difficult for the court members to reject the bias petition on the grounds of its political motivation.

> The explanations, with which the petition was substantiated in detail, are not intended to refuse a particular judge who is possibly objectionable because of his impartiality for some reasons. But this is necessary for a

legitimate and serious refusal. On the contrary, they aim to denounce the impartiality of all courts of the Federal Republic of Germany to decide on the present indictment.[63]

The judges and prosecutors have found themselves being put under general suspicion in this way. The defenders knew that these accusations of the defendants did apply to many but not to all judges and prosecutors and often withheld such allegations.[64] It should be pointed out, however, that the court members were a group of stakeholders who were led by their common interest. In their minds, that meant both to fight the enemies of the young state and to protect themselves for dealing with their pasts. However, this did not mean that they ignored the experiences the accused ones had gained in the past. For example, at the beginning of the proceedings, Neumann was able to describe in detail his entire life in court. Thereby, he paid special attention to the experiences he had made in the NS years. The judge let him make his statements. But he often asked him to be more objective and to adhere to the legal requirements, especially when Neumann tried to express his individual opinion in court, for example, about the Wehrmacht. The accused was able to provide statements on this because himself had been conscripted for less than one year. During this time, however, his opposition to the NS regime would have been developed, as he said. In doing so, he wanted to counter possible insinuations by court from the start.[65] Because, as in the GDR, younger West German KPD officials often had been trained in antifa schools during their time as POWs in the Soviet Union, which they had invaded as soldiers of the Wehrmacht during the war. After their return to West Germany, they had held leading positions in the party.[66] That would have been a good point of attack in trial. Therefore, Neumann pointed out that things had worked differently for him than for other West German KPD officials who joined the party after the war, as he did.

Instead of being attacked, the accused persons always tried to attack the court from the beginning of the trials. Thereby bias petitions were a regular means of their defense and became a tactical tool in this way, also to accuse judges and prosecutors by reason of their Nazi past. In the proceedings for the ban of the KPD before the Federal Constitutional Court (Bundesverfassungsgericht) several bias petitions against the judges were also submitted.[67] In order to substantiate his bias, the details of the respective judge's past were discussed in court. Although Josef Wintrich, for example, the president of the responsible criminal division of the Constitutional Court, was transferred for disciplinary reasons by the Nazis, his impartiality was doubted by the East German lawyer Friedrich Karl Kaul who defended the KPD.[68] In contrast to the defense lawyers in the proceedings against Neumann and his comrades, Kaul went into detail on the judge's personal background, which brought him to his conclusion that he was biased.[69] Kaul didn't care that his allegations against this judge were possibly wrong. According to the East German fascism theory the West German justice was generally to be charged. According to this theory the legacy of National

Socialism lay solely in the FRG. In this way, the KPD as the sister party of the East German SED projected the Nazi past on West Germany.[70] On these grounds he also challenged the impartiality of the president of the senate in the banning trial. But this bias petition, in which Kaul also compared West German anti-communism with that of the Nazi years, was rejected.[71] In his eagerness to accuse West German jurists as fascists, he had obviously not dealt more closely with the fact that the members of the responsible criminal senate of the Federal Constitutional Court were predominantly 'exonerated persons' – in contrast to the BGH.[72] But although Kaul overstepped the mark in Wintrich's case, it must be noted that, in contrast to Wintrich, the Jewish lawyer Kaul had to flee from Germany and spent the NS years in exile.[73] Especially in the first years after the war, persecutees of the Nazi regime had deliberately decided to go to East Germany, which officially made anti-fascism its basis and took action against Nazi criminals on a large scale.[74] However, this changed over time and the current loyalty of former Nazi officials and Wehrmacht officers for the Soviet Union and their engagement for anti-fascism became decisive in order to be employed in the civil service in the GDR. The commitment for a future socialist society became more important.[75] But soon investigations against these persons began again due to a possible burden from the Nazi past. For the FRG, there should be no chance to attack East Germany, now that the GDR intensified its campaigns against the West German 'class enemy.'[76]

Campaigns against West German justice

Since the mid-1950s, there were often attacks from the outside of the court, by the KPD and from the GDR. In different campaigns evidences were collected which should help to show that the accusations of the defendants against the West German judges and prosecutors were true and that many of them were former Nazis. In addition, the West German constitutional state should be denounced in this way. For example, the KPD published a bulletin on the court proceedings during the banning trial before the Federal Constitutional Court. In the FRG, the KPD (as well as other KPD-orientated organizations such as the *Zentralrat*) published such lawsuit-related information with the support of the East German SED. On the one hand, the communists followed the party's requirement with these campaigns. On the other hand, they also tried to elucidate the public about the West German continuities with the Nazi past and to generate greater attention for their own memories as victims and persecutees of the NS regime. In addition to articles on the 'refascistization' of the FRG, the KPD's bulletin on the party's banning trial also included comparisons between 'persecuted communists' and 'war criminals.'[77] Among other things, the past of Hans Ritter von Lex, the government's chief counsel in the KPD banning trial, was thematized.[78] But unlike the KPD's lawyers accusations against judge Wintrich, in von Lex's case it was true that he had worked in the Reich Ministry of Interior (Reichsinnenministerium) during the NS years.[79]

After it had become even more difficult for communists to publish their propaganda in West Germany after the KPD ban in 1956, the GDR increasingly sent brochures to the FRG. As part of East German campaigns against justice in the FRG, 'Hitler's hanging judges' were named in some of these books and brochures.[80] In 1957, three brochures were published in the context of this campaign which listed in total the names of 362 individuals and named their positions in the NS regime. In 1965, a 'Braunbuch' was released which listed 1,900 names of former NS staff in West German politics, economics, and justice. In 1967, the second edition was published which even scandalized the past of President Heinrich Lübke as a 'concentration camp builder.' As an engineer, he was involved in the construction of different projects which were of military importance for the Nazis but until today it is controversial if he was also responsible for the construction of a concentration camp.[81] The last edition of the 'Braunbuch' was released in 1968 and included the names of 1,400 offenders' profiles, among them were the names of 828 high officials from justice. In the FRG, these brochures and books were dismissed as propaganda from the GDR, which was true. Nevertheless, an intention to elucidate West German public via providing this information can also be assumed here. At least, SED politician Albert Norden, son of a rabbi who was murdered by the Nazis, who was responsible for agitation and led these campaigns, was about showing that a state (like the FRG) in which former Nazi judges and prosecutors could make a career should not describe itself as a constitutional state.[82] In this way, the pressure on West German politics increased to engage in some of these cases because West German media reported on this topic.[83] Today, it is also known that the error rate in the last of these campaigns was less than 1%.[84] In the FRG, these campaigns had consequences: high judges resigned or were retired, like Federal Prosecutor General Wolfgang Immerwahr Fränkel in 1962.[85] However, there were hardly any trials against former NS jurists and when it came to that, they mostly ended up with acquittals.[86] That means, when the information of the unsightly pasts of the judges and prosecutors became part of the public or even led to proceedings against them, they could still claim to have obeyed valid law during the NS period and thereby they followed the dominant narrative in the FRG. In this 'structural dilemma,' in which the judicial institutions and the people working in them were confronted with the Nazi past, they could always invoke on 'superior orders' (Befehlsnotstand) they had followed.[87]

Even though the GDR, the KPD (and other KPD-orientated organizations) mainly used such campaigns to legitimize their kind of anti-fascism and to delegitimize the FRG, the campaigns had an effect on elucidating the West German public about the NS years. Non-communist West German jurists also dealt with these campaigns and their results. On the sidelines of a conference of the *Initiativausschuss*, its members discussed the personal continuities of former NS jurists in the FRG and talked about Fränkel's dismissal. In doing so, they appreciated that the West German press treated these issues critically – 'according to our perspective.'[88]

The defenders as mediators?

A group of defenders which existed since November 1955 and grew until the beginning of the 1960s was the *Initiativausschuss für die Amnestie und der Verteidiger in politischen Strafsachen* (Committee for an Amnesty – Defenders in Cases of Political Justice). It was founded in Frankfurt on the Main by prominent lawyers and scholars but also politicians from the SPD and the liberal party were involved. Among them, there were even a few lawyers who had worked together with the KPD orientated *Zentralrat* before. But often these lawyers had not followed the *Zentralrat's* guidelines of a 'political argumentation' in court back then. At that time, the defenders had already argued as they thought it was right, because they seemed to see the guidelines as an 'annoying tutelage.'[89] The leading members of the *Zentralrat* were annoyed of their behavior but they were dependent on these lawyers because they needed their professional assistance.[90] And the defenders also stayed professional in the court proceedings. 'The tactics of the defenders stayed within the conditions of the conventional practice of political justice.'[91] In court, personal attacks against judges and prosecutors were a taboo for the most of them. The defenders hardly made any use of the 'political argumentation' in court, especially not the members of the *Initiativausschuss*. That was probably not only due to the fact that they basically rejected any kind of influence from the outside: judges and prosecutors did not allow such attempts anyway.[92] Nevertheless, the members of the *Initiativausschuss* were in contact with the KPD (thus also the SED) and their organizations (such as the *Zentralrat*), because they provided the members of the *Initiativausschuss* with information about the proceedings against communists and legal developments in the FRG in general. However, the defense lawyers refused to allow their work to be influenced by these parties and organizations. In 1961, for example, they received a documentation on the West German 'unjust state' from them. But from the start, the defenders insisted 'that they have complete freedom to make changes to the draft version.'[93] The *Initiativausschuss* was not controlled externally, neither in its actions outside the court room nor in the context of political defense before the court.[94]

But even if the lawyers of the *Initiativausschuss* did not use the guidelines of the *Zentralrat* and thus they also did not use memory as a strategic instrument against West German judiciary in general, they let their clients refer about their personal biographies in the past during the trials. In March 1960, a journalist was sentenced to five months imprisonment for writing an insulting article; the sentence was suspended on probation. In the court decision the defendant's past was included. During the NS years, he had been a student at the University of Cologne. But in 1933 he had to leave Germany because he was Jewish and a communist. He went into exile to the Netherlands where he went into hiding in 1942. His parents died in the Bergen-Belsen concentration camp and other relatives had been murdered in Auschwitz.[95] It was important for the defense lawyers that their clients reported such awful occasions from their pasts to make the court understand the actions of their clients.[96] In this way it was possible to show why the defendants acted like they acted and to oppose the juridification of the court proceedings. Furthermore, it also seems to be possible that telling these experiences was impossible for the defenders and members of the *Initiativausschuss* themselves, too, because several among them had been in exile or in the resistance or were among the persecuted persons during the NS period.

Members of the *Initiativausschuss* were, for example, Wolfgang Abendroth who was a political scientist, socialist jurist, and an expert in constitutional law and Walther Ammann who defended many (assumed) communists as a lawyer. Abendroth was organized in several resistance groups during the NS years, like the communist opposition (KPO) and the group *Neu Beginnen*, a Marxist organization which fought National Socialism. In 1937, he was arrested by the Gestapo and was imprisoned in penitentiary for four years where he even was tortured. In 1943, he was conscripted for the penal military unit 999 (Strafdivision 999). In this division were many anti-fascists who also fought against the NS system during the time they had been forcibly conscripted to the Wehrmacht. In 1944, when they were in Greece, Abendroth deserted to the Greek resistance group ELAS.[97] Ammann who was one of the central stakeholders in the *Initiativausschuss* had been in the Catholic resistance during the Nazi years.[98] Because of similar experiences they were able to understand the memories of their clients better as persons who did not share those.

For these reasons it seemed also to be important for the defenders that these memories should not be forgotten. In addition to Ammann, another central person in the *Initiativausschuss* was the lawyer Diether Posser (All-German People's Party (Gesamtdeutsche Volkspartei, GVP), later SPD). Posser was a colleague and friend of Gustav Heinemann (GVP, later SPD), which whom he had a law office. He defended many (alleged) communists in West German courts.[99] Unlike Abendroth or Ammann, Posser was not in the resistance during World War II but on the fronts. Nevertheless, since his childhood he was a member of the *Bekennende Kirche* (Confessing Church). Therefore, he was not affected heavily by the NS ideology. This can also be seen in his critical engagement with the NS years.[100]

Since the ban of the KPD in 1956, the members of the *Initiativausschuss* had an intense exchange on political justice. They addressed their meetings, reports, and publications to journalists, politicians, and academics. Its members wanted to create a broader lobby to contain the political justice in the FRG and to achieve an amnesty for convicted communists.[101] Outside the court, one of its most active members, Posser, criticized the extensive interpretation of the law in political justice[102] – similar to the journalist Müller-Meiningen jr. Even for Posser, the trials were clearly politically motivated. Although he always emphasized that he was not a communist and although he always noted that he did not sympathize with communism, it was important for him to defend communists in court. Possibly Posser's most significant point of criticism was that he considered 'their treatment as incompatible with the constitution.'[103]

Although the judges and prosecutors had tried to blend out 'the political' in the trials and to focus solely on the law, Posser and his colleagues tried to bring 'the political' back into the court proceedings. In Diether Posser's opinion, the trial should go beyond the criminal charges. But he meant something different than, for example, the 'aggressive defensive strategy' of the KPD-orientated *Zentralrat*. For him, it was important to show that his clients shared political approaches with those people who were not suspected to be hostile to the constitution. In fact, he knew that many judges and prosecutors had a Nazi past, but he was discreet in this case and avoided any public confrontation. He made a speech at a meeting of the *Initiativausschuss*:

> It has always been important for us to oppose comparisons that put today's political justice on one level with the justice in the 'Third Reich'. [...] But that we can present our criticism publicly – even if others are hostile to us – forbids this comparison.[104]

Their primary concern was to defend democracy and the rule of law. Their main concern was not necessarily to fight anti-communism, but above all to ensure that communists, like all other citizens, benefitted from their rights. That the members of the *Initiativausschuss* refused from comparisons between the NS judiciary and the current judiciary probably had something to do with their main goal – to achieve an amnesty for convicted communists. But it should be noted that many former NS civil servants (including judges and prosecutors) stayed in similar positions as in the NS system. Amnesties had already existed in West Germany, but the beneficiaries were mainly NS civil servants and even Nazi offenders. These amnesties were successful because of lobby groups of lawyers and politicians who had themselves been high officials during the NS years and were well connected with influential politicians.[105] The members of the *Initiativausschuss* had to cooperate with those people – not only in court but also to achieve their own political goals. A rapprochement to these people should not be endangered because the members of the *Initiativausschuss* needed their support to achieve an amnesty for communists.[106] Diether Posser, for example, emphasized several times that the lawyers would equally advocate all persecuted people affected by political justice.[107] But because political justice was mainly initiated against the political left, they dealt with it. However, he stressed that their intention was not to protect certain political groups, but that the law was crucial for their actions. In contrast to the *Zentralrat*, it was not only about political convictions for them.[108] From their point of view, the repressive measures against communists in the FRG could not be equated with the persecution during the NS years. They always emphasized that the FRG was a constitutional state. But to make sure it stayed one, they had to remain vigilant. That is why they stressed that people should no longer be persecuted in the FRG because of their political opinions – neither communists nor others. For them, political justice in general, and the KPD ban in particular posed a threat to constitutional democracy. Because political justice was applied to those who expressed different political opinions, they feared that the political opponent would be labeled as a criminal.[109] To counteract these effects of political justice, also in the context of remembering the persecution of political opponents during the NS years, in their view it was urgent that the government issued an amnesty for convicted communists.[110]

In addition to dealing with the past, for the members of the *Initiativausschuss*, daily politics also played a crucial role relating to the amnesty issue. In order to test the chance of reunification of both German states, a rapprochement to the Eastern bloc seemed also to be important for Posser and his colleagues. An amnesty should help to calm down the bloc confrontation. This pragmatism of Diether Posser and his colleagues stands for a more liberal position toward West German communists. These lawyers were convinced that everyone has the same rights and that a strong democracy also tolerates communist's opinions (as long as they did not fight democracy).[111] Their commitment in this matter was also based on the fact that people, who agreed with communists in certain political issues, were also suspected of being communists. These people had to expect political prosecution, too.[112]

The members of the *Initiativausschuss* were aware that they partially had to work together with 'denazified' persons within the judicial and political system to have a chance to achieve their political goals (such as an amnesty for communists and a reform of political justice). But beyond these fields, they not only tried to inform a broader public about political justice, thereby they also thematized the experiences communists had made during the NS period. They wrote critical articles and books on this topic, they gave interviews to newspapers and newscasts and were guests in political talk shows on TV.[113] Richard Schmid, for example, a member of the *Initiativausschuss*, friend of Fritz Bauer, and president of the higher regional court in Stuttgart published various columns in *Die Zeit*, a nationwide newspaper.[114] In his articles he primarily dealt with the current legislation in political justice, but he also occasionally wrote about the persecution of communists during the NS years or he drew parallels between justice during the NS years and some problematic proceedings against communists in the FRG, but with the addition that these cases were exceptions.[115] Among other things, Schmid described the case of Alfred Kantorowicz in detail. Kantorowicz was a Jewish jurist, journalist, author, and professor of literature at the East Berlin Humboldt University who fled to the FRG in 1957 because (as a member of the SED) he came into conflict with the party line and feared that he would become a victim of political purges. In the FRG, he had to sue in court for nine years to get his refugee ID which was entitled to him in West Germany and which was important for him to receive pension payments.[116] In his article, Richard Schmid described that the court excluded a political persecution of Kantorowicz by the GDR authorities because he had been a communist himself – since 1931. Schmid supposed that from the perspective of the court, Kantorowicz had 'the wrong past.' In his eyes, the judges resented the fact that, unlike many civil servants, he had not been a member of the NSDAP (which he could not have been as a Jew and persecutee of the NS regime, of course). By sharpening his argument in this way, Schmid tried to use the example of Kantorowicz's case to show that former NSDAP members and other 'denazified' civil servants had it generally much easier to obtain 'rights and benefits' in the FRG than communists. Even if they now criticized communism, as Kantorowicz did.[117] By using the opportunity to publish regularly in one of the best-known West German newspapers, Schmid was able to generate a larger public for the topic of political justice against communists, in general. Because he also mentioned the past of former persecutees, resistance fighters, and refugees, he also tried to raise public interest on this issue.[118]

In addition to individual members of the *Initiativausschuss*, this group also tried to gain more influence on public debate, especially on politicians in responsible positions. Through various petitions, letters to politicians, and brochures political justice received more and more attention. Even if it was the primary goal of the *Initiativausschuss* to improve political justice in the FRG, they also tried to create a memory-political area for experiences, communists had made in the NS years, by often trying to substantiate their arguments with examples from the lives of their clients and other (alleged) communists.[119] Later, some of the members of the *Initiativausschuss* took up political offices – Posser became minister in North Rhine Westphalia, his friend Heinemann became minister of justice in 1966, and Federal President in 1969. In 1968/69, not only political justice was reformed as a part of a reform of the penal system under the lead of the minister of justice Heinemann, but an amnesty for communists was also issued, which the *Initiativausschuss* had worked on for so long.[120] At the same time, however, an amnesty was issued 'via the back door' which favored former employees of the Reichssicherheitshauptamt (RSHA, Central Security Office of the Reich) which had been the central authority that had managed most of the repressive agencies in the NS years.[121] The simultaneity of both amnesties indicates that an amnesty only for communists could not be achieved in a state apparatus to which many former NS civil servants still belonged. In this context, the strategy of the *Initiativausschuss* seems far-sighted: to rely on factual negotiations in its concrete demands for an amnesty and for defusing political justice, and not to use the past of former Nazi persecutors as a means of attack. Nonetheless, that its members referred to the experiences that communists had made during the NS years and tried to achieve public attention for this topic, shows that they tried to create a larger area for the communists' memories in public, at the same time.

Conclusion

From the beginning of the 1950s until the KPD ban in 1956, the defendants mainly confronted the judges and prosecutors in court to get attention for the experiences, they have made in their pasts. At the same time, they followed the guidelines of such organizations like the KPD orientated *Zentralrat*. On the side of the SED it was possible to influence the West German court proceedings in this way. According to the East German fascism theory the legacy of National Socialism lay solely in the FRG. In this way, the GDR projected the Nazi past on West Germany and tried to disguise such entanglements in their own country. In this context, it was possible to discredit West German justice and politics by comparing it with the Nazi past. While defendants and communist activists brand the judges and prosecutors as former NS staff, the accused judicial personal blamed these persons to politicize the trials and to use the courts for political struggle. This could not be denied, especially because the defendants and activists often used an 'aggressive defensive strategy' in the proceedings. But it would be one-sided to ignore that many of the allegations made by the defendants against the judges and prosecutors based on a correct groundwork. The number of former NS civil servants who came into judicial office was high.[122] That these people now acted in the name of democracy and the rule of law was unthinkable for the communist activists. Therefore, that some of the defendants tried to elucidate West German society about their own pasts and the pasts of their opponents in court by using an 'political argumentation' cannot only be classified as a strategy, additional it seemed to be a mixture of political struggle and a feeling of inferiority in court. The judicial staff tried to prevent this confrontation, because they tried to avoid attacks on the constitutional state in general. But individually they feared that their own pasts could become public. Their demands for the juridification of the trials cannot be attributed solely as the wish for proceedings that were objective as possible, but also as a self-protection from a confrontation with the own past specifically, which included the refusal to come to terms with the NS past, especially of the jurists in general. They were not only in a more powerful position and their attempt to maintain silence about their pasts was not only in their own deepest interest, but this was also political supported. Western integration not only meant economic and political rooting in 'the West' and a rejection of reconciliation with 'the East,' but also a demarcation from the communist neighboring state and from the NS years. Thereby, anti-communism was the central ideology in the FRG, which also had effects on the public memory of the communist movement. That began to change since the beginning of the 1960s, when groups like the *Initiativausschuss* slowly gained influence. As external players its members were convinced that everyone has the same rights (also communists) and stood for a more liberal position toward the radical left. They wanted them to be part of the political discourse, of the public life, and they wanted them to participate in democracy. This intention meant not only defending them in court and to engage for a reform of political justice and for an amnesty for communists but also to mediate between the defendants on one side and the judges and prosecutors on the other side. In addition to the political goals the *Initiativausschuss* pursued in public they also used the chance to remember the anti-fascist memory of the communists in their meetings and via the media. Even if they usually did not personalize the destinies of their clients but generally remained the lives of affected persons in the past, even if they did not discuss the involvement of the judges and prosecutors in these years in specific cases, they referred to it generally. They made the pasts of the victims of the NS regime (including the ones of their clients) better known to a broader public and helped to initiate public debates. In this context, they could help an alternative narrative to find a place in the prevailing memory of the Nazi past.

Notes

1 See Patrick Major, *The Death of the KPD: Communism and Anti-Communism in West Germany, 1945–1956* (Oxford: Clarendon Press, 1997), 3.
2 See Major, *Death*, 5.
3 See Alexander von Brünneck, *Politische Justiz gegen Kommunisten in der Bundesrepublik Deutschland 1949–1968* (Frankfurt on the Main: Suhrkamp Verlag, 1978), 20–39, Dietrich Staritz, 'Die Kommunistische Partei Deutschlands,' in *Parteien-Handbuch: Die Parteien der Bundesrepublik Deutschland 1945–1980*, ed. Richard Stöss (Opladen: Westdeutscher Verlag, 1986), 1672 ff.; Dominik Rigoll, *Staatsschutz in Westdeutschland: Von der Entnazifizierung zur Extremistenabwehr* (Göttingen: Wallstein, 2013), 77 f.
4 See Major, *Death*, 253.
5 See Rigoll, *Staatsschutz*, 106.
6 See Major, *Death*, 279.
7 See Ibid., 279.
8 See Brünneck, *Politische Justiz*, 242, Lutz Lehmann, *Legal und opportun. Politische Justiz in der Bundesrepublik* (Berlin: Voltaire Verlag, 1966), 108.
9 As an exception the legal-historical work of Alexander von Brünneck should be mentioned here. See Brünneck, *Politische Justiz*.
10 See Major, *Death*.
11 See Josef Foschepoth, *Verfassungswidrig! Das KPD-Verbot im Kalten Bürgerkrieg* (Göttingen: Vandenhoeck & Ruprecht, 2017); Thomas Darnstädt, *Verschlusssache Karlsruhe: Die internen Akten des Bundesverfassungsgerichts* (Munich: Piper, 2018).
12 See Jens Niederhut, 'Anwälte zwischen Politik und Recht. Zur Rolle der Verteidigung in den politischen Prozessen gegen Kommunisten in der Bundesrepublik Deutschland der 1950er Jahre,' *Jahrbuch für historische Kommunismusforschung* 15 (2016): 235–252.
13 An exception is Dominik Rigoll's work on state protection, which among other things examines the generational experience of activists and civil servants in the context of West German security policy. See Rigoll, *Staatsschutz*. The memoirs of defense lawyer Diether Posser must also be mentioned here as an interesting historical source. See Diether Posser, *Anwalt im Kalten Krieg: Ein Stück deutscher Geschichte in politischen Prozessen 1951–1968* (2nd edn.) (Munich: C. Bertelsmann Verlag, 1991).
14 See Stefan Berger, Sean Scalmer, Christian Wicke, 'Memory and Social Movements: An introduction', in *Remembering Social Movements: Activism and Memory*, eds. Stefan Berger, et al. (London, New York: Routledge, 2021), 3.
15 See James M. Jasper and Jan Willem Duyvendak, eds., *Players and Arenas: The Interactive Dynamics of Protest* (Amsterdam: Amsterdam University Press, 2015).
16 See Niederhut, *Anwälte*, 239.
17 See Zentralrat zum Schutze demokratischer Rechte, *Abschrift der Anklageschrift gegen Mitglieder des Zentralrats zum Schutze demokratischer Rechte und zur Verteidigung deutscher Patrioten und der ADJ vor dem BGH*, 23 September 1957, SAPMO-BArch NY 4238/97.
18 The German communist movement used the term fascism instead of National Socialism. That was due to Marxism-Leninism, in which the core of fascism is anti-communism. In this way it was possible to create a clear enemy image (namely anti-communism) and to subordinate anti-Semitism to it officially. See Sabina Schroeter, *Die Sprache der DDR im Spiegel ihrer Literatur. Studien zum DDR-typischen Wortschatz* (Berlin: De Gruyter, 1994), 190 f.
19 See Annette Rosskopf, *Friedrich Karl Kaul. Anwalt im geteilten Deutschland (1906–1981)* (Berlin: Berlin Verlag, 2002), 74.
20 Jeffrey Herf, *Divided Memory: The Nazi Past in the Two Germanys* (Cambridge, MA: Cambridge University Press, 1997), 268.
21 Ibid., 208.

22 In 1951, for example, the so-called '131 law' stipulated that 150,000 soldiers who had been released from army during denazification were reemployed again and were legally entitled to pensions. See Norbert Frei, *Vergangenheitspolitik: Die Anfänge der Bundesrepublik und die NS-Vergangenheit* (Munich: C.H. Beck, 2012), 69–99.
23 See Rigoll, *Staatsschutz*; Franziska Kuschel and Dominik Rigoll, 'Saubere Verwaltung, sicherer Staat. Personalpolitik als Sicherheitspolitik in BMI und MdI,' in *Hüter der Ordnung: Die Innenministerien in Bonn und Ost-Berlin nach dem Nationalsozialismus*. Sonderausgabe für die Bundeszentrale für politische Bildung, eds. Frank Bösch and Andreas Wirsching (Bonn: BpB, 2018), 287 f.
24 See Frei, *Vergangenheitspolitik*; Marc von Miquel, *Ahnden oder amnestieren? Westdeutsche Justiz und Vergangenheitspolitik in den sechziger Jahren* (Göttingen: Wallstein, 2004); Andreas Eichmüller, *Keine Generalamnestie. Die strafrechtliche Folge von NS-Verbrechen in der frühen Bundesrepublik* (Munich: Oldenbourg, 2012).
25 See Irmtrud Wojak, *Fritz Bauer 1903–1968. Eine Biographie* (Munich: Beck, 2009), 342.
26 See Claudia Fröhlich, 'Der Braunschweiger Remer-Prozess 1952. Zum Umgang mit dem Widerstand gegen den NS-Staat in der frühen Bundesrepublik,' in *Schuldig. NS-Verbrechen vor deutschen Gerichten* (Beiträge zur Geschichte der nationalsozialistischen Verfolgung in Norddeutschland, 9), ed. KZ-Gedenkstätte Neuengamme (Bremen: Ed. Temmen, 2005), 17–28.
27 Fritz Bauer, 'Im Kampf um des Menschen Rechte (1955),' in *Vom kommenden Strafrecht*, ed. Fritz Bauer (Karlsruhe: C.F. Müller, 1969), 7. Translation by the author.
28 Fröhlich, *Remer-Prozess*, 20.
29 Ibid., 25.
30 See Major, *Death*, 282 f.
31 See Zentralrat zum Schutze demokratischer Rechte, *Prozessinformation Nummer 3*, 25 April 1958, SAPMO-BArch NY 4238/97; Mareen Heying and Florence Hervé, eds., *Frauen im Widerstand 1933–1945* (Cologne: Papyrossa, 2012), 97.
32 Zentralrat zum Schutze demokratischer Rechte, *Prozessinformation Nummer 3*, 25 April 1958, SAPMO-BArch NY 4238/97. Translation by the author.
33 See Norbert Frei, *Der Führerstaat. Nationalsozialistische Herrschaft 1933 bis 1945*, (8th edn.) (Munich: Deutscher Taschenbuchverlag, 2007), 51.
34 Indictment, *Trial against Members of the ADJ and the Zentralrat zum Schutze demokratischer Rechte*, 23 September 1957, SAPMO-BArch NY 4238/97. Translation by the author.
35 See Brünneck, *Politische Justiz*, 20 ff.
36 See Till Kössler, *Abschied von der Revolution: Kommunisten und Gesellschaft in Westdeutschland 1945–1968* (Düsseldorf: Droste Verlag, 2005), 400.
37 See Zentralrat zum Schutze demokratischer Rechte, *Indictment*, 23 September 1957, SAPMO-BArch NY 4238/97; and Major, *Death*, 280.
38 See Brünneck, *Politische Justiz*, 92.
39 Extract from Oskar Neumann's testimony, transcript of the trial, 14 June 1954, Institut für Zeitgeschichte München, ED 407/5. Translated by the author.
40 See Rosskopf, *Kaul*, 107.
41 Major, *Death*, 24.
42 Bias petition by Oskar Neumann, June 1954, Institut für Zeitgeschichte München, ED 407/9.
43 See Major, *Death*, 281.; Axel von der Ohe, 'Der Bundesgerichtshof und die NS-Justizverbrechen,' in *Erfolgsgeschichte Bundesrepublik? Die Nachkriegsgesellschaft im langen Schatten des Nationalsozialismus*, eds. Stephan Alexander Glienke, Joachim Perels et al. (Göttingen: Wallstein, 2008), 314.
44 See Brünneck, *Politische Justiz*, 224 f.
45 See bias petition by Oskar Neumann, June 1954, Institut für Zeitgeschichte München, ED 407/9.

Memory as a strategy? **177**

46 See Zentralrat zum Schutze demokratischer Rechte, *Informationen: Renazifizierung der Bundesrepublik*, 4 May 1956, Institut für Zeitgeschichte München, ED 711/1, 212–222.
47 See Peter Reichel, *Politik mit der Erinnerung: Gedächtnisorte im Streit um die nationalsozialistische Vergangenheit* (Munich: Hanser Verlag, 1995), 35 ff.
48 See Shida Kiani, *Wiedererfindung der Nation nach dem Nationalsozialismus? Konfliktlinien und Positionen in der westdeutschen Nachkriegspolitik* (Wiesbaden: Springer VS, 2013), 47–67; Reichel, *Politik*, 10, 35 f.
49 See Kössler, *Abschied*, 54 f.
50 Ernst Müller-Meiningen jr., 'Hexenprozesse 1953 – ein bedenklicher Ausweg,' *Süddeutsche Zeitung*, 21/22 November 1953, 4. Translation by the author.
51 See Kössler, *Abschied*, 403.
52 Letter from Claudia Kuhr to Friedrich Wilhelm Geier, 21 July 1954, Institut für Zeitgeschichte München, ED 407/10. Translation by the author.
53 Legacy of Oskar Neumann, Institut für Zeitgeschichte München, ED 407/10.
54 See Zentralrat zum Schutze demokratischer Rechte, *Indictment*, 23 September 1957, SAPMO-BArch NY 4238/97.
55 See Niederhut, *Anwälte*, 244–247.
56 See trial against Neumann and others, protocol of the proceedings, 14 June 1954, Institut für Zeitgeschichte München, ED 407/5, 3.
57 See Jörg Requate, *Der Kampf um die Demokratisierung der Justiz. Richter, Politik und Öffentlichkeit in der Bundesrepublik* (Frankfurt on the Main: Campus-Verlag, 2008), 30.
58 See Erik Gieseking, 'Der Prozess gegen Otto John, Deutschland 1956,' in *Lexikon der politischen Strafprozesse*, eds. Kurt Groenewold, Alexander Ignor, et al., http://www.lexikon-der-politischen-strafprozesse.de/glossar/john-otto-2, [accessed15. May 2020].
59 See Miquel, *Ahnden*, 390.
60 See Posser, *Anwalt*, 123.
61 See Major, *Death*, 281.
62 See Brünneck, *Politische Justiz*, 229.
63 Trial against Neumann and others, protocol of the proceedings, 14 June 1954, Institut für Zeitgeschichte München, ED 407/5, 3. Translation by the author.
64 See Niederhut, *Anwälte*, 244 ff.; Brünneck, *Politische Justiz*, 229.
65 Trial against Neumann and others, protocol of the proceedings, 14 June 1954, Institut für Zeitgeschichte München, ED 407/5, 7 f.
66 See Kössler, *Abschied*, 74 f.; Major, *Death*, 13–14, 208 ff.
67 See Foschepoth, *Verfassungswidrig*, 242.
68 See Rosskopf, *Kaul*, 86–87.
69 See Gerd Pfeiffer and Hans-Georg Strickert, eds., *KPD-Prozess. Dokumentarwerk zu dem Verfahren über den Antrag auf Feststellung der Verfassungswidrigkeit der Kommunistischen Partei Deutschlands*, (1st vol.) (Karlsruhe: C.F. Müller, 1955), 94–96.
70 See Reichel, *Politik*, 35 ff.
71 See Major, *Death*, 289.
72 See Dominik Rigoll, 'Streit um die streitbare Demokratie. Ein Rückblick auf die Anfangsjahrzehnte der Bundesrepublik,' *Aus Politik und Zeitgeschichte* 32–33 (2017): 43.
73 See Rosskopf, *Kaul*, 27–30.
74 See Mario Keßler, *Die SED und die Juden – zwischen Repression und Toleranz: Politische Entwicklungen bis 1967* (Berlin: Akademie Verlag, 1995), 31.
75 See Kuschel and Rigoll, *Verwaltung*, 299 ff.
76 Ibid., 303.
77 N.N., 'Patrioten eingekerkert – Kriegsverbrecher frei: Tatsachen beweisen die Faschisierung in Westdeutschland,' in *Fünfte Folge des Bulletins 'Über den Kampf gegen das geplante Verbot der Kommunistischen Partei Deutschlands, um Frieden und Demokratie,*

nationale Einheit und Unabhängigkeit,' ed. Central Committee of the KPD (Düsseldorf: Central Committee of the KPD, 1953), 13.
78 Ibid.
79 See Justin Collings, *Democracy's Guardians: A History of the German Federal Constitutional Court, 1951–2001* (Oxford: Oxford University Press, 2015), 41 f.
80 See Weinke, *Verfolgung*, 76.
81 See Manfred Görtemaker and Christoph Safferling, *Die Akte Rosenburg. Das Bundesministerium der Justiz und die NS-Zeit* (Munich: C.H. Beck, 2016), 194–202. The aggressive East German occurrence against Lübke probably was also related to the fact that the GDR was afraid that the FRG would reveal Nazi crimes in their country because that did not correspond to their anti-fascist self-presentation. See Weinke, *Verfolgung*, 351.
82 See Görtemaker and Safferling, *Akte Rosenburg*, 195 f.
83 See Manfred Görtemaker, 'Die heile Welt der Rosenburg. Das Bundesministerium der Justiz und die NS-Vergangenheit,' in *Die Ämter und ihre Vergangenheit: Ministerien und Behörden im geteilten Deutschland 1949–1972*, eds. Stefan Creuzberger and Dominik Geppert (Paderborn: Schöningh, 2018), 67 f.
84 See Görtemaker and Safferling, *Akte Rosenburg*, 202.
85 See N.N., 'Nicht geküsst,' in *Der Spiegel*, 1 August 1968; N.N., 'Vorführung empfiehlt sich,' *Der Spiegel*, 11 July 1962; Rigoll, *Staatsschutz*, 170 ff.
86 See Joachim Perels, 'Der Umgang mit NS-Tätern und Widerstandskämpfern nach 1945,' in *Kritische Justiz* 30 (1997), 370.
87 See Reichel, *Politik*, 45.
88 Walther Ammann, '6. Rundbrief, September 1962,' Institut für Zeitgeschichte, ED 712/1, 51.
89 Zentralrat zum Schutze demokratischer Rechte, 'Indictment, 23 September 1957,' in SAPMO-BArch NY 4238/97. See Niederhut, *Anwälte*, 244 ff.
90 See ibid.
91 Brünneck, *Politische Justiz*, 313.
92 See Rosskopf, *Kaul*, 107.
93 Internal report from 'Hans' to 'Peter' about the consultations with the comrades 'Hugo' and 'Emanuel' in the period between 10 July and 18 July 1961, 'Anleitung und Berichterstattung der Kommission Juristen, 21 July 1961,' in SAPMO-BArch BY 1 4262/210-217, 7. Translation by the author.
94 See Niederhut, *Anwälte*, 251.
95 See Posser, *Anwalt*, 192.
96 See ibid.
97 See Gregor Kritidis, ed., *Wolfgang Abendroth oder: 'Rote Blüte im kapitalistischen Sumpf'* (Berlin: Dietz, 2015), 12 ff.
98 See Friedrich Martin Balzer, ed., *Justizunrecht im Kalten Krieg. Die Kriminalisierung der westdeutschen Friedensbewegung im Düsseldorfer Prozess 1959/60* (Cologne: Papyrossa, 2006), 377.
99 See Posser, *Anwalt*.
100 See Joachim Perels, *Recht und Autoritarismus. Beiträge zur Theorie zu realer Demokratie* (Baden-Baden: Nomos, 2009), 345–347.
101 See Brünneck, *Politische Justiz*, 314–315.
102 See Diether Posser, 'Politik und Justiz. Ein Wort zum Verbot der KPD und zur politischen Justiz,' in *Stimme der Gemeinde* 17 (1956): 531.
103 Posser, *Anwalt*, 297. Translation by the author.
104 Diether Posser, 'Presentation, Arbeitstagung und Gesamtaussprache des Initiativausschusses, 4/5 May 1957,' BArch Koblenz, N1367-213, 29. Translation by the author.
105 See Frei, *Vergangenheitspolitik*.
106 See Brünneck, *Politische Justiz*, 321 f.; Diether Posser and Walther Ammann, 2. 'Denkschrift über Probleme der Justiz in politischen Strafsachen, 1957,' in BArch

Koblenz, N1367-213, 15. The first draft law, which was debated in parliament and which provided for an amnesty for communists, was also intended to benefit former Nazis. This was because the draft law had been developed by the liberal party's national wing, which was a melting pot of former Nazis. See N.N., 'General-Amnestie. Großmutters Grundsätze,' *Spiegel* 52 (1959): 24.

107 See Diether Posser, 'Discussion, Arbeitstagung und Gesamtaussprache des Initiativausschusses, 4/5 May 1957,' 33; Diether Posser and Walther Ammann, 2. 'Denkschrift über Probleme der Justiz in politischen Strafsachen, 1957,' in BArch Koblenz, N1367-213, 1–16.

108 See Diether Posser, 'Discussion, Arbeitstagung und Gesamtaussprache, 4/5 May 1957,' in BArch Koblenz, N1367-213, 33.

109 See Diether Posser and Walther Ammann, 2. 'Denkschrift über Probleme der Justiz in politischen Strafsachen, 1957,' in BArch Koblenz, N1367-213, 16.

110 See Walther Ammann, 'Die Rechtsprechung zur Geheimbündelei und zu den Untergrundvereinen (§§ 128, 129 StGB) sowie die weitere Praxis in politischen Strafsachen seit Mai 1957, 2. Arbeitstagung und Gesamtaussprache des Initiativausschusses, 26 October 1957,' in Institut für Zeitgeschichte München, ED 712/2, 7.

111 See Diether Posser, 'Erfahrungen aus Vorverfahren, Hauptverhandlungen und Strafvollzug bei politischen Überzeugungstätern, Arbeitstagung und Gesamtaussprache des Initiativausschusses, 4/5 May 1957,' in BArch Koblenz, N1367-213, 30; Diether Posser and Walther Ammann, 2. 'Denkschrift über Probleme der Justiz in politischen Strafsachen, 1957,' in BArch Koblenz, N1367-213, 16.

112 See Walther Ammann, 'Die jüngste Entwicklung der politischen Strafjustiz unter besonderer Berücksichtigung der Rechtsprechung zum KPD-Verbot, Bericht über die 13. Tagung des Initiativausschusses, 23/24 April 1966,' in Institut für Zeitgeschichte München, ED 712/2, 79a-87.

113 See Lehmann, *Legal*, 71–110.

114 Schmid had defended members of persecuted political groups in court during the NS years and founded an illegal political group himself. He was arrested in 1938 and sentenced for high treason by the Volksgerichtshof (People's Court of Justice) in 1940. See Perels, *Recht*, 338 f.

115 See Richard Schmid, 'Rechtsschutz ist Staatsschutz. Eine Erwiderung auf Bundesanwalt Wagner,' *Die Zeit* 10 (1966), http://www.zeit.de/1966/10/rechtsschutz-ist-staatsschutz [accessed 15 May 2020]; Richard Schmid, 'Auf dem Wege zum Überwachungsstaat. Das neue Vereinsgesetz und das KPD-Verbot,' *Die Zeit* 11 (1965), http://www.zeit.de/1965/11/auf-dem-wege-zum-ueberwachungs-staat [accessed 15 May 2020].

116 See Dietmar Petzina, "Zwischen den Stühlen der Mächtigen.' Alfred Kantorowicz – heimatlos in Ost und West,' in *Zur Kultur der DDR. Persönliche Erinnerungen und wissenschaftliche Perspektiven*, ed. Frank Hoffmann (Frankfurt on the Main: Peter Lang Edition, 2016), 111–138.

117 See Richard Schmid, 'Der Fall Kantorowicz,' *Die Zeit* 27 (1964), https://www.zeit.de/1964/27/der-fall-kantorowicz [accessed 15 May 2020].

118 See Perels, *Recht*, 340.

119 See as an example, 'Appeal to the Public by the Initiativausschuss, January 1956,' in BArch Koblenz, N1367-213.

120 See Sarah Langwald, 'Anwälte der KommunistInnen: Der Initiativausschuss für die Amnestie und der Verteidiger in politischen Strafsachen,' in *Das KPD-Verbot 1956. Vorgeschichte und Folgen der Illegalisierung der KPD in Westdeutschland*, eds. Bernd Hüttner and Gregor Kritidis (Berlin: Rosa-Luxemburg-Stiftung, 2016), 25.

121 See Weinke, *Verfolgung*, 301–306; Rigoll, *Staatsschutz*, 203–205.

122 For example, from the mid-1950s to the 1960s, the proportion of judges who had made careers in justice during the NS years was about 80% at the Federal Court of Justice. An exception was the Federal Constitutional Court; see Ohe, *Bundesgerichtshof*, 314.

10

'WE BELIEVE TO HAVE GOOD REASON TO REGARD THESE COMRADES, WHO DIED IN MARCH, TO BE OURS.' THE REMEMBRANCE OF THE *MÄRZGEFALLENEN* BY WORKERS' ORGANIZATIONS DURING THE WEIMAR REPUBLIC

Jule Ehms

Contemplating memories and memory culture in memory studies have always involved reflecting on collective identities and how the former relates to the latter.[1] Assuming that group identities are not just given but socially constructed and that they have to be continuously reconstructed, memory can play a crucial role in these processes. Or as Jan Assmann states: 'Groups base [...] their awareness of their unity and uniqueness particularly on events that take place in the past. Societies need the past mainly for the purpose of self-definition.'[2] Historians have not only discussed the role of memory with respect to societies and nations but also regarding political organizations and social movements. Concerning workers and their movements – which were so far not popular subjects of memory studies – Laurajane Smith, Paul Shackel, and Cary Campbell, for example, dedicated a book to 'the ways in which [members of the working class and their communities] draw on the past [...] to re-interpret and re-work contemporary [their] identity.'[3] More than that, authors have argued that political identity is, in turn, also constitutive for how movements remember the past and that political identity and social memory are therefore interdependent. This article draws especially on this mutuality and discusses, by the example of the German syndicalist movement, how 'memory work' and 'identity work' are interconnected.

After World War I, the political landscape in Germany, especially concerning the labor movement, had changed crucially. New parties and unions came into existence or suddenly gained in importance, including communist and syndicalist ones – forming own political movements (and communities[4]) and undermining the dominance of the German Social Democracy. Whereas the former tried to push for a 'real revolution' that would result in the abandonment of all classes, the Social Democracy was a key player in the establishment (and preservation) of the Weimar Republic. All these organizations strived to express their own political identity to gather worker's support. This competition influenced the collective memory and remembrance traditions of the, now more diverse than ever, German labor movement. Or in the words of the historian George Haupt:

> With the great split that occurred as a result of the collapse of the Second International and which was deepened by the October Revolution, the history of the working-class movement was definitively confiscated by hostile protagonists and subjected to the entire weight of their demands.[5]

On the following pages, I demonstrate how the division within the German labor movement influenced the way the three, the syndicalist, communist, and social democratic, communities remembered one specific event of the early Weimar years. In early 1920 the young republic faced a tremendous political crisis when due to a coup d'état, the so-called Kapp Putsch, the German government was forced to retreat. Although the coup was, thanks to a massive general strike, not successful, the workers' uprisings that followed reopened the question of how post-war Germany should look like. Syndicalist and communist, as well as social democratic organizations, were crucially involved in this 'impact event.'[6] Using the example of the little town Sömmerda (today's Thuringia, Central Germany), I will illustrate, how the three political communities developed their own narratives and commemoration of the Kapp Putsch and of the fights that followed. I will focus on the anarcho-syndicalist Free Worker's Union of Germany (*Freie Arbeiter-Union Deutschlands*, in short FAUD), which reported throughout the years how syndicalists in Sömmerda remembered their fallen comrades and to what extent their attempts conflicted with the commemoration procedures of the other strands of the labor movement. With the reports of the FAUD, we possess respectively unusual accounts of a developing differentiation of one memory culture, in this case, the memory culture of the German labor movement. Furthermore, whereas previous research discussed the culture of remembrance regarding the Kapp Putsch in general[7] and/or paid particular attention to the social democratic and communist culture of remembrance,[8] syndicalist memory culture in Germany has not been covered yet.

In Part 1, I will briefly outline the events during the Kapp Putsch. Part 2 introduces the remembrance culture of the labor movement during the Weimar Republic that drew on traditions developed before 1914. Part 3 recounts the early remembrance of the so-called *Märzgefallenen*, the fallen workers in the events of March 1920, and Part 4 captures the dispute among diverse workers' organizations over the legacy of the *Märzgefallenen* and how the remembrance culture changed, illustrating the highly political nature of memory and its role in the construction and expression of political identity.

The Kapp Putsch of 1920

In the spring of 1920 a group of conservatives and right-wing military officers, led by the Prussian civil servant Kapp and general Lüttwitz, tried to take over the government and to abandon the newly established democratic constitution. To prevent the putsch, the president of the Reich Friedrich Ebert proclaimed a general strike. Several workers' organizations, including the social democratic, Christian, and liberal unions, followed this call. The Communist Party published its own proclamation one day later. For the first and last time during the Weimar Republic, different workers' organizations joined forces and successfully defended the status quo. That their visions for the time after the republic's successful defense diverged widely did not compromise their shared concern.

In several cities, however, workers did not only go on strike, but they also armed themselves since the Reichswehr, the armed forces of the Weimar Republic, as well as local security forces, were divided among groups being loyal to the republic, in support of the putsch or remained neutral. Furthermore, the ambitions of the striking workers became more radical. Numerous workers did not just want to defend the republic but picked up demands of the revolutionary struggles of 1918/19. Therefore, more radical organizations continued to strike and to fight after the old government had been reestablished and the social democratic unions called the workers to resume work. These fights, which cost many workers their lives, occurred all over the Reich (most intensely in the Ruhr area, in Western Germany, with about 1,000 dead[9]) and were carried out above all by communists and anarcho-syndicalists. The latter were organized in the FAUD.

The FAUD was founded in December 1919 and the only union in Germany with an explicit syndicalist program and a reference to anarchism, aiming for the overthrow of capitalism and the state. For a short period, this program seemed to be convincing. In 1921, the FAUD numbered around 150,000 members.[10] Especially during the first years of the Weimar Republic, these members led strikes, joined the local soldiers' and workers' councils, and participated in several attempts at collectivization enterprises. However, the period of flourishing syndicalism in Germany did not last for long. By 1923 the FAUD had collapsed. By 1925, the syndicalist union had shrunk to 25,000 members[11]; by the 1930s, only around 6,000 workers remained.[12] In 1933, the FAUD, like all unions, was officially banned, but its members continued to offer a relatively persistent resistance against the new Nazi regime.

One of the cities the FAUD was well represented (even after 1923) was Sömmerda, a small town in Central Germany. According to the reports of the *Syndicalist* in 1920, the official organ of the FAUD, all workers of Sömmerda were organized within the syndicalist union.[13] United, these workers joined the general strike, formed workers' corps, and established a messenger service to other revolutionary councils in the area. According to the syndicalists, on March 24th, the Reichswehr – again under the control of the social democratic government – invaded Sömmerda without further notice.[14] Several workers were killed, although not during the fights, but after the village was already taken. As the FAUD of Sömmerda reported, at least six syndicalist comrades were shot or beaten to death by raging Reichswehr soldiers.[15]

The remembrance tradition of the German labor movement

The commemoration of the victims of the March events began several days later with funerals, often accompanied by giant processions. Even the first cenotaphs were already constructed.[16] By remembering the *Märzgefallenen* the German workers' movement referred back to an established remembrance tradition. The habit to inhume deceased leaders or victims in the presence of huge demonstrations had already been part of the workers' culture since the 1900s.[17] Before World War I though, the workers' movement was much less divided than after the war. The common remembrance of crucial events or important personalities was therefore not unusual in the nineteenth century. At the beginning of the Weimar Republic, however, the splitting of the workers' movement was evident and, as will be shown shortly, affected the way the events of March 1920 were commemorated.

The remembrance of the Kapp Putsch and the following uprising was indeed prominent in times of the Weimar Republic.[18] But also other events of the labor movement played an important, some of them an even more important role in the remembrance tradition of the communists, syndicalists or social democrats. In fact, the commemoration of the *Märzgefallen* during the Weimar Republic did only partly refer to those fallen 1920, but also to the victims of the revolution of 1848/9. On March 18th, 1848, the military killed over two hundred democrats. From then on, March 18th became a ritual day of remembrance during the time of the German Empire.[19] Even in times of greatest repression, socialists commemorated the victims with speeches, recitals, and songs.[20] Also during the Weimar Republic, the remembrance of 1848 was still alive among different strands of the labor movement. Memorial events for the victims of the Kapp Putsch were organized similarly and its protagonists explicitly pointed to the happenings of 1848/9.[21] Also, some worker's organizations saw themselves still in the tradition of this revolution.[22]

But parties and unions did not just relate to the revolution of 1848/9, but also to the Paris Commune of 1871.[23] And since the Paris Commune was founded on March 18th, the memorial events conducted for the *Märzgefallenen* during the Weimar Republic did, not surprisingly, address the happenings of 1848/9 as well as of 1871.[24]

The most important memorial day was, of course, May 1st and, although differently interpreted, equally celebrated by syndicalists, communists, and social democrats.[25] Introduced in Germany in 1890, the commemoration of May Day quickly became a central part of the proletarian celebration culture, especially during the Weimar Republic.[26] Unions and parties did not only use this day to once more call to action, praise solidarity and to propagate their programs but to remember the origins of May Day, the so-called Haymarket Riot of 1886 that lead to the arrest and killing of five activists. Occasionally, the celebration was conducted by several organizations together.[27] However, the remembrance was also used to dissociate the own organization from political opponents. According to the syndicalists, for example, both, social democrats and communists, would denigrate the idea of May 1st with their parliamentarian politics. Due to the wrong strategy, the FAUD members claimed, the demands of the working class have not been fulfilled.[28] This differentiation of a shared memory culture increased over the years and, as will be demonstrated, can be traced through the commemoration regarding the events of 1920.

However, the 'memory work' of the several strands of the labor movement did not just diverge increasingly but also conflicted with the remembrance practice of other political, especially conservative and right-wing, communities. These conflicts characterize the remembrance of the war dead during the Weimar Republic in general. Similar to the commemoration of the March events different agents could not agree on how to remember their dead which mirrors how much the Weimar society was divided. Regarding the commemoration of World War I diverse movements, communities, or associations tried to exclude each other from their memorial events or disturbed those of the others. Some memorials were even desecrated.[29] Thus, the conflict within the labor movement on how to remember the Kapp Putsch is not a unique example of a deeply contested memory culture in the time of the Weimar Republic.

The early commemoration of the *Märzgefallenen*

In Sömmerda, the killed comrades were buried by the end of March 1920,[30] but an additional funeral service was organized for April 25th, with several thousand people attending.[31] In this way, the Syndicalists began to commemorate the Kapp Putsch as did communist and social democratic workers. For instance, while the people of Sömmerda revealed a *Märzgefallenen* memorial in 1921, a similar monument was put up in the same year in Hagen (Rhineland-Westphalia). In the syndicalist dominated Sömmerda, the memorial event started with a mass demonstration which proceeded from the city center toward the cemetery.[32] A workers' and a women's choir performed political songs, a poem '*Die Märzgefallenen*' was read, and at least two short speeches given. Likewise, in Hagen a demonstration (here with over 2,500 people) moved from the city toward the cemetery, choirs sung, and speeches were held. But contrary to Sömmerda, this event was organized by social democrats.

Altogether several hundred memorials were raised all over the German Reich (especially near mass graves),[33] mostly as tombs for the fallen workers of the respective town.[34] Additionally, memorial plaques commemorated shootings.[35] But also major monuments were built which became the center of commemoration events of the labor movement every year. Prominent figures of the workers' movement spoke at these commemorations, for example, Rudolf Rocker, probably the most prominent figure of German anarcho-syndicalism, or communist Ernst Thälmann. This was new in this respect that the workers' movement has only partly been involved in commemorating the war dead so far. The Social Democracy was one of the groups in the interwar period establishing World

War I memorials. For the communists, remembering the war and the fallen soldiers was of little, for the syndicalists of no importance. These movements almost exclusively focused on their victims killed in political uprisings – like the *Märzgefallenen*.[36]

During the first years of the Weimar Republic, different labor organizations conducted these memorial activities together and shared their 'liuex de mémoire.'[37] In Sömmerda not only syndicalists remembered the killed workers, but several (also non socialist) organizations and associations put wreaths at the site of the memorial. In Hagen, for example, also the economic-liberal Hirsch-Dunckersche unions, which objected to any class-struggle but participated in the defense of the republic, called for commemoration.[38] These memorial events, regardless of their initiators, followed mostly the same pattern as the example of Sömmerda and Hagen have shown.[39]

Those services were not only conducive to mourning and to support the bereaved, but also provided a sense of purpose: Rudolf Rocker held a one-hour speech during the service in April 1920 in Sömmerda and explained that, thanks to the fights, the reactionary forces have been pushed back. According to Rocker, the fallen had given their lives for the good of humanity, had fought for a liberal socialism and a liberated society. The bereaved, thus, could indeed be proud.[40] In doing so, Rocker, only shortly after the 'impact event,' identified the deceased in a particular respect. Several studies have discussed this 'offer of identification' with respect to the imagination of a national community.[41] In this case, however, the dead were not remembered as soldiers, but as workers. The survivors did not refer to the nation or the fatherland as the 'unit of action,' but to a (although not yet specified in detail) political community.[42]

One year later, the FAUD commemorated the fallen workers once more and raised a memorial stone. The *Syndicalist* again covered the dedication ceremony, offering the following construal of the March fights:

> In the same way nature revolves, humanity will revolve and for this renewal those comrades, lying in the dark ground before us, sacrificed their lives. Socialism was the goal they fought and suffered for. And just as this memorial and tomb in its glorious natural growth stand in front of us, we will consider the goal of our killed comrades to be our goal and continue to fight until it is achieved.[43]

Once more the FAUD provided a sense of purpose: the workers did not die in vain, but their lives were given for a brighter and more equitable future. More than that, 'an inspirational connection with the present'[44] was made: the promise, syndicalists would continue the struggle. Just as the historian Enzo Traverso describes Marxist memory culture and historiography as 'a memory for the future, insofar as it announced the battles to come,'[45] also the syndicalist memory – even years later – tied the remembrance of the actual defeat to hopes and promises: 'It is necessary to carry out the legacy of the infinitely great, terrifying band of martyrs, that gave their last, deployed their lifeblood to free the world proletariat from all state and economic fetters.[46] In remembering the Kapp Putsch the syndicalists referred to their visions for the future, pointing toward and thus mobilizing for future collective actions. Not just the dead were in this way identified but also the survivors. By referring to shared goals and values, the dead and the survivors were both included into one (political) community and a certain future behavior was expected.[47]

The dispute over the legacy: who is entitled to commemorate the *Märzgefallenen*?

Still, as the unity of the workers' movement increasingly vanished, also the common remembrance ceremonies stopped. According to historian Günter Gleising, by the mid-1920s the commemoration was split.[48] In Hagen, for example, from 1924 on, the memorial events of the Communist Party of Germany (*Kommunistische Partei Deutschlands,* KPD) and the Social Democratic Party of Germany (*Sozialdemokratische Partei Deutschlands,* SPD) were strictly separated[49] At the Friedrichsfelde cemetery in Berlin, political differences even resulted in communists and social democrats burying their comrades at different sites of the cemetery.[50]

The historian Klaus Tenfelde noted how immediately after the events of 1920, class hatred had shattered the ability of the bereaved of various victim groups to mourn together.[51] After a few years, surprisingly not from the beginning, also the political conflict between the diverse strands of the labor movement had eventually affected the memory culture of these communities – at least the question of how the March events should be represented had to be renegotiated.[52]

What were the main points of divergence? The social democrats wanted to commemorate only the victims of the Kapp Putsch whereas the communists sought to include those of the so-called March Actions of 1921.[53] During these uprisings, mainly initiated and led by the Communist Party, about 200 workers had lost their lives.[54] Additionally, the organizations' interpretations of the March events varied significantly. Communists and syndicalists emphasized the revolutionary character of the fights of 1920.[55] The social democrats, in contrast, focused on the prevention of the Kapp Putsch as the defense of the republic and tried to celebrate the republic's achievements.

As already mentioned, the syndicalists did celebrate the fallen workers side by side with other labor organizations.[56] However, for the FAUD the conflict about the interpretation of the March events and especially about the question of whom these victims 'belonged' to played a role from the beginning. In spring 1921 the FAUD in Witten (Rhineland-Westphalia) reacted indignantly to the social democratic union's fundraising campaign to support the bereaved of the March events. According to the syndicalists,

> the free unions have no reason and no right to collect money for the *Märzopfer* [victims of March] because it was them, who – after the three-day general strike – stabbed those for freedom fighting brothers in the back […]

once their faithless comrades had taken back their ministry armchairs. [...] Has this been solidarity? But we will be solidary because we have the duty, but also the right to do so. Because 80% of the workers were members of the Free Workers Union and Communists, whereas the free unionists followed the orders of their faithless fat cats.[57]

By 1932 the FAUD in Sömmerda, still keeping the remembrance tradition alive, stated once again, that those workers killed had certainly not fought because they followed the slogans of the social democratic government, but to disarm the bourgeoisie.[58]

Evidently, the shared experience of the March events did not serve to overcome the division within the left. On the contrary, the syndicalists offered their group-specific perspective that underlined the difference between the own community and the social democratic, and later on also from the communist, movement. Notably, the use of emotional speak emphasizes the disappointment of the syndicalists in terms of the other workers' organizations and helped certainly in trying to express the distinctive collective identity of the movement.

That the FAUD participated in the remembrance of the fallen workers for so long was not obvious even though its members had been deeply involved in the general strike, the uprising and the fights. At least some popular syndicalists (for example, members of the FAUD secretary) disapproved of the involvement of FAUD members in the events after the general strike, causing a debate in the *Syndikalist* on the use of violence in general.[59] Whereas at least armed self-defense was predominantly accepted within the FAUD, the syndicalists stressed the power of the general strike, which for them was the 'most powerful expression of will the proletariat has ever been able to.'[60] It is therefore not surprising that even several years later, the collective strike was still a central aspect of the FAUD's remembrance of the March events:

> The socialist proletariat can celebrate no better than to draw once again a lesson from the events of the last 12 years; and we syndicalists should especially today wherever we have the chance to talk to the workers, remind them, that it was the general walkout that brought down Kapp [...].[61]

The proletariat should prepare itself for the general strike, the syndicalists continued, since the working class was still far from free. Once more, the FAUD linked the past to the future.

The conflict between syndicalists and other organizations was fought out in their respective newspapers, but also disturbed the actual memorial events as the example of Sömmerda reveals once more. In 1927, the *Reichsbanner*, an association of several parties (but mostly social democrats) to defend the republic, tried to conduct their own ceremony. As the *Syndicalist* described, the bereaved prevented the Reichsbanner members from putting down a wreath decorated with a black-red-golden ribbon, since those colors symbolized the state 'that murdered their beloved ones.'[62] The members of the *Reichsbanner* had to take the wreath back and only had a chance to place it at the monument at night. Nevertheless, on the following morning, the sons of one of the fallen workers and members of the local syndicalist youth organization moved the wreath to the back side of the memorial.[63] This incidence illustrates once more how 'memory work' also includes the struggle to gain visibility and thus to foster the relevance of the own movement.

Despite this incidence, the workers of Sömmerda regardless of their political background continued to celebrate the March events together in a 'quite dignified manner' – at least until 1931.[64] This time the FAUD had to deal with communists, who invited the syndicalists to prepare the memorial with them. Soon, however, it became clear the KPD had no interest in a contribution by the FAUD. It rejected the proposals of the Syndicalist Youth and allowed for only one, a communist, speaker. Furthermore, during the commemoration in Schallenburg (a nearby village of Sömmerda) the speech of a FAUD member was prevented and the decoration the syndicalists had prepared for the event demolished. For these reasons, the syndicalists decided against a joint celebration and KPD and FAUD visited the cemetery one after the other. Furthermore, the latter claimed the fallen workers once more for itself: 'We believe to have good reason to regard these comrades, who died in March, to be ours, since they died as those. There was no KPD in Sömmerda back then.'[65] The rhetoric alone reminds of the construction of national identities. But in this instance, by the interpretation of past events, not a 'common past' was formed that would invite the survivors to remember it collectively.[66]

The competition over who is remembered by whom and how illustrates how easily (and quickly) memory can become a subject of contestation. The memory of the workers who died during the Kapp Putsch was almost instantly woven into the political agenda of the respective workers' organizations. Communists, syndicalists and social democrats claimed the fallen workers fought for a certain ideal: be it the existence of the republic, the dictatorship of the proletariat or free socialism. All three groups did not only offer their respective explanation of the events but within a few years started to compete for the control of the interpretation of the March events. Considering that at the beginning of the Weimar Republic these groups tend to commemorate side by side, the fluidity of collective memories, as well as the powerful role of an own mnemonic narrative in cultivating collective identity, becomes apparent.

A common commemoration and mourning that could have expressed the integrity of the working class movement were abandoned on behalf of mutual accusations. Adolf Meinberg, a member of the KPD, cautioned against a division of the labor movement already in March 1920, during a funeral service in Dortmund:

> The dead of this grave belong to all of the parties. The counter-revolutionary attack united them. […] This should and must be the dead's warning to the living, this is what they died for. They were killed so that the unity of the proletariat can be achieved.[67]

However, the unity of the German labor movement could not be restored – even when the rise of fascism made joint actions necessary. In fact, none of the communities found an answer to the dilemma of facing the same political enemies but having made a collaboration with each other to fight these enemies almost unthinkable. The ongoing competition on how to interpret and commemorate the Kapp Putsch and the uprising afterward did not cause the fragmentation of the labor movement but certainly reinforced it.

The crumbling unity of the workers' movement was also reflected by its commemoration calendar in general. As stated above, on the one hand, the different communities were still part of the same tradition. On the other hand, they were looking for the establishment of their own revolutionary heritage and, thus, included other historical events in their memory culture.

Social democrats were part of the annual celebrations of the republic around November 9th, the day the Weimar Republic was proclaimed.[68] The communists, however, perceived this date as 'a day for mourning.'[69] Instead of honoring the Weimar Republic, they celebrated the anniversaries of the October Revolution (with rallies, demonstrations, concerts, and papers).[70] Despite the diverse opinions on which revolution should be honored, SPD and KPD agreed on the importance of January 15, 1919, the date of Rosa Luxemburg's and Karl Liebknecht's murder, and organized commemorations and demonstrations.[71]

Additionally, as mentioned before, the KPD also remembered the fallen of the 1921 riots. The FAUD though, so far as I see, did not include the commemoration of the March Actions of 1921 into its memorial tradition, even though its members participated in the strikes and the armed revolt. One reason for this might have been the disapproval of violent uprising on the part of some FAUD members, another being the fact that those riots were initiated by the communists. Instead of attending to the March Actions or even celebrate the Russian Revolution, the FAUD preferred to commemorate the Kronstadt rebellion of 1921, an event which until today plays a huge role within the collective memory of the anarchist movement.

But the communities within the labor movement did not just compete with each other over the appropriate memorial of the March events. Also, the far-right claimed its own construal of what happened in the spring of 1920. Memorials were raised by the far-right Freikorps, for example.[72] Naturally, the narrative of the Freikorps differed from the stories told by the workers' organizations.[73] Due to the, as above described, not just heterogeneous remembrance practice but the hostility among the different agents toward each other during the Weimar Republic, the execution of memorial events was occasionally restricted. Especially during the late years of the Weimar Republic more demonstrative forms of commemorations have been forbidden, only wreath-laying ceremonies were possible.[74] In the case of the syndicalists, the police accompanied the memorial events – for protection or surveillance or both – from the first years of the 1920s until the 1930s.[75]

Furthermore, the refusal of the construction of a memorial by the syndicalists[76] or the prohibition of commemorations[77] show that the remembrance of the *Märzgefallenen* by workers' organizations was not unconditionally tolerated by the state or the local governments.[78] In the Ruhr area only one memorial regarding the events of 1920 was founded by the state.[79] In Mülheim an der Ruhr a memorial commission, including the FAUD, communist parties, workers' choirs and sports groups, struggled in vain for years to get the approval of the city council.[80]

After the fascist takeover in 1933, workers' organizations and with them the expression of their collective and communicative memory was suppressed, criminalized and to some extent wiped out. Most memorials remembering the March events got destroyed and graves devastated. Instead, new monuments for the Freikorps, the Reichswehr or the Weimar security police were raised.[81]

After 1945, the rivalry for the memorial of the *Märzgefallenen* in some way revived: the labor movement but also military units pursued the commemoration. Memorials were rebuilt, albeit not always without discussion.[82] Within the GDR the commemoration of the March victims played a much more official role than in West Germany, although state representatives usually refused to acknowledge the significance of parts of the labor movement other than the KPD.[83] Nowadays, the memory of the March events is almost completely lost, with respect to state memory culture as well as within the labor movement.[84] Occasionally social democrats, communists and antifascists still visit the memorials[85]; in 2003 even a new monument was raised in Wuppertal.[86] Overall, however, the March events do not play an important role in the collective memory of the German labor organizations.

Conclusion

The social (or collective) identities of the different labor organizations in Germany were based on a permanent differentiation of the own to other political groups; the 'difference to the outside emphasized, the difference to the inside however deemphasized.'[87] This need to express disparity is reflected in the way the March events were commemorated. As the example of the remembrance by the FAUD has shown, by construing the uprising as a syndicalist endeavor the FAUD attempted to convince potential members that the rival movements, above all the Social Democracy, would only poorly represent the interests of the working class.

In this way, the syndicalists offered an identification for the dead as well as for the survivors. They did not only linked themselves to the fallen workers but at the same time linked the past to a certain vision of the future, in this case, the continued struggle for a liberated society. Correspondingly, besides the expression of the own political agenda and the appearance of the own organization in public, the memorial functioned as a renewal of 'political hope and emotional strength.'[88] By remembering past victories and lost chances, future triumphs appear to be possible. For this reason, we can assume that the remembrance of successful resistance or social struggles is especially relevant to those communities that fight for social change and (have to) believe that the status quo is significantly alterable.

To conclude, the same event, a shared plot so to speak, was linked to respective narratives. The example of the *Märzgefallenen* highlights that memory work not only serves the function to establish an 'excessive unity' regarding an imagined community,[89] but also or simultaneously to dissociate the own movement from certain agents and to explicitly exclude them. However, I caution against overrating the 'competition for cultural hegemony'[90] between the diverse communities. Indeed, the groups laid different emphases on which events to commemorate and offered various interpretations even to that extent that memories '[had] essentially become a weapon between rivals within the movement.'[91] On the other hand, there were nevertheless such striking overlaps and similarities between the remembrance traditions of the three groups that we still have to speak of one remembrance culture. All three communities did continue to remember the two major events of the international labor movement, May 1st and the Paris Commune, as well as proceeded to remember the fallen of March 1848 and of March 1920. Although these events were interpreted differently, in the end, syndicalists, communists, as well as social democrats, spread the same message during these memorial days[92]: that the fight for an equal society beyond capitalism will and has to go on. However, this was still insufficient to bind the German labor movement together and to overcome mutual hostility. In this respect, the ambiguity of a shared and also differing memory culture illustrates perfectly how the German labor movement was composed of several political communities whose identities were based on still shared but also different political concepts and values.

Sources

Der Syndikalist. Organ der Freien Arbeiten-Union Deutschlands (Anarcho-Syndikalisten).
Die Internationale. Organ der Internationalen Arbeiter-Assoziation.
Die Rote Fahne. Zentralorgan der Kommunistischen Partei Deutschlands (Sektion der Kommunistischen Internationalen).
Unsere Stimme. Organ der Kreis-Arbeiterbörse Nordsachsen.
Vorwärts. Berliner Volksblatt. Zentralorgan der Sozialdemokratischen Partei Deutschlands.

Notes

1 Astrid Erll, *Kollektives Gedächtnis und Erinnerungskulturen. Eine Einführung* (Stuttgart: Metzler, 2005), 105f.
2 Jan Assmann, *Cultural Memory and Early Civilization: Writing, Remembrance, and Political Imagination* (Cambridge; New York: Cambridge University Press, 2011), 114.
3 Laurajane Smith, Paul A. Shackel, and Gary Campbell, eds., 'Introduction: Class Still Matters,' in *Heritage, Labour, and the Working Classes, Key Issues in Cultural Heritage* (London; New York: Routledge, 2011), 1–16, here: 1.
4 Following Jenéa Tallentires' very generalized definition, 'community' is to be understood as a social group 'formed around shared political, material and social factors.'

Social memory plays a substantial role in the imagining of the identity of, in this case, a political community as it does for the identity of a social movement (since a social movement is itself or can include several political communities). Jenéa Tallentire, 'Strategies of Memory: History, Social Memory, and the Community,' *Histoire Sociale / Social History* 34, no. 67 (2001): 197–212, here: 197, 198.
5   Georges Haupt and Dale Tomich, 'Why the History of the Working-Class Movement?,' *New German Critique*, no. 14 (1978): 7–27, here: 16.
6   For example, a historical event of paradigmatic influence on the memory culture of specific groups. Anne Fuchs, *After the Dresden Bombing: Pathways of Memory 1945 to the Present* (University of St. Andrews, Palgrave Macmillan, 2014), 10.
7   For example, Joana Seiffert, 'Bürgerkrieg im Ruhrgebiet. Erinnerungsort Ruhrkampf,' in *Zeit-Räume Ruhr: Erinnerungsorte des Ruhrgebiets*, ed. Stefan Berger et al. (Essen: Klartext Verlag, 2019), 822–845; Klaus Jürgen Tenfelde, 'Fragmentiert, verschüttet: Der Bürgerkrieg 1920 und die Denkmalskultur im Ruhrgebiet,' in *Revolution und Arbeiterbewegung in Deutschland 1918–1920*, ed. Karl Christian Führer (Essen: Klartext-Verl, 2013), 413–430.
8   See the article of Stefan Berger in this volume. See also: Paul Stangl, 'Revolutionaries' Cemeteries in Berlin: Memory, History, Place and Space,' *Urban History* 34, no. 03 (December 2007): 407–426; Barbara Könczöl, 'Dem Karl Liebknecht haben wir's geschworen, der Rosa Luxemburg reichen wir die Hand' – Der Wandel des 15. Jaunuar als politischer Gedenktag von KPD und SED (1920 bis 1989),' in *Jahrbuch für Historische Kommunismusforschung 2005*, ed. Hermann Weber et al. (Berlin: Aufbau, 2005), 171–188; Christian Saehrendt, *Der Stellungskrieg der Denkmäler: Kriegerdenkmäler im Berlin der Zwischenkriegszeit (1919–1939)* (Bonn: Dietz, 2004).
9   Tenfelde, 'Fragmentiert, verschüttet,' 422.
10 Ulrich Klan and Dieter Nelles, *Es lebt noch eine Flamme: rheinische Anarcho-Syndikalisten/-innen in der Weimarer Republik und im Faschismus* (Grafenau-Döffingen: Trotzdem-Verlag, 1986), 123.
11 'Deutschland. Bericht der Freien Arbeiter-Union Deutschlands (Anarcho-Syndikalisten) für den II. Kongreß der Internationalen Arbeiter-Assoziation,' *Die Internationale*, no. 5, Juni 1925, 119.
12 Wolfgang Haug, '"Eine Flamme erlischt." Die Freie Arbeiter Union Deutschlands (Anarchosyndikalisten) von 1932 bis 1937,' *Internationale wissenschaftliche Korrespondenz zur Geschichte der deutschen Arbeiterbewegung* (IWK), no. 25 (September 1989): 360.
13 'Sömmerda,' *Der Syndikalist*, no. 13 (1920); In fact also other sources state, in 1920 the FAUD was the only union present in Sömmerda. Frank Harves, 'Die Freie Arbeiter-Union Deutschlands in Sömmerda/Thüringen von 1919–1933' (Magisterarbeit, Bochum: Ruhr-Universität Bochum, 1997), 25.
14 'Sömmerda,' no. 13 (1920),
15 'Sömmerda,' (1920).
16 Günter Gleising and Anke Pfromm, *Kapp-Putsch und Märzrevolution 1920* (Bochum: RuhrEcho Verl, 2013), 74.
17 Gleising and Pfromm, *Kapp-Putsch und Märzrevolution 1920*, II:58.
18 Fuchs, *After the Dresden Bombing*, 10.
19 Bernd Buchner, *Um nationale und republikanische Identität. Die deutsche Sozialdemokratie und der Kampf um die politischen Symbole in der Weimarer Republik* (Bonn: Dietz, 2001), 168.
20 Gleising and Pfromm, *Kapp-Putsch und Märzrevolution 1920*, 68/9.
21 Ibid., 76; During the already mentioned remembrance in Dortmund in the year 1921, for example, the poem 'Die Toten and die Lebenden' (The Dead to the Living) from July 1848 was recited. Meinberg, Aufstand an der Ruhr, fn 1, 143.
22 'Berliner Märzerinnerungen,' Vorwärts. Berliner Volksblatt. Zentralorgan der Sozialdemokratischen Partei Deutschlands, March 18, 1931.
23 Gleising and Pfromm, *Kapp-Putsch und Märzrevolution 1920*, II:529.

24 'Der 18. März,' Vorwärts. Berliner Volksblatt. Zentralorgan der Sozialdemokratien Partei Deutschlands, March 18, 1921.
25 The SPD, for example, stressed how the fight for the eight-hour day, introduced by the social democratic government in 1918, was linked to the May celebration.
26 Buchner, *Um nationale und republikanische Identität*, 263.
27 In 1925 and 1926 a surprising number of May 1st rallies were organized by both, the KPD and SPD. Buchner, *Um nationale und republikanische Identität*, 272.
28 'Maikampf!,' *Unsere Stimme. Organ der Kreis-Arbeiterbörse Nordsachsen*, no. 4. (May 1928).
29 Saehrendt, *Der Stellungskrieg der Denkmäler*, 14/15; Wolfgang Kruse, 'Strukturen, Entwicklungslinien und Perspektiven der öffentlichen Erinnerung an die Toten moderner Kriege in Deutschland und Westeuropa,' in *Mittel- und langfristige Perspektiven für den Waldfriedhof Halbe: Abschlussbericht der Expertenkommission und Beiträge*, ed. Günter Morsch, Jürgen Danyel, and Anja Tack (Berlin: Metropol, 2009), 107–108.
30 'Sömmerda,' no. 13. (1920).
31 'Trauerfeier in Sömmerda,' *Der Syndikalist*, no. 18 (Supplement) (1920).
32 'Sömmerda,' (1921).
33 Gleising and Pfromm, *Kapp-Putsch und Märzrevolution 1920*, 77.
34 The most famous monument would be in Weimar, designed by Bauhaus founder Walter Gropius, inaugurated May Day 1922. Buchner, *Um nationale und republikanische Identität*, 346.
35 Erhard Lucas, *Märzrevolution 1920: Verhandlungsversuche und deren Scheitern; Gegenstrategien von Regierung und Militär; die Niederlage der Aufstandsbewegung; der weiße Terror* (Frankfurt: Verl. Roter Stern, 1978), III:465.
36 Saehrendt, *Der Stellungskrieg der Denkmäler*, 26, 93.
37 Thälmann spoke for instance at a memorial event held on the cemetery Pelkum (Rhineland-Westphalia) in 1925. In December 1920 however, it has been syndicalists (maybe among other organizations) who collected donations to raise a monument in Pelkum for a mass burial site with 195 victims. 'Aufruf zum Denkmalfonds für das Massengrab von 105 Genossen in Pelkum bei Hamm i.Westf.,' *Der Syndikalist*, no. 50 (1920); Gleising and Pfromm, *Kapp-Putsch und Märzrevolution 1920*, II:288.
38 Uwe Schledorn, *70 Jahre Kapp-Putsch. Ein Beitrag zur Geschichte des 'Märzgefallenendenkmals' auf dem Hagener Rembergfriedhof*, ed. Hagener Geschichtsverein, SPD Unterbezirk Hagen (Hagen: SPD Hagen, 1990), 20.
39 Demonstration to the memorial or cemetery, speeches, choir performances, and wreath-laying were the usual components – at least for the labor movement. Other movements or groups included (aside from their respective symbols) also a religious representative.
40 'Trauerfeier in Sömmerda,' *Der Syndikalist*, no. 18 (Supplement) (1920).
41 For example, Reinhart Koselleck, 'War Memorials: Identity Formations of the Survivors,' in *The Practice of Conceptual History: Timing History, Spacing Concepts* (Stanford, CA: Stanford University Press, 2002).
42 This is not surprising for a civil war scenario, when the front line does not (at all) correspond with alleged national commonalities. Manfred Hettling, 'Einleitung. Nationale Weichenstellungen und Individualisierung der Erinnerung,' in *Gefallenengedenken im globalen Vergleich: nationale Tradition, politische Legitimation und Individualisierung der Erinnerung*, eds. Manfred Hettling and Jörg Echternkamp (München: Oldenbourg, 2013), 11–42, here: 35.
43 'Sömmerda,' *Der Syndikalist*, no. 15 (Supplement) (1921).
44 Smith, Shackel, and Campbell, 'Introduction,' 11.
45 Enzo Traverso, 'Marxism and Memory,' in *Left-wing Melancholia: Marxism, History, and Memory* (New York: Columbia University Press, 2016), 54–84, here: 59.
46 Anton Rosinke, 'Aufruf!,' *Der Syndikalist*, no. 7 (February 15, 1930).

47 Hettling, 'Einleitung. Nationale Weichenstellungen und Individualisierung der Erinnerung,' 16.
48 Gleising and Pfromm, *Kapp-Putsch und Märzrevolution 1920*, 92.
49 Uwe Schledorn, 'Grabmal der Revolutionskämpfer auf dem Rembergfriedhof in Hagen (Westf.),' in *Sie starben, damit wir leben: der Kapp-Putsch 1920 und das Märzgefallenendenkmal in Hagen*, ed. Hagener Geschichtsverein, Hagener Geschichtshefte (Hagen: Lesezeichen, 1997), 43–77, here: 44.
50 Joachim Hoffmann, *Berlin-Friedrichsfelde. Ein deutscher Nationalfriedhof: kulturhistorischer Reiseführer* (Berlin: Das Neue Berlin, 2001), 93.
51 Tenfelde, 'Fragmentiert, verschüttet,' 418.
52 Why has a separate commemoration not been established right after 1920? I could imagine the experience of fighting side by side and the shared pain was a strong motive to commemorate together. But as the relation between the organizations continued to deteriorate and the first difficulties arose regarding the commemoration ceremonies, a splitting was easier than to negotiate with the respective opponents year after year.
53 Gleising and Pfromm, *Kapp-Putsch und Märzrevolution 1920*, II:166.
54 Sigrid Koch-Baumgarten, *Aufstand der Avantgarde: Die Märzaktion der KPD 1921* (Frankfurt; New York: Campus, 1986), VI:299.
55 Gleising and Pfromm, *Kapp-Putsch und Märzrevolution 1920*, II:529/30.
56 In Bergkamen, according to the memorial commission's report, the monument was donated by the local syndicalists, the unveiling was joined by the SPD, KPD, and the Gelsenkirchner Union (a disaffiliation of the FAUD). Further organizations sent wreaths. Wilhelm Hevermann, 'Die Denkmalsenthüllung der Märzgefallenen vom Kapp-Putsch 1920 in Bergkamen,' *Der Syndikalist*, no. 47 (1921); Also in Erfurt (Thuringia), August 1921, represents of all the groups of the workers' movement spoke during the dedication of three tombstones. Willibald Gutsche, and *Der Kapp-Putsch in Erfurt* (Erfurt: SED-Bezirksleitung, 1958), 1921.
57 'Vereins-Nachrichten. Arbeiterbörsen Witten und Umgegend,' *Der Syndikalist*, no. 10 (1921).
58 'Die Tragödie von Sömmerda. Eine Erinnerung,' *Der Syndikalist*, no. 12 (26 March 1932).
59 'But always, the confusion bear fatal fruit. In the Ruhr area, in the Rhineland and Westphalia the workers disarmed the […] soldiers – and rightly so. In the flush of victory, they forgot to burst the murder machines and believed it would be "freedom" if they would now start a war by themselves and do what the enemy did. […] And again it's death alone reaping the harvest. […] General strike is the weapon, which, intelligently led, will defeat the strongest mine-throwing power and still does not murder.' Frigor, 'Freiheit oder Gewalt,' *Der Syndikalist*, no. 14 (1920).
60 R[udolf] R[ocker], 'Die große Lehre,' *Der Syndikalist*, no. 12 (1920).
61 H.R., 'Unser Märzgedenken: Vor 10 Jahren! Die Lehren des Generalstreiks,' *Der Syndikalist*, no. 11 (15 March 1930).
62 J. Ehmer, 'Das Reichsbanner auf den Gräbern der Märzgefallenen in Tunzenhausen und Sömmerda,' *Der Syndikalist*, no. 13 (Supplement) (March 1927).
63 Harves, Die Freie Arbeiter-Union Deutschlands in Sömmerda/Thüringen von 1919–1933, 43.
64 'Wie die KPD in Einheitsfront macht. Die Vorgänge in Sömmerda bei der Märzgefallenenfeier,' *Der Syndikalist*, no. 15 (15 April 1931).
65 'Wie die KPD in Einheitsfront macht.'
66 Priska Daphi, *Becoming a Movement. Identity, Narrative and Memory in the European Global Justice Movement* (London; New York: Rowman & Littlefield International, 2017), 26.
67 Adolf Meinberg, *Aufstand an der Ruhr: Reden und Aufsätze*, ed. Hellmut G. Haasis and Erhard Lucas (Frankfurt (M): Verlag Roter Stern, 1973), 144.

68 On the attempt to construct a 'republican patriotism' that 'centered on the achievements of the Weimar constitution,' see, for example, Manuela Achilles, 'With a Passion for Reason: Celebrating the Constitution in Weimar Germany,' *Central European History* 43, no. 04 (December 2010): 666–689.
69 'Zum 7. November,' *Die Rote Fahne. Zentralorgan der Kommunistischen Partei Deutschlands* (Sektion der Kommunistischen Internationalen), November 7, 1920.
70 Call for demonstrations and rallies, for example, in: *Die Rote Fahne. Zentralorgan der Kommunistischen Partei Deutschlands* (Sektion der Kommunistischen Internationalen), November 7, 1920; 'Revolutionskundgebungen der KPD,' *Die Rote Fahne. Zentralorgan der Kommunistischen Partei Deutschlands* (Sektion der Kommunistischen Internationalen), November 7, 1930.
71 See, for example, 'Den Toten der Revolution. Eine Gedenkfeier der Arbeiterjugend,' *Vorwärts. Berliner Volksblatt. Zentralorgan der Sozialdemokratischen Partei Deutschlands*, 13 January 1931. But apparently also here the remembrance involved conflicts; in 1920 the SPD called to stay away from a demonstration Communists had organized. 'Straßendemonstationen für Liebknecht und Luxemburg,' *Vorwärts. Berliner Volksblatt. Zentralorgan der Sozialdemokratischen Partei Deutschlands*, 16 January 1920; Barbara Könczöl, 'Dem Karl Liebknecht haben wir's geschworen, der Rosa Luxemburg reichen wir die Hand', 173–177.
72 For example, in Remscheid (Rhineland-Westphalia), 'Denkmal und Grab für Freikoprs, Westfriedhof, Remscheid,' Ruhrecho 1920, http://www.ruhr1920.de/orte/061.html [accessed 15 May 2020].
73 For example, the inscriptions of the memorial stones in Essen and Kiel refer to the Freikorps as them 'faithfully performed their duty.' 'Essen-Steele (Wasserturm), Nordrhein-Westfalen', Denkmalprojekt, http://www.denkmalprojekt.org/2013/essen-steele_wasserturm_1920_nrw.html [accessed 15 May 2020]; 'Kiel (Nordfriedhof, 3. Marine-Brigade), Schleswig-Holstein,' Denkmalprojekt, http://www.denkmalprojekt.org/2016/kiel-nordfriedhof-(3.marine-brigade-von-loewenfeld)_sh.html [accessed 15 May 2020].
74 Gleising and Pfromm, *Kapp-Putsch und Märzrevolution 1920*, II:288.
75 See, for example, 'Freie Arbeiter-Union Holsterhausen.'
76 Heinrich Oesterwind, 'Aufruf an das revolutionäre Proletariat Rheinlands-Westfalens! Massen-Gedächtnis-Demonstration und Kranzniederlegung,' *Der Syndikalist* 5, no. 9 (1923).
77 For instance, in Holsterhausen (Essen, Ruhr area). 'Freie Arbeiter-Union Holsterhausen,' *Der Syndikalist*, no. 21 (1921).
78 According to Günter Gleising, the construction of memorials on cemeteries needed authorization, which depended on the power relations within the city hall. Gleising and Pfromm, *Kapp-Putsch und Märzrevolution 1920*, 77.
79 Tenfelde, 'Fragmentiert, verschüttet,' 419.
80 Therefore, only individual graves were raised. Gleising and Pfromm, *Kapp-Putsch und Märzrevolution 1920*, II:364.
81 Lucas, *Märzrevolution 1920*, III:466; for example, in Essen in 1934 (incidentally, only in 1989 an information plate to inform about the historical context of this NS memorial was added). Ludger Fittkau and Angelika Schlüter, eds., *Ruhrkampf 1920 Die vergessene Revolution. Ein politischer Reiseführer* (Essen, Ruhr: Klartext, 2015), 73.
82 In Remscheid, workers' organizations demanded the construction of a new memorial since the first one was destroyed by the Nazis. The Christian Democratic Union polemicized those workers killed in 1920 fought for the dictatorship of the proletariat, the Lützower Freikorps, however, for the republican government. Nevertheless, in 1948 the foundation stone for a monument was laid. Lucas, *Märzrevolution 1920*, III:466.
83 Annegret Schüle, *Anarchosyndikalismus in Sömmerda*, ed. Landeszentrale für politische Bildung Thüringen, (Erfurt, 2004).

84 After the KPD was forbidden in West Germany in 1956 the remembrance of the March events in many places died out. Gleising and Pfromm, *Kapp-Putsch und Märzrevolution 1920*, 98.
85 For example, 'Gedenken an Todesopfer rechter Gewalt in DU-Walsum!,' Antifa Duisburg, https://antifaduisburg.noblogs.org/post/2012/03/28/gedenken-an-todesopfer-rechter-gewalt-in-du-walsum/ [accessed 15 May 2020]; 'Kranzniederlegung am Denkmal der Kämpfer gegen Reaktion und Faschismus in Werne,' VVN-BdA Bochum, http://vvn-bda-bochum.de/archives/category/themen/aufstand [accessed 15 May 2020].
86 https://www.denkmal-wuppertal.de/2013/02/kapp-putsch-denkmal-der-blitz-von-unten.html.
87 Jan Assmann, *Das kulturelle Gedächtnis: Schrift, Erinnerung und politische Identität in frühen Hochkulturen* (München: Verlag H.C.Beck, 2013), 40.
88 Smith, Shackel, and Campbell, 'Introduction,' 11.
89 Manfred Hettling, 'Erlösung durch Gemeinschaft. Religion und Nation im politischen Totenkult der Weimarer Republik,' in *Politische Kollektive: die Konstruktion nationaler, rassischer und ethnischer Gemeinschaften*, ed. Ulrike Jureit (Münster: Westfälisches Dampfboot, 2001), 217.
90 Astrid Erll et al., ed., 'Memory and Politics,' in *Cultural Memory Studies: An International and Interdisciplinary Handbook* (Berlin; New York: Walter de Gruyter, 2008), 179.
91 Haupt and Tomich, 'Why the History of the Working-Class Movement?,' 16.
92 More similarities could be found if we consider the manner of how the memorial events were carried out, the symbols used, and the songs and poems performed.

References

Achilles, Manuela. 'With a Passion for Reason: Celebrating the Constitution in Weimar Germany'. *Central European History* 43, no. 04 (December 2010): 666–689.

Assmann, Jan. *Cultural Memory and Early Civilization: Writing, Remembrance, and Political Imagination*. Cambridge; New York: Cambridge University Press, 2011.

———. *Das kulturelle Gedächtnis: Schrift, Erinnerung und politische Identität in frühen Hochkulturen*. Beck'sche Reihe 1307. München: Verlag H.C.Beck, 2013.

Buchner, Bernd. *Um nationale und republikanische Identität. Die deutsche Sozialdemokratie und der Kampf um die politischen Symbole in der Weimarer Republik*. Bonn: Dietz, 2001.

Daphi, Priska. *Becoming a Movement. Identity, Narrative and Memory in the European Global Justice Movement*. London; New York: Rowman & Littlefield International, 2017.

Denkmalprojekt. 'Essen-Steele (Wasserturm), Nordrhein-Westfalen', accessed May 15, 2020. http://www.denkmalprojekt.org/2013/essen-steele_wasserturm_1920_nrw.html. 'Kiel (Nordfriedhof, 3. Marine-Brigade), Schleswig-Holstein', accessed May 15, 2020. http://www.denkmalprojekt.org/2016/kiel-nordfriedhof-(3.marine-brigade-von-loewenfeld)_sh.html.

Doerr, Nicole. 'Memory and Culture in Social Movements'. In *Conceptualizing Culture in Social Movement Research*, edited by Britta Baumgarten, Priska Daphi, and Peter Ullrich, 206–226. London: Palgrave Macmillan, 2014.

Duisburg, Antifa. 'Gedenken an Todesopfer rechter Gewalt in DU-Walsum!', accessed May 15, 2020. https://antifaduisburg.noblogs.org/post/2012/03/28/gedenken-an-todesopfer-rechter-gewalt-in-du-walsum/.

Erll, Astrid. *Kollektives Gedächtnis und Erinnerungskulturen. Eine Einführung*. Stuttgart: Metzler, 2005.

Fittkau, Ludger, and Angelika Schlüter, ed. *Ruhrkampf 1920 Die vergessene Revolution. Ein politischer Reiseführer*. Essen, Ruhr: Klartext, 2015.

Fuchs, Anne. *After the Dresden Bombing: Pathways of Memory 1945 to the Present*. Basingstoke: Palgrave Macmillan, 2014.

Gleising, Günter. *Kapp-Putsch und Märzrevolution 1920. Ereignisse und steinerne Zeugen. Gräber und Denkmäler zwischen Rhein und Weser erzählen Geschichte*. Vol. II. Bochum: RuhrEcho Verl, 2014.

Gleising, Günter, and Anke Pfromm. *Kapp-Putsch und Märzrevolution 1920*. Bochum: RuhrEcho Verl, 2013.

Gutsche, Willibald. *Der Kapp-Putsch in Erfurt*. Schriftenreihe zur Geschichte der deutschen Arbeiterbewegung in Thüringen. Erfurt: SED-Bezirksleitung, 1958.

Harves, Frank. *Die Freie Arbeiter-Union Deutschlands in Sömmerda/Thüringen von 1919–1933*. Magisterarbeit. Bochum: Ruhr-Universität Bochum, 1997.

Haupt, Georges, and Dale Tomich. 'Why the History of the Working-Class Movement?' *New German Critique* 5, no. 14 (1978): 7.

Hettling, Manfred. 'Einleitung. Nationale Weichenstellungen und Individualisierung der Erinnerung'. In *Gefallenengedenken im globalen Vergleich: nationale Tradition, politische Legitimation und Individualisierung der Erinnerung*, edited by Manfred Hettling and Jörg Echternkamp, 11–42. München: Oldenbourg, 2013.

Hoffmann, Joachim. *Berlin-Friedrichsfelde. Ein deutscher Nationalfriedhof: kulturhistorischer Reiseführer*. Berlin: Das Neue Berlin, 2001.

Klan, Ulrich, and Dieter Nelles. *Es lebt noch eine Flamme: rheinische Anarcho-Syndikalisten/-innen in der Weimarer Republik und im Faschismus*. Grafenau-Döffingen: Trotzdem-Verlag, 1986.

Koch-Baumgarten, Sigrid. *Aufstand der Avantgarde: Die Märzaktion der KPD 1921*. Vol. 6. Frankfurt; New York: Campus, 1986.

Könczöl, Barbara. 'Dem Karl Liebknecht haben wir's geschworen, der Rosa Luxemburg reichen wir die Hand" – Der Wandel des 15. Jaunuar als politischer Gedenktag von KPD und SED (1920 bis 1989)'. In *Jahrbuch für Historische Kommunismusforschung 2005*, edited by Hermann Weber, Ulrich Mählert, Bernhard H. Bayerlein, Horst Dähn, Bernd Faulenbach, Jan Foitzik, Ehrhart Neubert, and Manfred Wilke, 171–188. Berlin: Aufbau, 2005.

Koselleck, Reinhart. 'War Memorials: Identity Formations of the Survivors'. In *The Practice of Conceptual History: Timing History, Spacing Concepts*, edited by Reinhard Koselleck, 285–326. Stanford, CA: Stanford University Press, 2002.

Lucas, Erhard. *Märzrevolution 1920: Verhandlungsversuche und deren Scheitern; Gegenstrategien von Regierung und Militär; die Niederlage der Aufstandsbewegung; der weiße Terror*. Vol. 3. Frankfurt: Verl. Roter Stern, 1978.

Meinberg, Adolf. *Aufstand an der Ruhr: Reden und Aufsätze*, edited by Hellmut G. Haasis and Erhard Lucas. Frankfurt (M): Verlag Roter Stern, 1973.

Ruhrecho 1920. 'Denkmal und Grab für Freikoprs, Westfriedhof, Remscheid', accessed May 15, 2020. http://www.ruhr1920.de/orte/061.html.

Schledorn, Uwe. *70 Jahre Kapp-Putsch. Ein Beitrag zur Geschichte des 'Märzgefallenendenkmals' auf dem Hagener Rembergfriedhof*, edited by Hagener Geschichtsverein. SPD Unterbezirk Hagen. Hagen: SPD Hagen, 1990.

———. 'Grabmal der Revolutionskämpfer auf dem Rembergfriedhof in Hagen (Westf.)'. In *Sie starben, damit wir leben: der Kapp-Putsch 1920 und das Märzgefallenendenkmal in Hagen*, edited by Hagener Geschichtsverein, 43–77. Hagen: Lesezeichen, 1997.

Schüle, Annegret. *Anarchosyndikalismus in Sömmerda*, edited by Landeszentrale für politische Bildung Thüringen. Erfurt, 2004.

Seiffert, Joana. 'Bürgerkrieg im Ruhrgebiet. Erinnerungsort Ruhrkampf'. In *Zeit-Räume Ruhr: Erinnerungsorte des Ruhrgebiets*, edited by Stefan Berger, Ulrich Borsdorf, Ludger

Claßen, Heinrich Theodor Grüttner, and Dieter Nelles, 822–845. Essen: Klartext Verlag, 2019.
Smith, Laurajane, Paul A. Shackel, und Gary Campbell. 'Introduction: Class Still Matters'. In *Heritage, Labour, and the Working Classes*, edited by Laurajane Smith, Paul Shackel, and Gary Campbell, 1–16. London and New York: Routledge, 2011.
Stangl, Paul. 'Revolutionaries' Cemeteries in Berlin: Memory, History, Place and Space'. *Urban History* 34, no. 03 (December 2007): 407–426.
Tallentire, Jenéa. 'Strategies of Memory: History, Social Memory, and the Community'. *Histoire Sociale / Social History* 34, no. 67 (2001): 197–212.
Tenfelde, Klaus, Jürgen. 'Fragmentiert, verschüttet: Der Bürgerkrieg 1920 und die Denkmalskultur im Ruhrgebiet'. In *Revolution und Arbeiterbewegung in Deutschland 1918–1920*, edited by von Karl Christian Führer, 413–430. Essen: Klartext-Verl, 2013.
Traverso, Enzo. 'Marxism and Memory'. In *Left-wing Melancholia: Marxism, History, and Memory*, edited by Enzo Traverso, 54–84. New York: Columbia University Press, 2016.
VVN-BdA Bochum. 'Kranzniederlegung am Denkmal der Kämpfer gegen Reaktion und Faschismus in Werne', accessed May 15, 2020. http://vvn-bda-bochum.de/archives/category/themen/aufstand.

11

MEMORY AS POLITICAL INTERVENTION

Labor movement life narration in Australia, Jack Holloway and May Brodney

Liam Byrne

In 1916 an extraordinary and unique event convulsed Australian society. In October that year, Australian voters were polled in referendum to decide if Australian men should be conscripted for overseas military service. Australia had joined the war effort in 1914 as a dominion of the British Empire. Over the course of the war more than 333,000 served in the Australian Imperial Forces, with at least 59,000 perishing.[1] Few Australians were untouched by the sacrifices of the war, and this made the conscription debate an especially polarizing affair. The Yes case alleged imperial and national disloyalty on behalf of their opponents, dubbed the 'Antis.' The Antis, predominantly consisting of the labor movement, alleged that the pro-conscriptionists were seeking to introduce European-style militarism into the land. This, it followed in their argument, would destroy the industrial and political freedoms the trade unions had fought so hard to attain. Indicative of the heated racialized politics of the time, both accused the other of sacrificing the racist White Australia policy. It was a time of sprawling, confused, and vituperative mobilization and public debate. Nowhere else in the world during the 'Great War' was such a crucial matter of war aims put to the populace.[2] When the votes were tallied, extraordinarily, the Australian people voted no. There would be no conscription in Australia.[3]

It was a defining moment in the politics of the nation, and in particular, for its labor movement. Australian labor was, at this time, of international significance. It had produced the first workers' party in the world to govern a nation: the epochal Australian Labor Party (ALP) administration of 1904. Its political influence ensured passage of a range of progressive reforms, with industrial arbitration particularly prized by labor leaders. The trade union movement was able to operate freely and without repression, and its political representatives within the ALP were an established element of the governing system. Labor was the hegemonic political expression of the organized workers' movement with no substantial challengers to its influence from the constellation of small socialist groups. The ALP's position as an integral component of Australia's democracy was demonstrated by its election to national government in September 1914, tasking it with leading the country's war effort.[4]

This created tension between the Labor government and the movement which had sponsored it into power.[5] Labor ministers and MPs were criticized for introducing measures, which reduced the living standards of the working class. By mid-1915, socialist criticism of the Labor government and the Prime Minister, Billy Hughes, was deafening. In late 1915, Hughes reneged on Federal Labor's promise to hold a referendum that would give his government the power to introduce price controls. The broader labor movement howled in outrage. Then, in 1916, after several months touring Britain, Hughes proposed a referendum with the intent of introducing conscription. The union movement mobilized against this alleged treachery. After they defeated Hughes at the polls, they expelled the prime minister and his supporters from the Labor Party, and the labor movement. It was a famed labor split that convulsed the movement. The ensuing losses from its ranks were great enough to ensure that Labor would not govern the nation again for more than a decade.

The conscription victory became a key reference point in the mythos of the Australian labor movement. In subsequent years participants would write widely read reflections on their experiences and the meaning of the campaign, the central Victorian trade union building adorned its walls with plaques to commemorate the victory, and past participants would long hark back to the great battle of 1916 to prove their loyalty to the movement.[6] Through such means, the conscription campaign of 1916 became an integral component of the Australian labor movement's conceptualization of itself, and its understanding of its own history and sense of purpose.

In this chapter I consider the contested meaning of the conscription battle and the 1916 'split' in the life writing of two labor activists and leaders: E.J. 'Jack' Holloway, and May Brodney, née Francis. In 1916 Jack Holloway was one of the most powerful trade unionists in Australia, and a pivotal figure of anti-conscriptionism. He served as President of the Trades Hall Council (THC) in Victoria (the peak representative body of trade unions in the state) and was the first national President of the ALP. Brodney (at the time Francis) was also actively involved in the movement, as a trade union delegate to the THC, and as secretary and founder of the radical socialist grouping, the Militant Propagandists of the Labor Movement (MPLM). Both proclaimed themselves to be socialists, and both advocated radical action against conscription.

In the 1950s and 1960s these veterans of the anti-conscription movement produced conflicting accounts of its events and interpretations of its meaning to further their own political projects. By this time Holloway was an elder of the labor movement. He had been elected as a Labor MP in 1927, and served as a minister in the governments of 1941–9, retiring from parliament in 1951. In 1954 he penned an unpublished reflection of his life story, its title indicating the trajectory of his career: *From Labor Council to Privy Council*.[7] The text was drafted as the ALP experienced another bitter split, this time as right-wing Catholics abandoned the party for an alleged softness toward communism. It was a traumatic experience that Holloway dwelled upon in his recollections.[8] A decade later, Holloway's text found publication, in part, with his chapter on conscription forming the basis of a pamphlet produced in commemoration of the fiftieth anniversary of the campaign.[9] This text was released as the Australian conservative government introduced conscription as part of its military commitment to American forces in Viet Nam. As it did so, Labor experienced further convulsions as the party leader Arthur Calwell, himself a stalwart of 1916, faced internal opposition to his staunch anti-conscription position from the ambitious reformer Gough Whitlam. Whitlam succeeded Calwell as Labor's leader and brought the ALP back to power after 23 years of federal opposition in 1972, and was widely credited with modernizing Labor's policies, identify, and electoral approach. In 1966 Whitlam was Calwell's deputy, but believed Calwell's strong stance to be an electoral liability.[10]

Brodney was spurred by this account of the movement to issue a rejoinder. She had remained an inveterate radical. A founding member of the Communist Party in 1920, Brodney had been a fixture of the radical left, and a prominent figure in its causes.[11] Holloway's text on conscription, she believed, obviated the true radicalism of the time, and was indicative of his own journey from socialist to moderate labor politics.

Through their life narrations, these veterans contested the memory and legacy of 1916, and did so intending to intervene into political debates underway in the movement. As such, they constructed and contested the movement's collective memory. This chapter uses these case studies to consider the nature of personal memory and life writing in the context of social movements, its contribution to the 'collective memory' of the movement, and the forms of the writing themselves. As will be discussed further below, life writing is integral to the construction and perpetuation of working-class culture. Memory and reminiscences provide a means through which historical meaning can be transmitted from one generation to the next, solidifying the sense of shared experiences, and providing a meaningful way to interpret the position of the class and its members within broader capitalist society. What is remembered in these accounts, what is forgotten, and how do such recollections help and hinder in appreciating the motivations and actions of those that gave substance and meaning to labor as a movement? What does this suggest about the existence of 'official' movement memory, and forms of internal movement counter-memory – narratives about the past that challenge those sustained by the movement's leadership?

Literature on collective memory and social movements

Life narration is an important element of the construction and perpetuation of cultures of work, and working-class culture.[12] Autobiographical writing and oral testimonies play a crucial role in defining proletarian identity within an industry, nation, or political tradition. In the political realm, labor biography has been central in maintaining loyalty and cohering identity, though this biography has been disproportionately weighted toward labor parliamentarians, party-operatives, and union leaders.[13]

As Tim Strangleman has demonstrated, such working-class narratives depict the author's process of induction into working life, summoning the sensory and emotional experiences of this time of transition. Speaking of one working-class memoir, Strangleman analyzes the transformative experiences it presents 'wherein the boy becomes a man through the work performed or the anticipation of it.'[14]

In such a story, the subject comes of age through induction into the rituals and practices of the world of work. Their identity is defined by the act of having a profession. Though each industry has its own specific culture and key reference points, this narrative arc of personal self-definition through entry into the world of work can be related to more broadly within a working-class readership. By heightening the emotional and symbolic resonance of such experiences, this type of writing imbues meaning for subsequent generations of the working class.

In the labor movement, similar inductions into the political practices and rituals of labor are integral to the meaning and identity the movement requires to maintain itself across generations. Life narrations are a pivotal device through which the significance of the movement's practices, structures, and sense of self are imbued with a general meaning and passed from one generation to the next. They assist in tying otherwise disparate moments together in a single thread of meaning: so that opposition to conscription in the service of Empire in 1916 is unified with the movement against conscription to 'fight communism' in Viet Nam in 1966.

So how is such memory used, and contested, within a social movement? There is a disparate and eclectic literature that specifically considers memory within social movements, though there has been no systematic exploration of the relationship between memory and movement, a fact that is often bemoaned.[15] In this sparse, yet growing, literature it is generally accepted that a movement's collective identity is constructed in reference to the past. A crucial element in this construction is the remembrance of things past, and the narration of the movement through autobiographical recollection.

Unsurprisingly, these works are largely framed in reference to Maurice Halbwachs' pioneering work on collective memory.[16] Though his conceptualization has been consistently critiqued, Halbwachs' insight that individual experience can be expressed and understood only through collective social coding remains significant in overcoming the tendency to either overly personalize and individualize memory, or to innately connect the concept of collective memory to state/national memory. It provides the basis to study social movements as individuals in motion, bounded in a collective by both personal motives and general claims.[17]

Despite his substantial discussion of class in his most famous text, *On Collective Memory*, the form of collective identity that most scholars have focused on has been the nation, rather than that engendered by social movements.[18] This requires scholars to develop a new analytical apparatus, suited to comprehend the nature of social movements as collectives, and their modes of recollection and narrative construction. Memory studies has not necessarily been hospitable terrain for this theoretical work. As Enzo Traverso has noted, the rise of contemporary memory studies has accompanied the decline of Marxism and other radical mobilizations against the capitalist status quo. The forms of memory focused on in this literature are those which emphasize suffering, loss, and sorrow, rather than that which facilitates and spurs further active mobilization. This has led to a neglect, he argues, of 'future-oriented' 'strategic' memory, with focus instead on memory as a form of mourning.[19] Less attention is paid to the strategic imperatives and functions of memory: memory as a form of political intervention, crafted by and responding to immediate imperatives and future aims.

But this is not to suggest that social movement memory has been neglected altogether. There is an emerging literature which grapples with the role of memory in constructing movement identity, narratives, and strategies. This is often embodied in monuments, ritual, and symbolism. The personal transmission of memory – either experienced or inherited – has also been recognized as a powerful means of developing and disseminating movement knowledge. At times, this can operate to form and entrench movement mythologies, which may function to bolster movement identity, but at the cost of misrepresenting the realities of its past. The most famous study in this vein was Elizabeth Armstrong and Suzanna Crage's work on the 'Stonewall' myth, and the manner in which this epochal episode's hegemony in the mythology of Gay Liberation has displaced and obscured other meaningful events in the movement's development.[20]

The broader point to be drawn from this example is that memory and memorialization can function as a form of myth-making that, despite doubtful claims to historical accuracy, perform a significant function in cohering movement identity by providing a common reference point. Acknowledgment of such references denotes inclusion within a movement. Shibboleths of this type are vital for movements which do not necessarily have stable boundaries with broader publics.

As Erik Nevue demonstrated in his important study of the contested legacies of *Mai '68*, memory's political significance to a social movement is not just in the construction of identity, but in the active mobilization to achieve set aims based upon that identity.[21] In this sense, movement memory is not simply reflective, but active and projective, intending to draw upon and from the past to enhance the mobilizing capacities of a movement in the present and into the future.

But a social movement is not a singular thing, and neither is its memorialization, commemoration, remembrance, and myth-making. Social movements often include different factions, tendencies, and perspectives. Some, such as the labor movement, incorporate both a professional core and broader layers of non-professional activists at the grassroots. To understand movement memory, it is necessary to consider the specific placement of memory agents within a social movement, and the manner in which this positioning impacts the forms and intentions of memorialization. It is vital to account for, as Timothy Gonaware has argued, the 'specific interactive processes in which participants actively bring the past forward to the present,' as a form of 'collective movement anchoring.'[22] It is also important to recognize that the act of memorialization in a movement is as potentially constrictive as it is creative. Memories can inform a movement by locating it within a particular tradition of mobilization and claims, but this can also constrain further action by stifling the creative impetus, locking contemporary activists into the perspectives and techniques of those who came before.[23] This has a particular resonance in social movements which are framed around the creation and perpetuation of institutions that may have, or develop, an interest in stability and continuity.

As social movements are not homogenous entities – though they are often represented as such in the public sphere – their memories are internally contested. Usually, there is some form of 'official' memory narrative that is constructed within a movement. This is not necessarily consistent throughout time. It is constructed by agents conceptualized within the literature as alternately: 'remembering agents,' 'memory activists,' 'memory entrepreneurs,'[24] or 'political entrepreneurs.'[25] Often, the implication is that this is a negative, and that the cultivators of official movement memory are impeding other forms of commemoration.

Neveu, for instance, in discussing the first official movement memory of May 1968 in Paris, borrows from Weber's sociology of religion to describe the 'clergy of apparatchiks, party historians and activists, selected as witnesses in proportion to their orthodoxy' who not only helped to frame one set memory of the event, but to subsequently perpetuate it.[26] Further references to these phenomena are existent in Alessandro Portelli's work on uchronic memory, referencing the 'official' version of history that is 'sanctioned by the party leadership and by the power establishment.'[27]

This form of 'official' memory is often coded in party platforms and statements of purpose, official histories, speeches, institutes, and elsewhere. It is often repeated in the life stories of key leaders, usually politicians. It is remembered through place, song, chants, and symbolism. It is not, however, always negative – though the tight control over the 'memory' of events has served a political purpose, and seems to have often been used to justify leadership policy. It has often been used, for instance, to police the bounds of loyalty – particularly by Communist Parties which have tended toward centralized control over party-operations and meaning creation.[28]

Within social movement such as the labor movement, which has built substantial institutions to sustain its mobilization over the course of many decades, memorialization and the construction of a movement memory that is inherited by successive generations are also often positive and creative forces. Neither are these forms of memory and memorialization hegemonic, but are, instead, open to contest by other memory agents. James Scott's work on 'hidden transcripts' has been adapted and utilized by memory scholars such as Neveu and Frederick Harris to understand this challenge.[29] Scott argued that among the arts of domination is the imperative for the subjugated to perform and enact certain practices, termed 'public transcripts,' defined as the representations of behavior that conform with the expectations of the powerful. But beneath these performances lie 'hidden transcripts,' characterized as the 'discourse that takes place "offstage," beyond direct observation by powerholders.'[30] It is by considering the 'discrepancy *between* the hidden transcript and the public transcript we [that] we may begin to judge the impact of domination on public discourse.'[31]

This conceptualization has been adapted for the specific study of memory. In his work on the civil rights movement, Harris explores 'hidden transcripts' as the collective memories of 'marginalized groups' where the 'shared past is articulated below the radar screen of elites and dominant institutions and nurtured through kinship and community networks.'[32] Neveu, in particular, discusses an alternate, radical, memory of the rebellious French May 1968, distinct from that of its remembrance in the public sphere and its official movement memory. This was a 'more political, more class-sensitive, and anti-capitalist' version that persisted in 'a cultural space of narratives, clichés and remembrances.' This account was 'unseen' as 'it was expressed in private spaces, carried by cultural forms not legitimate enough to trigger public discussion in the core of the press-media system.'[33] Such forms of memory can persist beneath the most observable representations, transmitted through oral accounts – or written testimony.

Movement memory, as a whole, can function as a hidden transcript. But in large, powerful, institutionalized movements, I would suggest that a similar process occurs internally. An 'official' movement memory is constructed by powerbrokers and intellectuals, and this is often taken to represent the memory of the movement. But such memory tends to be challenged and contested, often by more radical perspectives, which can be categorized as a form of hidden transcript. The discrepancies between the two can indicate much about the construction of memory within a movement, and the political motivations that drive it. Movement memory is contestable and contested, with what is remembered and what seems forgotten of equal relevance when considering how such memory operates.

This political impulse is directly connected to memory's function in continued mobilization. Memory is, the accumulated literature suggests, a key means to bring 'the past' to the present to enable and sustain movement mobilization.[34] It should also be temporally conceptualized as a means of bringing the past into the future, and of revealing alternate futures in the past.[35] Movement memory can indicate the possible futures that were dreamed of, planned, and mobilized toward in past periods. Memory is also used to intervene in debates to guide the future direction of social movements: in terms of techniques, but also in ultimate aim.[36] As a result, the contest over a movement's memory is not just a dispute on what has been, but on the potentialities to come.

Jack Holloway's story: defining labor's boundaries

In 1954 Jack Holloway completed his memoir of a life spent in labor politics. At 130 typed pages, the manuscript was a substantial narration. It was not just the tale of times that had passed, but a political statement, an intervention into the major issue facing the movement. At its core was his account of the struggle against conscription in 1916, and the Labor Party split it engendered. These events were reconsidered in light of the breach in the ALP that culminated in the 'split' of 1954–5, when a section of right-wing Catholics led a break from Labor, and the formation of the Democratic Labor Party (DLP).

The DLP split was a distressing event, as former friends and comrades were severed by new loyalties and allegiances. Holloway was writing as a party elder who had seen this process before, with a unique and specific wisdom to share. Many in the movement had asked him, he explained, 'if the present split in the Labor Party is a serious one and how can it be explained?'[37] Through his narration of 1916 he sought to shed light on the troubled time that the movement found itself in, to interpret the meaning of these new events, and to offer hope for the way forward.

Holloway's narrative was structured around the particular interpretation of class loyalty that he proposed could protect and consolidate the movement, preserving its sense of meaning. In his interpretation, the DLP split was the result of the meddling of powerful interests from outside the labor movement, namely, those with connections to the Catholic Church, and in fact, the Church itself.[38] Holloway reflected on his own life as one of singular devotion to the cause of labor, devoid of alternate pulls upon his loyalty to the movement. It is a narrative of lessons learned in the movement, explicitly intended to pass knowledge from one generation to the next to equip it for the task it confronted of rebuilding a shattered party after its split.

This interpretation and consideration of the requirement of the time informed Holloway's narrative of the events of 1916, crafting a story of the campaign that downplayed its internal political divisions to tell a compelling, yet simplified, tale of Hughes and his cronies (influenced by powerful forces outside of the movement which loosened their ties to labor) and those who kept the faith. This simplified narrative of heroes versus villains diminished consideration of the substantial debates and differences that existed among opponents of Hughes, especially between socialists and moderates. What makes this account even more interesting is Holloway's own obscured socialist past.

Edward Holloway was born in 1875 in Tasmania, and his early life was one of hardship. Like so many other working-class youths at the time he left the state education system in his early teens to take up full-time work, in Holloway's case, in a boot makers factory. He was allocated his sobriquet of Jack at this early stage of his life by a manager who did not deign to learn the boy's name, simply shouting at him across the factory floor 'Jack.' Holloway answered, and he would for the rest of his life.[39]

Jack moved to Melbourne aged 15 and joined the cause of labor, becoming a member of the Boot Makers Union. From the factory floor he worked his way through the movement due to his persistent and passionate union activity. Soon, he represented his union to the Trades Hall Council, the powerful peak representative body of unions in the state. In the mold of many a proletarian autodidact he read voraciously, spending countless hours at the public library, and reading in the aisles of the Coles Arcade bookshop.[40]

Alongside his union commitment and membership of the Labor Party, Holloway was a declared socialist. Despite many accusations from its conservative rivals, the ALP was not a self-proclaimed socialist organization at this time. The party's social basis was the union movement, and powerful moderate unions such as the rural-based Australian Workers Union held sway over its parliamentary parties (on the state and federal level) and internal decision-making processes. There was a significant socialist minority within the party and the union movement, but it tended to lack the organizational influence of the moderates. In 1906 this situation began to change when Tom Mann founded the Victorian Socialist Party (VSP).

Best known for his long career as a British syndicalist and communist leader, Tom Mann resided in Australia from 1902 to 1909. From 1902 to 1905 he worked as the Victorian Labor Party's organizer, seeking to change the party from within. In 1906 he founded the VSP as a means to draw together the state's disparate and disconnected radicals into a single organization that could propagate the socialist creed, with the aim of eventually transforming the ALP into a socialist party. At its height the VSP had 2,000 members, making it the largest pre-communist socialist organization in Australia. Holloway was one of many young activists who were drawn into politics under Mann's influence, though he studiously avoided mentioning this affiliation with the VSP in his memoir.[41]

By 1908, however, syndicalist influences plunged the VSP into a factional dispute civil war, between those who believed the VSP should work within the official institutions of the labor movement (such as the Labor Party), and those who wished to organize separately, with the aim of replacing these official institutions altogether.

Holloway left the VSP at this point, pursuing politics through his union work and the Labor Party. But the VSP would leave its mark on the young man who still considered himself a socialist pursuing radical aims. It is notable, however, that this story of his political training within the VSP is largely obviated in his account. Holloway does make oblique references to economics classes, but neglects that these were classes in Marxist economics.[42] What he does dwell over are the relationships he built in this time. It was here, for instance, that he met John Curtin, future Labor Prime Minister, under whom Holloway would serve as minister during World War II. There was another association of note, with the young Edward Russell, a bright and ambitious young man who was also a socialist at this time, but who in 1906 won election as a Labor senator, before, in 1916, walking out of Labor with Hughes.[43] Holloway's narrative of betrayal would become a key means through which Holloway communicated his warning of the cost of breaking the bounds of loyalty to the movement, as we will see.[44]

Soon, Holloway was the most influential left-wing union leader in the state, and arguably in the country. By 1914 he was leading his union, while serving as Victorian Labor's President, and President of the Trades Hall Council. He had established himself as a figure of power and prominence, leading a confident and influential movement. Then came the war.

Holloway's account of the outbreak of war is somewhat muted. This was a controversial and defining event, one that challenged the politics and principles of socialists and labor activists across the globe. But Holloway chooses to elide the substantial debates and questioning that gripped the movement at the time, instead emphasizing the unity of labor as it entered this new and uncertain period. He makes particular reference of the contributions made by two unions to the imperial war effort. The first was the Australian Workers Union, the strongest union in Australia, known for its position on labor's right wing. The second was the left-wing Railways Union.[45]

But Holloway moved swiftly from the outbreak of war to the battle over conscription, and his own influence over the struggle:

> [in the] early years of my leadership of the industrial and political wings of the Victorian Labor Movement, I was thrust into the leadership of the greatest and most bitter battle of its history. This was the fight to prevent the evil thing from the Old World, conscription of human life for wars far beyond one's own frontiers.

Through this statement, Holloway effectively conflates his experience with that of the movement as a whole, and his account of the time proceeds through this lens. Holloway's is an insider's account based on recollections and first-hand assessments of the characters involved. His is a heroic narrative, in which the trade unions put up a united front against the measure. To his telling, the tension was between those who stayed true to the principles of Labor – by being anti-conscription – and those who strayed from the path. So the main narrative becomes of heroes and villains, rather than conflicting ideologies. Holloway spends a good deal of the text reflecting on the individuals of the time; those who acted honorably and those who did not.

One major recollection is of two Labor MPs in the state of Victoria, Frank Tudor and Senator Edward Russell, the former member of the Socialist Party. Holloway recalled a moment in which he, as state President of the ALP, went to see both men to tell them that after Hughes had announced his and the government's support for conscription, the broader labor movement had determined it was time for them to resign from the Federal Cabinet in protest. Tudor, Holloway relates, was relieved and delighted. In Holloway's telling, Tudor was utterly loyal to the movement, and gratefully took the opportunity to declare his colors.[46]

Russell, on the other hand, was less pleased with this outcome. He prevaricated, and ultimately refused. His loyalty to the movement had proven to be shallow. As Holloway recounted, at 'the first test of Party solidarity which threatened him with a little temporary loss of privileges and income, he refused to accept the majority Party decision.' This decision was not represented as being the consequence of politics or ideology, but deriving from the undue influence of the prestige of government office. Their respective fates were indicative. Russell was cast out from the movement that had brought him to power and influence, and as a result, 'he was never a happy man again.'[47] Russell's fate was, indeed, a tragic one. His mental health degenerated until his early death in 1925.[48] Tudor, on the other hand, would go on to become Leader of the Labor Party, feted and respected for his decision to remain loyal to the wishes of the movement.

The respective fates of Tudor and Russell were indicative of the broader morality tale Holloway constructed around conscription and the split of 1916. The split was a defining moment for Labor. In November of 1916, after his defeat in the referendum, Hughes walked out of Labor's party room in parliament house, refusing to receive recrimination from Tudor and other loyalists. This was the beginning of the schism. In December, at a special Labor conference presided over by Holloway, a motion was moved to formally expel Hughes and his supporters from the ALP, and the broader labor movement.[49] None who supported the cause of conscription in the campaign were allowed to remain within labor's ranks. It was a seismic event, and for Labor's prospects of leading national government, a damaging one.

Reflecting back, Holloway put forward a different interpretation. Acknowledging the damage experienced, he went on to note: 'there were compensations. The ranks were closed and we sensed a purifying effect: in the wilderness we looked to higher standards of solidarity as we set about rebuilding.'[50] It was a statement to soothe the fraying nerves of those undergoing a similar rupture within the party, nearly four decades on. This was Holloway, as an elder statesman of the movement, seeking to marshal political and personal memory to understand and intervene in a decisive issue of the time.

This act of memory as political intervention was part of the construction of an 'official memory' – the utilization of personal narrative to give shape and form to a legend of the movement, one attuned to the challenges and realities of the contemporary period, with its future direction in mind. This 'official memory' was not, in this sense, simply negative, enforcing a politically expedient line on the appropriate narrative of the labor movement. Rather, it was an important means for Labor leaders and activists to consolidate the party and justify its purpose in a troubling time of crisis.

But the tale of Holloway's narrative does not end there. Holloway's manuscript went unpublished. This was not for want of trying. But in that context an account of the internal movement dynamics by one who had not claimed the highest office himself was not deemed worthy of publication. This does not mean that this account, and the politics that informed it, served no practical and immediate use for the movement. Twelve years later, Holloway's account of 1916 was reproduced for a different purpose. In 1966 Australia was fighting in Viet Nam, and conscription had been reintroduced the previous year. Labor Leader Arthur Calwell – an activist in the 1916 campaign – was strongly against both. After losing the election in 1966 Calwell's hard line, and his leadership, was under challenge from Gough Whitlam, an epochal reformer who wished to 'crash through' the orthodoxies of the old guard to refashion Labor's purpose and program for governing.[51]

For Calwell, opposition to conscription was not a policy to be judged by electoral expediency, it was an article of faith, a core component of his very understanding of the meaning of the labor movement. Holloway's account became a useful means through which to conduct his argument that opposition to conscription was vital for Labor, no matter what its popularity (or lack thereof) in the electorate. Calwell donated to the cost of publication (and wrote the postscript) for the chapter in Holloway's memoir to become a pamphlet celebrating the 50th anniversary of the conscription campaign.[52]

Holloway had shaped a heroic narrative of 1916 that served, once more, to present an 'official' version of movement memory. By utilizing his life story to develop and present this narrative, Holloway was asserting an authority derived from experience. As shall be demonstrated, this approach was challenged by May Brodney, a socialist critic of the labor movement's moderate leadership, who drew on her own experiences of 1916 to challenge the dominant narrative of anti-conscription and its meaning for labor.

May Brodney's radical rebuttal: conscription and the movement's hidden transcripts

Brodney's political life, in contrast to Holloway's, was lived largely on labor's radical edge.[53] Throughout her activist career she consistently sought to drag the movement to the left, and she frequently crossed swords with moderate union and Labor leaders in her attempts to do so. She never lost faith in the radical potentials of the labor movement, but believed that to unleash this potential it was necessary to pull apart the obfuscations and mythologies of its moderate leaders.

This belief prompted her turn to life narration in an attempt to correct the historical record, and preserve the socialist legacy of the movement for the benefit of its contemporary and future radicals. She was particularly outraged by Holloway's version of the events of 1916. In her correspondence, Brodney expressed her agitation at Holloway's pamphlet for 'giving a false impression of the attitude of the Labor movement.' Holloway himself, she alleged, was not the unambiguously stalwart 'Anti' he presented himself to be. To her recollection, Holloway was too tenuous in his response to Hughes' proposal, concerned more with his own position of power than principle. When radicals such as Brodney were already campaigning, Holloway would not take a public position against conscription despite his personal assurances that he opposed the measure.[54] She wished to correct this record, and ensure that the tradition of socialist agitation was placed at the center of the narrative of labor's defining struggle.

Similarly to Holloway, Brodney's acts of memorialization were captured in two forms: a published text discussing 1916 through a personal prism, and an unpublished life narration. There is an important difference between the two memory agents captured in the location of their records. While Holloway's records are kept under his name in Australia's National Library, Brodney's are to be found in a collection held at the State Library of Victoria under the name 'Alfred Tennyson Brodney' – her husband. Despite a life of independent activism, political thought, and influence, Brodney's records are effectively collapsed into that of Alfred (in his own right an important figure on Australia's left),[55] indicating the gendered nature of memorialization and the archive. Holloway's recollections were also at a more developed state of preparation than Brodney's, with her work consisting primarily of sketches and notes that indicate the direction of her life narration, and the political intent behind it.

This draft of an autobiography was not Brodney's first work of memorialization. In 1963 Brodney published a historical account of the radical organization, the Militant Propagandists of the Labor Movement (MPLM).[56] The forum for this account was *Labour History*, the academic journal of the Australian Society for the Study of Labor History. While this was an academic journal, it is important to note that part of its self-defined mission and purpose was to provide a forum for debate and discussion within the labor movement, and it intentionally published articles that would appeal to non-academic labor activists and leaders.[57] As such, Brodney's memorialization was a substantial text, intended for wide dissemination in the movement.

In this text and her autobiographical writings, Brodney developed a narrative that ran directly counter to Holloway's. While Holloway's tale focuses on his rise from the grassroots to Labor's upper echelons, Brodney's is about finding the radical perspective that would guide her through the trials and tribulations of the subsequent years. For Holloway, loyalty to Labor is the ultimate act of faith, whereas for Brodney, it is loyalty to the idea and practice of socialism that defines the heroes and villains of her story.

Brodney grew up in a political household. Both her parents were Irish-migrants, and supporters of the rebel Fenian movement in their homeland.[58] From an early age, she recalled her intense interest in politics, to the point of asking her father to take her to the Victorian parliament to witness its debates. The world of formal politics was, at this time, an almost exclusively male sphere. Brodney was determined to change this, and her first political involvement was with the Women's Political Association (WPA) led by Vida Goldstein, a prominent and influential campaigner for women's suffrage (achieved in 1902 federally and on a state level in 1908).[59]

The WPA did not limit its aims to suffrage alone, but campaigned for equal pay, property rights, and other elements of gender equality. It had a vibrant intellectual culture of public meetings and lectures. Brodney recalled her first experience of such a public meeting, stating that afterwards she was 'walking on air I was so excited.'[60] The organization also produced a paper, the *Woman Voter*, that Brodney would sell on street corners and outside progressive political meetings. It is here that she began to encounter and build relationships with Melbourne's radicals.[61]

But the defining event that brought Brodney to the center of Victorian socialist politics was the outbreak of war in 1914. She was outraged by the imperialist clash, but also the jingoistic nationalism it sparked in Australia. In one evocative episode she recalled selling an anti-war newspaper with a comrade at a major thoroughfare and being set upon by an angry crowd. Word spread that they were 'pro-German' and the ferocity of the assault increased. In Brodney's words the: 'crowd behaved more like wild animals than human beings, and it was only with difficulty that the police got us out.'[62]

The war split the WPA. Brodney recounted the 'storm' that hit the WPA at the declaration of the conflict, with the organization rupturing over pro/anti-war attitudes.[63] Dislodged from her political network by her radical stance Brodney was drawn into the problems of industrial organization, dedicating herself to protecting the rapidly eroding industrial conditions in her workplace. The similarly poor conditions for women in other industries led Brodney to advocate for, and attempt to initiate, 'a union for all women workers whatever work they did.'[64]

Brodney's efforts were prompted when her employer attempted to steal extra labor time from its female-dominated workplace by refusing to use time clocks to mark the end of shifts. Her agitation around this matter led to an introduction to a radical friend of her neighbors, Jack Cosgrave, secretary of the Cycle Trades Union.[65] While impressed with her efforts to organize working women, Cosgrave expressed his shock that she had 'formed what he called a "scab union",' that is, a union not affiliated with the Trades Hall Council, which to Cosgrave 'was apparently the greatest crime a worker could commit.'[66] Cosgrave took the issue of women's representation straight to the leadership of the THC.[67] This spurred Brodney to leave her employment and take a job in military production so she could join the Clothing Trades Union, and become a union activist. Though the scheme for an all-woman union fell away at this point, Brodney became a union radical, quickly ascending to its wages board, and official positions with the union's women's section.[68]

In 1916, as it became clear that the threat of conscription was looming, Brodney, now an influential women's union delegate, joined with Cosgrave to launch the Militants. Prompted by the threat of conscription, it was a far-reaching project intending to organize at the grassroots to radicalize the movement, the militant energies of which had been smothered beneath the bureaucracy of the moderate leadership, advancing its own meager program of reforms instead of fighting for radical change.[69] After a few months Cosgrave, the inaugural secretary of the group, fell sick and Brodney took his place as secretary of the Militants.

Brodney used a biographical frame in her writing on this period to address what she believed was the major ellipses on MPLM's role in the campaign, neglected due to the heroic narrative constructed by the likes of Holloway which obviated the internal differences in the movement, particularly that between moderates and radicals. Holloway, she accused, was 'giving a false impression of the attitude of the Labor movement.'[70]

Brodney's intent was to tear Holloway's narrative apart. This was not driven by personal malice alone (though it would be to belie her reputation for sectarianism to deny this imperative). Rather, this was the logical consequence of her political perspective, and the project that had sustained her through decades of labor activism. For Brodney, labor's true existence was found not in the parliamentary party and among the top levels of trade union leadership, but rather, at the grass roots. This reflected her political convictions, and likely her experience of gendered discrimination within the movement. Women, such as Brodney, could rise to positions of prominence and influence in the labor movement in the early twentieth century. But this was strongly attenuated by patriarchal attitudes that ensured such promotion was contained to women's unions, and did not encroach on the male leadership of the trade unions as a whole. In the 1920s the situation declined for women unionists, as a series of amalgamations eroded the place and power of women-led unions, and the position of the women who led them.[71] There was, as a result, a certain level of alienation between women labor activists, and the movement's male-dominated leadership.

But equally, Brodney was motivated by her conviction in socialism, and a desire to correct the historical record. This included personal attack on Holloway. In speaking of the response to the outbreak of war in August 1914, the great test of loyalty to the principles of internationalism, she recalled: 'Some like the late E. J. Holloway claimed to be socialists but as ambitious men did not declare themselves against the war because it was unpopular to do so.'[72]

In her account, parliamentarians were not differentiated according to their loyalty or disloyalty to Labor. They were, rather, by their very position in the capitalist state, tainted by a conservatism that made them, at best, untrustworthy allies, who had to be brought into line by the workers at the grassroots. In prosecuting this case, Brodney heavily relied on the utilization of her personal narrative to reinterpret the events of 1916. In this account, she emphasized the role of the Militants (and as a result, her own role in the campaign), as the decisive factor that prevented wavering MPs from capitulating to Hughes, resulting, ultimately, in victory for the 'Antis.'

Perhaps the most striking example is in her account of Frank Tudor, and his motivations for publicly declaring his opposition to conscription. Whereas for Holloway, Tudor repudiated conscription willingly, Brodney argued that he only did so because Militants organized in his electorate of Yarra and forced him to take this stance.[73] In her telling, Tudor was a wavering and untrustworthy ally who had made comments in public speeches hinting toward possible support for conscription.[74] As secretary of the Militants Brodney wrote to Tudor, receiving a response that was 'evasive.' As a result, Militant activists visited every Labor branch within the boundaries of Tudor's electorate, carrying motions condemning conscription. As a result of this groundswell, Tudor 'finally, if somewhat reluctantly, did declare that he opposed conscription.'[75]

Brodney's narrative was not just intended to critique Holloway's construction of a simple loyalty/disloyalty binary through which the campaign's history was told, but to resuscitate a radical element to 1916 that she felt had been smothered beneath the official memory of the movement. This too was bound to the act of recollection, as she sought to assign the MPLM with the creative agency in launching the anti-conscription campaign. She argued that it was, in fact, Militants who first brought the issue to the Melbourne Trades Hall Council, in the form of a motion moved by Cosgrave. Cosgrave's motion, crucially, sought not just to launch a campaign against conscription, but to use the industrial muscle of the labor movement – a general strike – to ensure victory. This motion was not successful.[76]

Brodney observed that this was defeated as a result of a motion moved by another left-wing union leader, but backed by 'the reactionaries.' This motion rejected immediate action, but did call for the gathering of trade unions from across Australia in a grand meeting that would be held that July, launching the national campaign against conscription. For Brodney, this did not go far enough, as it did not unleash the radical energies the Militants desired. But it did, she acknowledged, bring the movement together to fight a successful campaign. While criticizing this outcome, Brodney also takes credit for it, writing that 'I think we can claim it was the Militants, both by propaganda, organization and this resolution who played a major part in this move.'[77] She would later go so far as to say: 'I am very sure, that if it had not been for the early propagandists such as the "militant propagandists" in Victoria, and similar minorities in other States, the official movement may well have been conscriptionist.'[78]

For Brodney, the conscription campaign of 1916 was one in which moderates were brought into line with the wishes of labor's grassroots by the organized actions of socialists such as herself. This narration reflected Brodney's own career and project as a labor activist. Sexism and her radical outlook ensured Brodney did not assume high office within the institutions of the labor movement. Her capacity to influence the movement's direction predominantly derived from her capacity to mobilize support and place pressure upon labor's leaders. But by the time her account of 1916 was written this influence had been left behind. Brodney ceased to be a union delegate (in the clothing-industry) in 1929, and though she eventually joined the Labor Party in 1940, she held no substantial positions of influence again before her death in 1973.[79]

In the decades that followed the success of the anti-conscription movement, Brodney was writing to intervene in the politics of labor. Her intervention was intended to correct the historical record as the means to protect and maintain a tradition she feared was being smothered beneath the bureaucracy and parliamentarianism of the movement. The year 1916 was an important touchpoint in this struggle, it was a means to accrue prestige for her own brand of politics, and to demonstrate that labor's mythological moments were bound with its radical traditions. It was, in this sense, a hidden transcript, intended to keep alive a tradition she feared forgotten, a preservation of a legacy to inspire and fuel future struggles, in direct contrast to the mythos of the movement's moderates.

Conclusion

The burgeoning literature on memory and social movements has identified the function of memory in creating and consolidating movement identity. This work, however, has a tendency to consider movements in the singular. Even in works which do identify the interplay between different forms of memory, one type of memorialization, the 'official' movement memory, is often depicted as a predominantly negative device for control, imposing stagnant mythologies to the service of contemporary expediencies.

In this chapter I have sought to demonstrate the expediency and mobility of memory and the agents of memorialization as they shift through time and circumstance. Social movements are not singular things, but complex and often contradictory currents of thought, identity, and activism, constantly transforming in response to changing circumstance. Within such periods of transition and change, memory can perform a key function of cohering and preserving movement identity. It can be a salve in a time of hurt, and a weapon in the contest over control of a movement's purpose and meaning between its different factions. Holloway and Brodney both used memorialization as a form of political intervention, and did so as part of directly competing political projects. At stake was not just the remembrance of things past, but the future trajectory of the labor movement.

The interplay between Holloway and Brodney's memorialization of 1916 is, of course, just one small example from within the broader interaction through which a movement's memory is formed, constructed, and contested. This example suggests the significance of understanding both the nature of official movement memory and its hidden transcripts, without privileging the role of either. Each form of memorialization is significant to the construction and maintenance of a movement's sense of self and purpose, and the contest over memory can be a creative, rather than disruptive, force.

Notes

1 Stuart Macintyre, *The Oxford History of Australia: Volume 4, 1901 – 1942, The Succeeding Age* (Melbourne: Oxford University Press, 1986), 177.
2 Robin Archer, 'Stopping War and Stopping Conscription: Australian Labour's Response to World War I in Comparative Perspective,' *Labour History* 106, no. 1 (2014): 43–67.
3 The story of these months has been told and retold, for an effective summary: Joan Beaumont, *Broken Nation: Australians in the Great War* (Sydney: Allen & Unwin, 2013), 219–261.
4 Stuart Macintyre, *The Labour Experiment* (Melbourne: McPhee Gribble Publishers, 1989), 36.

5 Ian Turner, *Industrial Labour and Politics: The Dynamics of the Labour Movement in Eastern Australia 1900 – 1921* (Sydney: Hale& Iremonger, 1979), 76–81, 93–97.
6 Sean Scalmer, 'Legend and Lamentation: Remembering the Anti-Conscription Struggle,' in *The Conscription Conflict and the Great War*, eds. Robin Archer, Joy Damousi, Murray Goot, and Sean Scalmer (Clayton: Monash University Publishing, 2016), 188–210.
7 E.J. Holloway, *From Labor Council to Privy Council*, Personal Papers, MS 2098. Folder 1, 22–23, National Library of Australia (NLA).
8 Ross Fitzgerald, *The Pope's Battalions: Santamaria, Catholicism and the Labor Split* (St. Lucia: University of Queensland Press, 2003).
9 E.J. Holloway, *The Australian Victory over Conscription in 1916–17* (Melbourne: Anti-Conscription Jubilee Committee, 1966).
10 Jenny Hocking, *Gough Whitlam: A Moment in History* (Carlton: The Miegunyah Press, 2008), 262–268.
11 Raelene Frances, 'Brodney, Maria May,' *Australian Dictionary of Biography*, accessed: http://adb.anu.edu.au/biography/brodney-maria-may-9587.
12 Tom Strangleman, 'Working Class Autobiography as Cultural Heritage,' in *Heritage, Labour and the Working Classes*, eds. Laurajane Smith, Paul A. Shackel, and Gary Campbell (London: Routledge, 2011), 147–159.
13 Mark Hearn and Harry Knowles, 'Representative Lives? Biography and Labour History,' *Labour History* 100, no. 1 (2011): 127–144.
14 Strangleman, 'Working Class Autobiography as Cultural Heritage,' 152.
15 Frederick C. Harris, 'It Takes a Tragedy to Arouse Them: Collective Memory and Collective Action during the Civil Rights Movement,' *Social Movement Studies* 5, no. 1 (2006): 19–43; Timothy Kubal and Rene Becerra, 'Social Movements and Collective Memory,' *Sociology Compass* 8, no. 6 (2014): 865–875.
16 Harris, 'It Takes a Tragedy to Arouse Them,' 19.
17 Mary Fulbrook, 'History-Writing and 'Collective Memory',' in *Writing the History of Memory*, eds. Stefan Berger and Bill Nevan (London: Bloomsbury, 2014), 65–77, here: 73.
18 Maurice Halbwachs, *On Collective Memory* (Chicago, IL: The University of Chicago Press, 1992). As Berger and Niven note, the concept has most frequently been deployed to appreciate 'the relationship between state power and memory,' Stefan Berber and Bill Nevan, 'Introduction,' in *Writing the History of Memory*, eds. Stefan Berger and Bill Nevan (London: Bloomsbury, 2014), 1–24, here: 9.
19 Enzo Traverso, *Left-Wing Melancholia: Marxism, History, and Memory* (New York: Columbia University Press, 2016), xiv, 10.
20 Elizabeth A. Armstrong and Suzanne M. Crage, 'Movements and Memory: The Making of the Stonewall Myth,' *American Sociological Review* 71 (2006): 724–751.
21 Erik Neveu, 'Memory Battles over Mai 68,' in *Conceptualizing Culture in Social Movement Research*, eds. Britta Baumgarten, Priska Daphi, and Peter Ulrich (London: Palgrave, 2014), 275–299.
22 Timothy B. Gongaware, 'Collective Memory Anchors: Collective Identity and Continuity in Social Movements,' *Sociological Focus* 43, no. 3 (2010): 214–239.
23 Ibid., 233.
24 Kubal and Becerra, 'Social Movements and Collective Memory,' 865–875.
25 Harris, 'It Takes a Tragedy to Arouse Them,' 19.
26 Neveu, 'Memory Battles over Mai 68,' 287.
27 Alessandro Portelli, 'Uchronic Dreams: Working Class Memory and Possible Worlds,' *Oral History* 16, no. 2 (1988): 46–56, 53.
28 See Portelli and Neveu.
29 Harris, 'It Takes a Tragedy to Arouse Them,' 20.
30 James C. Scott, *Domination and the Arts of Resistance: Hidden Transcripts* (New Haven, CT: Yale University Press, 1990), 4.
31 Ibid., 5.

32 Harris, 'It Takes a Tragedy to Arouse Them,' 20.
33 Neveu, 'Memory Battles over Mai 68,' 290.
34 Gongaware, 'Collective Memory Anchors,' 214–239, here: 233; Timothy B. Gongaware, 'Keying the Past to the Present: Collective Memories and Continuity in Collective Identity Change,' *Social Movement Studies* 10, no. 1 (2011): 39–54, here: 42.
35 Portelli, 'Uchronic Dreams,' 46–56. Jane Palmer, 'Past Remarkable: Using Life Stories to Trace Alternative Futures,' *Futures* 64 (2014): 29–37.
36 Portelli, 'Uchronic Dreams,' 46–56; Palmer, 'Past Remarkable,' 29–37.
37 Holloway, *From Labor Council to Privy Council*, 130.
38 Ibid., 131–134.
39 Ibid., 3–5.
40 Ibid., 22.
41 The VSP's internal culture and this training of future labor leader has been discussed: Liam Byrne, 'Constructing a Socialist Community: The Victorian Socialist Party, Ritual, Pedagogy, and the Subaltern Counterpublic,' *Labour History* 108, no. 1 (2015): 103–122.
42 Holloway, *From Labor Council to Privy Council*, 23.
43 Geoff Browne, 'Russell, Edward John,' *Australian Dictionary of Biography*, accessed: http://adb.anu.edu.au/biography/russell-edward-john-8300
44 Holloway, *From Labor Council to Privy Council*, 23.
45 Ibid., 27.
46 Ibid., 41.
47 Ibid., 41.
48 Browne, 'Russell, Edward John'.
49 Australian Labor Party, *Report of the Proceedings of the Special Commonwealth Conference* (Melbourne: Labor Call, 1917).
50 Holloway, *From Labor Council to Privy Council*, 41.
51 See note 9.
52 Holloway, *The Australian Victory over Conscription in 1916–17*.
53 Frances, 'Brodney, Maria May,'
54 'Correspondence with Sam Merrifieled re: historians' misunderstanding of the I.W.W. and stereo plate of cartoon,' Brodney papers, Box 4, Folder 8 (May Brodney Papers), State Library of Victoria (SLV).
55 Raelene Frances, 'Brodney, Alfred Tennyson,' *Australian Dictionary of Biography*, accessed: http://adb.anu.edu.au/biography/brodney-alfred-tennyson-bob-10002
56 M. Brodney, 'Militant Propagandists of the Labour Movement,' *Labour History*, no. 5 (1963): 11–17.
57 Eric Fry, 'The Labour History Society (ASSLH): A Memoir of Its First Twenty Years,' *Labor History*, no. 77 (1999): 83–96, here: 87–88.
58 May Brodney, 'Draft of Beginning of Autobiography,' Brodney Papers, Folder 23 (i), MS 10882, SLV, 1.
59 Ibid., 1–2.
60 Ibid., 2.
61 Ibid., 3.
62 Brodney, 'Militant Propagandists of the Labour Movement,' 13.
63 Brodney, 'Draft of Beginning of Autobiography,' 9.
64 Ibid., 9.
65 Ibid., 10–11.
66 Ibid.
67 Ibid., 11.
68 Ibid., 12.
69 Brodney, 'Militant Propagandists of the Labour Movement,' 15.
70 Brodney, 'Correspondence with Sam Merrifieled Re: Historians' Misunderstanding of the I.W.W. and Stereo Plate of Cartoon.'

71 Melanie Nolan, 'Sex or Class? The Politics of the Earliest Equal Pay Campaign in Victoria,' *Labour History*, no. 61 (1991): 101–122, here: 116; Cathy Brigden, 'The Legacy of Separate Organizing: Women in the Victorian Trades Hall Council in the Interwar Years,' *Labor Studies Journal* 36, no. 2 (2011): 245–268, here: 254–258.
72 Brodney, 'May Brodney's Notes re I.W.W.,' Brodney Papers, Box 10, folder 31, SLV, 5.
73 Brodney, 'Militant Propagandists of the Labour Movement,' 15.
74 Ibid.
75 Ibid.
76 Ibid., 14.
77 Ibid., 15.
78 Brodney, 'Correspondence with Sam Merrifield'.
79 Frances, 'Brodney, Maria May'.

12

REMEMBERING THE MOVEMENT FOR EIGHT HOURS

Commemoration and mobilization in Australia

Sean Scalmer

Australian workers won the eight-hour day from the middle 1850s. A campaign led by the stonemasons of Melbourne, April 1856, heralded broader success. The precocity of the advance helped to establish Australia's reputation as a workers' paradise. It also inspired a vigorous commemorative practice that would persist for nearly a century.

Labor's commemoration was immediate. The first celebration was in fact only three weeks after the achievement of the victory. In early May 1856, unionists resolved at a public meeting on 'a day being set apart' as a means to 'mark out to ourselves and the world' the import of the eight-hours standard. A fete in the Cremorne Gardens, Whit Monday, was agreed.[1] It was preceded by a procession through the city, as perhaps 1,200 tradesmen walked in irregular file, behind a large tricolor flag that bore the inscription 'Eight Hours' Labor. Eight Hours' Recreation. Eight Hours' Rest'. At the gardens, around 350 men and women sat down to roast beef and plumb pudding and then as many as 3,000 gathered for dancing and for fireworks.[2] Speeches were planned, though it appears that Victorians by now were more anxious to enjoy themselves than to submit to ceremonial oratory:

> It was evident the people had got the measure which they had for some time been agitating, and were not disposed for a repetition of the old arguments at that time...the committee very wisely determined upon giving the good folks their own way, and reserving themselves for the next occasion.[3]

The celebrations were revived on the first anniversary of the victory. A meeting of quarrymen in early April declared their judgment that after 'twelve months' experience', the eight-hours system was 'one of the greatest blessings the working classes ever enjoyed'. They further announced a 'determination to act upon it ourselves, and by every legal and constitutional means to assist those who have not yet partaken of its benefits'.[4] A meeting of slaters a week afterwards echoed these judgments.[5] Also in mid-April, a more substantial public meeting of upwards of two thousand workers – mostly from the building trades – gathered in the Olympia Theatre, resolving to combine again in a procession and a fete.[6]

The event was a success: some two thousand workers marched, four abreast; 'most imposing' crowds thronged the footpaths and gazed from windows; perhaps five thousand attended the Cremorne Gardens celebrations, enjoying not only the opportunity to picnic, but also a circus, an aviary, and an animal menagerie.[7] It was, apparently, a 'decided advance on the inaugural display'.[8] Victoria's press adjudged the gathering 'highly creditable to those engaged'.[9] Substantial profits from the sale of tickets underwrote a major contribution to a building fund for a 'Trades Hall': a future place of social gathering and education for Melbourne's workers.[10]

Doubtless the success encouraged emulation; within a few years, a singular celebration had become a regular annual event. Already, in 1856, an 'Eight Hours League' had been established.[11] In 1859, an Anniversary Committee agreed upon 'Rules…for the better guidance of future Eight Hours Demonstrations',[12] and from this point the commemorations took on the stable and repetitive form of a ritual practice. The size and spectacle of the anniversary nonetheless increased, year upon year. In 1879, the Anniversary was gazetted as a public holiday. By the early 1880s, more than 100,000 typically gathered in Melbourne's streets. 'Eight Hour Day' was henceforth understood as: 'the workers' day of days'[13]; the 'Emblem day of all the year'[14]; 'the greatest day in Labor's world'[15]; 'The Greatest Demonstration in Australasia', and 'The Great Event of the Year'.[16] European observers noted the event with some envy.[17] Some years before the rise of 'May Day', Australian workers had developed their own, unique form of local celebration.

The memorialization of the eight-hour day is an historical case that contrasts with the paradigmatic episodes that have structured the field of 'memory studies'. It is an example of *labor movement* commemoration, tied to a battle for improved working conditions, whereas most studies have considered the commemorative practices of non-labor movements, struggling for recognition.[18] It is a celebration of a victory, whereas earlier work has given greater attention to episodes of mourning, martyrdom, and loss.[19] It is *historically venerable*, whereas most studies undertaken so far consider the period since World War II (even eminent historians of labor have tended to date mass commemorative practices from the end of the nineteenth century).[20]

The peculiarities of this case make for distinctive insights. Because of the great time span of the eight-hour commemoration, it is possible to trace changes in memory politics over time, and to give special attention to the role of generational difference in shaping historical memory. Because this commemoration is embedded in a campaign for material advancement, it empowers an investigation of how memory politics can shape struggles for redistribution as well as recognition. Because it is an example of a movement celebration, it allows one to consider whether memories of victory rather than loss have implications for movement identity, possibility, and orientation.

It was in the city of Melbourne that the eight-hour commemoration was most elaborate, sustained and important. Considering this case, I seek to answer four questions. First, why did workers come to celebrate and remember this victory? Second, why did the commemoration persist? Third, what was its contribution to the labor movement's mobilization? Fourth, what are the implications for understandings of social movements and memory?

Why did workers seek to commemorate their eight-hour success? The answer lies partly in the favored political repertoire of Victorian workers and partly in the nature of their opposition. Unions had won 'eight hours' by persuasion more than coercion. James Stephens, the leader of the movement, emphasized that workers needed 'public opinion' to 'go with them', if they were to win their goals.[21] The 'means' of the eight-hour campaign were generally likened to those outstanding and venerated examples of earlier 'moral force' politics, the movements to abolish slavery and the corn laws.[22] This meant that emphasis was placed on the dissemination of information 'by means of the public press, public lectures and discussions'.[23] Advocates wrote numerous letters to Melbourne's newspapers.[24] They delivered lectures on the cause.[25] They commissioned an essay prize on 'The Eight Hours and Early Closing Questions' (expressly to be written in a 'popular' style and language) and then organized for the publication of the winning composition.[26] They convened large public meetings.[27] They passed resolutions.[28] They sent deputations.[29] They met with employers.[30]

Direct industrial action by workers supported these interventions. Unionists announced in mid-April an intention to henceforth work an eight-hour day, and to 'walk in procession' through Melbourne's streets, on 21 April.[31] They fulfilled this plan in large numbers – some 700 or so – meeting afterwards at a public hotel to reiterate their commitment.[32] They also withdrew labor, briefly, when two employers refused to concede. But unionists denied that this was a 'strike', seeking a less threatening terminology ('it was a libel to call it a strike').[33]

These methods were sufficient for the building trades to secure the treasured trinity of three 'eights'. But immediate victory was aided by the buoyancy of an economy propelled by the gold rushes and by a labor market in which the skilled artisan was highly prized. Once achieved, the maintenance of the standard was by no means assured. Unionists faced public opposition. One daily denounced the 'stupid mischievous blockhead' who 'set this agitation going'.[34] Another warned that 'capital is a sensitive thing'.[35] And even the sole newspaper that supported the campaign advised workers against following their 'passions' and 'prejudices', counseling submission to 'the laws of trade'.[36] While some employers were sympathetic, others sought to reimpose a longer day of ten hours.[37] Failing businessmen blamed their insolvency on the system.[38] Many workers continued to labor in excess of the declared standard.[39]

The decision to commemorate the eight-hour day in 1856 and soon afterward should therefore be understood as an attempt to defend a fragile industrial achievement. It was not so much a confident remembrance of a secure victory as an effort to buttress a treasured but unstable gain. It deployed methods of public performance that had earlier been used as a means of political pressure. If it was an act of commemoration, it was also a form of political mobilization. If it propagated the memory of a past victory, it was also a contribution to a movement's maintenance, and to its extension.

Why did the commemoration persist? Though labor's achievements were fragile, the context was otherwise relatively hospitable. Residing in a prosperous new city in a settler-colony, Melbourne's residents enjoyed the capacity to assemble in public; working-class men possessed the right to vote. City authorities regularly ceded the right to march. There were no competing state festivals, and in consequence labor's grand day could be embraced as a common civic occasion.

The political environment permitted unionists to remember in public. Workers continued to exploit this opportunity, year upon year, for two reasons. First, because it served to support the movement. Second, because a generation of activists – the 'men of the fifties' – felt a strong emotional tie to the founding of the eight-hour day, and as they aged they worked with vigor to maintain and then to extend its public remembrance.

The celebration of the eight-hour day strengthened the labor movement in several ways. It promoted the value of 'eight-hours' demand. It drew attention to the number of beneficiaries. It publicly asserted the strength of the movement. It demonstrated the worthiness of the workers. It promoted the unity of the campaign, and of the broader labor movement. And it conveyed to labor's supporters a message of the importance of political struggle.

First, the celebration of the anniversary was a public statement of the value of the eight-hour standard. By assembling in large numbers, workers signaled their devotion to the system. Newspapers reported that it was the 'greatest holiday of the year amongst working men', outranking New Year's Day, Boxing Day, and Easter Monday.[40] They acknowledged, too, that its popularity expressed a commitment to principle. The *Australasian*, for example, described the anniversary as

> the day of all days of the year to the artisans of Melbourne – the commemoration of victory, the attestation of a principle for which the working man will forever unfurl his banners, and, it must be supposed, shed his blood at need.[41]

The banners that workers carried in procession explicitly referenced the system and registered its promise. Leading the march was the old flag: 'Eight Hours' Labor. Eight Hours' Recreation. Eight Hours' Rest'. The Stonemasons' banner, the first of its kind carried in an eight hours demonstration, also included a representation of labor, recreation, and rest.[42] One part of the Millers' Operatives Society banner was a picture of the first flour mill in the colonies to adopt the eight-hours principle.[43] Other banners took on allegorical forms that symbolized the benefits of a shorter day and that expressed the workers' devotion. One trades' flag pictured a figure of female divinity, raising a wearied worker with one hand, while the other pointed to higher aspirations. Another depicted a dragon of oppression, crushed by the genius of liberty.[44] The bricklayers' banner was an image of the 'emancipation of labor': an angel stooping to raise the worker on one side; the arms of the bricklayer on the other.[45] The Seamen's Union banner included the figure of 'Hope' on one side and the ocean god of Neptune on the other. One observer suggested that: 'The god stands triumphantly, as if proud of the achievement his devotees have won, and glad of the place they occupy in the 'eight hours' procession'.[46]

Poems and songs amplified the message. William Pascoe's song, 'Eight Hours Anniversary', emphasized the value of the trinity:

> Eight hours for labor, eight hours for rest,
> And eight for whatever each man may think best,
> For study or pleasure, or parley or play:
> This rule or division no man can gainsay.[47]

J.A. Andrews' 'Eight Hours Day' was no less adoring, though it clearly aspired to a greater poetical sophistication:

> For where is the land can glory in treasure so rich as ours?
> Not even old England's standard, begirt by the chainless sea.
> Or bars that hold open the star-gate of Washington's liberty,
> Have shadowed a pearl so lovely (though widely their folds have flown)
> To match with this gem so radiant, that is all Australia's own?[48]

Second, it publicly established the beneficiaries of the eight-hours system. Participation in the anniversary procession was at first limited to those workers whose trades had recognized 'the Eight hours principle'.[49] It was not enough to be a member of a union; one needed also to reassure the Anniversary Committee that hours of work 'never exceeded eight hours'.[50] From the very beginning of the campaign, the success of one union therefore incited others to join the struggle: first the stonemasons, then the bricklayers, carpenters, joiners, plasterers, and slaters.[51] Members of trades working longer hours watched on as the aristocrats of labor proudly marched.

As new unions secured the privilege, so they joined the celebration.[52] It has been estimated that by 1881, 56 of the 76 unions in Melbourne had their origins in demands for an eight-hour day.[53] And if the exclusiveness of the march at first expressed a sense of superiority and social distance, it also offered a public measure of the movement's progress. Over time, the commemorative procession effectively became a display of the relative extension of the principle. The number of unions joining the procession expanded from as few as seven or eight in 1856 to nearly 50 at the turn of the century. These included so-called 'new unionists' (associated with an expansion of unionism beyond the old crafts): wharf laborers; implement makers; builders' laborers; engine-drivers; cigarmakers; felt hatters; railway workers; typographical workers; tobacconists; glass bottle makers;

wickerworkers; tailors; glass bevellers.[54] They became leading figures in the organization of celebrations.[55] By 1915 there were 111 separate sections, with new participants that included 'women bookbinders', clerks, gardeners, billposter, theatrical employees, musicians, and textile workers, among many others.[56] As more workers achieved the standard, so observers noted, with anticipation, that 'the ranks will be swelled'.[57] The eight-hours march thereby served to underline the growth of the movement, and its apparent ascendance from year to year.

Third, the claiming of the city's streets was a demonstration of strength. Even on the occasion of the first anniversary, the spectacle was imposing: a procession of nearly 2,000 persons, extending some half a mile; the display of union banners, marked by images that manifested workers' skills and their animating values; the thronging of the footpaths; the blast of music from the bands.[58] The increasing scale of the commemorations brought with it a heightened evocation of labor's massed power. By the mid-1880s the event encompassed 22 bands, 70 trade societies, and some 140,000 spectators.[59] Buildings throughout the city were decorated with bunting and flags[60]; even those citadels of the establishment, St. Paul's Cathedral and Parliament House, were so bedecked.[61] Housetops, trees, and lamp-posts were scaled by workers and their supporters.[62]

This was the era in which the crowd was just being imagined as a fearsome and threatening presence, and some journalists recorded a sense of strangeness and possible alarm. One report noted that the pageant 'took complete possession of the streets', stopping trams and 'pursuing a self-assertiveness'.[63] Another stated that the thick crowds made 'a very powerful and enduring impression'[64]; a third that 'the streets themselves' were 'the most striking portion of the show'.[65] Others still argued that the commemoration established for the public that 'this is a working man's country',[66] or that it conveyed 'the power of the people'.[67] Those with strong affiliations to labor were more expansive, arguing that the tramping of the workers' feet expressed the political potential of an increasingly dominant collective actor:

> "Tramp, tramp, tramp, the boys are marching." My word, it was a soul inspiring site, and likewise an exceeding suggestive one … Thinks I to myself, here's union, and consequently strongness; this here three mile o' men isn't to be imposed upon, and refuses sternly, but respectfully – respectfully mind you – to be trampled on.[68]

> Tramp! Banners boldly waving, bands stirringly playing, bodies rhythmically swaying: faces determined …. This process, to men who have eyes to see and ears to hear, symbolizes the great international march from gloom and bondage to sweetness and regeneration.[69]

The increasing permanence of labor's spatial presence in the city magnified these impressions. As early as 1859 a Trades Hall building had been constructed out of timber on the corner of Lygon Street and Victoria Parade with funds raised from a public campaign; it included a large public hall, library and café. This was conventionally the place where workers assembled on Anniversary morn. From 1874 the building was reconstructed on bluestone foundations according to the design of Joseph Reed, who was also responsible for the Public Library and Town Hall in Swanston Street as well as the Exhibition Building. The new building's ornate entrance portico, with its Corinthian columns, suggested a complement and a rival to the colonial legislature on Spring Street. An eight hours' monument, raised in 1903 and in 1923 placed on an adjacent corner, further established labor's claim to equal status in the colony, as it did the formative role of the eight-hour day.

Fourth, the commemoration publicly established the worthiness of Australia's artisans. The commemoration of the eight-hours victory was also a demonstration of pride in the act of labor. Not only tramping with banners in hand, unionists also attempted to display the skills that defined their trades. Borne on lorries drawn by draft horses, the societies thrilled the crowds with their proficiency. Farriers used a forge to make shoes for a pony; tinsmiths equipped knights in sheets of armor; felt hatters exhibited head-gear in all the stages of its manufacture; bakers used ovens to feed the people with huge loaves; stonemasons chipped at a block of bluestone; members of the typographical society worked off handbills en route; engineers, coachmakers and furniture makers displayed fine examples of their work.[70] The poetical tribute, 'The 21st of April' foregrounded the significance of labor to the process of commemoration, its opening lines strangely anticipating Bertolt Brecht's 'Questions From A Worker Who Reads':

> Who cut the marble gems of Greece –
> Frieze, Column, Temple, Tomb?
> Who carved the graceful capital
> Evolved from ancient gloom?
> Who reared the might Pyramids?
> Great Babylon so gay?
> But men like us, with chisel, trowel,
> Who keep this EIGHT-HOUR DAY.
> ....
>
> In every Land, in every Age,
> The Flower of Life's deep Play
> Is Labor! Which we Eight-Houred Men
> Apotheose to-day.[71]

If commemoration allowed unionists to project the skill and dignity that defined their labor, it also presented further opportunities for the display of collective worth. The procession itself was a display of discipline, order, and self-control. Observers were impressed by the respectable appearance of the tradesmen,[72] the absence of drunkenness and fisticuffs,[73] and the orderly conduct of the people.[74] Even Victoria's Governor celebrated the 'order' and 'regularity' of the march.[75] The 'well-organized' and 'controlled' character of the procession was especially emphasized by labor's supporters.[76] It was, moreover, a reflection of the self-government of the unions themselves – union officials commanded their own members within the march, while the elaborate deployment of different colored flags offered overall coordination.[77] The *Leader* argued that 'a stranger would have been struck by the unanimity and organization'.[78]

The carnival that succeeded the procession projected intellectual ambition, as well as order. Advocates of the eight-hour day had first justified the enhancement of recreation for its capacity to offer 'moral' and 'intellectual' advantages to the working class.[79] In consequence, the program of entertainment was soon broadened beyond banqueting and dancing to embrace more ambitious and elevating activities. Shakespeare's plays were performed.[80] Organists ventured works from Rossini and Mendelsohn; orchestras played selections from Carmen. And a major sports carnival came to encompass a great variety of events, especially foot-racing and cycling.[81] Commenting on the festival in 1888, the *Australasian* saw the termination of proceedings as a confirmation of the high moral status of the Victorian worker:

> It is to the credit of the whole of the Eight Hours people that Saturday evening should have closed so quietly. In no other British city, perhaps, would 50,000 people, all with money in their pockets and ample opportunities for dissipation, have held themselves in such admirable self-control, mixed mirth so thoroughly with reason, and gone home in such good and orderly fashion.[82]

Fifth, the cooperation of Victorian unionists in the act of commemoration both celebrated and reproduced a common and unified identity. For so many different trade societies to work together so closely was indeed a rare achievement at this time; it was recognized as such.[83] As one union leader put it: 'The result of the gathering was not only to cement the bond of union between the various trades, but to extend the feeling of unionism in all directions….(Cheers.)'[84]

This was a unity performed as much as proclaimed. The unfolding of the commemoration quite deliberately aimed to dramatize the pre-eminence of collective ties. The committee that organized the anniversary celebrations incorporated members of all participating unions and capped the number of delegates per association. The choreography of the 1859 procession was structured around the rotation of leadership, so that each section (representing a distinct craft) had an opportunity to take the front of the march.[85] Even when this arrangement was abandoned as impractical, in later years, a ballot of the unions was undertaken to determine the order of the procession.[86] Likewise, a ballot in 1869 determined the six banners that would be displayed at the celebratory evening ball.[87] These and other measures affirmed the equality of the trades and their joint participation in a common struggle.

The very process of annual celebration also acted to promote labor's unity over time, as well as between the trades. Year upon year, Anniversary Committee meetings passed the same resolution: '…that the Trades walk the same in the Procession as last year',[88] that 'the old route of former years be followed'.[89]

The repetition of the practice meant that participants did not simply remember the eight-hour victory, but also re-enacted the past commemoration of that victory. The persistence of the celebrations connected the activists of the past and the present in a common relationship to labor's founding struggle. They came to share an orientation to the original victory of 1856 as well as a form of collective action that sought to honor it. This act of sharing bound the movement together.

The process is perhaps best illustrated through the career of the 'Eight Hours' flag. Its continuity across the years of labor movement contention made it a material expression of the link between past and present. The 'worn appearance' (frequently noted),[90] and the simplicity of the design came to contrast with the more elaborate creations of later years. The flag's deterioration made the endurance of the anniversary physically visible. Its tattered presence connected anniversary marchers across the decades, so that the aging of the flag embodied the continuity of the movement and the common affection for the object an emotionally binding tie. From the early 1880s, observers noted the popularity of the standard:

> It is a perfect nonentity compared with the gorgeous silk banners which have since sprung up, but the working men will never use another so long as its threads hold together, so much do they prize it.[91]

Labor's propagandists amplified the theme. W.E. Murphy's *History of the Eight Hours Movement* (1896) provided a detailed account of the flag's creation, even fabricating an imagined declaration by its designer: 'I intend this banner to be handed down to those who shall maintain our glorious principles, therefore it must be made of lasting material and standing colors'.[92] One contributor to the radical newspaper, the *Tocsin*, argued that the flag's weavers should be honored by inclusion at the head of the anniversary march.[93] The newspaper photographed the 1898 Anniversary Committee alongside the banner, providing the caption: 'The New Men and the Old Flag'.[94] Beyond the flag, of course, laborites persistently emphasized the connection between the eight-hour day and the unity of labor. To cite one, representative Australian socialist: '"The Unity of Labor is the Hope of the World." This is the lofty and final meaning of the Eight-hour celebrations'.[95]

Finally, the anniversary was the commemoration of a victory. It therefore served to remind workers of the value of struggle and the necessity of political self-assertion. Union banners proclaimed this lesson, marked, as they were, by pithy directives to mobilize: 'Union is strength'[96]; 'Slaves No Longer'[97]; 'Hot and Ready'[98]; 'By Unity We Stand'[99]; 'He who would be free himself must strike the blow'.[100] William Pascoe's song, 'Eight Hours Day', summarized these lessons of the anniversary more expansively:

> Come, toilers all,
> Obey the call;
> Join in the celebration

> Of eight hours' day
> With spirits gay
> And joyful adulation.
>
> Be firm and bold
> Like those of old,
> Who won this just concession;
> Keep on your strife,
> Devote your life
> To struggle for progression.[101]

In the press and in speeches, Laborites recalled the eight-hour victory as a product of sacrifice and struggle: 'no easy victory', but a 'strenuous, uphill fight', resting on a 'grand indomitable spirit'.[102] It was alleged to encompass 'great personal risks'.[103] It was thought to rest on persistent 'workers' agitation',[104] and on 'the solid front of Unionism'.[105] Hilary Boland's poem, 'Labor Pioneers', summed up this view of the past:

> Let me sing one song of triumph, ere I lay the pen aside,
> They may read it in the places where the hosts of Toil abide;
> 'Tis the song of Labor marching, ever onward to the goal,
> Never looking to the rearward, strong of heart and staunch of soul,
> Just a song of toil and trouble, but they bravely fought their way,
> Till they placed the Labor banner where it proudly flies to-day.[106]

Remembered in these terms, the eight-hours successes of the 1850s provided a justification for further struggle in the present. In 'Past and Future!', a poem written especially for labor newspaper, the *Tocsin*, J.A. Andrews gloried in the victories of the stonemasons – the 'triumphs of our fathers' – but noted also the continuation of inequality – the threats of the 'Landlord', 'Worklord', and 'Wealthlord'. For Andrews, these were a 'bitter degradation' and a 'shame'. The resources and memories of history provided a reason to struggle against them, and to mobilize anew…

> Do we honour thus our fathers? Let their flags be hid in shame,
> Or become the flags of battle, earning newer, brighter fame!
> Let us onward to the conquest, for the children of our land,
> Of their country to abide in, and the labors of their hand
> …
> For a free united people on a free and noble shore!
> Bid the banners range for war![107]

The capacity of the commemorations to propel the labor movement forward contributed to their persistence. But a generation of labor activists – the eight-hour pioneers – were especially attached to the 1856 victory and particularly devoted to the promulgation of its lessons. As they aged, so they became more active in the memorialization of their own histories.

From the later 1860s, those who gathered to celebrate the eight-hour victory increasingly framed the campaign as a thing of the past: 'The movement had now reached an age that made it historical'.[108] The death of James Galloway – stonemason and early advocate – quickened this process. A campaign to raise a funerary monument was enacted, and in 1869 and 1870 funds were gathered from the Anniversary Committee and from other unions and short hours associations, to realize the ambition.[109] A fine and imposing monument was erected, out of Malmsbury stone.[110] The process of fund-raising promoted Galloway's contributions, suggesting that 'every man who worked only eight hours' was himself 'a living monument to the exertions of James Galloway'.[111] The poem recited at his graveside, as the monument was raised, honored Galloway as a kind of prophetic figure:

> Who gained the toiler an enduring prize,
> And first conceived that honest labor's foes
> Should be restrained by gen'rous human laws,
> Who taught that shorter hours of daily toil,
> Was birthright of the men of Austral soil.
> Thou died and left behind a deathless name,
> To be emblazoned on the scroll of fame

It cautioned its auditors to remember:

> And shall he lie neglected in the grave:
> Whose words were wisdom, and whose acts were brave?

It affirmed that Galloway was 'worthy of a monumental stone'. And it tried to imagine a permanence to his achievement that was threatened by the encroachment of death:

> Soon may the pile completed greet our eyes,
> To consecrate the spot in which he lies;
> And may its graven tablets not decay
> What age on age has slowly passed away.[112]

Galloway's passing was premature, and it was some decade later when a greater proportion of the movement's pioneers approached the end of their lives. Other forces contributed at this time to a growing interest in the movement's past. The right to eight hours, and to participate in the annual march, had spread by the early 1880s to new unions and new workers who had no direct involvement in the struggles of mid-century. It is notable that Melbourne's major dailies – conservative and liberal – both published detailed accounts of the campaign's history just as it won these greater successes. In 1883 the *Argus* profiled what it called the 'Rise and Progress of the Eight Hours' Movement',[113] while the *Age* explicitly linked its synchronous historical survey to the recent extension of the eight-hour system:

> Of the many who enjoy this boon, there must be thousands who are not acquainted with its history, and therefore a brief sketch of the origin and progress of the movement will be of interest.[114]

It was also in the middle 1880s that the Stonemasons' appointed a committee to confirm the origins of the movement, and particularly to establish the relative role of the leading figures. Its report was published and widely circulated.[115] It elevated the special claims of former Chartist (veteran of the Newport Uprising), James Stephens. It also promoted a 'National Testimonial' to aid Stephens in an improvident old age, drawing attention to the 'obligations' owed to him by his fellow workers.[116]

Stephens served as the inaugural President of a new organization that advanced the import of the early participants in the movement: the 'Pioneers of the Eight Hour Day Association'. First convened in March 1885, the group's purpose was to organize an annual 'social gathering' and to coordinate participation in the anniversary procession.[117] The connections with the life cycle were obvious. The Preamble to the Association described the group as 'a fitting tribute to ourselves that we should bound together as a brotherhood, and fraternally cheer each other by periodical intercourse during the remnant of our declining days'. It further imagined a process of generational succession, as the founding fathers passed the stewardship of the movement on to those who came afterward:

> as years cool and as we are one by one removed from the scene of action it shall be the sacred duty of the last Pioneer to hand the standard of triumph to our sons whose duty it shall be to carry on the work from step to step until every man, woman and child throughout the land who obtain their living by the sweat of their brow shall be participants in this glorious boon bequeathed them by their fathers.[118]

The intent was to claim a special status. The Pioneers presented themselves as 'men of the "fifties"' who had 'accomplished so much for the amelioration of the industrial classes'.[119]

Keen to demonstrate their collective import, they petitioned the Anniversary Demonstration Committee to take a place in the procession. When the Demonstration Committee initially replied that 'the most honoured place in the procession was at the head of their respective bodies' (that is, as members of the trade societies, and not as a separate group), the Pioneers were incensed.[120] After further pressure, the Association's members did eventually gain an accepted place as an identifiable collective at the rear of the procession, as well as the possibility of inclusion in commemorative photographs.[121] Still, they were not satisfied.

The next year, a deputation of veterans argued that 'as Pioneers of the Eight Hour Movement they should be recognized as such in the procession and … their place should be at the front and not the rear', even invoking a parallel with 'the Pioneers who fought at the Battle of Waterloo'.[122] Their request was granted, though only on the condition that they march (rather than ride).[123] As the Demonstration Committee probably foresaw, this was thought impractical by the Pioneers, and so they now accepted that they 'could ride in Draggs' at the rear of the procession.[124]

Tensions remained. One Pioneer complained that the younger radicals of the Trades Hall had slighted him and his brothers as 'old Fossils'.[125] The Association's Minutes recorded frustration that the 'young men who form the large majority' of trade societies 'fail to appreciate the work of our members'.[126] But the Pioneers resolved that their 'just claims' would be 'recognised at the true value',[127] and anger at apparent slights in fact inspired greater exertions. A Pioneers' Flag was created[128]; an identifying ribbon was obtained for wearing on the anniversaries[129]; and a regular place in the procession was maintained.[130] Stung by what they felt was a disrespect within the movement and a wider public ignorance of their import, they now brought forward schemes to heighten their acknowledgement.

In 1889, the Pioneers developed a scheme for a 'National Monument',[131] and at a public meeting in September they sought to win support. The address that publicized the plan expressed a desire to 'commemorate and perpetuate this greatest achievement of Labor that – as yet – has been accomplished in the history of the world'.[132] The Chair of the Pioneers, Benjamin Douglass, anticipated mass enthusiasm: 'All classes, he was convinced, would come forward, and there is no doubt about it'.[133]

The projection soon seemed optimistic. A committee met regularly. Promotional materials were despatched (thanks in part to free postage, gifted by a Liberal Government).[134] A model of the proposed monument was rapidly produced and publically displayed.[135] But already by early 1890 it was conceded that 'we are unable to report as favorably as we otherwise should have'.[136] A series of divisive and damaging industrial disputes coincided with the onset of a major financial collapse and a great depression. Trade societies, unsurprisingly, did not contribute to the monument fund as expected.[137]

In consequence, progress stalled and plans were recast. The original design embodied the allegorical and ambitious character of the movement's banners. It comprised a female figure of intelligence, carrying a lighted torch, and a male figure of labor: a hammer over his shoulder, a wedge in his right hand. Behind them a column read: 'Eight Hours'. The costs required to complete this design proved too vast, however, and a more modest construction was eventually pursued.[138]

The monument eventually upraised was designed by one of the pioneers, J. Rees, and then produced at Australian Pioneer Granite Works, Footscray. It stood approximately 25 feet high, and was decorated atop with a gilt ball or globe intended, reportedly, 'to suggest the world wide scope of the eight hours movement'. The granite base of the monument bore a simple inscription: 'To commemorate the Eight Hours movement. Initiated in Victoria 1856. Erected 1903'.[139] The final cost was some 2,000 pounds.[140] The Royal Victorian Institute of Architects thought it a poor effort: 'not fit for a site in an outlying suburb'.[141] Labor leaders admitted that it might be 'more magnificent', but were pleased, nonetheless, that it 'would bear evidence for all time of the work which had been done by the pioneers of the movement'.[142]

It was also the Pioneers who advocated in October 1889 for a 'complete and authentic history of this great social reform since its inception', suggesting even its distribution to all state schools, railway departments, and public offices.[143] The history was not completed and published until more than half a decade later, but W.E. Murphy – himself a veteran activist – canonized the work of the founding generation. Murphy's book was explicitly dedicated to the Pioneers 'with pleasure and with pride'.[144] It argued forcefully that Australians, 'without doubt', deserved 'the credit' of establishing the eight-hours system.[145] It included poetic tributes to the pioneers as possessors of 'true hearts set in steel-wrought frames'.[146] And it devoted great attention to the origins of the system, treating its consolidation and extension in only a scanty few pages. A second volume, published in 1900, surveyed developments in other lands only to confirm Australian precocity.[147]

In this way, generational assertiveness appeared to augment the movement's collective purposes. Both the desires of the pioneers and the benefits to the labor movement propelled the eight-hours commemoration onward, reproducing an image of Australian radicalism, winning a brave and significant victory that lighted the way for the workers of the world.

The story relayed helps to explain the culture of the Australian labor movement. But what are the implications for scholars less engaged with Antipodean events, and more concerned with understanding the relationships between social movements and history? Few studies have explored the relationship between social movements and memory.[148] Those that have so far been advanced have primarily considered the struggles of 'memory activists' to subvert official forgetting and to contest dominant understandings of the past.[149] They have identified the import of memory as a resource for the maintenance of movement identity.[150] But they have not grasped that commemoration can be used to pursue redistribution as much as recognition. And they have only rarely considered cases where a commemorative practice formed a central element of a social movement's emergence and mobilization.[151]

The examination of the eight-hour day in Melbourne establishes several important findings. First, unionists developed precocious and vital forms of memorialization from the middle of the nineteenth century that were cogent enough to imprint themselves upon Victorian society. Second, labor's commemorative practices not only contributed to the promulgation of a unified collective identity, but also helped to project labor's goals, advertise its affiliates, signify its strength, and educate its members on the import of struggle. Commemoration was more than a resource; it was also an effective form of action. There is good reason to accept that it aided Australian labor's remarkable rise from the 1850s through to the cusp of World War I. Third, many of the activists most concerned with memorialization were members of a particular generation, propelled by a sense of generational difference, and sometimes provoked by tensions with younger radicals. Fourth, the effects of these struggles went far beyond memory and narrative, but had implications for the working conditions and social lives of many citizens.

Clearly, the memorialization of the eight-hour day had many benefits. But there were also limits to this form of politics, and they merit some consideration. The form of Australian labor's commemorative practice raised two linked dangers. First, that the celebration of the victors might promote an unwillingness to support the struggles of those still battling to achieve political and economic rights. Second, that the celebration of the victory would obscure continuing inequalities, thereby overstating the gains that Australian workers had made and fostering quiescence.

Male craft unionists did support the eight-hours struggles of others, and the numbers enjoying the standard did greatly increase over time. Importantly, these did include female unionists. The unionization of women workers from the early 1880s was welcomed by the liberal press.[152] Female employees such as tailoresses and laundrywomen eventually joined the eight-hour day procession.[153] And just after eight-hour day in 1887 an annex to the main Trades Hall building, a Female Operatives Hall, was opened as a separate place for women to meet and organize.[154] The culture, assumptions, goals and leadership of the Victorian union movement remained masculinist. However, this did not imply a complete indifference or hostility to the extension of industrial rights to women workers.

Non-white workers, by contrast, were regarded with antipathy. As was noted in the press, Chinese workers did not participate in the eight-hours processions of the nineteenth century, despite their mass employment in the furniture trades, in particular.[155] Not only that, but some activists even connected the maintenance of the eight-hour system with a White Australia policy. At the anniversary banquet in 1888, the toast 'The Extension of the Eight Hours Principle' was met by a response from the Chair that:

> There was one thing – and only one thing – which threatened to subvert the eight-hours principle, and that was the presence of the Mongolian among us.[156]

It was not just that the eight-hour ceremonies reflected racism in Australia; the commemoration of the eight-hours principle appeared in fact to drive racial exclusions and prejudice.

This did not imply, however, that the celebration of the victory promoted acceptance of current economic arrangements. If labor propagandists treasured the achievement and remembered the struggle, they also dramatized the work to be done. Claude Marquet's influential cartoons perhaps expressed this attitude most fully. One of his fine creations, 'Labor "Rejoices"', showed the figure of

Labor carrying on his back the fatman who represented the 'Idle Rich', the Eight Hours banner in his left hand, slightly reworded: 'Eight Hours of This Daily!'.[157] Another, 'Still Too Heavy', showed Labor as carrying a cross of '8 Hours Labor'. One bystander asked whether 'this be another crucifixion?' Another explained: 'Not exactly! The giant Labor is merely rejoicing that the weight of his cross is now regulated by law!'[158]

In reflections on the eight-hour day, labor intellectuals pledged themselves to a still shorter working day,[159] to the battle to end unemployment,[160] and to the effort to eliminate poverty.[161] Most flatly rejected the notion that the anniversary celebrations were simply to 'commemorate' a 'moderately short working-day'. Rather, it was insisted, the purpose should be to express a 'determination' not just to 'conserve' the progress made, but even more to 'extend yet further the victories of labor over class, caste, and Mammon'.[162] Commemoration therefore did not imply incorporation. The vitality of labor's memories helped to drive its further advance.

The public commemoration of the eight-hour day has long been abandoned. Like the winning of the standard itself, it has passed from popular memory. Rediscovering that practice is a reminder of the labor movement's vital cultural life. It carries the implication that labor's forgetfulness may be connected with its contemporary political malaise.

Notes

1 'The Eight Hours Movement: Meeting of all Trades,' *Argus*, 6 May 1856; 'The Eight Hours Question,' *Argus*, 12 May 1856.
2 'The Eight Hours Movement,' *Argus*, 13 May 1856. For the tricolor flag: W.E. Murphy, *History of the Eight Hours' Movement, Volume I* (Melbourne: Spectator Publishing, 1896), 76.
3 'Labor Fete at Cremorne,' *Age*, 13 May 1856.
4 'Important Movement among the Quarrymen,' *Age*, 7 April 1857.
5 'The Trades' Movement,' *Age*, 14 April 1857.
6 'Anniversary of the Emancipation of Labor,' *Portland Guardian and Normanby General Advertiser*, 15 April 1857.
7 'Anniversary of the Eight-Hours' Movement,' *Age*, 22 April 1857; 'Victoria,' *Launceston Examiner*, 25 April 1857.
8 Murphy, *History of the Eight Hours' Movement, Volume I*, 95.
9 'Latest News from Melbourne,' *Bendigo Advertiser*, 22 April 1857.
10 'Town Talk,' *Bendigo Advertiser*, 27 April 1857.
11 Murphy, *History of the Eight Hours' Movement, Volume I*, 92.
12 Minutes (29 July 1859), Minute Books Eight Hours Anniversary Committee, University of Melbourne Archives, ML MSS 305, Box 5.
13 R.S. Ross, 'The Marching Army,' *Labor Call*, 23 April 1914, 10.
14 'Ode to Liberty,' in Murphy, *History of the Eight Hours' Movement, Volume I*, iii.
15 'Topical Echoes,' *Tocsin*, 26 March 1903.
16 'Eight Hours Day,' *Tocsin*, 21 April 1898, 9.
17 Émile Pouget, 'La conquête de la journée de huit heures,' *Le Mouvement socialiste* 151, no. 15 (March 1905), in: *L'action directe et autres écrits syndicalistes (1903–1910)*, Textes rassemblés et presents par Miguel Cheuca (Marseille: Agone, 2010), 235–239.
18 The role of oral history in the development of memory studies meant that many practitioners conceived the field as an attempt to bring forgotten and suppressed truths to light. The Holocaust has also served as a paradigm for studies of memory

and trauma. Summarizing the field, in an influential recent contribution, Michael Rothberg claims that 'debates about collective memory and group identity are primarily struggles over injustices of recognition'. See: Michael Rothberg, *Multidirectional Memory: Remembering the Holocaust in the Age of Decolonisation* (Stanford, CA: Stanford University Press, 2009), 20. One recent examination of the memory of the 'comfort women' (enforced sexual slaves of the Japanese Army) draws attention to the ways in which 'testimony, sympathy and remembrance' came to dominate over redistributive and material questions relating to legal redress. See: Hee-June Serenity Joo, 'Comfort Women in Human Rights Discourse: Fetishized Testimonies, Small Museums, and the Politics of Thin Description,' *Review of Education, Pedagogy and Cultural Studies* 37 (2015): 166–183.

19 Ann Rigney, 'Remembering Hope: Transnational Activism beyond the Traumatic,' *Memory Studies* 11, no. 3 (2018): 368–380. The paradigmatic labor movement festivals of the nineteenth century were the commemoration of the Paris Commune and May Day. Both emphasized the sacrifice of militants to the cause. One of the most influential studies of memory and working-class movements concerns a martyrdom: Alessandro Portelli, ed., 'The Death of Luigi Trastulli: Memory and Event,' in *The Death of Luigi Trastulli and Other Stories. Form and Meaning in Oral History* (Albany: State University of New York, 1991), 1–26.

20 Eric Hobsbawm famously identified the 'manufacture of mass traditions' with the period after the 1870s and the only labor movement case he studied in detail was May Day, beginning in 1890. See: Eric Hobsbawm, 'Mass-Producing Traditions: Europe, 1870–1914,' in *The Invention of Tradition*, eds. Eric Hobsbawm and Terence Ranger (Cambridge: Cambridge University Press, 1983).

21 'The Eight Hours Question,' *Argus*, 10 April 1856.

22 J.A. Aldwell, *The Prize Essay of the Melbourne Labor League, on the Eight Hours and Early Closing Questions* (Melbourne: Wilson, Mackinnon and Fairfax, 1858), 7; Report of stonemasons, in: 'The Eight Hours Movement,' *Argus*, 1 May 1856.

23 'Abridgement of the Hours of Labor,' *Argus*, 10 April 1856.

24 As noted in: 'Domestic Intelligence,' *Argus*, 25 April 1856.

25 For example, 'The Slaters' Annual Dinner,' *Age*, 22 April 1857.

26 Aldwell, *The Prize Essay of the Melbourne Labor League, on the Eight Hours and Early Closing Questions* See 'Prefatory Note' for popular style.

27 Mr. Sinclair, at meeting of coachbuilders, in: *'Minutes of the Victorian Eight Hours Labor League,'* n.d. [1859], Trades Hall and Literary Institute – rough minute books, 1858–1870, University of Melbourne Archives, ML MSS 308, Box 2. Note that the emphasis on public meetings as a tool of the campaign in NSW is emphasized in: John Niland, 'The Birth of the Movement for an Eight Hour Working Day in New South Wales,' *Australian Journal of Politics and History* 14 (April 1968): 75–87, here: 83–84.

28 24 March 1859, Trades Hall and Literary Institute – rough minute books, 1858–1870, University of Melbourne Archives, ML MSS 308, Box 2.

29 8 September 1859, Trades Hall and Literary Institute – rough minute books, 1858–1870, University of Melbourne Archives, ML MSS 308, Box 2.

30 Murphy, *History of the Eight Hours' Movement, Volume I*, 47–48.

31 Note this intention: 'The Eight Hours Question,' *Argus*, 15 April 1856.

32 'Domestic Intelligence,' *Argus*, 22 April 1856.

33 Mr. Spracklin, cited in: 'The Eight Hours Struggle,' *Age*, 22 April 1856.

34 The *Melbourne Herald*, cited in: *Report of the Committee Appointed by the Victorian Operative Masons' Society to Inquire Into the Origin of the Eight-Hours' Movement in Victoria*, Adopted Annual Meeting, June 11, 184, Melbourne: Labor Call Print, 1912, 6.

35 'The Eight Hours Question,' *Argus*, 21 April 1856.

36 'The Anniversary of the Eight Hours Movement,' *Age*, 21 April 1857.

37 This was the case with coachmakers in Melbourne. See: Operative Board of Trade Minute Book (22 September 1859), Trades Hall and Literary Institute – rough minute books, 1858–1870, University of Melbourne Archives, ML MSS 308, Box 2. For

a later example, see: 'The Eight Hours' Association: Meeting of Trades,' *Ballarat Star* (7 August 1869).
38 For example, 'New Insolvent,' *Age*, 6 May 1857.
39 Bradley Bowden, 'The Rise and Decline of Australian Unionism: A History of Industrial Labor from the 1820s to 2010,' *Labor History 100* (May 2011): 51–82, here: 54.
40 'The Eight Hours Anniversary,' *Leader*, 22 April 1882.
41 'Eight Hours Day Incidents,' *Australasian*, 28 April 1888.
42 'The Eight Hours' Demonstration,' *Record*, 25 April 1884.
43 'The Eight Hours Demonstration,' *Age*, 14 April 1891.
44 'Anniversary of the Eight-Hours Movement,' *Age*, 22 April 1857.
45 'Eight Hour Labor System: Anniversary Festival,' *Bendigo Advertiser*, 23 April 1857.
46 'The Eight Hours Demonstration,' *Record*, 25 April 1884.
47 William Pascoe, 'Eight Hours Anniversary,' *Bendigo Advertiser*, 19 April 1884.
48 J.A. Andrews, 'Eight Hours Day,' *Tocsin*, 20 April 1899, 2.
49 Minutes (18 March 1859), Minute Books Eight Hours Anniversary Committee, University of Melbourne Archives, ML MSS 305, Box 5.
50 Minutes (1 April 1859), Minute Books Eight Hours Anniversary Committee, University of Melbourne Archives, ML MSS 305, Box 5. See also: 'Eight Hours Anniversary Celebration,' *Age*. 5 February 1891).
51 This is the process and trajectory laid out in James Galloway to 'The Mechanics of Kilmore' (25 May 1856), in *Report of the Committee Appointed by the Victorian Operative Masons' Society to Inquire Into the Origin of the Eight-Hours' Movement in Victoria*, Adopted Annual Meeting (June 11 1884), Melbourne: Labor Call Print, 1912, 9–10.
52 'The Eight Hours Demonstration,' *Leader*, 25 April 1885.
53 Tom O'Lincoln, *United We Stand: Class Struggle in Colonial Australia* (Carlton North: Red Flag Publications, 2005) 29.
54 'Labor's Carnival,' *Tocsin*, 20 April 1899, 4.
55 For example, J.W. Billson, President of the Eight Hours Committee in 1899 was described as belonging to 'the School of New Unionism'. See: 'Our Illustrations,' *Tocsin*, 20 April 1899, 4.
56 'Order of Eight Hours Procession,' *Labor Call*, 22 April 1915, 5.
57 'The Eight Hours Demonstration,' *Age*, 20 April 1882.
58 'Eight Hour Labor System: Anniversary Festival,' *Bendigo Advertiser*, 23 April 1857.
59 'The Eight Hours Anniversary,' *Illustrated Australian News*, 30 April 1887.
60 'The Eight Hours Demonstration,' *Age*, 23 April 1883.
61 'The Eight-Hours Demonstration,' *Weekly Times*, 28 April 1883.
62 'The Eight Hours Demonstration,' *Leader*, 27 April 1889; 'Eight Hours Day in Melbourne,' *Leader*, 26 April 1890.
63 'Eight Hours Celebrations,' *Leader*, 25 April 1891.
64 'Eight Hours Processions,' *Weekly Times*, 27 April 1889.
65 'The Eight-Hours' Demonstration,' *Geelong Advertiser*, 22 April 1882.
66 'The Eight Hours Demonstration,' *Weekly Times*, 25 April 1885.
67 'The Eight Hours' Anniversary,' *Leader*, 22 April 1882.
68 'The Eight Hours Demonstration,' *Alexandra and Yea Standard, Gobur, Thornton and Acheron Express*, 30 April 1886, 3.
69 Ross, 'The Marching Army,' 10.
70 'The Eight Hours' Demonstration,' *Age*, 22 April 1884; 'Eight Hours Day,' *Australasian*, 23 April 1887; 'The Eight Hours Demonstration,' *Age*, 10 April 1886; 'The Eight Hours Procession,' *Bendigo Independent*, 22 April 1892.
71 'The Twenty-First of April,' *Tocsin*, 21 April 1898, 4.
72 For example, 'Eight Hours Procession,' *Weekly Times*, 27 April 1889.
73 For example, 'The Eight Hours Demonstration,' *Weekly Times*, 28 April 1883.
74 'The Eight Hours Anniversary,' *Weekly Times*, 22 April 1882.
75 'The Eight Hours Demonstration,' *Leader*, 25 April 1885.
76 'The Eight Hours Carnival,' *Tocsin*, 30 April 1903, 5.

77 'The Eight-Hours Demonstration,' *Australasian*, 28 April 1883.
78 'Eight Hours Day,' *Leader*, 29 April 1893.
79 An argument often put. See, for example: Aldwell, *The Prize Essay of the Melbourne Labor League, on the Eight Hours and Early Closing Questions*, 9.
80 For example, Minutes (4 April 1864), Minute Books Eight Hours Anniversary Committee, University of Melbourne Archives, ML MSS 305, Box 5.
81 The program of events for 1896 is included in: Murphy, *History of the Eight Hours' Movement, Volume I*, 121–142.
82 'Eight Hours Day Incidents,' *Australasian*, 28 April 1888.
83 For example, 'Eight Hours A Day,' *Advocate*, 25 April 1885.
84 'Pioneers Banquet,' *Leader*, 23 April 1887.
85 Minutes (8 April 1859), Minute Books Eight Hours Anniversary Committee, University of Melbourne Archives, ML MSS 305, Box 5.
86 Minutes (29 March 1860), Minute Books Eight Hours Anniversary Committee, University of Melbourne Archives, ML MSS 305, Box 5.
87 (7 April 1869), Minute Book, 1864–1873, Trades Hall, Melbourne, University of Melbourne Archives, ML MSS 308, Box 6.
88 For example, Minutes (10 April 1863), Minute Books Eight Hours Anniversary Committee, University of Melbourne Archives, ML MSS 305, Box 5.
89 (27 March 1872), Minute Book, 1864–1873, Trades Hall, Melbourne, University of Melbourne Archives, ML MSS 308, Box 6.
90 For example, 'The Eight Hours' Demonstration,' *Age*, 22 April 1884.
91 'The Eight Hours Demonstration,' *Age*, 23 April 1883.
92 Murphy, *History of the Eight Hours' Movement, Volume I*, 76.
93 'Eight Hours Day. 43rd Anniversary,' *Tocsin*, 20 April 1899.
94 'Eight Hours Anniversary Committee, 1898,' *Tocsin*, 21 April 1898.
95 Ross, 'The Marching Army.'
96 'The Eight Hours Demonstration,' *Record*, 25 April 1884.
97 'The Eight Hours' Demonstration,' *Age*, 22 April 1884.
98 'Anniversary of the Eight-Hours Movement,' *Age* (22 April 1857).
99 'The Eight Hours Demonstration,' *Leader* (27 April 1889).
100 Ibid.
101 William Pascoe, 'Song – Eight Hours Day,' *Bendigo Advertiser*, 21 April 1891.
102 'En Avant,' 'Eight Hours Day,' *Labor Call*, 6 April 1916, 2.
103 'The Day We Celebrate,' *Tocsin*, 23 April 1903, 8.
104 Walter Greig, 'Eight Hours and its Lesson,' *Labor Call*, 23 April 1914, 1.
105 R.W. 'Union Is Strength,' *Labor Call*, 22 April 1915, 18.
106 Hilary Boland, 'Labor Pioneers,' *Labor Call*, 6 April 1916, 18.
107 J.A. Andrews, 'Past and Future!,' *Tocsin*, 19 April 1900, 1.
108 'Eight Hours Anniversary,' *Mount Alexander Mail*, 22 April 1869.
109 'A Memorial to Mr. Galloway,' *Age*, 1 July 1869; (10 May 1871), Minute Book, 1864–1873, Trades Hall, Melbourne, University of Melbourne Archives, ML MSS 308, Box 6; 'Bakers' Short Hours Association,' *Ballarat Star*, 1 February 1870; 'The Galloway Monument,' *Williamstown Chronicle*, 1 October 1870.
110 Murphy, *History of the Eight Hours' Movement, Volume I*, 100.
111 'Monument to the Late Mr. Galloway,' *Williamstown Chronicle*, 3 July 1869.
112 Poem by 'Mr. Glaister,' reproduced in: 'The Galloway Monument,' *Williamstown Chronicle*, 5 November 1870).
113 'Rise and Progress of the Eight Hours' Movement,' *Argus*, 23 April 1883.
114 'The Eight Hours Movement – It is Origin and Progress,' *Age*, 23 April 1883.
115 *Report of the Committee Appointed by the Victorian Operative Masons' Society to Inquire Into the Origin of the Eight-Hours' Movement in Victoria*, Adopted Annual Meeting, 11 June 1884, Melbourne: Labor Call Print, 1912.
116 'National Testimonial to James Stephens (6 November 1883), in *Report of the Committee Appointed by the Victorian Operative Masons' Society to Inquire Into the Origin of*

the Eight-Hours' Movement in Victoria, Adopted Annual Meeting (11 June 1884) (Melbourne: Labor Call Print, 1912), 23–24.
117 'Pioneers of the Eight Hour Day Association' [henceforth PA], University of Melbourne Archives, Accession Number 77/114; Minutes (4 March 1885).
118 PA Minutes, 14 July 1887.
119 PA Minutes, 17 July 1890.
120 PA Minutes, 26 March 1885.
121 'Pioneers of the Eight Hours Movement First Annual Reunion. Melbourne (13 April 1885).' In: PA Papers.
122 PA Minutes, 16 March 1886.
123 Ibid.
124 PA Minutes, 23 March 1886.
125 PA Minutes, 4 August 1886.
126 PA Minutes, 5 July 1888.
127 PA Minutes, 5 July 1888.
128 PA Minutes, 14 May 1886.
129 PA Minutes, 19 April 1888.
130 By 1888, Pioneers spoke of a 'usual' arrangement. See PA Minutes, 9 March 1888.
131 PA Minutes, 4 July 1889.
132 PA Minutes, 2 September 1889.
133 Ibid.
134 PA Minutes, 9 January 1890.
135 PA Minutes, 19 November 1889.
136 PA Minutes, 9 January 1890.
137 PA Minutes, 3 April 1890.
138 'Eight Hours Monument,' *Leader*, 7 March 1903; 'The Eight Hours Movement,' *Bendigo Advertiser*, 22 April 1903; 'Eight Hours Memorial Unveiled,' *Weekly Times*, 2 May 1903.
139 'Eight Hours Memorial,' *Leader*, 25 April 1903.
140 Ibid.; 'Eight Hours Monument,' *Leader*, 7 March 1903.
141 Mr. Koch, President of the Royal Victorian Institute of Architects, 'Eight Hours Memorial Unveiled,' *Weekly Times*, 2 May 1903.
142 Mr. Beazley, cited in: 'The Luncheon,' *Age*, 28 April 1903.
143 PA Minutes, 3 October 1889.
144 Murphy, *History of the Eight Hours' Movement, Volume I*, viii.
145 Ibid., vii.
146 Hamilton Mackinnon, 'Ode to the Eight Hours' Pioneers,' in Murphy, *History of the Eight Hours' Movement, Volume I*, ix.
147 W.E. Murphy, *History of the Eight Hours' Movement, Volume II* (Melbourne: J.T. Picken, 1900).
148 As noted in: Linda Farthing and Benjamin Kohl, 'Mobilizing Memory: Bolivia's Enduring Social Movements,' *Social Movement Studies* 12, no. 4 (2013): 361–373, here: 363; Nicole Doerr, 'Memory and Culture in Social Movements,' in *Conceptualizing Culture in Social Movement Research*, eds. Britta Baumgarten, Priska Daphi, and Peter Ullrich (London: Palgrave Macmillan, 2014), 206–226, here: 207; Fredrick C. Harris, 'It Takes a Tragedy to Arouse Them: Collective Memory and Collective Action during the Civil Rights Movement,' *Social Movement Studies* 5, no. 1 (2006): 19–43, here: 19; Timothy Kubal and Rene Becerra, 'Social Movements and Collective Memory,' *Sociology Compass* 8, no. 6 (2014): 865–875.
149 For uses of this concept: Carol Gluck, 'Operations of Memory: "Comfort Women" and the World,' in *Ruptured Histories: War, Memory, and the Post-Cold War in Asia*, eds. Sheila Miyoshi Jager and Rana Mitter (Cambridge, MA: Harvard University Press, 2007), 47–87, here: 57; Nicole Doerr, 'Memory and Culture in Social Movements,' 206. Cognate concepts like 'memory entrepreneurs' (Erik Neveue, 'Memory Battles over Mai 68: Interpretative Struggles as a Cultural Re-Play of Social Movements,'

in *Conceptualizing Culture in Social Movement Research*, eds. Britta Baumgarten, Priska Daphi, and Peter Ullrich (London: Palgrave Macmillan, 2014), 275–299, here: 276) or 'initiators and enthusiasts of memory' (Alexander Etkind, *Warped Mourning* (Stanford, CA: Stanford University Press, 2013).) have also been advanced.

150 For example, Timothy B. Gongaware, 'Collective Memory Anchors: Collective Identity and Continuity in Social Movements,' *Sociology Focus* 43, no. 3 (2010): 214–239; Timothy B. Gongaware, 'Keying the Past to the Present: Collective Memories and Continuity in Collective Identity Change,' *Social Movement Studies* 10, no. 1 (2011): 39–54; Jeffrey K. Olick and Joyce Robbins, 'Social Memory Studies: From "Collective Memory" to the Historical Sociology of Mnemonic Practices,' *Annual Review of Sociology* 24 (1998): 105–140; Serguei Alex Oushakine Remember in Public: On the Affective Management of History,' *Ab Imperio* 1 (2013): 269–302.

151 A rare and valuable exception is: Elizabeth A. Armstrong and Suzanna M. Crage, 'Movements and Memory: The Making of the Stonewall Myth,' *American Sociological Review* 71 (2006): 724–751.

152 For example, 'Rise and Progress of the Eight Hours' Movement,' *Argus*, 23 April 1883.

153 'The Eight Hours Festival,' *Argus*, 28 April 1903.

154 'Trades Hall: A Female Operatives' Hall,' *Age*, 26 April 1887.

155 'Eight Hours Demonstration,' *Weekly Times*, 2 May 1903.

156 'The Eight Hours Anniversary Banquet,' *Argus*, 24 April 1888.

157 Claude Marquet, 'Labor "Rejoices",' *Labor Call*, 22 April 1915.

158 Claud Marquet, 'Still Too Heavy,' *Labor Call*, 23 April 1914, 15.

159 Tom Mann, cited in: 'Eight Hours Memorial,' *Leader*, 22 April 1903.

160 'The Whole Hog,' *Tocsin*, 19 April 1900, 4.

161 R.S. Ross, 'The Red Flag,' *Labor Call*, 19 April 1916, 14; 'Eight Hours Memorial,' *Leader*, 25 April 1903.

162 'The Eight Hours Anniversary,' *Tocsin*, 18 April 1901.

13

THE MEMORY OF TRADE UNIONISM IN GERMANY

Stefan Berger

Introduction: memory as a resource for trade unions

The German Trade Union Confederation's (Deutscher Gewerkschaftsbund, DGB) Saxon branch (DGB Sachsen) commissioned a film in 2015, which sought to explore what pupils in German Berufsschulen (schools attended by those who are being apprenticed, during their apprenticeships) knew about trade unions.[1] The result was thoroughly depressing: they knew virtually nothing and hardly anyone thought that this was an organization that had anything to do with them. One interviewee commented: 'Trade Unions? Is that not something for professors?' When they were told what trade unions have stood for and what concrete gains working people have been able to make through trade unions, most of those interviewed thought that trade unions were a good thing. The message of the film is clear: the lack of historical memory is a key obstacle to the trade unions' ability to recruit new members at a time when trade unions are frequently attacked publicly by their political adversaries as dinosaurs of the industrial age. Hence the revival and strengthening of memory is a necessary part of ensuring the continuing strength of trade unionism in contemporary German society. This is why the current chairman of the DGB, Reiner Hoffmann, has set up a commission entitled 'Commission on Memory Cultures of Social Democracy in Germany.'[2] He did not want to call it a commission on memory cultures of trade unionism, as he wanted to indicate that the task is not only an institutional one but a broader one, namely to strengthen memory cultures that are associated with the values and history of the left in Germany. Today, the left-wing political spectrum incorporates the trade unions, and also, as political parties, the Social Democrats, the Left Party, and the Green Party, as well as a range of left-of-center social movements that are engaged in environmental, peace, LGBT, women's, and third world movements, to mention only the most obvious and prominent ones. In strengthening memory cultures that are in line with the norms and values of the left, the DGB is hoping to make a contribution to revitalizing the project of the left that is currently facing a massive challenge by right-wing populist movements, not only in Germany but across Europe, and the wider world.[3] This chapter will explore to what extent the German trade unions have used memory as a political resource between their institutionalization in the second half of the nineteenth century and today, and it will ask how successful they have been in justifying themselves and their mission in the present with reference to the past. This is not an easy task, as there is not much research at all so far on the long history of the shaping of the memory of German trade unionism. Hence we shall only here be able to give hints and first hypothesis about the memory history of German trade unionism in the hope that others might be able to fill the vast empty spaces on this particular historical canvas.

German trade unions on the eve of World War I: memory and the struggle for recognition

The German trade union movement emerged in close association with political parties and wider ideological camps during the second half of the nineteenth century. Social Democratic trade unions were closely aligned with the Social Democratic Party (SPD) that was founded as General German Workers' Association (ADAV) in 1863.[4] It is the oldest continuous Social Democratic Party in the world, and, unlike in Britain, where trade unionism preceded the Labour Party by more than a century, the political movement preceded trade unionism and helped to build trade unions in the decades leading up to World War I. The close association of the Social Democratic trade unions with a political party that was ostracized in Imperial Germany as anti-national and intent on overthrowing the social order by revolutionary means meant that it was extremely difficult for those unions to be accepted by employers and the state alike. Furthermore they faced tough competition from trade unions that had a very different ideological orientation to Social Democracy. In particular the Catholic trade unions were often serious rivals to their Social Democratic counterparts. Thus, for example, in the Ruhr valley, one of the prime coal-extracting regions of Germany, the Catholic unions were stronger than their Social Democratic counterparts. Catholic social teaching was an important driving force behind the setting up of Catholic trade unions in Germany. Like their Social Democratic rivals, they were also closely associated with a political party, the Catholic Centre Party in Imperial Germany.[5] They shared a history of persecution, at least in the biggest German state, Prussia, as the Catholic church and all its institutions were heavily persecuted by the Protestant state as a disloyal force during the 1860s, during the so-called Kulturkampf. As a result of such experiences of persecution, distinct Social Democratic and Catholic milieux emerged in Imperial Germany that were both inward-looking and intent on strengthening its organizational culture and creating towers of strength in an environment perceived predominantly as hostile. The memory of persecution played a huge role in determining both their positioning in the present and their perspectives of the future. Despite their ideological differences, Social Democratic and Catholic trade unions could unite in common strike action, for example, in the famous 1905 miners' strike in the Ruhr, but more often they refused to join forces in what should have been a common struggle for better wages, working conditions, workplace safety and the general recognition of the principles of trade unionism. The Social Democratic and Catholic unions were by far the biggest and most important union movements in Imperial Germany, but there were others, notably a small liberal union movement,[6] the Hirsch-Dunckersche Gewerkvereine, who were also ideologically associated with the liberal parties in Imperial Germany, and the Polish trade union in mining, which had considerable strength only in the Ruhr valley.[7]

When the German revolution of 1918 ended the Imperial German state and ushered in the Weimar Republic, the trade union movement could look back on roughly half a century of struggles. The first trade unionists could write their memoirs and foundational anniversaries as well as the anniversaries of major industrial struggles were regularly celebrated with speeches, publications and whole host of anniversary literature – giving space for the memorialization of events, experiences and struggles associated with trade unionism. These tended to be memories of struggle, of crisis, of having pulled through difficult times, having overcome all sorts of adverse conditions, from reticent employers to a hostile state, in order to work tirelessly on behalf of their members for better wages and working conditions. Thus, for example, in mining, the 1889 strike which helped to establish the Social Democratic miners' union, the Alter Verband, was frequently the subject of memorializations within the Social Democratic labor movement.[8] This memory was starkly divided in ideological terms: where the Social Democrats remembered their persecution under the Anti-Socialist Laws between 1878 and 1890, the Catholic unionists remembered the Kulturkampf as a period in which they had been isolated. In both cases the memories of persecution led on the one hand to an internal rallying of the troops, an inward-looking solidarity which found expression in a heroic memory narrative, in which Social Democrats and Catholics had been suffering on behalf of the Protestant ruling elites of Prussia and Imperial Germany but had pulled through and only emerged stronger in spirit and organization after the end of the persecution. This memory discourse strengthened the external borders of the milieux not only vis-à-vis the state but also vis-à-vis other ideological groups. It helped to create the 'mentality of the tower' among Catholics and a 'negative integration' of social democracy into the Imperial German state.[9] There were, however, also occasional glimpses of solidarity across ideological divides, especially where the memorial literature referred to common struggles against a common enemy. This is the case of the memorial literature on the 1905 miners' strike in the Ruhr, where both Catholic and Social Democratic unions, on the one hand, affirm their respective ideological narratives, which are rooted in different foundational stories and different horizons of expectation but, on the other hand, they also accept the need for solidarity among workers, however misguided they thought the other union might be.[10] Thus, for example, on the occasion of the 30 year anniversary of the major miners' strike of 1889, in the wake of which the trade union Alter Verband had been founded, a jubilee volume appeared in Dortmund in 1909, penned by a journalist close to the Social Democratic union, reminding its readers, presumably mainly trade unionists, of the many struggles and achievements of the trade union movement since 1889. The message was clear: much had already been achieved even if it would take a long and arduous struggle to achieve full social equality. The gaze into the future was upbeat – there was no doubt in the brochure regarding the overall progressive direction of history: things were moving toward the eventual coming of a socialist society.[11] The Catholic trade union movement, as Jan Kellershohn has shown, remembered a different strike history in Imperial Germany, one that emphasized not 1889 and not class and socialism, but estates and the age-old right of the miner to be treated respectfully. The ideological divisions between Christian and Social Democratic unions were highly visible in the diverse memory narratives,[12] even if both narratives also had a common concern for achieving a better world for the miners of the Ruhr valley.

Individual memoirs of trade unionists also reflected a memory narrative of progress: they often compared the dire conditions when they were young, which frequently are portrayed as the main reason for becoming active in the union movement, with the improvement of conditions since – an improvement directly connected with the work of the trade unions. They left no doubt that much still had to be achieved, notably the recognition of trade unions as legitimate institutions representing workers' interests and the breakthrough to industrial bargaining with employers, but still, most memoirs left no doubt that the last decades had seen a change for the better. In that sense, the memoir literature of German trade unionists, which has yet fully to be mined, indicated that the integration into Imperial German society was not only negative. In many respects, even Social Democratic trade unionists felt themselves to be at least to some extent positively integrated into Wilhelmine German society before 1914, which also explains their willingness to support the German War effort in 1914.[13]

A special place in the memory culture of German trade unionism was reserved for the memory of iconic strike movements.[14] Strikes had often led to the establishment of more permanent trade union structures, as was the case with the miners' union Alter Verband, founded in the aftermath of a major miners' strike in 1889. These iconic strikes, sometimes victories, more often defeats, were also remembered as heroic moments of trade unionism on the way toward taking its rightful site in German society as representatives of the German workers.

Social Democratic trade unionists celebrated 1 May as Labor Day. The May Day manifestoes and newspapers as well as the speeches and demonstrations all contained an important memory aspect, as these were days, in which not only the 'Chicago martyrs' were remembered, in whose honor Labor Day had first been celebrated,[15] but also to remember the past struggles and the collective strength they had both shown and created.[16] It was a proud self-assertion of the power of trade unionism. Labor Day was also an occasion for the celebration of the internationalism of the Social Democratic movement. After all, Social Democracy had long been a stalwart of international proletarian solidarity. However, if we look at the memorial discourse around Social Democratic trade unionism, it is striking how the overwhelming majority of memory discourses and memorial practices center on national events, institutions, and occasions. Internationalism is either separated off into a memorialization of the development of the international trade union secretariats or it is side-lined altogether, indicating that this internationalism was only entering the everyday memorial practices of trade unionism in Imperial German skin-deep.[17]

It was striking that the memory of Social Democratic trade unionism in late Imperial Germany was one that talked little about the revolution. Instead it rested almost exclusively on struggles for workers' rights and wages in and around the factories. Such memory discourses were an attempt to distance the trade unions from the Social Democratic Party and from political goals more generally. Memory was mobilized in order to restrict trade unionism to reformist agendas around the representation of workers in the factories. It was a memory discourse contributing to the Mannheim agreement between Social Democratic unions and the Social Democratic Party, in which the unions asserted their independence from the SPD and refused any tutelage of the party over trade union affairs.[18] The reformism of German trade unions was based on memories of successes and achievements which also powered their willingness to enter into an agreement with the Imperial German elites to support the German War effort in exchange for major advances in the recognition of trade unions as legitimate representatives of workers vis-à-vis management.[19]

At the moment it is only possible to outline the memory discourse of German trade unionism in Imperial Germany with a very broad brush. It is likely that there were also more militant, more radical and more political memory discourses of trade unionists feeling more committed to revolutionary objectives than the mainstream of the trade union leadership in Imperial Germany. Yet in 1918, when the German revolution happened to the German labor movement, it was partly unable to lead that revolution, because it had long said good-bye to its revolutionary commitments.[20] They were referred to in memory discourses as ultimate aim, but the aim was kept in a never-never land of the future. The memory discourse of the German trade unions in other words had a considerable part in pacifying the union movement, and in making it concentrate on finding improvements in the here and now rather than looking for major societal changes.

Trade unions in the Weimar Republic: memories of an outsider as insider

If the memory discourse of German trade unionism in Imperial Germany was moving toward greater integration of trade unions into the structure of the

Imperial German state, the full acceptance of trade unionism and far greater possibilities for achieving concrete results for its core constituency only came with the Weimar Republic – a product of the German revolution of 1918 that had swept away the Imperial German elites. The institutional landscape of German trade unionism remained ideologically divided. If anything, the divisions were increased by the emergence of strong anarcho-syndicalist unions in the early years of the Weimar Republic and by the institutionalization of Communist unions. Social Democratic and Catholic unions moved closer together, as both now had overcome their status of outsiders and had become insiders in the Weimar Republic. Recognized as legitimate representatives of working-class interests, they had a far more powerful position vis-à-vis the employers. Furthermore, important legislation during the Weimar Republic further strengthened their hand not only at the factory level and in wage negotiations, but also in their influence on social policy more generally.[21]

Memorial events that involved trade unionists and autobiographical literature by trade unionists in the Weimar Republic showed that among Catholic and Social Democratic trade unionists, the achievement of political democracy in 1918/19 was seen as a major inspiration to work toward the realization of social and economic democracy. The memory of the revolution and its promises, was, however, an ambiguous one: some trade unionists, especially Catholics and Social Democrats, pointed to the huge advances that trade unionism had been able to make because of the progressive character of the Weimar constitution. Even here, though, the memory of the promises of 1918, especially the promises of cooperation made by employers, fearful of the revolution in 1918, was widely seen as a betrayal. The Central Working Community (Zentrale Arbeitsgemeinschaft, ZAG) between employers and trade unionists had led to hope for a permanent cooperation out of mutual recognition and respect.[22] Instead, many trade unionists complained bitterly that once the immediate fear of Bolshevization had receded, employers did everything to undermine the agreements of the ZAG, in particular the eight-hour day and any moves in the direction of greater economic democracy. The works' council law of 1921, initially only welcomed by the Catholic unions, was, by the end of the Weimar Republic, also celebrated as a major achievement of economic democracy by many Social Democratic unionists, as it allowed workers' representatives in many companies a greater say over management decisions and decisions directly affecting the working lives of trade union members at the factory level.[23] Many of them were trade unionists. Another achievement that is often celebrated in labor movement autobiographies is access to education – the Weimar Republic made it easier for workers to get access to diverse forms of education and the autobiographies show a pride in educational achievements. Very few workers and labor activists would attend university, but even a more limited educational achievement was widely celebrated as pointing into the right, progressive future.[24]

Social Democratic and Catholic trade unionists, either as trade unionists, or as civil servants of the Labor Ministry of the national government, played an important role in the deliberations of the International Labor Office (ILO) in Geneva in the interwar period. Here they worked hand-in-hand with state officials that were often sympathetic to their demands, and with representatives of employers interested in developing good corporatist relations with trade unionists and the state. However, as Sandrine Kott has demonstrated, memory discourses were most important in the deliberations of the ILO in that they allowed the German representatives to construct the German social insurance system as a positive lieu de memoire within the ILO. Hence, memory served particular national interests in an organization founded to encourage international exchanges and the standardization of international policies. Kott describes the memory politics of the German representatives in the ILO as 'national internationalism' – an attitude, she argues, which was to allow a few of them to support National Socialist and social imperialist ventures between 1933 and 1945. In this sense, a commitment to national memory by trade union representatives hindered the breakthrough to truly transnational and international agendas within the ILO.[25]

Those trade unionists committed to revolution, anarcho-syndicalists and Communists, emphasized a memory of betrayal in the Weimar Republic. The rot had started with reformist trade unionism in Imperial Germany which led directly to the truce with the Imperial German elites at the outbreak of World War I and a betrayal of revolutionary internationalism. Betrayal of the true revolutionary working-class interests in 1914 was followed by further betrayal in 1918/9 when the revolution had been contained and stopped short of reaching a true transformation of capitalist society. This memory of betrayal led to a reconfirmation of proletarian internationalism in the form of the Third and Fourth Internationals and, on the part of the Communists, the idealization of Bolshevism, or the idealization of an ideal proletarian internationalism on the part of anarcho-syndicalists.[26]

Trade unions in the early federal republic: remembering the destruction of the union movement and persecution under National Socialism

The key event in the memory discourse of German trade unionism in the early years of the Federal Republic was the destruction of the German trade union movement by National Socialism on 2nd May 1933, one day after the National Socialists had made Labor Day a national holiday in Germany. For the National Socialists these two events symbolized one and the same thing. The interests of the German workers, the 'honor of German labor,' in the language of the National Socialists, now lay with National Socialism.[27] The National Socialist movement sought to appeal to workers by making them a range of symbolical and materialist offers in order to lure them into the racial state. The declaration of Labor Day as national holiday was one such offer. The destruction of the union movement one day later was hammering home the same message: those who had claimed to represent working-class interests were no longer seen as doing so. They had to be defeated and eliminated as opponents of the new order that National Socialism was about to install in Germany. Subsequently many trade union officials were murdered, tortured, persecuted, imprisoned and many had to leave Germany and go into exile.[28]

The truly traumatic memory of oppression under National Socialism led to a memorial discourse that was squarely focused around suffering and resistance. Those who survived, like Hans Böckler, who was to become the first chairman of the DGB in 1949, were initially full of mistrust against the employers: had they not undermined trade unionism in the Weimar Republic? Had they not welcomed Hitler and cooperated with him, as it served their interests for higher profit? Had they not welcomed the destruction of the trade union movement? Bitter memories made him initially refuse any acceptance of employers' federations. He did not even want to negotiate with them, as he saw them as having been personally responsible for the victory of National Socialism in Germany. And yet, it did not take long for him to change tune. Under the impact of the Cold War he moved toward accepting the forms of corporatism and social partnership that were to become typical for the Federal Republic.[29]

Böckler was characteristic of one part of the post-war trade union elite in that he had withdrawn largely into private life under National Socialism. Like many others he had not chosen the path of active resistance, although he did have contacts to resisters like Wilhelm Leuschner and had to go into hiding after the attempt on Hitler's life in July 1944. Unlike others, however, he did escape the camps, torture, and death. The memory of those choices and of what could have been must have had a sub-conscious impact on the positioning of trade unionists after 1945. Indeed, it made a difference whether trade unionist had been active resisters or exiled, like Otto Brenner, or if they had, by and large, withdrawn from 'active service' to re-emerge onto the scene after 1945. Both types of trade unionists were united in celebrating and memorializing those who had paid the ultimate price for their resistance to National Socialism, both were also united in their antifascism, but the memory of relative passivity arguably created an inner distance to those who had chosen to resist. Subliminally those different choices after 1933 thus influenced the way in which trade unionists related to the memorialization of National Socialism. Those like Hans Gottfurcht who belonged to a younger generation than Böckler and who had gone into exile, drew far more radical conclusions for a new social order that he thought had to be established in Germany after 1945, whereas Böckler found it easier to relate his memories to a politics that continued where he had left off on 2 May 1933.[30] The fact that many post-war trade unionists had no direct experience of persecution, oppression, and resistance meant that they could be more lenient when persons tried to move into the trade union movement who had been in sympathy with the National Socialists before 1945.[31]

In the post-war memorial discourses of trade unionists on the destruction of the trade union movement in May 1933, the words of Wilhelm Leuschner were present everywhere in the calls to form a united trade union movement. Leuschner, a trade unionist who had been murdered in the camps for taking part in the attempted coup against Hitler on 22 July 1944, had allegedly said, a day before he was executed by the National Socialist henchmen at the concentration camp Plötzensee: 'Tomorrow I will be hanged. You need to create unity!' For the first time in German history Christian, Social Democratic and Communist trade unionists came together after 1945 to create a united trade union movement, the Confederation of German Trade Unions (DGB). The desire for unity was, however, a short-lived moment with regard to the Communists. The onset of the Cold War led to a virulent anti-Communism in the Western zones of occupation and the early Federal Republic. The DGB unions slowly but surely forced Communists out of positions of leadership and marginalized them within their organizations. The same was true for left socialists who insisted on maintaining a transformative anti-capitalist vision of the future, such as Viktor Agartz.[32] As Dieter Nelles has shown, this exclusion of certain memories meant that the International Transport Workers' Federation (ITF) and its internationalist antifascist struggle did not become part of the German trade unions' memory discourse, because the stronger national orientation of leading German trade unionists found the positions of the ITF anathema to their own beliefs.[33] The constant reference to 'unity' in the dealings of former Social Democratic and Christian trade unionists papered over very real differences that had continued to exist during the years of National Socialism. The memory trope of 'unity' was one way of not allowing those differences to surface in the post-war years.[34] The 1950s were characterized by a process of the trade unions finding their place within a West German society emerging out of the ashes of the National Socialist past. Unionists fought over whether to understand trade unions as a force opposing capitalism and the capitalist structures that had been restored in the Federal Republic, or whether to form a partnership with capital – a conflictual partnership, in which conflict was regulated and based on mutual acceptance.[35] Ultimately, it was the latter position that was to win the day. The foundations for the German social partnership model, also sometimes referred to as Rhenish capitalism, had been laid. The positive memory of many trade unionists of the works' councils in the Weimar Republic and their reconstitution in the Federal Republic worked toward a relatively rapid acceptance of the new social order, as trade unionists could start in 1945 where they had left off in 1933.[36]

Overall, the unified trade union movement faced three crucial tasks in the early years of the Federal Republic: first to build a unified trade union movement via the memory of the movement's defeat by National Socialism, second, to force the Communists out of the movement by invoking the memory of totalitarianism, and, thirdly, to shed a more radical, transformative perspective by referring to memories of the successful integration of trade unionism into German society from the Kaiserreich to the present day. For all three tasks, memory was crucial.

Trade unionism from the heydays of Rhenish capitalism to the challenges of neoliberalism: memory as a forgotten resource for trade unionism?

Unlike in the Weimar Republic the overwhelming majority of the employers after 1945 accepted trade unions as an integral part of the industrial relations system and embarked on the road to the form of corporatism that was to characterize the Bonn republic: a conflictual partnership between unions and employers, mediated by a state setting the macro-economic framework for economic development. The dominant people's parties of the Federal Republic, the SPD, and the Christian Democratic Party (CDU) both had strong trade union wings, although the trade unions were undoubtedly more powerful within the SPD than the CDU. It had, however been a key disappointment to the trade union movement that co-determination on the model of the coal and steel industry had not been extended to other sectors of the economy with the co-determination laws of 1952. Whereas in the coal and steel sector of the economy, 50% of seats on the executive boards of companies were taken by trade unionists, the 1952 law foresaw that unionists would only take one-third of seats on executive boards of other companies. When the Social Democrats came into national government for the first time in the history of the Federal Republic in 1969, trade unionists saw their chance to change this, only to be bitterly disappointed again by the 1976 law on co-determination, which fell again far short of their expectations. The trade unions had used memory politics extensively in their quest to widen co-determination in Germany. They argued that the National Socialist past made it especially necessary to democratize the economic sphere. The trade unions saw themselves as an agent fulfilling a lesson from the past – more economic democracy followed directly out of the failure of both political and economic democracy at the end of the Weimar Republic.[37] The co-determination debates in the early 1950s and early 1970s accompanying the formulation of new co-determination laws were resonant with memories of the Weimar years.[38] Yet ultimately the unions' memory discourse was not strong enough to determine politics in this respect.

Nevertheless, the trade unions in the Federal Republic were a powerful force that politics and employers alike had to reckon with. Some of the wage agreements that they were able to achieve were legendary. Their influence on social policy and the shaping of the West German welfare state was considerable. In outlook there were important differences. Some, like the metalworkers' union (IGM), were more militant and willing to strike to push through their demands.[39] Others, like the miners' union (IGBE, today's IGBCE) hardly ever went on strike and still were able to exert considerable influence. Like in the Weimar Republic and Imperial Germany, anniversaries were duly celebrated. Thus, on the occasion of the 80th anniversary of the miners' strike of 1889, in 1969, in politically tumultuous times, the memory of 1889 was invoked to show the long continuity of organized and disciplined industrial struggle leading to success.[40] On the other hand, as Karl-Christian Führer has argued, the famous 1974 strike of the public services union (ÖTV), which pushed through wage increases of up to 14%, was, with hindsight, a traumatic event for the trade union. Although successful, the subsequent interpretation of the strike as showing the recklessness of trade unions and their inability to take into account the common good meant that the unions, throughout the 1980s, remained very cautious in its negotiating strategies. The memory of 1974 was not a triumphant but an embarrassed memory.[41]

In the heydays of trade union power and confidence in West Germany, during the 1970s, critics of Rhenish capitalism and of the power of the trade unions within Rhenish capitalism, used the memory trope of the 'trade union state' in order to claim that the unions, through their close alliance with the SPD, exerted undue influence over government. This was already a trope that had been used by employers and right-wing politicians during the Weimar Republic to fight the trade unions. Trade unionists were quick to point this out and link it to the unfortunate demise of the Weimar Republic. Their counter-discourse pointed to what appeared to them as irresponsible behavior of the employers during the late 1920s, exemplified by the lock-out in the steel industry in 1928 symbolizing the refusal of employers to negotiate with trade unions. The memory politics of the trade unions amounted to a call not to go back behind what had been achieved in the early Federal Republic. The memory horizon of Weimar served as a negative 'other' to the social relations that had been forged after 1945.[42]

The DGB followed the same strategy when it criticized the cuts in social policy in the early 1980s. The Weimar Republic had been fatally destabilized by cuts to the welfare state. The Federal Republic, they argued, should be aware not to make the same mistakes.[43] At the same time, as Sandrine Kott has pointed out, the German trade unions, in 1969, celebrated the ILO and its history, like never before. Paying tribute to the memory of the ILO was one way of countering the beginning neoliberal critique of corporatist models. For the trade unions the memory of the ILO was underlining the importance and positive value of these corporatist models. Hence the ILO was used in the memory discourse of the German trade unions to defend their national positions. Characteristically the unions made virtually nothing of the considerable international development policies of the ILO, as they saw these international commitments rather as a burden than a normative principle to be highlighted.[44]

The unions also used their memorial practices in the 1970s and into the 1980s to celebrate their early successes in the Federal Republic – from improving the real wages of employees and workers to securing safer work environments, from increasing entitlements for holidays to achieving a shorter working week and further to many other small achievements that had catapulted the trade union movement to become one of the major movers and shakers of the Bonn republic from the 1950s to the 1970s. In the 1970s and 1980s unions like IG Metall developed the idea that their training courses for trade union officials had to contain courses that allowed historical orientation. History was very much seen as a resource for contemporary struggles. Memory of past defeats and successes had to be made fruitful for the present.[45] Trade unionists were also often to the fore in the West German history workshop movement, in which hundreds of local groups investigated the history of industrial workers, their everyday concerns, their hopes, and aspirations including their struggles for greater recognition and more social equality that often involved trade unions.[46] Up to this day there are many local trade union groups who come together regularly in order to exchange views on the past and present and these forms of lived communicative memory remain important forums in which past, present, and future are connected in the lives of trade unionists.[47]

If the attacks of neoliberalism on the trade union movement had never been as successful in Germany as they had been, for example, in Britain, this might well have to do a lot with such successful memory politics. Of course, there were political reasons too. As mentioned above, the Christian Democrats, who returned to office after 1982, had a strong trade union wing and were therefore unwilling to embark on trade union bashing in a similar way that the Conservative Party in Britain under Margaret Thatcher did after 1979. The small German Liberal Party (FDP) became the spearhead of a globalized neoliberalism during the 1980s and 1990s but it never was powerful enough to put its neoliberal program into practice. Hence, despite much talk about change after 1982, the governments by Helmut Kohl were always careful to keep a constructive dialog with the trade unions and the trade unions, in turn, were able to influence social policies, and speak for their members in wage negotiations and especially in forging socially responsible schemes in the face of factory closures, involving retraining schemes, generous early retirement schemes for older workers and generous compensation payments for those made unemployed.[48]

All of this is not to say that neoliberalism was not a major challenge to German trade unionism, in particular in the wake of German unification after 1990. The union movement continued to lose members, as neoliberals attacked them as the last dinosaurs of the industrial age and as the individualization of life styles and the erosion of working-class milieux meant a significant weakening of collective identities that had helped to underpin the culture of trade unionism in Germany. This crisis, it would appear, coincided with a profound disinterest in the history and memory of the trade union movement. Much of this disinterest had to do with the way in which history had been discussed in the trade union movement in the early 1980s. Two major history conferences in 1979 and 1983, organized by the DGB, discussed the topic of National Socialism specifically and the historical legacy of trade unionism more generally. The trade unions, from the immediate post-war years to the present day, have been a major antifascist force and they have, time and again, underlined this through their memory politics. Thus, for example, they published books on the resistance of trade unionists to National Socialism and they linked the historical memory to the fight against the far right in Germany, in the early 1950s with the Socialist Reich Party (SRP), the 1960s with the National Democratic Party (NPD), in the 1980s with the

Republican Party and the German People's Union (DVP) and in contemporary Germany with the Alternative for Germany Party (AfD).[49] But the big historical conferences of the early 1980s also had to fend off a challenge from Marxist and Communist trade union historians, like Frank Deppe, Georg Fülberth, and Jürgen Harrer, who charged the trade unions with having failed in their mission to fight against and transform capitalism. History, for them, became the whip with which to lash the unions and remind them that they had once stood for something different than social partnership and Rhenish capitalism.[50] Deppe and his collaborators accused the trade unions of having failed workers in World War I, in the German revolution of 1918/9 and toward the end of the republic. They accused the trade unions of not being more radical, opposing capitalism per se, during the history of the Federal Republic. Historians, closer to the mainstream of reformist trade unionism defended the path of the German trade unions.[51] While we need closer examination of the impact of these debates, it would appear likely that this experience turned many trade unionists away from history and memory. It may not be a coincidence that the Hans-Böckler-Foundation of the DGB hardly funded any history projects at all from the late 1980s to the 2000s. Having still used memory politics quite extensively to defend themselves in the 1970s, the unions, under political pressure, did now mainly focus on the here and now of their core concerns: defending wages, working conditions, softening blows from deindustrialization and protecting the achievements of social policy that benefitted their members.

Not only did the here and now prevent trade unionists from paying attention to historical memory, but the trade unions also seemed to have lost their historical optimism in a better future for themselves and their constituencies, the more they were fighting defensive struggles to retain what had been achieved in previous decades. No longer was the movement characterized by an excess of optimism, as had still been the case in Imperial Germany, the Weimar Republic, and the early years of the Federal Republic. Now the fighting mood of optimism had given way to a deep-rooted pessimism about how the West German social model could be preserved in the light of an international neoliberal onslaught against a socially responsible and just world order. By 2009 a discussion between trade unionists on the historical consciousness of the trade unions concluded that there was no longer a substantial historical consciousness present among the vast majority of trade unionists.[52] It is characteristic that the trade unions decided in the 1990s not to secure and develop one of their most precious memorial assets, their archives. Instead they handed them over to the Friedrich-Ebert Foundation, a political foundation close to the Social Democrats, which looked as though the unions were getting rid of a 'problem' rather than celebrating an 'asset.'

Trade union houses that exist in virtually all bigger German cities and trade union schools, of which there are still many in Germany also are hidden away and often neglected rather than being transformed into center points of a historical memory that has relevance for contemporary struggles. The major history museums of the Federal Republic all marginalize the history of trade unionism and the still powerful trade union movement to date does little to correct this.[53] There are few attempts to celebrate the history of trade unionism and to make it meaningful for the present. When the Technoseum in Mannheim organized a major exhibition on the German labor movement, including the trade union movement, with the input of the contemporary labor movement, it amounted to a rather traditional(ist) and tired narrativization of a heritage that would seem to most visitors as being firmly rooted in the past – with precious few attempts to link that past to the present. The very title of the exhibition: 'through darkness into the light' picks up a well-known slogan of the nineteenth-century German labor movement, but it also insinuates that the light has been reached and that history is not providing anymore guidance and challenges for the work of contemporary trade unionists.[54] There is to date no permanent museum which would seek to collect, display, and narrativize in more exciting ways the many objects associated with trade unionism, for example, posters, flags, banners, pamphlets, photographs, films, plates, and a range of other material objects. Nor is there an attempt to have a central monument constructed to remind the German public of some the key achievements of German trade unionism. The memorial to the eight-hour day in Melbourne,[55] for example, could serve as inspiration to the German trade union movement to think about a monument for social justice or for co-determination and social partnership which should not stand in Berlin, but in the Ruhr, which has been the prime laboratory for co-determination and social partnership in Germany. True, in 2010 there has been a local attempt in the Ruhr to create a memorial dedicated to the strike history of German miners: artist Silke Wagner created the monument entitled 'Glückauf: Bergarbeiterproteste im Ruhrgebiet,' which seeks to connect the past to the present. The successful miners' strikes are linked to the hope that those working precariously and receiving poor wages in contemporary times may unite gain to fight social injustice in the same way that the miners had done in the past (Figure 13.1).[56] An excellent online site on the history of trade unionism in Germany exists,[57] but it would need a lot more dedicated memory politics and history politics work in order for it to be an effective resource.

However, if the interest in history and memory waned between the mid-1980s and the 2000s, it did not disappear altogether. When the miners' union protested against the closure of more mines in the late 1980s, it printed posters which reminded everyone that in the late nineteenth century, in the context of the 1889 miners' strike, miners had been going to the emperor to get themselves heard; now, the poster said, they would go to the national government in Bonn. [Image 2: Handgemaltes Protestplakat, 1980er Jahre (IG Bergbau Chemie Energie, Ortsgruppe Bergkamen-Oberaden), Ruhr Museum, Essen/Foto: Rainer Rothenberg. Abgedruckt in: Ulrich Borsdorf/Heinrich T. Grütter (Hg.): Ruhr Museum. Natur. Kultur. Geschichte, Essen 2010, S. 368.] Even in the 1990s the trade unions did not forego altogether an active memory politics. Thus, in 1999 the trade unions celebrated extensively the foundation of the DGB in

FIGURE 13.1 Silke Wagner: Glückauf. Bergarbeiterproteste im Ruhrgebiet. Photo: Roman Mensing, artdoc.de.

1949. It was, however, striking that the celebrations were, by and large, directed inwards – toward the organization. The public reception would also merit a closer analysis, but an initial glimpse into the media coverage of 50 years DGB would suggest that the external perception of the trade unions was much less generous than its internal view.[58]

Conclusion: memory and the future of trade unionism

This broad survey of the memory culture of German trade unionism over more than one hundred years suggests that the trade unions in Germany did have a relatively intensive memorial culture, in which the past played a significant role. The unions have continuously celebrated their foundational jubilees remembering great defeats, like the destruction of the union movement by the National Socialists, and great victories, like co-determination. The substantial number of ego-histories of trade unionists also forms an important part of the collective memory of German trade unionism, as does the literature (and other media) produced around key events such as May Day. Much needs to be done to analyze in greater depth the functioning of this memory culture, its internal differentiation and its external effects. We know far too little about the key agents of this memory discourse, what counter-memories it provoked, and how effective it was in both achieving internal cohesion among trade unionists, that is, in forging a collective identity, and, at the same time, in fostering the societal aims that trade unionism was pursuing at different times over the long twentieth century. I have argued here that the trade union memory was characterized by immense optimism about the future from the late nineteenth century to the 1980s. This optimism was based on a firm belief in the certain victory of the just cause that the unions fought on behalf of its core constituency, workers, and employees. Through the worst periods of persecution and attempted destruction, in Imperial and National Socialist Germany, the memory of struggles and of perseverance served the purpose of re-assuring trade unionists that their cause cannot be defeated, even if they had to lay down their lives in the pursuit of a better world for its members. This future-oriented memory, which can also be described as the construction of a 'practical past,'[59] was hardly ever characterized by utopian thinking. Instead a very sober programmatic orientation, which sometimes resulted in attempts to provide prognoses for the future, dominated. Together with Thomas Welskopp I have argued elsewhere that the future-orientation of the German Social Democratic movement as a whole was characterized by three types of imagination: programmatic, prognosis, and utopia.[60] On balance the union imagination was squarely belonging to the first two of those types.

On the basis of a very preliminary survey it would appear that, at some point during the latter half of the 1980s, the German trade unions began to lose this optimism about the future which coincided with a decreased interest in the past and in the memorialization of trade union history. Much of this, I have argued, had to do with the fact that the neoliberal attacks on trade unionism as dinosaur of an industrial age that was rooted firmly in the past showed its effects. History was no longer seen as a resource but as a burden, and trade unionists fled into the defensive concerns of the present, where it appeared to them that they had more than enough on their hands. Future-orientation thus gave way to presentism, which would be in line with general developments in the perception of time regimes, at least if we are to follow François Hartog's influential argument in this respect.[61] Yet it would appear that this is not the end of the story. In fact, we have seen for a number of years now attempts to revive memory cultures of trade unionism that see memory and history as an important resource in the contemporary struggles of German trade unionism. The Hans-Böckler-Foundation together with the SPD's Friedrich-Ebert-Foundation and Die Linke's Rosa-Luxemburg Foundation started a number of initiatives from around 2004/5 onwards that are aimed at strengthening the historical memory of German trade unionism. This includes both work in academia and work in the trade union movement. The organization of regular seminars in labor history (biannually, in conjunction with partner institutes in the universities), the promotion of historical education inside the trade unions, the support for the foundation of a German Labour History Association that explicitly welcomes links between the academic and non-academic worlds[62] – all of these are signs of a political will to forge a new memory culture that can act as shield for trade unionism and allow trade unions to deal with the many challenges that await them in a more constructive way.[63] Weak trade unions, a study of the International Monetary Fund has concluded, are one of the key reasons why social inequality is increasing in the contemporary world.[64] More attention to memory and history will not reverse this trend single-handedly, but our brief and preliminary review of the memory politics of German trade unionism shows how memory can be an important resource for trade unions. They ignore this resource at their peril.

Notes

1 The film was produced by Arbeit und Leben Leipzig. Unfortunately it is currently no longer available online.
2 https://www.boeckler.de/erinnerungskulturen.htm# [accessed 27 May 2019]
3 Leo Panitch and Greg Albo, eds., *The Politics of the Right* (special issue of Socialist Register) (2016).
4 Toni Offermann, *Die erste deutsche Arbeiterpartei: Organisation, Verbreitung und Sozialstruktur von ADAV und LADAV, 1863 – 1871* (Bonn: J.W.H. Dietz, 1979).
5 Klaus Tenfelde, 'Die Entstehung der deutschen Gewerkschaftsbewegung: vom Vormärz bis zum Ende des Sozialistengesetzes,' in *Geschichte der deutschen Gewerkschaften von den Anfängen bis 1945*, ed. Ulrich Borsdorf (Cologne: Bund, 1987), 15–165.
6 R.W. Branz, 'The Hirsch-Duncker Unions in the Weimar Republic, 1918–1933,' *Internationale Wissenschaftliche Korrespondenz zur Geschichte der Arbeiterbewegung* 31 (1995): 151–167.
7 John J. Kulczycki, *The Polish Coalminers' Union and the German Labour Movement in the Ruhr, 1902 – 1934: National and Social Solidarity* (Oxford: Berg, 1997). For a general introduction to the history of the German labor movement see Stefan Berger, *Social Democracy and the Working Class in Nineteenth and Twentieth-Century Germany* (London: Longman, 2000).
8 Jan Kellershohn, 'Streik,' in *Zeit-Räume Ruhr: Erinnerungsorte des Ruhrgebietes*, eds. Stefan Berger, Ulrich Borsdorf, Ludger Classen, Heinrich Theodor Grütter and Dieter Nellen (Essen: Klartext, 2019), 846–863.
9 Michael Schneider, *Christliche Gewerkschaften, 1894–1933* (Bonn: J.W.H. Dietz Nachf., 1982); Reinhard Richter, *Nationales Denken im Katholizismus der Weimarer Republik* (Münster: Lit, 2000); Dieter Groh, *Negative Integration und revolutionärer Attentismus: die deutsche Sozialdemokratie am Vorabend des ersten Weltkrieges* (Frankfurt/Main: Propyläen, 1973).
10 Kellershohn, 'Streik.'
11 Anton Bredenbeck, *1889. Die erste Erhebung der Bergarbeiter. Zur Erinnerung an den großen Bergarbeiterstreik vor 20 Jahren* (Dortmund: Gerisch, 1909).
12 Jan Kellershohn, 'Streik und Erinnerung: der Bergarbeiterstreik von 1889 als erinnerungspolitische Ressource,' in: https://www.boeckler.de/pdf/p_ek_ap_04_2019.pdf [accessed 1 June 2019].
13 Otte Hue, *Die Bergarbeiter: Historische Darstellung der Bergarbeiter-Verhältnisse von der ältesten Zeit bis in die neueste Zeit* (2 Vols) (Stuttgart: J.W.H. Dietz, 1913); Stefan Berger, 'In the Fangs of Social Patriotism: The Construction of Nation and Class in Autobiographies of British and German Social Democrats in the Interwar Period,' *Archiv für Sozialgeschichte* 40 (2000): 259–287.
14 Klaus Tenfelde and Heinrich Volkmann, eds., *Streik: zur Geschichte des Arbeitskampfes in Deutschland während der Industrialisierung* (Munich: C. H. Beck, 1981).
15 Philipp S. Foner, *May Day: A Short History of the International Workers' Holiday, 1886 – 1986* (New York: International Publishers, 1986).

16 Gottfried Korff, '"Heraus zum Ersten Mai": Maibrauch zwischen Volkskultur, bürgerlicher Folklore und Arbeiterbewegung,' in *Volkskultur: zur Wiederentdeckung des vergessenen Alltags (16. – 20. Jahrhundert)*, eds. Richard von Dülmen und Norbert Schindler (Frankfurt/ Main: Fischer, 1984), 246–281, 423–427.
17 Ulf Teichmann is currently preparing a study on the memorial culture of May Day in Germany. It will be published on the website of the Commission on the Memory Culture of Social Democracy: https://www.boeckler.de/erinnerungskulturen.htm# [accessed 27 May 2019].
18 Klaus J. Becker and Jens Hildebrandt, *100 Jahre "Mannheimer Abkommen": zur Geschichte von SPD und Gewerkschaften* (Ludwigshafen: Llux, 2006).
19 Susanne Miller, *Burgfrieden und Klassenkampf: die deutsche Sozialdemokratie im ersten Weltkrieg* (Düsseldorf: Droste, 1974).
20 Stefan Berger, 'Demokratiegründungen am Ende des ersten Weltkrieges und europäische Erinnerungskulturen,' in *Neue Perspektiven auf die deutsche Revolution 1918/19*, eds. Stefan Berger, Wolfgang Jäger und Anja Kruke (Bonn: J.W.H. Dietz, 2021), forthcoming.
21 Klaus Schönhoven, *Reformismus und Radikalismus: gespaltene Arbeiterbewegung im Weimarer Sozialstaat* (Munich: C.H. Beck, 1989).
22 Michael Schneider, *Unternehmer und Demokratie. Die freien Gewerkschaften in der unternehmerischen Ideologie der Jahre 1918 bis 1933* (Bonn: J.W.H. Dietz, 1975).
23 Werner Milert and Rudolf Tschirbs, *Die andere Demokratie: betriebliche Interessenvertretung in Deutschland, 1848 – 2008* (Essen: Klartext, 2012); Werner Milert is currently preparing a study looking at the practice of works' councils at factory level in different areas of industry. See http://www.isb.ruhr-uni-bochum.de/forschung/mitbestimmungspraxis.html.de [accessed 1 June 2019].
24 Franz-Josef Jelich, 'Bildungsaspiration und – partizipation von Arbeiterkindern und – jugendlichen der Weimarer Republik,' in: https://www.boeckler.de/erinnerungskulturen.htm# [accessed 18 Jan. 2021].
25 Sandrine Kott, 'Keine Erinnerungsgemeinschaften in der ILO? Das Beispiel deutscher Gewerkschafter und der Sozialversicherung,' in: https://www.boeckler.de/pdf/p_ek_ap_02_2019.pdf [accessed 1 June 2019].
26 Jeffrey Herf, 'German Communism's Master Narratives of Anti-Fascism: Berlin – Moscow – East Berlin, 1928 – 1945,' in *Divided Memory: The Nazi Past in the Two Germanies*, ed. Jeffrey Herf (Cambridge, MA: Harvard University Press, 1997), 13–39: Andreas G. Graf, ed., *Anarchisten gegen Hitler: Anarchisten, Anarcho-Syndikalisten, Rätekommunisten in Widerstand und Exil* (Berlin: Lukas Verlag, 2001).
27 Alf Lüdtke, '"Ehre der Arbeit": Industriearbeiter und Macht der Symbole. Zur Reichweite symbolischer Orientierungen im Nationalsozialismus,' in *Arbeiter im 20. Jahrhundert*, ed. Klaus Tenfelde (Stuttgart: Klett-Cotta, 1991), 343–394.
28 Michael Schneider, *Unter dem Hakenkreuz: Arbeiter und Arbeiterbewegung, 1933–1939* (Bonn: J.W.H. Dietz, 1999).
29 Ulrich Borsdorf, 'Die Zerschlagung der Gewerkschaften verarbeiten: das Beispiel Hans Böckler,' in *Gewerkschaftsgeschichte als Erinnerungsgeschichte: der 2. Mai 1933 in der gewerkschaftlichen Erinnerung an den Nationalsozialismus und der gewerkschaftlichen Positionierung der Zeit nach 1945*, ed. Stefan Berger (Essen: Klartext, 2015), 45–56.
30 On Gottfurcht see Ursula Bitzegeio, 'Selbstreflexion und Lernprozesse im Londoner Exil: Hans Gottfurcht und das eherne Gesetz der Oligarchie,' in *Gewerkschaftsgeschichte als Erinnerungsgeschichte*, ed. Berger, 57–67.
31 Several such cases are discussed by Klaus Mertsching, 'Die Auseinandersetzung des DGB mit dem Erbe der NS-Zeit,' in *Gewerkschaftsgeschichte als Erinnerungsgeschichte*, ed. Berger, 214–224.
32 Christoph Jünke, 'Wirtschaftsdemokratische Neuordnungskonzept nach dem Faschismus am Beispiel von Viktor Agartz,' in *Gewerkschaftsgeschichte als Erinnerungsgeschichte*, ed. Berger, 68–77.

33 Dieter Nelles, 'Der verdrängte Widerstand: die Erinnerung an den Widerstand der Internationalen Transportarbeiterföderation (ITF) in den deutschen Gewerkschaften,' in *Gewerkschaftsgeschichte als Erinnerungsgeschichte*, ed. Berger, 303–323.
34 Holger Heith, 'Die Zerschlagung der deutschen Gewerkschaften als Thema der Bildungs- und Jugendarbeit der Industriegewerkschaft Bergbau und Energie (IGBE),' in *Gewerkschaftsgeschichte als Erinnerungsgeschichte*, ed. Berger, 279–288.
35 For the concept of 'conflictual partnership,' see Walter Müller-Jentsch, *Gewerkschaften und soziale Marktwirtschaft seit 1945* (Leipzig: Reclam, 2011).
36 Werner Milert, 'Erinnerungsort Betriebsrat: Erfahrungen und Anknüpfungspunke gewerkschaftlicher Interessenvertreter nach dem Zweiten Weltkrieg,' in *Gewerkschaftsgeschichte als Erinnerungsgeschichte*, ed. Berger, 240–266.
37 Thomas Köcher, *"Aus der Vergangenheit lernen – für die Zukunft arbeiten!"? Die Auseinandersetzung des DGB mit dem Nationalsozialismus in den 50er und 60er Jahren* (Münster: Westfälisches Dampfboot, 2004).
38 Werner Milert, 'Erinnerungsgeschichte der betrieblichen Mitbestimmung,' in: https://www.boeckler.de/erinnerungskulturen.htm# [accessed 27 May 2019], forthcoming.
39 Kurt Thomas Schmitz, 'Die IG Metall und ihre Geschichtsschreibung. Überblick und Ausblick,' *Gewerkschaftliche Monatshefte* 39:2 (1990): 112–120.
40 Wolfgang Köllmann and Albin Gladen, eds., *Der Bergarbeiterstreik von 1889 und die Gründung des "Alten Verbandes" in ausgewählten Dokumenten der Zeit* (Bochum: Berg Verlag, 1969).
41 Karl-Christian Führer, 'Gewerkschaften und Erinnerungskulturen der sozialen Demokratie: ein Problemaufriss am Beispiel der ÖTV,' unpublished paper, in possession of the author.
42 Hans Otto Hemmer and Ulrich Borsdorf, '"Gewerkschaftsstaat" – Zur Vorgeschichte eines aktuellen Schlagworts,' *Gewerkschaftliche Monatshefte* 25:10 (1974): 640–653.
43 'DGB: Wir nähern uns den Verhältnissen von Weimar,' *Die Welt*, 30 November 1983; Peter Gillies, 'Der DGB, die Armut und der kühne Vergleich mit Weimar,' *Die Welt*, 1 December 1983. Cited in: Christoph Lorke, 'Gleichheitsversprechen und ihr Erinnern im geteilten und vereinten Deutschland,' in https://www.boeckler.de/erinnerungskulturen.htm# [accessed 18 Jan. 2021].
44 Kott, 'Keine Erinnerungsgemeinschaften.'
45 J. Wehberg, '1989: Bildungspolitik und politische Bildungsarbeit der Gewerkschaften. Hinweise zu ihrer historischen Entwicklung,' in *Mit der Vergangenheit in die Zukunft. Felder gewerkschaftlicher Politik seit 1945*, eds. H.E. Bremes and M. Schumacher (Münster: Westfälisches Dampfboot, 1989), 69–88; on the centennial and jubilee literature see also: Gerhard Beier, 'Glanz und Elend der Jubiläumsliteratur. Kritische Bestandsaufnahme bisheriger Historiographie der Berufs- und Industriegewerkschaften,' *Gewerkschaftliche Monatshefte*, 19:10 (1968): 607–614.
46 Manfred Scharrer, *Macht Geschichte von unten. Handbuch für gewerkschaftliche Geschichte vor Ort* (Cologne: Bund, 1988).
47 On the memory work of German trade unionism after 1945 compare Michael Schneider, 'Erinnerungskultur der Gewerkschaften nach 1945: Bestandsaufnahme und Perspektiven,' in: https://www.boeckler.de/pdf/p_ek_wp_02_2018.pdf [accessed 2 June 2019].
48 Robert Lorenz, *Gewerkschaftsdämmerung: Geschichte und Perspektiven deutscher Gewerkschaften* (Bielefeld: transcript, 2013), 67–252.
49 Bodo Zeuner, *Gewerkschaften und Rechtsextremismus: Anregungen für die Bildungsarbeit und die politische Selbstverständigung der deutschen Gewerkschaften* (Münster: Westfälisches Dampfboot, 2007).
50 Frank Deppe, Georg Fülberth, and Jürgen Harrer, eds., *Geschichte der deutschen Gewerkschaftsbewegung* (Cologne: Pahl-Rugenstein, 1977).
51 Erich Matthias and Klaus Schönhoven, eds., *Solidarität und Menschenwürde. Etappen der deutschen Gewerkschaftsgeschichte von den Anfängen bis zur Gegenwart* (Bonn: J.W.H.

Dietz, 1984); Ulrich Borsdorf, ed., *Geschichte der deutschen Gewerkschaften von den Anfängen bis 1945* (Cologne: Bund, 1987); Hans-Otto Hemmer u. Kurt-Thomas Schmitz, eds., *Geschichte der Gewerkschaften in der Bundesrepublik Deutschland: von den Anfängen bis heute* (Cologne: Bund Verlag, 1990).
52 U. Schulz, 'Tagungsbericht "Nutzen und Nachteil der Gewerkschaftsgeschichte für die Gewerkschaften", 15.05.2009 –17.05.2009, Bochum,' *H-Soz-Kult*, 24 June 2009, in: https://www.hsozkult.de/searching/id/tagungsberichte-2651?title=nutzen-und-nachteil-der-gewerkschaftsgeschichte-fuer-die-Gewerkschaften&q=Schulz%20Nutzen%20und%20Nachteil&page=2&sort=&fq=&total=31&recno=21&subType=fdkn [accessed 2 June 2019].
53 Wolfgang Jäger, *Soziale Bürgerrechte im Museum: die Repräsentation sozialer Demokratie in neun kulturhistorischen Museen* (Essen: Klartext, 2020).
54 *Durch Nacht zum Licht? Geschichte der Arbeiterbewegung 1863 – 2013* (Mannheim: Technoseum, 2013).
55 See the contribution of Sean Scalmer in this volume.
56 Silke Wagner, *Glückauf. Bergarbeiterproteste im Ruhrgebiet*, 2010, https://www.emscherkunst.de/kunstwerk/glueckauf-bergarbeiterproteste-im-ruhrgebiet/ [accessed 2 June 2019].
57 https://www.gewerkschaftsgeschichte.de/ [accessed 3 June 2019].
58 DGB-Bundesvorstand, eds., *Bewegte Zeiten. Mitgestalten, Mitbestimmen, Mitverantworten. 50 Jahre DGB, Düsseldorf 1999; Bewegte Zeiten – Arbeit an der Zukunft. Dokumentation der wissenschaftlichen Konferenz des DGB "50 Jahre DGB" am 11. und 12. Oktober 1999 in München* (Gewerkschaftliche Monatshefte, 12, 1999); vgl. auch den VHS-Dokumentarfilm des DGB-Bundesvorstandes, *Bewegte Zeiten. 50 Jahre DGB* (1999).
59 Hayden White, *The Practical Past* (Evanston/Illinois: Northwestern University Press, 2014).
60 Thomas Welskopp, 'Die deutsche Sozialdemokratie programmiert die "neue Zeit": die Zukunft der Sozialdemokratie von den Anfängen bis zum ersten Weltkrieg,' and Stefan Berger, 'Von der Begrenzung der Zukunft zur Suche nach Zukunft: die Zukunft der Sozialdemokratie vom ersten Weltkrieg bis heute,' both in Die *Zukunft des 20. Jahrhunderts: Dimensionen einer historischen Zukunftsforschung*, ed. Lucian Hölscher (Frankfurt/Main: Campus, 2017), 39–74.
61 François Hartog, *Regimes of Historicity. Presentism and Experiences of Time* (New York: Columbia University Press, 2015).
62 https://germanlabourhistory.wordpress.com/ [accessed 3 June 2019]
63 Jörg Neuheiser, Christine Bartlitz, and Violetta Rudolf, 'Mehr Geschichte wagen: Plädoyer für einen mutigeren Umgang der Gewerkschaften mit (ihrer) Zeitgeschichte,' (2016), in: https://www.boeckler.de/pdf/p_fofoe_WP_018_2016.pdf [accessed 3 June 2019].
64 Florence Jaumotte and Carolina Osorio Buitron, 'Inequality and Labour Market Institutions,' published by the International Monetary Fund, *Staff Discussion Note* 15, 14 July 2015, in: http://www.imf.org/external/pubs/ft/sdn/2015/sdn1514.pdf [accessed 3 June 2019].

14

PROTEST CYCLES AND CONTENTIOUS MOMENTS IN MEMORY ACTIVISM

Insights from postwar Germany

Jenny Wüstenberg

The transformation of memory through contentious action does not often enter into public awareness in a prominent way. When it does though, it leaves a lasting impression. It is not hard to conjure up the iconic images of Lenin statues being carted off – images that marked the irreversible end to the Cold War. Another example is found in the television broadcasts of Saddam Hussein being unceremoniously hoisted off his pedestal, symbolizing the end to his brutal reign. And just recently, the dismantling of Confederate statues and other symbols of racist violence in various North American cities has made headline news.[1] Among them, the mobilization of the far right in Charlottesville, Virginia, ostensibly to keep Confederate General Robert E. Lee in place, has had the most dramatic (and deadly) consequences.[2] Such moments, in which the politics of memory, and the involvement of grassroots movements in them, briefly take center stage, are usually regarded as the byproducts of important transformative episodes in history.

In this chapter, I want to problematize this limited notion of temporality when it comes to grassroots mobilization surrounding memory culture. On the one hand, I argue that the work of 'memory activists' is not confined to those publicity-worthy moments: movements for remembrance engage in much 'quiet' memory work in the 'medium-term' that is explicitly targeted at public commemoration – both before and after their activity receives public attention (if it ever gets any at all). This work, that may happen over months and years (rather than decades), is pivotal for the transformation and reproduction of dominant narratives about the past, as well as of the institutional arrangements that govern memory policy. It can be understood as part of a 'protest cycle,' emerging in periods of broader political and social upheaval. Moreover, various memory activist groups are characterized by key patterns that shape their emergence, the nature of their public interventions, and their development over time. Second, I argue that it is important to take into account the impact of 'contentious moments' (defined as occurrences, brief in duration, that spark or are accompanied by controversy or even conflict) in terms of their role in catalyzing broader memory-political processes. Scholars of memory have a tendency to analyze changes of mnemonic narratives and politics over (sometimes longer periods of) time, often without paying much attention to the role of agency in these changes. Attention to key events and patterns evident in the medium-term not only introduces important elements of contingency into an account of memory politics, but also restores 'to these struggles the very real prospect for human agency that inhere in them.'[3]

In order to think through these concerns for memory studies, I take a cue from the discussion about temporality in social movement studies, that is, I consider how to understand social movement mobilization and impact from a temporal perspective. In my 2017 book, I argue that memory activists become especially influential during contentious moments, when their (equally important but quieter) 'memory work' morphs into more visible 'memory protest.' In this chapter, I take a closer look at the role of key events, broader cycles of contention, and medium-term patterns in explaining grassroots memory action. I begin by summarizing how civil society activists have intervened in German memory politics from 1945 to the present, emphasizing their impact on the institutional arrangements governing commemoration.[4] I then briefly outline the relevant concepts of temporality in social movement studies and apply them to the case of German memory activism. In particular, I examine the qualitative and quantitative transformation of memory politics of German memory politics from the early 1980s onwards from three different temporal perspectives: long-term, medium-term, and immediate. In this context, I draw on the concept of 'cycles of contention' as one that is useful in thinking through memory activists' relationship to other movements as well as key patterns of mobilization and demobilization and acknowledge the crucial role played by 'contentious moments' where public memory can experience sudden sea changes.

Activist memory politics in Germany, 1945 to the present[5]

Between 1945 and the present, memory politics in Germany have been profoundly transformed; it is probably one of the most widely studied cases of coming to terms with a dark past. However, the role played by civil society and social movements in this story has largely been neglected. In fact, grassroots activists were engaged in shaping public memory from the very beginning. Holocaust survivors and displaced persons rapidly formed associations that sought, sometimes with the help of the Allies, to mark the sites of their suffering and safeguard the memories of the victims. For example, the International Camp Committee at Buchenwald conducted a first commemorative event only eight days after liberation by American troops.[6] At Bergen-Belsen, the Bergen-Belsen Jewish Committee inaugurated a monument recalling the thirty thousand Jewish victims of this camp in September 1945.[7] In addition to such local efforts, several national victims associations were founded, most prominently the Union of the Persecuted of the Nazi Regime/Association of Antifascists (VVN-BdA, *Vereinigung der Verfolgten des Naziregimes-Bund der Antifaschisten*), which initially existed in both the Soviet and the Western zones of occupation. In the East, the group was quickly replaced by a state-sanctioned association, which proceeded to promote the ideological line and commemorative agenda of the Stalinist regime. Grassroots memory activism was, like any autonomous civic effort, suppressed in the GDR until there was some measure of political liberalization in the 1980s. In West Germany, conditions were not repressive, but victims of the Nazi regime received little official support in the first two decades after the war. The federal government vilified the VVN-BdA as Communist and as funded by the East German state and even attempted to outlaw it. The Holocaust was not silenced entirely, but the stories of survivors were not actively sought out or publicized.[8] The first Chancellor Konrad Adenauer used Holocaust commemoration strategically and, as a consequence, some sites, like Bergen-Belsen and the Bendler Block in Berlin (where the anti-Hitler plot of 1944 had been centered), received some public exposure. But even these sites would not have received the attention they did without the sustained efforts of civic associations that were made of mostly of Holocaust survivors and family members of those killed. Under these challenging conditions, victims' groups did succeed in placing numerous memorials, but they did not do much to alter the prevailing 'Vergangenheitspolitik'[9] of the Federal Republic during the 1950s and 1960s that was aimed at sidelining responsibility for Nazi crimes and in exonerating the vast majority of perpetrators.

The much more successful memory activists of this era were those seeking to commemorate 'German suffering,' particularly veterans' associations and the many local and cross-regional organizations representing Vertriebene (expellees). Ethnic Germans from Eastern Europe were a highly influential force in the 1950s and 1960s especially, with their own political party and effective organizational structures (although they also faced discrimination from local populations). Expellees' commemorative output was impressive, resulting in thousands of memorial markers that recalled the lost homeland without acknowledging the cause of the loss. Veterans similarly created many local memorials (often simply adding to World War I memorials) that did not link the horror of war to responsibility for Nazi aggression. One of the most prominent examples is the *Heimkehrermahnmal* in Friedland near Göttingen (Figure 14.1), which was erected by the Federation of Homecomers, POWs and Relatives of the Missing (*Verband der Heimkehrer Kriegsgefangenen und Vermisstenangehörigen, VdH*). Both veterans' and expellees' groups successfully tapped into the prevailing anti-Communist climate in the Federal Republic, which also supported a vigorous memory culture surrounding the victims of the 1953 uprising in the GDR and later those who died trying to cross the inner German border. The Union of Victims of Stalinism (*Vereinigung der Opfer des Stalinismus, VOS*) was another early memory association that received both grassroots and official support. Prominent members of the federal government and local dignitaries such as the West Berlin mayor regularly attended their commemorative events.

FIGURE 14.1 Heimkehrermahnmal in Friedland near Göttingen: 'Memorial built by the Federation of Homecomers, POWs and Relatives of the Missing 1967' (Photo: author, 2016).

In sum, these memory activists did not challenge official memory politics so much as underwriting and supporting it. The mnemonic rhetoric of government officials of the 1950s and early 1960s, which mostly avoided directly addressing Germans' responsibility for Nazi crimes, while making sure not to alienate Cold War allies, was mostly in line with that of these activists. Both tended to refer to the period of 1933–45 through vague phrases such as 'dark times,' 'years of violence' without explaining historical context or assigning blame to anyone beyond Hitler and his inner circle. Representatives of expellees, veterans, or victims of Stalinism did not represent an oppositional social movement, but rather civil society as a supportive structure for state governance, in the sense Robert Putnam has outlined.[10] Groups of Holocaust survivors and reconciliation associations were no doubt oppositional in terms of their demands for commemoration, but their voices were not heard loudly or frequently. The political and cultural climate of the early Federal Republic was not favorable to their objective of placing Holocaust memorials prominently in public space. Having emerged from genocidal persecution and having acquired a modicum of acceptance in the new political system, survivors were often reluctant to use contentious tactics, preferring to work through institutional channels to gain the respect of established politicians. As German society began to change during the 1960s, however, so did the relative position of various memory activists vis-à-vis the state.

The student movement of the 1960s is conventionally credited with transforming how the Nazi past was confronted in the Federal Republic. However, though '1968' was important, the shift did not happen quite as suddenly as this shorthand implies. The memory-political climate both began to shift earlier and was influenced strongly by the emerging social movement scene on the 'post-revolutionary' 1970s. In direct response to a wave anti-Semitic graffities, tens of thousands protested in January 1960 in Berlin against anti-Semitism and neo-Nazism – an unprecedented level of mobilization in this issue area.[11] A confrontation with the Nazi past was also increasingly undertaken by liberal intellectuals and artists, and was manifested in the judicial reckoning with the Holocaust, most prominently in the Auschwitz trials. The shift could be felt in a gradual withdrawal of official support from 'German-centric' commemoration. For instance, the *Heimkehrermahnmal* had been begun in the wake of Adenauer's publicity-conscious campaign to free the remaining POWs in the Soviet Union. By the mid-1960s, the federal government had quietly handed over the project to the VdH.[12] Moreover, the student movement's vocal condemnation of continuing fascist structures and personnel and its Marxist critique remained largely abstract and did not immediately filter down to 'on the ground' memorialization efforts. The student revolution, however, did have an indirect and important impact on memory activism. The waning of the most radical protest phase resulted in the creation of a vibrant social movement scene of alternative projects, coffee shops, publishing houses, and community centers during the 1970s,[13] which facilitated not only the well-known environmental, women's, and peace movements but also two smaller and closely allied movements that directly targeted commemoration. These took off in the early 1980s and peaked in terms of membership and activities in the mid-1980s to early 1990s. Today, many groups that had formed these movements continue to exist and intervene in local memory politics, but no longer form an oppositional challenge to official memory culture.

The first of these was the History (Workshop) Movement (*Geschichtsbewegung* or sometimes *Geschichtswerkstättenbewegung*), which was made up of dozens of 'history workshops' and 'alternative archives' that sought to examine local history from the ground up. Its motto was 'dig where you stand!' (*grabe wo du stehst!*). One of the initial purposes of these explicitly left-wing initiatives was the safeguarding of historical evidence about sister struggles and the desire not to leave the writing of history to the 'establishment.' For this reason, history workshops became pioneers of oral history interviewing, the history of everyday life, and alternative approaches to exhibition design. They also sought to involve lay people, and especially underrepresented populations, in the writing of their own history. And they had a much less formal style than the somewhat stuffy academic historiography. Emblematic of this approach were the History Movement's self-made newsletter and its annual 'history festivals' (*Geschichtsfeste*) – both means through which the disparate local groups could exchange information and develop an identity as a larger movement. The 1986 festival was entitled 'Tango and Theoretical Work' (*Tango und Theoriearbeit*), suggesting the movement's different approach to the past. The History Movement's core goal was not memorialization per se. However, because of its concern for identifying historical traces in the landscape, politicizing the past, and drawing from it for a more democratic presence, and because they engaged in much practical memory work, they ended up being the driving force behind the numerous new memorials – and behind the creation of critical publicity for existing memory sites. To name just two examples: the Marburg History Workshop since the late 19080s until today has engaged in protest activity and counter-memorialization at a local monument that recalled uncritically a military regiment that had been engaged in war crimes during World War II. The Workshop not only conducted and publicized research about the regiment, but also picketed annual memorial events of veterans and tried to place an 'irregular' memorial recalling the deserters from the Nazi army (Figure 14.2). Similarly, the Berlin History Workshop over many years illegally 'renamed' a bridge over the Landwehr Canal the 'Rosa-Luxemburg-Bridge,' and by 2013 had successfully persuaded the city to officially change the name. The Workshop also helped to initiate such important Berlin memorial sites as the Topography of Terror, the Memorial at the former forced labor camp in Schöneweide, the T4 memorial to victims of Euthanasia and the 'decentralized' Holocaust memorial around the Bayrischer Platz in Schöneberg – as well as putting together countless exhibits and historical city (and boat) tours.

The second key memory movement of the 1980s and 1990s, the Memorial Site Movement or *Gedenkstättenbewegung*, was less explicitly urban and left-wing, but drew supporters from many of the same circles as the history workshops. Often, workshoppers were also directly involved in the Memorial Site Movement. This movement was organized around local struggles to commemorate sites of Nazi terror. At the more well-known locations, such as Dachau, Bergen-Belsen or Neuengamme, the new initiatives could build on the work of existing victims' associations, though sometimes a generational and culture clash had to be overcome first. However, there were also many initiatives at so-called 'forgotten' memory sites – such as satellite camps, routes of death marches, or former Gestapo offices. The initiatives brought together activists with diverse backgrounds – students, schools, union members, church groups, victims' representatives – depending on local context and interest. They also encountered varying situations on the ground: sometimes they faced stiff resistance from residents, business owners or politicians who did not want their town 'tarnished' by the 'dark past.' Other times, they quickly found allies within local governments

FIGURE 14.2 Members of the Marburg History Workshop next to the Marburger Jäger regiment during a commemorative ceremony (Photo: Michael Heiny, Marburger Geschichtswerkstatt, 1989).

and organizations, aiding the institutionalization of critical memory as I discuss below. Despite the fact that memorial initiatives were concentrated on local concerns and coalition-building, they quickly realized that other groups in the Federal Republic were confronted with similar challenges. Starting in the early 1980s, they actively networked and traded experiences through a newsletter (*Gedenkstättenrundbrief*), regular meetings (*Gedenkstättenseminare*), and also a coordinating office (*Gedenkstättenreferat*), which was at first based with Action Reconciliation/Service for Peace (ASF) and then at the Topography of Terror Foundation in Berlin. Through these efforts, the Movement developed a sense of identity and solidarity that continues to this day – even though the activists no longer face much resistance and have in fact often become part of the state, the memory politics of which they set out struggling against. I will again name just two examples of memorial site initiatives here. First, the *Aktives Museum Faschismus und Widerstand in Berlin e.V.* was founded as an effort to mark the site of the former Gestapo headquarters in central Berlin and to create a different kind of interactive museum there. The activists of the *Aktives Museum* used both protest tactics and persistent lobbying, but largely retain their identity as a force for critical memory – that is a self-reflective confrontation with the past that demands an unsettling of established narratives, the taking of historical responsibility, and a dismantling of values that facilitate discrimination, nationalism, and war – to this day. Initially facing reluctance to act, they eventually succeeded in creating one of the most important memorial institutions in Germany – and one that now also hosts additional memorial sites as a kind of umbrella institution.

The *Initiative Gedenkstätte Neuengamme* sought to safeguard the historical traces of the former concentration camp on the outskirts of Hamburg when it was still being used as a regular prison. Victims' associations had succeeded in placing markers on the perimeter of the site, but the *Initiative* – again through protest and publicity – succeeded in getting the prison closed and the site converted into a memorial institution, with a permanent exhibition, a research unit and archive, and links to many former satellite sites. Initiatives like these can be found all over Germany, some of them founded more recently, but all of them with the explicit goal of promoting a critical approach to the Nazi past and a democratic memory culture by promoting values of tolerance, anti-nationalism, self-critique, care for the weak, and a strong culture of debate.[14]

The History and Memorial Site Movements together make up the most important initiator of memorials to the Nazi past in the Federal Republic and thus, a crucial participant in the transformation of its memory politics. According to a Brigitte Hausmann, during the 1980s 'about half of the monuments were initiated by history working groups, homeland associations (Heimatvereine), peace groups and citizen initiatives, by associations for Christian-Jewish cooperation and memorial initiatives.'[15] This crucial role continued into the 1990s and the new century, though they no longer face nearly as much resistance to their demands. Without this leftist memory activism, we would not have the decentralized memory landscape we have in Germany today, nor would many memorials be able to operate without sustenance from civic support groups. Many of the (former) activists are now (and have been for decades) staff or even leaders of memorial institutions, and have deeply influenced them through their 'march into the institutions.' This has had a profound effect on memorial institutions. Even as activists became employees of the state, they retained their civic identity. They brought their memorial principles into the institutions – such as their emphasis on historical authenticity; anti-monumentality and decentralized commemoration; non-emotionality; and attention to perpetrators, marginalized victim groups, and 'forgotten' sites. They also brought their political culture of open debate and inclusion of civil society with them, and sought to manifest it in institutional structures, for instance through the integration of civic groups into decision-making committees. In this way, they created what I have called 'hybrid institutions:' organizations (Gedenkstätten, local and regional museums, memorial sites with educational offerings) that are state regulated and funded, but staffed by individuals who are socialized in civil society and retain a civic identity. But these activists-turned-civil servants have also carefully guarded their hard-fought victories and have been reluctant to open up to new ideas.

With the fall of the Berlin wall, the memorial-institutional environment became more complex, but also received a further boost, as honest confrontation with the Nazi past became part of the state's raison d'être and official funding programs. The next wave of memory activists, those who sought to commemorate life and repression in the German Democratic Republic, had to contend with the institutional environment as it was shaped by the memory activists of the History and Memorial Site Movements. On the one hand, this was a clear advantage, as these 'GDR memory activists' began their advocacy in a society that valued highly both commemoration and civic engagement more generally. Moreover, the federal government rapidly provided funding mechanisms for memory projects dealing with the legacies of dictatorship. On the other hand, local memory activists felt that they were mostly alone in demanding the safeguarding of sites of repression, for example, in Bautzen, Torgau, Erfurt, or Cottbus. Moreover, the funding criteria and memorial aesthetics put forward by state institutions such as the regional foundations for memorials (that is, Stiftung Brandenburgische Gedenkstätten) were strongly shaped by the previous generation of activists as argued above. Sometimes this meant dealing not only with competing 'pasts' (such as in Buchenwald, Sachsenhausen, or Torgau) but also with a clash of personalities and personal histories. In West Germany since the 1980s, the commemoration of 'German suffering' and national commemoration had largely been the domain of conservative parties and organizations. The much-maligned initiatives and scandals of the Kohl administration ('Bitburg,' plans for a war memorial in Bonn, etc.) were indications of this. For this reason, traditionally anti-Communist groups such as the VOS and the BdV were suspicious of the leftist memory activists who had not paid much attention to human rights violations in the GDR. On the flip side, advocates for confronting the Nazi past often suspected those 'GDR memory activists,' who advocated for a prominent remembrance of repression under the Communist regime, of seeking to relativize the centrality of the Holocaust in German political culture. Some of the most contentious episodes in recent German memory politics were based on these cultural battles and personal animosities between various kinds of memory activists and their institutional allies.

These clashes also showed up in rhetoric and memorial design ideas. For example, advocates for GDR sites such as Berlin-Hohenschönhausen and Leistikowstrasse in Potsdam argued that exhibitions had to be gripping and emotional in order to bring home the point that the past was still fresh and perpetrators still around.[16] A good example of this is the design of the former prison in Cottbus, where many political prisoners had been held, which depicts the overcrowding of cells and the humiliation through the careless rifling through of personal belongings (Figure 14.3). This violated the principle – valued by the two Movements of the 1980s – that history should be presented with emotional distance so as to not overwhelm the audience and allow for a reflective learning process. Such disagreements resulted in heated debates and the – sometimes warranted – feeling on the part of GDR victims' groups that they were being excluded from deciding the nature of the sites of their own suffering. Representatives of 'hybrid' memorial institutions often quite blatantly employed the definitional and funding power of the state in order to sideline these new activists as 'unprofessional.'[17] However, some GDR memorial activists have also successfully used these contentious processes to assert their own demands and to find their way into memorial institutions. Despite the generally favorable institutional environment,

FIGURE 14.3 Center for Human Rights Memory in Cottbus, staged to show how guards humiliated prisoners by rifling through their belongings in their cells (Photo: author, 2014).

without persistent memory activism, many sites recalling life and dictatorship in East Germany would likely not exist at all today and they would certainly look different. As may already have become clear in this account of the history of memory activism then, there do appear to be patterns of mobilization, movement strategies and institutional integration in German memory politics. In the next section, I analyze these patterns and apply some concepts familiar to social movement theorists to this field.

Temporalities in German memory activism

The history of postwar Germany shows that though grassroots activity is a virtually constant component of memory politics, it has had differential rates of success. I argue that it is particularly when memory activism becomes contentious that it profoundly influences mnemonic values and public remembrance. *Non-contentious memory activism* can be of two varieties. Either it is in line with mainstream memory narratives (as was the case with expellee or veteran activism in the immediate postwar era) and thus fulfills a *reproductive* function. The other variety is not visible or powerful enough and so can easily be ignored by elites and by society at large (like that of some Holocaust survivor groups during the same period). Memory activists have struggled to have their interpretations of the past acknowledged throughout the postwar period, but they have not always succeeded in transforming mnemonic norms in the emerging democratic society. They are likely to have a *transformative* effect when their actions provoke public outrage or pressure on other actors to either shift positions or dig in their heels, thereby producing more protest.

I have distinguished between two – not entirely separate or separable – modes of activism: memory work and memory protest. I contend that it is when memory work turns into protest – either because memory work challenges dominant mnemonic norms or because activists use contentious tactics – that public memory is more likely to be transformed.[18] Here, I would like to examine this point in light of social movement theorists' discussion of temporality. I argue that two temporal concepts in particular, protest cycles and contentious moments, can help us think through and challenge memory studies' tendency to disregard agency in general and the role of grassroots activists especially.

Doug McAdam and William Sewell contend that in social movement research, some types of temporalities have been implicitly privileged over others (and also that much work on social movements does not address temporality at all). The two most prominent concepts of time are long-term change processes (associated especially with the work of Charles Tilly) and cycles of contention (Sidney Tarrow). McAdam and Sewell write that two important temporalities have been neglected: transformative events and cultural epochs.[19] I will leave the question of cultural epochs in the analysis of memory developments aside here (although I believe an interesting case could be made that the notion of cultural epochs can help explain broad strokes of remembrance cultures). Long-term change processes such as industrialization, urbanization, and state formation can have destabilizing effects on existing power relations and facilitate the formation and mobilization of oppositional groups.[20] Long-term factors such as generational and technological change are an important part of many explanations of why German society underwent the profound shift from unwillingness to take responsibility for the Nazi past to making the confrontation with it a central feature of its political culture and identity. Memory politics, the argument goes, change with the *Zeitgeist*, which, in turn, can change when the generation of perpetrators and victims is no longer dominant in public life. Another point often made is that the growing interest in the Nazi past in German society was part of the more general memory boom that resulted from globalization, technological change, and a concomitant desire to ascertain historical roots and traditions. Both of these long-term change processes are no doubt important, but they cannot explain Germany's unique memory politics and the extraordinary shift they underwent during the 1980s. Moreover, both ignore how key actors intervene and shape them. In other words, they are necessary, but not sufficient conditions for mnemonic change.

The application of the two remaining notions of temporality, protest cycles and transformative events, addresses the problem I raised at the outset of this chapter. That is, that memory activism tends to receive public attention rarely, and when it does, it is presented as a *symptom* of long-term political change, rather than as the primary *driving factor* behind mnemonic change. Moreover, the important but quiet work of memory activists, as well as their relationship to phases of broad societal unrest, is rarely analyzed. A tearing down or the inauguration of a monument then appears as a short outburst, those who made it happen and how are usually absent from the public sphere.

The protest cycle concept was put forward by Sidney Tarrow and for a while played a central role in social movement studies, aiming to theorize the observation that collective mobilization tends to occur in waves, during periods of 'generalized social unrest' that drive forward movements in different issue areas and that they pass through a regular set of stages.[21] Tarrow defines a cycle of contention as

> a phase of heightened conflict across the social system: with a rapid diffusion of collective action from more mobilized to less mobilized sectors; a rapid pace of innovation in the forms of contention; the creation of new or transformed collective action frames; a combination of organized and unorganized participation; and sequences of intensified information flow between challengers and authorities.[22]

However, the concept was relatively quickly subjected to critique – including by Tarrow himself. In *Dynamics of Contention*, McAdam, Tilly, and Tarrow noted that they had come to understand that trajectories of contention 'do not pass through invariant stages and that the driving force in their progression lies in the interaction of the actors,' and that they now saw 'the cyclical model as one empirical form of trajectories,' leaving them 'free to turn directly to the mechanisms and processes that power them.'[23]

This significant recognition notwithstanding, I contend that the core elements of the 'protest cycle' concept can still help us think through memory activism in three ways. First, it highlights that mobilization usually happens not in an isolated fashion on one particular issue, but in the context of broader upheavals in society. Second, the idea of a protest cycle directs attention to a 'medium-term' temporality, which is to memory work done over the years, months, and weeks (but not decades or centuries) preceding a key event or achievement. Third, while a model positing distinct types and a succession of phases in a cycle is clearly too rigid, the 'cycle' does push us to consider patterns in memory activism and the extent to which one tends to follow another. This kind of analysis allows for more systematic comparison of different memory activists across time and space and seeks explanations for why key developments occur when and how they do. The notion is especially interesting for analyzing memory politics, which are often viewed as uniquely linked to particular (national) contexts and historical reference points, rather than recognizing that memory activism is a form of social movement action that can and does exhibit comparable dynamics of radicalization and institutionalization,[24] diffusion processes across movements in various issue areas, and shared repertoires and collective action frames.[25]

The first point – that memory movements are likely to emerge during periods of generally heightened social movement activity – is clearly illustrated by my discussion of the History Workshop and Memorial Site Movements. These were embedded in and took advantage of a vibrant 'scene' of new social movements (especially the anti-nuclear and environmental movements that were at a peak in the early 1980s) in the context of which there was a rapid diffusion of collective action and development of protest repertoires. These Movements were also temporarily able to entice less organized portions of the population to participate in demanding a more critical approach to the past. These elements gave the Movements an advantage and helps to explain their extraordinary success in persuading the German public and the state to (mostly) give up resistance and to institutionalize critical memory.

Combining the second and third points – that there are medium-term patterns of mobilization, often appearing in a particular sequence – it is instructive to think about how memory activists of different eras might fit into a pattern of mobilization. Based on my analysis of various memory activists in postwar Germany, I next identify a series of phases – roughly following one another, but often overlapping or switching places as well. Some of these will be familiar to students of movement studies and indeed occurred through mutual influencing of various movements during a cycle of contention. Others, however, are specific to activists targeting the representation of the past.

1   *Identification of a particular historical episode in the past or a particular site as the focus of action.* This may be done with by individuals or groups with a personal connection to the episode/site (survivors, relatives, staff of a site's new usage) or that have for some reason become interested in it (historians, interested lay people, students). These can be regarded as 'early' (and sometimes initially unsuccessful) risers, such as the victims' groups of the 1940s and 1950s. Such persons can then help to inform and create public awareness, potentially increasing the scope of collective action. For example, prior to the formation of local initiatives that became part of the Memorial Site Movement, a small group of individuals had always developed a sense of the local topography of National Socialism, as well as an understanding of the larger and developing debate about the need to work through the past.

2   *A group of people begin to gather regularly for the purpose of undertaking memory work*. I have defined memory work, as

> those activities that are the primary occupation of memory initiatives, including: holding meetings [to discuss the past]; networking with stakeholders and potential benefactors; creating forums for debate; lobbying; conducting historical research (through archival work, interviews and the collection of materials); safeguarding of evidence (sometimes under adverse conditions); presenting findings in exhibits, publications, and guided tours; and organizing commemorative events (large and small).[26]

This joint activity can then lead to a process of group identity formation, mobilization of a broader set of supporters, organization-creation, and innovation in the forms of contention.

3   *Formation of an oppositional identity and movement radicalization*. This usually happens in reaction to a (perceived) lack of openness in society or among elites to confront the past or to provide it space in public sphere. In many cases, a trigger of radicalization is the occurrence of an 'outside threat' to an important mnemonic site. In Wuppertal, for instance, activists rallied when the local government announced plans to construct a parking garage on the site of a destroyed synagogue.[27] In 1987, former Nazi rallying grounds in Nuremberg were chosen to be made into a shopping mall, thus crystalizing the mnemonic opposition.[28] In Frankfurt/Main, a broad coalition occupied the site of archeological remains of a Medieval Jewish ghetto in order to prevent its razing for the purposes of building a public transportation administrative building.[29] Another source of oppositional identity are of course internal deliberative processes through which participants reach the realization that their struggle contradicts the prevailing mnemonic norms.

4   *The development of new frames of meaning*. This element of the protest cycle may actually come at any point or happen parallel to other phases, but it is crucial. As Tarrow has argued, protest cycles bring new or changed symbols, frames, or ideologies, typically arising first within a social movement and then spreading outward.[30] In memory politics, one might regard the call for historical justice and the recognition of the plight of victims as crucial new collective action frames. More specific examples of mnemonic frames might be the Memorial Site Movement's insistence of non-monumentality and authenticity as a counter-frame to nationalistic remembrance rituals; systematic attention to 'forgotten' victim groups and places; and its call to deal directly with sites and identities of perpetrators. GDR memory activists extended many of these frames to their own memory struggles but also specifically developed frames of meaning such as the importance of emotionality at historic sites (sometimes trumping authenticity or historical accuracy).

5   *The shift to memory protest*. This shift to contentiousness can happen for two reasons: first, because the content of commemorative activity clashes with

existing mnemonic norms or challenges the government's official line. Thus, the mere voicing of alternative memory frames makes them contentious. Second, the 'socialization' of the group (the existence of activist traditions and a willingness to employ various repertoires) can lead people to employ contentious tactics, intentionally provoking a reaction from society. Often, this shift occurs for both of these reasons. Memory protest tactics can involve the whole range of the social movement repertoire and are linked with the explicit publicizing of historical information or the staging of public commemoration. Common for grassroots memory actors in Germany have been: staging rallies and other protest actions such as occupations or sit-ins; putting up exhibitions and memorials in provocative places or manners; undertaking hunger strikes (a tactic used especially by early memory activists and more recently by GDR victim groups); repurposing existing memorials through signs or graffiti; and illegally placing monuments or commemorative symbols. The Memorial Site and History Movements developed new ways to present and publicize historical evidence and expanded existing repertoires, including by applying tactics (sit-ins, street theater etc.) known to them through left-wing sister movements to the field of memory.

6 *Finding and cooperating with mainstream or institutional actors.* A common feature of the memory movement cycle is that there is a process of finding and allying with elites and institutions – or put differently, of varying state responses to contention. This process can vary in speed and intensity. Often, there is a kind of back and forth between activists and authorities over several years. As I describe,

> activists, after mounting publicity work, lobbying, and staging protests against political recalcitrance, might have been able to achieve an initial success of a small memorial marker or limited funding for an historical project. With growing public awareness and activist self-confidence, as well as a shift in attitudes within political and bureaucratic circles, more [becomes] possible.[31]

Thus, we might identify several rounds of commemoration and cooperation with institutions. At Neuengamme, for example, the activists, even after succeeding in acquiring a documentation center, kept calling for the prison to be closed and the entire site be handed over to become part of the memorial. They also increasingly included Neuengamme's satellite camps in their demands. There usually comes a point, however, at which the activists' rhetoric about having to struggle against long odds to overcome an ingrained refusal to confront the past honestly can be seen as just that: rhetoric. There is a tipping point at which the movement meets with more support than opposition and has a powerful set of institutional allies.

7 *The next phase for successful activists is that they develop a regularized relationship with institutions.* This can take the form of an informally or formally arranged structure through which activists are integrated in governance of memorial

sites, for instance, by being represented on government councils or advisory boards. In this way, the memory movement's importance as a public partner is cemented and their demands defined as legitimate. In the cases I studied, these kinds of arrangements were often accompanied or followed by the integration of activists as institutional staff or even in leadership positions. This, then, marks the 'march through the institutions,' which also entails that a movement's communicative culture and mnemonic principles are adopted by institutions, as I suggested above.

8 *The final portion of the cycle is the movement's decline,* either through lack of success or through the absorption of the movement's purpose and principles by institutions, and a resulting reduction in activist enthusiasm and support. Thus, while many history workshops and memorial initiatives continue to exist in Germany today, they no longer form a movement with a replenishing pool of participants and a common cross-regional identity. Their initial demands have largely been met and many of the early activists continue their work from within institutions.

While this account of the memory protest cycle is no doubt schematic and the eight phases are presented as artificially separate, they are nevertheless useful for analytical purposes. My research suggests that those activists who make the move from 'memory work to memory protest,' pass through all of these phases – though not necessarily in the same order or speed. The model can be used to examine the links between memory movements and a larger wave of protest, to differentiate memory from other types of activism, as well as to ask why some memory activists are more successful than others.

The local and regional campaigns to transform the memory and topography of the Nazi past, as well as efforts to mark sites of repression in East Germany, quite neatly the patterns I describe here. However, when comparing the early advocates for confrontation with the Nazi past, especially the associations of Holocaust survivors, to the Memorial Site Movement of the 1980s, which were not part of the same cycle of contention, the following becomes clear: while the survivors certainly clearly identified the important sites and episodes (Phase 1) and undertook extensive memory work, such as organizing events to recall their comrades, autonomously creating memorial markers, safeguarding historical traces, etc. (Phase 2), their efforts stalled somewhere between Phases 3 and 4. That is, they did not successfully radicalize and develop new frames of meaning, nor did they succeed in making memory contentious in a way that rattled the prevailing consensus in the early postwar period. Their activities did not become part of a full-fledged wave of contention. As a result, they never reached the phases where they were able to impact the institutional arrangements of public remembrance. Of course, a large part of the explanation for this failure must be sought in the unfavorable political opportunity structure faced by Holocaust survivors – an aspect that I have not discussed here, but do extensively elsewhere.[32] I want to emphasize that the lack of institutional impact does not take away from victims' associations' crucial role as producers of memory work, as guardians of historical evidence and recorders of oral histories, and as providers of support to survivors. Memory activists' importance does not lie only with their impact on mainstream memory culture.

A further useful function of a medium-term perspective on memory activism is that it helps identify the shift from memory work to memory protest as a tipping point, which can bring about the transformation of mnemonic frames and facilitate the location of elite or institutional allies. Next I look more closely at transformative events as the most immediate form of temporality discussed by social movement scholars.

Contentious moments in German memory activism

To bring us full circle, I now return to the transformative events, such as the spontaneous tearing down of statues, with which I opened this chapter. Drawing on the work of Aristide Zolberg, Tarrow[33] argues that such moments seem to recur in the history of social movements and suggests that 'the impossible becomes real – at least in the minds of participants.'[34] This notion may appear exaggerated for scholars who emphasize the gradual transformation of memory cultures. However, there are events when memory debates rapidly undergo dramatic shifts, when depicting the past in established ways is suddenly no longer acceptable, when large numbers of or symbolically important actors mobilize for a mnemonic cause when previously they were disinterested, when new audiences are drawn to historical concerns, and when new resources can be harnessed. As McAdam and Sewell have pointed out, such moments have strangely been neglected by scholars of social movements, despite the fact that anyone who has participated in one is likely to have felt the pivotal nature of particular events.[35]

Elaborating on the role played by the 'neglected temporality' of events, McAdam and Sewell argue that key moments act like Weber's 'switchmen': 'that is, events are the central sources of "evidence" out of which insurgents (and other parties to the conflict) construct their shared understandings of the system's vulnerability at every stage of the protest cycle. They thus mediate between long- and medium-term change processes and the ebb and flow of protest activity, distilling and illuminating the former and shaping the latter.'[36]

In memory politics, I identify two kinds of pivotal moments. First, there are mnemonic events that cannot be planned or predicted by activists, but which can be taken advantage of when they happen. One of the most influential moments in German memory politics was the 1985 speech by President Richard von Weizsäcker on the occasion of the 40th anniversary of the end of World War II, which was widely lauded as a turning point by the national and international media. He depicted 8 May 1945 not as defeat, but as liberation and also distinguished between the victims of Nazism and the suffering of Germans. My research on memory struggles shows that this moment was harnessed by many local activists to demand that a particular site be marked or converted into a memorial site.[37] In other words, the speech and the public reaction to it acted as a catalyst for (local) publics to recognize the issues at hand and for activists to frame their work in a much broader manner.

The second kind of moment is the kind that is created intentionally by activists, often at the point where memory work is shifted to memory protest. First and foremost, such moments may be 'publicity stunts,' organized to enhance visibility of a mnemonic issue or site, but they can become transformative events. For example, in 1985 (three days before von Weizsäcker's speech), the *Aktives Museum* in Berlin orchestrated a 'symbolic dig' on the grounds of the former Gestapo headquarters. This action is now regarded as a critical junction, which relatively rapidly lead the city to conduct actual archeological investigations that unearthed the remains of the Gestapo torture cells. From this moment on, it was practically impossible for the city *not* to address the site in a prominent way. Similarly, when GDR memory activists chained themselves to a temporary memorial at Checkpoint Charlie in Berlin, made up of crosses commemorating those who died at the German-German border, they forced the local and federal governments to address how the German capital remembered the separation and human rights violations in the GDR. The activists had transformed the terms of the debate about the necessity of marking sites of memory.

My point about contentious moments is not that they single-handedly transform public remembrance. However, I believe they deserve more attention than they have thus far gotten, as key events that puncture and propel forward (or backward) medium and longer-term transformations. Precisely because memory work often takes place outside of broad public view, contentious events are crucial in crystallizing to activists and publics alike what the state of the debate about the past is, what is widely acceptable, and what is doable for activists. Transformative moments can be the cause of sudden realizations about the past for publics (what Germans would call 'aha-moments'), can help recruit new activists and resources, and trigger more action through the diffusion of mnemonic frames and collective action repertoires. If there is a critical amount of support for activists and the 'establishment' digs in, this can be part of the chain reaction after a moment of madness and lead to more mobilization. Key events, however, can also have the opposite effect of showcasing to activists that their position is one of weakness, strengthening the positions of the mnemonic mainstream, reproducing it, and casting activists as the minority.

This explicit attention to temporality to the field of memory activism has been preliminary and more work remains to be done. For instance, a systematic examination of key mnemonic moments in German history and their impact on the development and impact of movements for memory is needed. My account does however warrant the conclusion that the highly public and symbolic 'tearing down' or 'putting up' of memorials are only the top of the iceberg when it comes to recognizing the work done by grassroots activists. The slow and often quiet labor that makes the big events possible, and the backstory to and aftereffect of the big events, both deserve more scholarly and public attention. A more nuanced examination of the temporality of memory movements will go a long way toward understanding the role of agency and contingency in the field of memory politics.

Notes

1 'Where Confederate Monuments End Up,' *CNN*, 16 August 2017, https://www.cnn.com/2017/08/16/us/where-confederate-statues-end-up/index.html, 'From Lofty Perch, New Orleans Monument to Confederacy Comes Down,' *The New York Times*, 19 May 2017, https://www.nytimes.com/2017/05/19/us/confederate-monument-new-orleans-lee.html?_r=0, 'Halifax Removes Contentious Statue of Port City's Founder, Edward Cornwallis' *The News*, 31 January 2018, http://www.ngnews.ca/news/halifax-removes-contentious-statue-of-port-citys-founder-edward-cornwallis-182140/
2 'The Statue at the Center of Charlottesville's Storm' *The New York Times*, 13 August 2017, https://www.nytimes.com/2017/08/13/us/charlottesville-rally-protest-statue.html
3 Doug McAdam and William H. Sewell Jr, 'It's About Time: Temporality in the Study of Social Movements and Revolutions,' in *Silence and Voice in the Study of Contentious Politics*, eds. Ronald R. Aminzade, Jack A. Goldstone, Doug McAdam, Elizabeth Perry, William H. Sewell Jr., Sidney Tarrow and Charles Tilly (New York: Cambridge University Press, 2001), 89–125, here: 125.
4 I focus on activists that targeted those memory politics at the heart of post-1945 West and later unified Germany, revolving around World War II, the Holocaust, the experience of Germans during the World Wars, histories of migration before and after 1945, the division of Germany, and repression and resistance under Stalinism and post-Stalinism. I do not discuss here activism surrounding social transformations such as (de)industrialization, nor the recent mobilizations concerning colonial legacies.
5 This chapter, and this first section in particular, draws heavily on the findings of my *Civil Society and Memory in Postwar Germany* (Cambridge: Cambridge University Press, 2017).
6 Gedenkstätte Buchenwald, ed., *Die Geschichte der Gedenkstätte Buchenwald. Begleitheft zur Dauerausstellung.* (Weimar, 2007).
7 Stiftung Niedersächsische Gedenkstätten, ed., *Bergen-Belsen. Geschichte der Gedenkstätte – History of the Memorial* (Celle, 2012).
8 Robert G. Moeller, 'Remembering the War in a Nation of Victims – West German Pasts in the 1950s,' in *The Miracle Years – A Cultural History of West Germany, 1949–1968*, ed. Hanna Schissler (Princeton, NJ: Princeton University Press, 2001), 83–109.
9 Norbert Frei, *Vergangenheitspolitik – Die Anfänge der Bundesrepublik und die NS-Vergangenheit* (München: C.H. Beck Verlag, 1997).
10 Robert Putnam, *Making Democracy Work* (Princeton, NJ: Princeton University Press, 1993).
11 Anja Corinne Baukloh, '"Nie wieder Faschismus!" Antinationalsozialistische Proteste in der Bundesrepublik der 50er Jahre im Spiegel ausgewählter Tageszeitungen,' in *Protest in der Bundesrepublik – Strukturen und Entwicklungen*, ed. Dieter Rucht (Frankfurt: Campus Verlag, 2001), 71–101.
12 Birgit Schwelling, 'Die "Friedland-Gedächtnisstätte",' *Zeithistorische Forschungen – Studies in Contemporary History* 5, no. 2 (2008): 189–210.
13 Sebastian Haunss and Darcy K. Leach, 'Social Movement Scenes – Infrastructures of Opposition in Civil Society,' in *Civil Societies and Social Movements – Potentials and Problems*, ed. Derrick Purdue (Oxon: Routledge Press/ECPR studies in European political science, 2007), 71–87.
14 Jenny Wüstenberg, *Civil Society and Memory in Postwar Germany* (Cambridge: Cambridge University Press, 2017), 8.

15 Brigitte Hausmann, *Duell mit der Verdrängung? Denkmäler für die Opfer des Nationalsozialismus in der Bundesrepublik Deutschland 1980 bis 1990* (Münster: Lit Verlag, 1997), 13.
16 Jenny Wüstenberg, 'Pluralism, Governance, and the New Right in German Memory Politics,' *German Politics and Society*, Issue 132, 37, no. 3 (Autumn 2019): 89–110.
17 Wüstenberg, 'Pluralism, Governance, and the New Right in German Memory Politics;' Thomas Lindenberger, 'Governing Conflicted Memories: Some Remarks about the Regulation of History Politics in Unified Germany,' in *Clashes in European Memory. The Case of Communist Repression and the Holocaust*, ed., Muriel Blaive, Christian Gerbel, and Thomas Lindenberger (Innsbruck: StudienVerlag, 2011), 73–87.
18 Wüstenberg, *Civil Society and Memory*, 8.
19 McAdam and Sewell Jr., 'It's About Time,' 89.
20 Ibid., 91.
21 Ibid., 96.
22 Sydney Tarrow, *Power in Movement – Social Movements and Contentious Politics* (2nd edn.) (Cambridge: Cambridge University Press, 1998), 142.
23 Doug McAdam, Sidney Tarrow, and Charles Tilly, *Dynamics of Contention* (Cambridge: Cambridge University Press, 2001), 66–67; see also Donatella della Porta and Mario Diani, *Social Movements: An Introduction*, (2nd edn.) (Oxford: Wiley-Blackwell Publishers, 2006), 188.
24 McAdam, Tarrow, and Tilly, *Dynamics of Contention*, 66.
25 Pamela E. Oliver, and Daniel J. Myers, 'Networks, Diffusion, and Cycles of Collective Action,' in *Social Movements and Networks. Relational Approaches to Collective Action*, eds. Mario Diani and Doug McAdam (Oxford: Oxford University Press, 2003), 173–204.
26 Wüstenberg, *Civil Society and Memory*, 18.
27 Heidi Behrens, Paul Ciupke, and Norbert Reichling. '"… Und im Nachhinein ist man überrascht, wie viele Leute sich das auf die Fahnen schreiben und sagen, ich habe es gemacht." Akteursperspektiven auf die Etablierung und Arbeit von Gedenkstätten in Nordrhein-Westfalen,' *GedenkstättenRundbrief* 171 (September 2013): 3–18.
28 Paul B. Jaskot, 'The Reich Party Rally Grounds Revisited. The Nazi Past in Postwar Nuremberg,' in *Beyond Berlin. Twelve German Cities Confront the Nazi Past*, eds. Gavriel D Rosenfeld and Paul B. Jaskot (Ann Arbor: The University of Michigan Press, 2008), 143–162, here: 151.
29 Michael Best, ed., *Der Frankfurter Börneplatz. Zur Archäologie eines politischen Konflikts* (Frankfurt: Fischer Taschenbuch Verlag, 1988).
30 Tarrow, 'Cycles of Collective Action,' 286.
31 Wüstenberg, *Civil Society and Memory*, 95.
32 Ibid.
33 Tarrow, 'Cycles of Collective Action,' 281.
34 Ibid., citing Aristide R. Zolberg, 'Moments of Madness,' *Politics and Society* 2, no. 2 (1972), 206.
35 McAdam and Sewell Jr., 'It's About Time,' 102.
36 Ibid., 123.
37 see for instance, '20 Jahre Verein EL-DE-Haus' *El-DE Info Nr. 10* (September 2008), and Jan Otakar Fischer, 'Memento Machinae. Engineering the Past in Wolfsburg,' in *Beyond Berlin. Twelve German Cities Confront the Nazi Past*, eds. Gavriel D. Rosenfeld and Paul B. Jaskot (Ann Arbor: The University of Michigan Press, 2008), 89–115, here: 100.

15

'SOCIAL MOVEMENTS, WHITE AND BLACK

Memory struggles in the United States South since the Civil War'

W. Fitzhugh Brundage

During the century after the American Civil War self-appointed arbiters and voluntary associations crafted public memory in the United States, especially the South. Public authorities played only a small role in this important cultural work until the second half of the twentieth century. Ultimately, groups who could marshal resources, a measure of popular support, and access to power had the greatest success imposing their historical memory on the American public sphere. For much of the past century and a half, white Southerners took full advantage of their disproportionate political and economic power to ensure that the region's civic traditions and public spaces enshrined their favored version of history. African Americans, nevertheless, continuously contested the glorification of the 'Old South,' slavery, the Confederacy, and white supremacy. After the restoration of political and civil rights to African Americans during the 1960s, southern blacks expanded and escalated their campaign for a revision of the region's public memory. In turn, a coalition of white southerners has mobilized to defend formerly sacrosanct symbols of white memory and southern 'heritage,' thereby ensuring that the region's past remains a contentious arena of public life.

A brief survey of the different agents who were responsible for the production of historical memory in different parts of the Western world during the late nineteenth century throws into high relief the role of voluntary groups active in the American South. In France, for example, the national state used its administrative apparatus to affect everything from the market for art and museum holdings to civic rituals. Agents of the French government exerted influence through patronage and funding to sway the strategies of cultural arbiters even in the hinterland. The same was true in Britain. The monarchies of Queen Victoria, Edward VII, and George V cultivated 'ceremonial splendor' with the aim of inspiring allegiance to the Crown and the empire even at a time when royal power was in decline. Even in Germany, where civic associations remained instrumental in erecting national monuments and staging celebrations throughout the nineteenth century, the reign of William II at the end of the century was marked by ostentatious public works, monuments, and rituals in which the emperor himself played a prominent role. By actively influencing, directing, or subsuming most campaigns to craft public memory, European states strove to organize their citizenries into cohesive 'modern' societies.[1]

Such ambitious cultural policies had no parallel in the United States. In the American republic the tradition of limited government extended to the realm of public culture, where cultural voluntarism, rather than state intervention, prevailed. With no meaningful tradition of royal cultural patronage inherited from the colonial era, Americans forged only the weakest link between the national government and national culture. The skeletal administrative structure of the national government and the dispersed authority inherent in American federalism offered few resources with which to shape a national cultural policy. Only tireless pestering could pry funds from state coffers to subsidize monuments, statues, and other public expressions of memory.[2]

Throughout the nineteenth century state governments abjured responsibility over historical memory to voluntary associations, which served as self-proclaimed intermediaries between the state and a broader and ill-defined constituency – the so-called 'public.' Because public authorities and ruling elites embraced a narrow conception of state obligations, citizens necessarily looked to voluntary associations to meet needs that public officials were either incapable or indisposed to address.

These characteristics of nineteenth-century American public culture placed a premium on the ability of any would-be custodians of public memory to manufacture 'public' support. Demonstrations of public interest, however crudely generated and staged, established the authority of voluntary associations to speak for the 'public.' Consequently, voluntary organizations were keen to represent their campaigns as spontaneous expressions of popular enthusiasm. Any organized group that could summon sufficient support and funds might influence public representations of the past, and even place demands on the state to recognize that memory.

Thus, the American South offers a conspicuous example of successive generations forging social movements that mustered tens of thousands to promote and perpetuate social memory. At least three generations of white southerners crafted an American landscape dense with Confederate monuments, while generations of African American southerners simultaneously responded with their own campaigns to promote and perpetuate a counter-memory.

-I-

The urgent need of the generation of white southerners who fought the Civil War to find a salve for the sting of defeat mobilized diverse groups' intent on rehabilitating the region. Sometimes these self-appointed memory activists worked at cross purposes but more often their efforts complemented one another and helped promote the impression of a region-wide movement that enjoyed broad popular support.

In addition to regaining a place in the Union, replacing slavery with a new form of labor, and rebuilding the southern economy, white Southerners confronted the equally vexing challenge of making sense of a catastrophic war that achieved none of its avowed purposes. That white southerners would commemorate their sacrifice during the war was almost certainly inevitable. But how best to commemorate the war defied simple answer. The slaveholder's republic had not been just defeated; it had been humiliated. Hundreds of thousands of white southerners had died or been wounded in a vainglorious struggle. Its white population had been demoralized. Any effort to mitigate a defeat of this magnitude would have to rally broad popular interest and mobilize as many cultural resources as possible.[3]

Given the conspicuous role of white clerics in defending slavery before the war and championing of the Confederate cause during the conflict, it was not surprising that white ministers emerged as important postwar architects of white southern memory. They had no doubt that God's hand was evident in the South's defeat. But the collapse of the southern nation did not prompt them to abandon their conviction that God favored white southerners and had a transcendent purpose for them. Rather than interpret defeat as evidence of God's wrath, white southerners instead concluded that they were latter day Israelites of the Old Testament and that God had used the ungodly Yankees to chasten his chosen people. In this manner, white clerics after the war fashioned a bulwark against suggestions that white southerners had been treasonous or immoral. The crucial and enduring contribution of southern white clerics was to sacrifice the war and the Confederate warriors who fought in it.[4]

Confederate veterans were no less keen than white clerics to erase the stigma attached to their defeat. Within a few years of the war's close local benevolent associations with ties to veterans proliferated across the former Confederacy. Most were small, closely knit organizations that performed both memorial and charitable work within their immediate communities until 1869 when former Confederate officers in New Orleans, who harbored larger ambitions, launched the Southern Historical Society. These veteran historians devoted themselves to compiling Confederate records, publishing justifications for the Confederacy, and excusing the South's defeat. Their signal accomplishment was to codify the explanation for the war's outcome. The Confederacy, they vouched, had been just and its generals and soldiers uncommonly brave and tenacious. These qualities, however, could not outlast the superiority of northern industry and numbers. Had the two contending armies been evenly matched in material and forces, they boasted, Confederate victory would have been swift.

More generally, veterans were catalysts for and recipients of public veneration in the emergent commemoration of the Confederacy. The image of aged and hobbled veterans as objects of charity, to a great degree, is an accurate measure of their place in the southern public life. But while they were the focus for reverence their ability to control the memory of the Civil War was ephemeral. The United Confederate Veterans (UCV), an organization of affiliated veterans' groups formed in 1889, exerted considerable influence over white memory between 1890 and 1910. At its peak, more than 1,500 local 'camps' of the organization dotted the South and perhaps as many as 80,000 veterans filled their ranks. Its official organ, the *Confederate Veteran* carried its message to an estimated 50,000 readers. But the life span of the UCV was only as long as that of its members and it lost influence rapidly after 1910 when death began to rapidly thin its ranks.[5]

Around the turn of the twentieth century a new generation assumed effective leadership of the commemoration of the Confederacy. What Confederate veterans needed and wanted most was the adoration of their society and this they could not provide themselves. Consequently, those white southerners who had not fought, especially women, had an essential role to play in Confederate commemoration. White women created and sustained the most enduring social movement of Confederate commemoration. Founded in 1894, the United Daughters of the Confederacy (UDC) quickly became the most potent voluntary organization devoted to public memory in the region, claiming a membership of more than 100,000 by the outbreak of World War I.[6]

This impressive mobilization of white women was a testament to Victorian conventions of mourning that assigned to women prominent roles in public remembrance. White men deemed and white women accepted as 'peculiarly fitting to women' the duties of mourning and, by extension, memorialization. With the hierarchical order of the South shaken by war, many elite white women recoiled from the perceived social chaos and committed themselves to reestablishing antebellum class and racial hierarchies. In this manner, white women's memorial associations functioned as choruses that reassured white men of their manliness and authority, and of feminine deference.

White women first transformed their wartime soldiers' aid societies into memorial associations devoted to commemorating the Confederate dead. The first task undertaken by such groups was the creation of Confederate cemeteries and rituals of remembrance. The pathos of widows gave rise to Confederate Memorial Day in 1866 and within four years it was a region-wide holiday. For countless white women, Confederate Memorial Day was the year's most important public event. They devoted months to recruiting school children, writing and distributing flyers, meeting with public officials, publishing articles in local newspapers, inviting orators, cleaning up cemeteries, and tending to the minutia inherent in any public occasion. On the day itself, women performed the central ritual – the decoration of the graves. They also marched along the parade routes and sometimes even spoke to the gathered crowds.[7]

With each passing decade after the war, white southern women cluttered more and more of the landscape of the South with monuments to Confederate heroes. As the organized might and political influence of white women's groups waxed at the end of the nineteenth century, their claims on public space expanded as well. In the immediate postwar years women's groups had erected cemetery monuments in keeping with their mission to give public expression and permanence to their mourning. By the dawn of the twentieth century they were funding showy statues to Confederates in the region's most conspicuous civic spaces. The ultimate expression of their ambitions was the grandiose plan to etch upon the face of Stone Mountain near Atlanta, Georgia the largest bas relief carving in the world, which would glorify Robert E. Lee and other Confederate heroes.[8]

After the 1920s, the promotion of Confederate memory no longer mobilized the numbers of white southerners it once had. By then, when the prodigious work on Stone Mountain began, the consolidation of Confederate commemoration was largely complete. Its central tenets were in place and together, white clerics, veterans, and organized women had colonized the region's public spaces and civic life with celebrations of the Confederacy and southern 'heritage.' Like priestesses tending an altar, dedicated members of the UDC remained vigilant against textbooks that traduced the Confederacy and conscientious about the observation of Confederate Memorial Day. So ubiquitous was their handiwork that they and many outsiders concluded that the public memory of white southerners was virtually hegemonic across the region.

-II-

Giving voice to a shared understanding of history was no less urgent for African Americans after the Civil War. In the wake of emancipation, African Americans anticipated a truly public culture in which all segments of southern society – black and white – would enjoy the right to voice their concerns and claims. But whereas southern whites marshaled the full array of cultural forms at their disposal to commemorate the Confederacy, blacks had to make do with comparatively meager resources. Poverty and oppression sharply circumscribed their efforts. Nevertheless, blacks defiantly insisted upon the public expression of their memory by creating a robust ceremonial life. Through public ceremonies blacks displayed their recalled past, enabling vast numbers of blacks to invent, learn, and practice a common memory.

Blacks during the late nineteenth century understood that by entering into public space and performing communal pageants, they thrust black history into the region's public culture. Such celebrations ensured that the black sense of the past was more than a learned exercise accessible principally to literate, elite African Americans. Instead, black memory was made manifest in recurring events that incorporated the breadth of the black community, from the college trained preacher to the illiterate day laborer, from the battle scarred veteran to the impressionable school child.[9]

Ministers and politicians took the lead in marshaling their communities to commemorate their heritage. As leaders of largely autonomous black-led institutions, black ministers were well placed to assume the lead in this cultural work.

They also could place the saga of black history in a larger Biblical narrative of suffering and redemption. Consequently, they often not only organized but also presided over commemorative ceremonies. African American politicians, similarly, used the occasions as opportunities to link past struggles to contemporary partisan politics and to urge the continued mobilization and cohesion of the black electorate.

By the end of the nineteenth century, they had filled the calendar with at least a half-dozen major holidays and countless lesser occasions during which African Americans celebrated their heroes and hallowed events. They virtually laid claim to Independence Day, which most white southerners refused to celebrate until the Spanish-American War revived their patriotic ardor. Blacks also celebrated holidays that commemorated the Civil War. To the extent that Lincoln's birthday was acknowledged in the South it was by African Americans. Their eager participation in Charleston, South Carolina in 1865 and elsewhere helped to establish Memorial Day in late May as the preeminent commemoration of national sacrifice. Most importantly, blacks invented their own commemorative festivals, including Emancipation Day marking the anniversary of Lincoln's Emancipation Proclamation, and the birthday of Frederick Douglass after the beloved abolitionist's death in 1895.[10]

The stability of the genre reflected the ritualized context of the ceremonies. After formal introductions and opening prayers, the celebrations typically continued with readings of such cherished texts as the Declaration of Independence and the Emancipation Proclamation. Next came recitations, often by schoolchildren, of appropriate poems and essays. The climax arrived when the day's principal speaker delivered the oration, which typically enumerated the race's progress. What may sound to modern ears like tedious recitations of arcane data about black schools, business investments, and property holding were to black audiences a confirmation of their steady advance in the face of long odds. If the record of black accomplishment augured a promising future, the challenge of overcoming white oppression remained. Public celebrations, especially the orations that often capped them, provided an opportunity to inveigh against white racism and to praise God's mercy before the gathered black community. Repetition of form and argument suited the needs of a people who had only limited means of historical production but were eager for the systematic organization and retrieval of their past.[11]

Even as segregation sequestered more and more of black life, blacks continued to stage processions that demonstrated – to themselves and to whites – their civic spirit and version of history. Indeed, parades took on added significance in the age of segregation because they offered African Americans a unique opportunity to present complex self-portraits of their communities while simultaneously making the same claims to use prominent public spaces for public assembly that whites took for granted. The *Savannah Tribune*, on the eve of Memorial Day in 1918, explained the importance of processions for African Americans. Parades allowed all blacks, regardless of occupation or status, to come together in common cause. 'The vanguard of the race,' the newspaper pledged, 'will be there as well as the denizens of Negro ghettos, unlettered and unkept – the complete kaleidoscope of racial gamut, but all of common mind and bent upon a common goal.' And why was such a display of 'unanimity and solidarity' so important? Because, by participating in what the newspaper predicted would be a 'mammoth parade,' 'every worthy colored man, woman, and child ... would dedicate himself to the great causes of racial interest.'[12]

After World War I, educators and civic activists assumed leadership of African American commemoration. Ministers were not so much displaced as superseded in the promotion of black memory. Southern African Americans recognized that public ceremonies were insufficient to nurture historical awareness systematically and continuously. Blacks continued to stage rousing public commemorations across the first half of the twentieth century, but they increasingly looked to public schools and colleges as a quasi-public sphere in which they could best promote historical awareness and contest the version of history promoted by white southerners. In one of the most profound ironies of segregation in the South, blacks used state and private resources to turn schools into essential sites of collective memory that performed a role comparable to that of museums, archives, and schools in the white community. That the inadequately funded black schools and colleges became centers of black public life would have surprised and shocked many white southerners.[13]

Between roughly 1920 and 1950 the campaign to incorporate 'Negro history' into the education of blacks mobilized a broad coalition of black professional historians, schoolteachers, parents, and students. A prerequisite for the campaign was the gradual, albeit uneven, improvement in black educational opportunities across the region. By World War II, two-thirds of black children attended school and more than a fifth of eligible black children enrolled in high school. Simultaneously, advances in teacher training spread so that by the thirties some rural schools boasted black teachers with credentials equal or superior to their white counterparts. These changes encouraged not only a broadening of students' ambitions but also an enriching of the intellectual life of black schools.[14]

Black teachers became the conduits through which the scholarship of activist black historians reached even the most benighted parts of the South. Carter Woodson, a Harvard educated historian, and a constellation of other professional scholars devoted themselves to overturning inherited wisdom about almost every facet of African American history. Building on the long-established tradition of black commemorative celebrations, Woodson and his allies launched Negro History Week in 1926. Scheduled each February in recognition of the anniversaries of the birthdays of Frederick Douglass and Abraham Lincoln, Negro History Week went beyond existing traditions. Pageants, plays, and performances quickly became an essential component of the event. Performances displayed a new forthrightness about the horrors of slavery, including the slave trade, the ever-present threats of rape and violence, and even the justice of slaves resorting to violence to throw off their shackles. Whether in a play about Crispus Attucks, an African American colonial hero, or a public reading of the writings of Frederick Douglass, blacks were depicted as steadfast in their pursuit of and devotion to freedom. And just as the benign depictions of slavery so popular among whites were countered in the Negro History Week activities, so too were white interpretations of Reconstruction as a descent into corruption and tyranny.[15]

The Negro History campaign boasted notable early successes. Unlike earlier failed efforts to organize a national Emancipation Day, Negro History Week formalized national recognition of black history. So successful was the event that it came to be celebrated virtually coast to coast and in many communities replaced Emancipation Day as the preeminent celebration of black history. Moreover, as early as 1935 nearly a third of black high schools in the South offered black history courses and many even made these courses compulsory for graduation. By the end of the thirties Delaware, Oklahoma, and South Carolina had joined North Carolina in adopting Woodson's preferred texts for their black schools and in several other states officials left the choice of texts to the discretion of school districts, thereby granting black teachers additional control over the history curriculum.[16]

During the age of Jim Crow blacks could not lay claim to public spaces in the manner or to the degree that southern whites did. Yet on select occasions when African Americans did perform as communities in the civic spaces and within their segregated sphere they shared a black history that was a counterweight to the public memory of whites. When Angela Davis, a prominent black activist and scholar, opened her recycled textbook in her elementary school, she read of the 'War of Southern Independence.' But her teachers ignored the intended message of the textbooks and made sure that 'Black identity was thrust upon us.' Carl T. Rowan, a distinguished black journalist, recalled that his high school history teacher instilled a healthy dose of race pride by celebrating the accomplishments of Booker T. Washington, W. E. B. Du Bois, and other black notables. She explained to Rowan and his classmates the enduring impact of an education that empowered rather than crippled; 'What you put in your head, boy, can never be pulled out by the Ku Klux Klan, the Congress, or anybody.'[17]

-III-

The drawn-out process of ending Jim Crow and restoring African American civil rights necessarily raised questions about whether and how the divergent memories of white and black southerners would be acknowledged in previously segregated spaces in the South. Addressing the preponderance of white memory in the region's public spaces was never a major focus of civil rights activists prior to the 1960s, who predictably concentrated on more immediate concerns. They acknowledged, assailed, and regretted the narratives that white southerners told about the region's past, but directed the bulk of their energies against the conspicuous mechanisms of white supremacy – above all, segregated education, voting restrictions, public segregation, and economic discrimination. They assumed that once they uprooted the institutional foundations of white power, its cultural detritus, in time, would be swept aside as well.

The long struggle to overcome southern white resistance to the Supreme Court's 1954 *Brown v. Board of Education* decision, however, focused the attention of black educators, students, and parents on the curriculum and atmosphere in the newly integrated schools. The often half-hearted and sometimes openly dismissive responses of white authorities to black complaints fuelled protests, boycotts, and even violence at schools across the region. At some formerly all black schools, black students and parents fumed over the cancellation of Negro History Week assemblies while at formerly all-white schools blacks were offended by cursory acknowledgment of black history in general. Everywhere anger over displays of Confederate flags by white students provoked black students and parents to action.[18]

A particular point of friction was the continued use of objectionable textbooks and lesson plans in the South's now desegregated public schools. Because black students now often encountered the invidious racism of the textbooks commonly used in southern schools but now without the comparative protection provided by black teachers and schools, black parents and white allies demanded root-and-branch textbook revision. The major civil rights organizations joined the chorus demanding that school administrators revise curricula and adopt new texts.[19]

Revision of texts and curricula came slow to the South. Throughout the 1960s publishers continued to sell 'segregation' editions to southern schools, which typically appeased southern white prejudices by ignoring black history and avoiding sensitive topics. Ignoring federal subsidies for school districts that adopted 'multiracial' text books, white administrators displayed a mixture of lethargy and outright hostility to new texts. In Virginia, for example, desegregation did not redress the explicitly segregationist history taught to fourth, seventh, and eleventh graders. Throughout the 1950s and 1960s the assigned state history textbooks emphasized the purported benefits of slavery for African Americans and downplayed the disfranchisement of blacks after 1902 because 'there were enough hard feelings already.' With mounting urgency during the late 1960s blacks, joined by growing numbers of whites, criticized the textbooks as 'out-and-out propaganda' until the Virginia board of education finally voted unanimously to discontinue their use after 1972.[20]

Grassroots campaigns by black parents and students compelled administrators to add Black History Week ceremonies into the calendars of all schools. Carter Woodson's long-delayed hope that white students would be exposed to African American history finally came to pass during the 1970s. Even Governor George Wallace, the one-time advocate of 'segregation forever,' endorsed Black History Week (the successor to Woodson's Negro History Week) in Alabama in 1973 and by 1980 public schools in every southern state participated in its celebration.[21]

While campaigning for curricular reforms, black educators, parents, and students also began to chip away at the Confederate commemorative landscape of the South by advocating for the renaming of desegregated public schools. Blacks understandably bridled at having to attend public schools named after slaveholders, Confederate generals, or white politicians who had championed white supremacy. In St. Bernard Parish in Louisiana, for instance, black parents had tolerated that Milladoun Elementary was named after a nearby antebellum plantation. But plans to replace the dilapidated building with a new school named after Confederate general P. G. T. Beauregard outraged them. Similarly, a grassroots movement in New Orleans during the 1980s campaigned to remove the names of all slaveholders from local schools. The school board eventually adopted a policy against retaining names of 'former slave owners or others who did not respect equal opportunity for all.' Within five years faculty and students had renamed 22 schools including P. G. T. Beauregard Elementary (now named after black jurist Thurgood Marshall) and Jefferson Davis Elementary (now named after the city's first black mayor, Ernest N. Morial).[22]

Although some commentators ridiculed the renaming of schools as meaningless grandstanding, it reflected the longstanding importance that African Americans placed on schools as sites of community pride. Having witnessed the loss of many black school traditions during school desegregation, black teachers, students, and parents sought to transform the identities of the schools that they inherited after integration. Michael L. Lomax, a prominent African American politician and educator, answered the critics, highlighting the combination of power and powerlessness that lay behind efforts to give schools new identities. 'It's a very direct statement that I will celebrate my own history and I will compel you to recognize my heroes and heroines,' he explained. 'But it is also more of a statement of frustration in exercising power over one of the few things that you can exercise power over, which is the name of a street or a building.'[23]

By the 1980s the expansion of state-guaranteed rights in the South that began with the *Brown* decision and culminated in the Voting Rights Act of 1965 enabled black activists to begin to bring long unaddressed historical concerns before public bodies. A 'rights revolution' in American jurisprudence substantially broadened citizens' understandings of their entitlements and rights, especially to due process. Blacks turned to the courts for the settlement of public disputes, including persisting claims of historical injustice. African American litigants, for example, invoked the Fourteenth Amendment equal protection clause in suits to take down the Confederate flag flying atop the state capitol in Alabama and to remove Confederate symbols from the Georgia state flag. The suits claimed that continued displays of Confederate symbols in public spaces fostered an exclusionary and racist atmosphere that precluded blacks from the exercise of their rights. While the practical aim of these suits was to remove Confederate symbols from specific public spaces, the broader goal was to establish unequivocally that all Confederate symbols are tinged with racism and that the public spaces of the South should be cleansed of them. Other legal advocates proposed using the Thirteenth Amendment protection against 'badges of inferiority' to strip Confederate symbols from public schools and institutions. Here again the aim was to demonstrate that the state had a legal obligation to regulate public displays of Confederate symbols. Although these arguments failed to persuade most state and federal courts, blacks made clear their intent to persist until they purged the region of Confederate symbols and other reminders of white supremacy.[24]

-IV-

While some southern whites accepted black empowerment and efforts to revise the South's civic spaces, other whites recoiled with alarm, even disgust at what they perceived to be mounting threats to southern 'heritage.' They lamented that the Jim Crow South had given way to the desegregated 'Sunbelt' South, that suburbanization had transformed huge swathes of the region into landscapes indistinguishable from those elsewhere in the nation, and that immigrants from Latin America and Asia seemed poised to overwhelm the South's 'native' white population. For these white southerners alienated by the region's evolution, their 'heritage' was the last bulwark against their absorption into a cosmopolitan national culture they reviled.

A comparatively small but robust coalition of the Sons of Confederate Veterans (SCV), so-called neo-Confederates, and avowed white supremacists mobilized white southerners to defend their 'heritage' during the 1980s and 1990s. Founded in 1896, the SCV failed for nearly a century to muster a large membership or to exercise much influence. But during the 1970s and 1980s new recruits, including Civil War reenactors and men vigilant against any insults to southern white 'heritage,' invigorated its ranks. The new membership also included white supremacists who looked to the Confederacy as inspiration for the creation of a white Euro-American homeland. The League of the South, founded in 1994, added a patina of intellectual rigor to this neo-Confederate revival by warning white southerners that cosmopolitan academics, liberal and irreligious politicians, foreign organizations, and other sinister forces were intent on the destruction of the white South's values and heritage. The South, they protested, had historically been and should remain an Anglo-Celtic homeland. Equally important, the white South had come closer to creating the ideal Christian republic than any other society so the defense of white southern 'heritage' was, literally, the defense of everything that was sacred.[25]

With gathering energy during the 1990s, the SCV and allied groups picketed, lobbied, campaigned, and litigated to prevent 'heritage violations,' which included 'any attack upon our Confederate Heritage, or the flags, monuments, and symbols which represent it.' Particular energy was devoted to bringing suit against school districts and municipalities that sought to restrict the public display of the Confederate Battle Flag. Although the SCV usually failed in these efforts, it stoked the fears and resentments of members and allies steeped in a white regional memory that dwelled on white southerners' victimhood at the hands of a succession of Union generals, outside agitators, northern legislators, and activist judges.

The defense of Confederate heritage increasingly contaminated the region's public life during the 1990s. Previously, the defense of white southern 'heritage' was the preoccupation of white Democrats in the South. During the 1970s Republican insurgents eager to expand the party in the region embraced white southern 'heritage' as a means to exploit white resentments and yoke them to the party's fortunes. As part of President Richard Nixon's 1972 reelection campaign, Republican strategists sought to peel off white voters in the South who recoiled from the Democrats' commitment to racial equality, school desegregation, and opposition to the Vietnam War. This so-called 'Southern Strategy,' which appealed to white suburban southerners who were anxious to preserve *de facto* segregation in the suburbs, allowed the Republican Party to exploit the anxieties of whites without having to categorically oppose racial integration.[26] Nevertheless, the Democratic Party retained the allegiance of many white southerners. The party still included old-line politicos who only grudgingly acceded to the new reality of growing black political empowerment while playing up their regional loyalties in thick southern accents.

Only in hindsight is it evident that 1972 marked the emergence of the new face of Republicanism in the South: Jesse Helms. He had previously been a minor figure in national affairs even while he pioneered the politics of white resentment in North Carolina. Taking advantage of his position as an executive at a Raleigh, North Carolina television station during the 1960s, he had begun delivering nightly broadcast editorials. He honed a stridently conservative message that he presented as down home, common sense traditional values. He did not literally need to wave the Confederate flag to reassure whites that he would protect their interests and defend southern 'heritage.' His accent, his invocations of traditional values, and his visceral contempt for civil rights activism made such appeals superfluous.[27]

Ronald Reagan's 1980 campaign and subsequent presidency expanded on the foundation built by Helms. Reagan himself evidenced little sympathy for Confederate heritage, but he was not embarrassed to glad-hand race-mongers and voters who had previously championed segregation. Notably, he delivered a major campaign speech endorsing 'states' rights' in Philadelphia, Mississippi, the site of a notorious murder of three civil rights activists during the 1960s. No location was more fitting for Reagan's implicit renunciation of a century of Republican commitment to racial equality or appropriation of the time-honored defense of the Confederate cause.

Reagan's handiwork prepared the way for the surprisingly rapid consolidation of Republican strength in the South. Jesse Helms' tenacious opposition to the establishment of a national holiday in honor of Martin Luther King, Jr. was a sign of how far the party of Lincoln had traveled in only a few years. Helms and his conservative allies mocked King's historical importance, criticized his opposition to the Vietnam War, and tarred him as a communist. Reagan gave credence to Helms' slanders until finally caving in and signing the legislation creating the holiday in 1983. Helms, Reagan, and the naysayers had made their point even in defeat; any observer understood that Republican support for the holiday was half-hearted at best and that, in the eyes of many conservatives, it was a tawdry concession to illegitimate 'special interests.'[28]

The emergent coalition of Republicans and Confederate devotees demonstrated its newfound influence in the struggle over the state flag of Georgia during the 1990s. Demands to revise the state flag roiled the state's politics for more than a decade. In response to the Supreme Court's *Brown* decision, segregationist politicians in 1956 had redesigned the state flag to include the Confederate battle flag. When the 1996 Atlanta Olympics brought international scrutiny to the state, Democrats and some business leaders advocated the removal of the divisive Confederate symbol from the state flag. Other politicians, especially Republicans, exploited the issue to depict Democrats as captives of urban black activists and outside business elites hostile to white southern 'heritage.' During the 2002 gubernatorial campaign, Republicans pummeled Democratic Governor Roy Barnes for his role in the adoption of a new state flag, rallying the support of rural white males who harbored grievances against what they perceived to be metropolitan, liberal, and elitist policies. For conservative whites, the new state flag became a symbol of 'political correctness,' affirmative action, multiculturalism, moral laxity, and other perceived modern ills. Similar battle lines emerged elsewhere, including Alabama and Mississippi, whose state flags also incorporated the Confederate battle flag. In South Carolina, controversy arose over the display of the Confederate flag above the statehouse.[29]

By the dawn of the twenty-first century the alliance between neo-Confederates and Republicans was so tight that only extraordinary circumstances persuaded southern Republicans to reevaluate their steadfast defense of all things Confederate.[30] For instance, not until after the 2015 massacre of nine African Americans at the Emanuel African Methodist Episcopal Church in Charleston, South Carolina by Dylan Roof, a white supremacist, did Republican leaders of the state grudgingly furl the Confederate battle flag that had graced the state capitol grounds for decades.

The removal of the Confederate battle flag from the South Carolina capitol was widely applauded as evidence of statesmanship and a new commitment to reconciliation within Republican ranks in the South. Yet arguably the most important response by Republicans has been the proliferation of 'heritage protection' laws. While Republicans retreated from defending the Confederate flag, they nevertheless were steadfast in their devotion to the preservation of Confederate monuments in the public spaces of the South. Alarmed first by the outcry after Roof's rampage, and then subsequently by the desecration of Confederate monuments by activists energized by the Black Lives Matter movement, Republican legislators in Alabama, Georgia, Mississippi, North Carolina, and Tennessee, took the lead in passing laws that imposed onerous requirements, typically including legislative approval, to alter names on buildings or to move or remove monuments. Riddled with ambiguities and resting on untested claims of legislative authority, these laws pose hardships on any community intent on revising its civic landscape. Communities graced with teams of lawyers may test the laws or try to navigate the legislatures, but their attempts almost certainly will end up in state or federal court. In the meantime, the contemporary landscape of the South, which is cluttered with thousands of memorials to the Confederacy, is likely to remain frozen for the near future.

After white nationalists and others staged a violent protest to oppose the removal of a statue of Confederate Robert E. Lee from a park in Charlottesville on August 12, 2017, white conservatives sought to divorce themselves from racist extremists even while defending those in Charlottesville who had rallied to celebrate Confederate heritage. President Trump's public comments three days after the tragic death of Heather D. Heyer, a counter-protester in Charlottesville, included a mash-up of arguments that had long circulated among Confederate apologists. He warned against the erasure of history and suggested that 'good people' had been present among the crowds of white nationalists. Conservative commentators subsequently drew comparisons between the campaign to remove Confederate symbols and the demolition of ancient monuments by ISIS in Syria and by the Taliban in Afghanistan as well as the destruction of Jewish art by Nazis in Germany, implying a moral equivalency between American anti-Confederate activists and the most reviled enemies of the United States. Such remarks were consistent with the long-familiar tactic of attacking the NAACP, which advocated boycotts against states that prominently honored the Confederacy, as a racist hate group. Remarkably, since 2017 white conservatives have contended that opposition to Confederate heritage is un-American.

★ ★ ★

Clashes over the past in the American South show no signs of abating. Both familiar and new controversies over Confederate symbols, museum exhibits, historical monuments, and the naming of public thoroughfares roil public life there. These controversies, which now are woven into state and local politics across the region, mobilize broad constituencies because they have been and will continue to be barometers of who exercises power and what history will inform and affirm the region's identity. This struggle over the region's civic landscapes almost certainly is inevitable, but it has been exacerbated during the past decade by pessimism about the direction of American race relations. Previous optimism that white supremacy was a relic that would wither has been shattered by ample evidence of police brutality (much of it captured on social media), the cumulative effects of unprecedented rates of incarceration of people of color, exploitative financial practices that targeted African Americans during the economic crisis of the Great Recession, and other examples of systemic racial discrimination. Against this backdrop, Dylan Roof's 2015 massacre and the 2017 Charlottesville neo-Nazi rally demonstrated that long-tolerated symbols of the Confederacy remain catalysts for violent and brazen demonstrations of racism. In the eyes of

African Americans mobilized by Black Lives Matter as well as white anti-racism activists the memorials are much more than mildly offensive relics of bygone mores; they are malevolent symbols of enduring oppression.

When facing off over the region's inherited commemorative landscape, southerners strive to secure the moral high ground by beseeching state legislatures, courts, and local governments to serve as arbiters of historical interpretation. This recourse to the political realm is unquestionably divisive, because it is as likely to yield disgruntled losers as gratified winners. These contests have provoked hand wringing about the worrisome escalation of 'culture wars' in the region. Previously, white elites exploited their wealth and power to enshroud their version of the past with the prestige of official recognition. Now, after the empowerment of African Americans across the region, historical sites and civic events are more likely to accentuate both the complexities of and the divergent perspectives on the past. These developments offer little solace to those who believe that their interpretation of history qualifies as historical 'truth,' and that other interpretations are illegitimate. White southerners whose views were once the privileged interpretation of the past can no longer assume that public sites or civic ceremonies will provide unambiguous celebrations of the Confederacy or southern 'heritage.' At the same time, black southerners bridle at the continuing celebration of Confederate History Month and recognition of slaveholders and white supremacists in the civic spaces of the region. Because no other contemporary institutions can resolve these disputes to the satisfaction of concerned southerners, state bodies, especially elected assemblies and the courts, have necessarily become the battlegrounds for many clashes over the past.

Yet, even while state bodies and public officials have become entangled in these controversies and state resources are recruited to defend or revise the region's public memory, grassroots organizations and social groups continue to exert decisive influence. Indeed, the limits of the state to control public memory in the face of mobilized groups were affirmed in North Carolina after 2017. Two years prior, the Republican-controlled state legislature of North Carolina assumed its edict would foreclose any threats to Confederate monuments in the state. But after the white supremacy rally in Charlottesville in 2017, demonstrators in Durham toppled the city's Confederate memorial. A year later, demonstrators in nearby Chapel Hill pulled down another Confederate memorial that had been the focus of controversy for decades. These acts of civil disobedience underscored that despite the legislature's claims of authority 'the public' still ultimately retained power over the region's memorial landscape and public memory.

The contest over historical memory in the American South highlights the tenacity of historical memory generated by social movements. For the century after the Civil War state governments across the region at most bolstered but never directed the cultural work of Confederate memorialists. Instead, it was successive generations of self-appointed architects of regional memory that created the current commemorative landscape of the South. Now, when the demand to revise that inherited landscape is cresting, even sympathetic state officials confront the obstacles of both organized resistance and traditions that limit government influence over civic culture. Consequently, the transformation of the American historical landscape almost certainly will come about not through government intervention but rather through sustained campaigns by social movements.

Notes

1 For the international context, see David Cannadine, 'The Context, Performance and Meaning of Ritual: The British Monarchy and the "Invention of Tradition," c. 1820–1977,' in *The Invention of Tradition*, eds., Eric Hobsbawm and Terence Ranger, (New York: Cambridge University Press, 1983), 101–164; Alon Confino, *The Nation as a Local Metaphor: Wurttemberg, Imperial Germany, and National Memory, 1871–1918* (Chapel Hill: University of North Carolina Press, 1997), esp. Part I; and Daniel J. Sherman, *Worthy Monuments: Art Museums and the Politics of Culture in Nineteenth-century France* (Cambridge, MA: Harvard University Press, 1989), esp. Part I.
2 On the limits of the nineteenth-century American state, see Nancy Cohen, *The Reconstruction of American Liberalism, 1865–1914* (Chapel Hill: University of North Carolina, 2002), esp. Chapters 1–2; Alan Dawley, *Struggles for Justice: Social Responsibility and the Liberal State* (Cambridge, MA: Harvard University Press 1991), Part I; and Stephen Skowronek, *Building a New American State: The Expansion of National Administrative Capacities, 1877–1920* (Cambridge: Cambridge University Press, 1982), esp. Part II.
3 W. Fitzhugh Brundage, 'Redeeming a Failed Revolution Confederate Memory,' in *In the Cause of Liberty: How the Civil War Redefined American Ideals*, eds. William J. Copper Jr. and John M. McCardell, Jr., (Baton Rouge: Louisiana State University Press, 2009), 126–136.
4 Mitchell Snay, *Gospel of Disunion: Religion and Separatism in the Antebellum South* (Chapel Hill: University of North Carolina Press, 1997); Christopher H. Owen, *The Sacred Flame of Love: Methodism and Society in Nineteenth-Century Georgia* (Athens: University of Georgia Press, 1998), 93–113; W. Scott Poole, *Never Surrender: Confederate Memory and Conservatism in the South Carolina Upcountry* (Athens: University of Georgia Press, 2004), 37–56; and Charles Reagan Wilson, *Baptized in Blood: The Religion of the Lost Cause, 1865–1920* (Athens: University of Georgia Press, 1980).
5 David Blight, *Race and Reunion: The Civil War in American Memory* (Cambridge, MA: Harvard University Press, 2001), 140–210; Gaines M. Foster, *Ghosts of the Confederacy: Defeat, the Lost Cause, and the Emergence of the New South* (New York: Oxford University Press, 1987), esp. Chapters 7–8; M. Keith Harris, *Across the Bloody Chasm: The Culture of Commemoration among Civil War Veterans* (Baton Rouge: Louisiana State University Press, 2014), 66–89; and Caroline E. Janney, *Remembering the Civil War: Reunion and the Limits of Reconciliation* (Chapel Hill: The University of North Carolina Press, 2013), 133–196.
6 On women, memorialization, and gender tensions, see W. Fitzhugh Brundage, *The Southern Past: The Clash of Race and Memory* (Cambridge, MA: Belknap Press of Harvard University Press, 2005), esp. Chapter 1; Jane Turner Censer, *The Reconstruction of White Southern Womanhood, 1865–1895* (Baton Rouge: Louisiana State University Press, 2003); Karen L. Cox, *Dixie's Daughters: The United Daughters of the Confederacy and the Preservation of Confederate Culture* (Gainesville: University Press of Florida, 2003); Sarah Gardner, *Blood and Irony* (Chapel Hill: University of North Carolina Press, 2003); LeeAnn Whites, *The Civil War as a Crisis in Gender, Augusta, Georgia, 1860–1890* (Athens: University of Georgia Press, 1995), 160–224.
7 Mrs. George T. Fry, 'Memorial Day – Its Origin,' *Confederate Veteran* 1 (May 1893): 149; *A History of the Origins of Memorial Day as Adopted by the Ladies' Memorial Association of Columbus, Georgia* (Columbus: Lizzie Rutherford Chapter of the Daughters of

the Confederacy, 1898), 24–25; Ellen M. Litwicki, *America's Public Holidays, 1865–1920* (Washington, DC: Smithsonian Press, 2000), Chapter 1.
8   Thomas J. Brown, *The Public Art of Civil War Commemoration: A Brief History with Documents* (Boston, MA: Bedford/St. Martin's, 2004); David B. Freeman, *Carved in Stone: The History of Stone Mountain* (Macon: Mercer University Press, 1997), Cynthia J. Mills and Pamela H Simpson, eds., *Monuments to the Lost Cause: Women, Art, and the Landscapes of Southern Memory* (Knoxville: University of Tennessee Press, 2003).
9   Brundage, *Southern Past*, 55–104; Kathleen Ann Clark, *Defining Moments: African American Commemoration & Political Culture in the South, 1863–1913* (Chapel Hill: University of North Carolina Press, 2005), Mitchell A. Kachun, *Festivals of Freedom: Memory and the Meaning of African American Emancipation Celebrations, 1808–1915* (Amherst: University of Massachusetts Press, 2003); Laurie Maffly-Kipp, 'Mapping the World, Mapping the Race: The Negro Race History, 1874–1915,' *Church History* 64 no. 4 (December 1995): 610–626; and Doris Hollis Pemberton, *Juneteenth at Comanche Crossing* (Austin, TX: Eakin Press, 1983).
10 Blight, *Race and Reunion*, Chapter 9; Cecilia Elizabeth O'Leary, *To Die For: The Paradox of American Patriotism* (Princeton, NJ: Princeton University Press, 1999), Chapter 7; Antionette G. van Zelm, 'Virginia Women as Public Citizens: Emancipation Day Celebrations and Lost Cause Commemorations, 1863–1890,' in *Negotiating Boundaries of Southern Womanhood: Dealing with the Powers That Be*, eds. Janet L. Coryell, et al. (Columbia: University of Missouri Press, 2000), 71–80.
11 Brundage, *Southern Past*, 88–99.
12 *Savannah Tribune*, May 4, 1918.
13 On black education, see James D. Anderson, *The Education of Blacks in the South, 1860–1935* (Chapel Hill: University of North Carolina Press, 1988); Louis R. Harlan, *Separate and Unequal: Public School Campaigns and Racism in the Southern Seaboard States, 1901–1915* (Rep.: New York: Atheneum, 1968); Leon F. Litwack, *Trouble in Mind: Black Southerners in the Age of Jim Crow* (New York: Knopf, 1998), Chapter 2; Neil R. McMillen, *Dark Journey: Black Mississippians in the Age of Jim Crow* (Urbana: University of Illinois Press, 1989), Chapter 3; and Robert A. Margo, *Race and Schooling in the South, 1880–1950: An Economic History* (Chicago, IL: University of Chicago Press, 1990).
14 Adam Fairclough, *Teaching Equality: Black Schools in the Age of Jim Crow* (Athens: University of Georgia Press, 2001), 50–51; Michael Fultz, 'African American Teachers in the South, 1890–1940: Powerlessness and the Ironies of Expectations and Protest,' *History of Education Quarterly* 35, no. 4 (Winter 1995): 406–407, 408, 418; Sonya Y. Ramsey, 'More Than the Three R's: The Educational, Economic, and Cultural Experiences of African American Female Public School Teachers in Nashville, Tennessee, 1869 to 1983' (Ph.D diss., University of North Carolina, 2000); Vanessa Siddle Walker, *Their Highest Potential: An African American School Community in the Segregated South* (Chapel Hill: University of North Carolina Press, 1996), esp. Chapter 1.
15 'Negro History Week – The Fourth Year,' *Journal of Negro History* (hereafter *JNH*) 14 no. 2 (April 1929): 111; *JNH* 15, no. 1 (January 1930): 3; *Baltimore Afro-American* February 22, 1930; *JNH* 17, no. 1 (January 1932): 3; *Norfolk Journal & Guide*, February 18, 1933; 'Negro History Week – The Eighth Year,' *JNH* 18, no. 2 (April 1933): 117; *Houston Informer*, February 24, 1934; *JNH* 22 (January 1937): 5; *JNH* 25, no. 1 (January 1940): 3–4; *Nashville Globe*, February 2, 1940; Myrtle Brodie Crawford, 'The Negro Builds a Pyramid,' *Social Studies* 32, no. 1 (January 1941): 27; *Norfolk Journal & Guide*, February 7, 1942.
16 'Negro History Week – The Tenth Year,' *JNH* 20, no. 2 (April 1935): 127–128.
17 Angela Y. Davis, *Angela Davis: An Autobiography* (New York: International Publishers, 1988), 90–91; Carl T. Rowan, *Breaking Barriers: A Memoir* (Boston, MA: Little Brown and Co., 1991), 32–33.
18 *Southern Patriot*, 36 (January 1972): 6; 36 (February 1972): 3; (March 1972): 6, 7; 36 (December 1972): 5. See also James V. Holton, 'The Best Education Provided: A

Social History of School Integration in Polk County, Florida, 1863–1994' (Ph.D. diss., George Washington University, 2002), 142–178.
19 *Thirty-Third Annual Celebration of Negro History Week* (Washington, DC: ASNLH, 1958), 3; 'House Committee Studies Treatment of Minorities in Text and Library Books,' *Publishers' Weekly* 190 (September 19, 1966): 40; Lerone Bennett, Jr., 'The Negro in Textbooks: Reading, 'Riting and Racism,' *Ebony* 22 (March 1967): 130–138; Jonathan Zimmerman, *Whose America?: Culture Wars in the Public Schools* (Cambridge, MA: Harvard University Press, 2002), 112–115.
20 *Roanoke Times*, February 18, 1948, A4; Virginia Senate Document No. 4, *The Teaching of Virginia and Local History and Government in the Public Schools* (Richmond, VI: Division of Purchases and Printing, 1949), 9; Frederic R. Eichelman, 'A Study of the Virginia History and Government Textbook Controversy, 1948–1972 (Ed.D. diss., Virginia Tech, 1975), 36, 98–120; Marvin W. Schlegel, 'What's Wrong With Virginia History Textbooks,' *Virginia Journal of Education*, 64 no. 1 (September 1970): 10; idem, 'What a Good Virginia History Textbook Should Be,' *Virginia Journal of Education* 64 no. 2 (October 1970): 6–7.
21 Zimmerman, *Whose America?* 126.
22 *Birmingham News*, July 26, 2001; *New York Times*, November 16, 1997, Sections 4–5. See also *Atlanta Constitution*, March 7, 1993, A1; *New Orleans Times-Picayune*, January 5, 1993, B6; January 22, 1992, B1; February 1, 1993, B5; April 3, 1994, B7; September 18, 1994, B7; July 1, 1995, B3; September 24, 1997, B1, B2; December 2, 1997, B3; *New York Times*, January 27, 1993, A16; November 12, 1997, A1; *Jacksonville Florida Times-Union*, February 21, 1999, D3; *San Antonio Express-News*, June 18, 1999, B4; *Birmingham News*, July 26, 2001, September 5, 2001; *Richmond Times-Dispatch*, October 1, 2003, B1; *Raleigh News & Observer*, December 28, 2003, D5.
23 *New York Times*, November 16, 1997, Sections 4–5.
24 Kathleen Rilley, 'The Long Shadow of the Confederacy in America's Schools: State-sponsored Use of Confederate Symbols in the Wake of Brown v. Board,' *William and Mary Bill of Rights Journal* 10, no. 2 (February 2002): 533–534; Alexander Tsesis, 'The Problem of Confederate Symbols: A Thirteenth Amendment Approach,' *Temple Law Review* 75, no. 3 (Fall 2002): 539–612. On the 'rights revolution' see Lawrence M. Friedman and Grant M Hayden, *American Law: An Introduction* (New York: Oxford University Press, 2017), 260–290; Samuel Walker, *The Rights Revolution: Rights and Community in Modern America* (New York: Oxford University Press, 1998), esp. 61–114.
25 *Birmingham News*, December 21, 2000, A1; February 13, 2001, B4, February 22, 2001, B4, February 27, 2001, B6, March 13, 2001, A2, May 19, 2001, August 9, 2003; Suzanne M. Alford, 'Student Display of Confederate Symbols in Public Schools,' *School Law Bulletin* 33, no. 1 (Winter 2002): 1–7; James M. Dedman IV, 'At Daggers Drawn: The Confederate Flag and the School Classroom – A Case Study of a Broken First Amendment Formula,' *Baylor Law Review* 53, no. 4 (Fall 2001): 877–927; David L. Hudson, Jr., 'Stars and Bars Wars: Confederate Flag-Wavers, Many of Them Students, Storm the Courts Under a Banner of Free Speech,' *ABA Journal* 86 (November 2000): 28; Ann Burlein, *Lift High the Cross: Where White Supremacy and the Christian Right Converge* (Durham, NC: Duke University Press, 2002).
26 Joseph Crespino, *In Search of Another Country: Mississippi and the Conservative Counterrevolution* (Princeton, NJ: Princeton University Press, 2007), Joseph Crespino, *Strom Thurmond's America* (New York: Hill and Wang, 2012), esp. 165–252; Kevin M. Kruse, *White Flight : Atlanta and the Making of Modern Conservatism* (Princeton, NJ: Princeton University Press, 2005); Matthew D. Lassiter, *The Silent Majority: Suburban Politics in the Sunbelt South* (Princeton, NJ: Princeton University Press, 2006); William A. Link, *Righteous Warrior: Jesse Helms and the Rise of Modern Conservatism* (New York: St. Martin's Press, 2008), esp. 131–270.

27 Link, *Righteous Warrior*, 99–166.
28 Daniel Thomas Fleming, "'Living the Dream': A History of the Martin Luther King Jr. Federal Holiday' (Ph.D dissertation, University of Newcastle Australia, 2016). See also Beth A. Messner and Mark T. Vail, 'A 'City at War': Commemorating Dr. Martin Luther King, Jr.,' *Communication Studies*, 60, no. 1 (Winter 2009): 17–31; Thomas J. Shields, 'The 'Tip of the Iceberg' in a Southern Suburban County: The Fight for a Martin Luther King, Jr., Holiday,' *Journal of Black Studies* 33, no. 4 (March 2003): 499–519.
29 'Traditionalists versus Reconstructionists: The Case of the Georgia State Flag, Part One' and 'Confederate Symbols, Southern Identity, and Racial Attitudes: The Case of the Georgia State Flag, Part Two,' in *Confederate Symbols in the Contemporary South*, eds. J. Michael Martinez, Ron McNinch-Su, and William D Richardson (Gainesville: University Press of Florida, 2000), See also K. Michael Prince, *Rally 'Round the Flag, Boys': South Carolina and the Confederate Flag* (Columbia: University of South Carolina Press, 2004); Rebecca B. Watts, *Contemporary Southern Identity: Community through Controversy* (Oxford: University Press of Mississippi, 2007), 87–116.
30 Ed Kilgore, 'The Political Uses of the Anti-Anti-Confederacy,' *NY Magazine*, April 19, 2018, http://nymag.com/intelligencer/2018/04/why-conservatives-love-defending-the-confederate-flag.html?gtm=top&gtm=bottom, visited October 15, 2018.

16
AFTERWORD

The multiple entanglements of memory and activism

Ann Rigney

This volume appears against the background of an increasingly intense dialogue between memory studies and social movement studies. In the last couple of years, the terms 'memory' and 'activism' seem to have found each other and settled in for a long-term relationship. Witness the appearance in rapid succession of such titles as *The Cultural Memory of Non-Violent Struggles* (Reading and Katriel 2015); *Memory Activism* (Gutman 2017), *Social Movements, Memory, and the Media* (Zamponi 2018), to mention only a few.[1] And now: *Remembering Social Movements*.

The rich array of cases addressed in this collection show in multiple ways how new social movements draw on an inherited repertoire of contention. But they do much more than this. They collectively add to our understanding of the memory-activism nexus (Rigney 2018).[2] By the memory-activism nexus I mean the mutual entanglements and feedback loops between *memory activism* (contentious action to promote certain memories), the *memory of activism* (acts of remembrance about earlier social movements), and *memory in activism* (the role of memory in new acts of contention). This is a multidimensional dynamic, which the present collection helps bring more sharply into focus at the same time as it adds a new layer of complexity. It does this by factoring in the ways in which movements actively promote the memory of their own activism in tandem with their active promotion of the various causes to which they are committed.

In practice, then, there are multiple crossovers between these memory activisms, the memory of activism, and memory in activism. But it remains useful to distinguish analytically between them to better grasp how they feed into each other. Of particular importance is the distinction between contentious action aimed at changing memory and contentious action, informed by memory, that is aimed at changing society. While changing memory may be a step-up towards changing society, this isn't always the case. On the contrary: action to change dominant narratives may sometimes be deployed to distract attention away from other forms of action. Witness, for example, the fact that public apologies on the part of the Canadian government for the past abuse of indigenous peoples have not fed into systemic changes that would improve the lives of those peoples in the present. In such cases, memory activism forms a substitute for reform rather than becoming a catalyst of change.

A classic example of memory activism is presented here by Lauren Richardson in her analysis of the campaigns for recognition of the Comfort Women in Korea, and how those campaigns have invoked the international discourse on human rights. Where the Korean case is presented as a single-issue campaign that is not entangled with broader issues, other chapters show how memory activism may also converge with other causes and other forms of activism. Jenny Wüstenberg shows with reference to post-war Germany how contentious actions to develop a more inclusive public memory, with due attention to the darker sides of the German past, follow rhythms of claim-making that are comparable to activism in other domains, including the occurrence of 'moments of madness' that mark turning points (see also Wüstenberg 2017).[3]

In certain cases, memory activism works in tandem with efforts to develop a more democratic society. Indeed, a more open memory culture is arguably a precondition for an open society. Sarah Langwald's analysis of the interplay between memory activism regarding the Nazi past and the trials against communists in the post-war German Federal Republic offers a case in point. However, as W. Fitzhugh Brundage's chapter on the memory of the Confederacy shows, memory activism does not necessarily serve inclusivity or openness. That Confederate heritage should be defended as a way of advancing white supremacy makes painfully clear that memory activism as such does not always feed into emancipatory causes.

That being said, activism as such always has a mnemonic dimension. This volume provides vivid illustrations of the different ways in which activism and memory feed into each, involving crossovers, entanglements, and feedback loops. Several essays show how the strategies adopted by social movements are informed by the 'implicit memory' (Zamponi 2018)[4] of predecessors, which offers models for action and a tactical as well as cultural repertoire. In an interesting variation on the principle that the implicit memory of one movement shapes the actions of later ones, Richard Rohrmoser shows how the memory of people's failure to stand up to national socialism enhanced their later willingness to campaign against nuclear weapons. Similarly invoking a negative form of memory, David Lowe shows how recollections of the destruction called by earlier instances of nuclear testing in Australia helped mobilise new generations of environmentalists. Finally, Iain McIntyre shows with respect to the US how recent activists drew on a radical musical tradition developed in the context of civil rights and labour activism in order to conduct environmentalist campaigns. Memories may cross over between movements and causes, then, linking them intersectionally and transferring their legacy to new generations involved in new campaigns.

Perhaps the biggest surprise in this volume is the importance of what several contributors call 'movement memory.' By this is meant the immense effort that activists themselves invest both in shaping how they themselves will be remembered in the future and in remembering the origins of their own movement. Whereas activism is rightly associated with futurity and with attempts to change the world, it transpires here that many activists are also avid archivists and memorialists. How can one look back and look forward at the same time? The life narratives of Indian feminists, discussed here by Devleena Ghosh and Heather Goodall, provide a fruitful lens through which to capture this process on an individual level. However, it is not only individuals but also movements that are involved in retrospectively shaping their identity while prospectively also signalling the way forward.

As Sean Scalmer shows with respect to the eight-hour day, the annual commemoration of this milestone in labour history helped to underwrite the importance of organised advocacy as well as offer a regular reminder that efforts can be rewarded with success. Stefan Berger's historical survey of the memory of trade unionism shows just how important such reminders are: stories of struggle and the overcoming of defeats ensure that transgenerational connectedness without which a movement may fall apart, its power to mobilise in the present weakened by its failure to remember its own past. Memorials are the material means to renew hope and demonstrate strength of purpose, while well-organised commemorative rituals in public spaces are also a way of displaying the movement's self-discipline and strength to the public at large.

Movement memory is more than just a by-product of its activism. The mnemonic extension of the present back into earlier fights and other generations is an active strategy for enhancing a movement's sense of worthiness, unity, numbers, and commitment, to invoke the combination of elements that Charles Tilly saw as being key to the success of contention.[5] Narratives of resistance and heroism, of defeat and martyrdom, of betrayal, of 'small acts of resistance' (Altinay et al. 2019)[6] all belong to the repertoire of movement memory. Borrowing from Hayden White (1973),[7] we can argue that activism has its own *metamemory* with which it emplots its own development and publicly displays its memory. Although the repertoire changes over time, there have also been remarkable continuities in the cultural forms most suitable for shaping movement memory. Martyrdom is one such persistent form, arguably as important as the romance of achievement.

The memory of activism is not always consensual, however. Like other objects of remembrance it is open to debate and re-interpretation. Struggles to re-define the movement's past are part and parcel of present-day movement politics. Memory activism directed towards the movement's past provides a resource for recalibrating their goals and strategies in the present. As Liam Byrne writes here, disputes about the past are not just about 'what has been' but about 'the potentialities to come' (p. 205). Byrne himself shows how the consensual memory of the campaign against conscription in Australia in 1916 was contested by later activists seeking to re-engage with the hopes and struggles of the earlier generation against the background of peace campaigns against the war in Vietnam. Similarly, Jule Ehms shows how different political movements jostled for the right to appropriate and interpret the memory of the *Märzgefallenen* of 1920, each anxious to claim the murdered demonstrators as 'their own' and use their memory to advance present agendas.

Memory dissensus within a movement would appear to have a positive function. It ensures that the past remains a resource for dealing with the present and prevents commemoration becoming reduced to a petrified annual ritual carried out in a congratulatory comfort zone, which makes renewed action in the present seem redundant. Too much memory, or rather too canonical or consensual a memory, can be a recipe for quiescence and sanitisation, diminishing the potential of the past to inspire contention and mobilise people to act. For that very reason, counter narratives and critical un-doings of consensus narratives, emphasising paths once taken but subsequently overlooked, offer a resource for resuscitating more radical claims. More than has hitherto been acknowledged, historiography is part of the repertoire of contention itself. In their survey of feminist historiography, Sophie van den Elzen and Berteke Waaldijk not only demonstrate the importance of history writing within the feminist movement, but also show how that auto-history has been constantly subject to critical revision as new generations of activists have sought to become more inclusive by overcoming the intersectional blind spots relating to class and race that plagued their predecessors.

Taken together, these chapters show that we need to elaborate even further on the idea that remembrance is performative (see also Rigney 2005, p. 17).[8] The term performative is used here in a general sense, flagging the fact that the acts of recollection constitutive of what is called 'memory' entail forms of action taking place in the present. The term 'performative' can also be used here in the strong sense of speech act theory, that is, to indicate utterances (the so-called 'performatives') that not only represent the world but also change it in some way. We 'do' things with words, as Austin's famous title put it, as well as with meaning-making through other media.[9] With this strong notion of performativity in mind, it is striking just how often memory has been linked to forms of action in the foregoing pages. Memory presents here as a verb rather than as a noun. Remembrance serves to instigate and legitimate public action (Wicke); to discredit and trivialise certain actions while generating public support for others (Langwald); to provide a warning to the living (Ehms); to police the bounds of loyalty, enhance the mobilising capacities of the movement in the present, and fuel future struggles (Byrne); to bear testimony to achievements, buttress precarious gains, and display a sense of purpose (Scalmer); to nationalise a movement, restrict its agenda to reform rather than revolution, forge an identity and achieve cohesion (Berger), and so on. The list of verbs could have been extended. Suffice these randomly chosen examples to indicate the thoroughly performative character of memory and the fact that commemoration is itself a form of action. Within the framework of social movements, the performativity of memory serves not only to connect members by reference to a common history, but also to shape their goals and allegiances.

If memory and activism are closely entangled in a feedback loop, as these chapters show, then where are the edges of movement memory? To put this differently: how are we to understand the interface between the memory work taking place within the framework of social movements and public memory in a broader sense? There's no easy answer to this question, though Red Chidgey's conceptualisation of memory in terms of an 'assemblage' may be helpful in thinking of the interface between movement memory and public memory in an open-ended and interactive way.[10] As Liam Byrne remarks here, movements do not necessarily have 'stable boundaries' with broader publics. This means that the ongoing feedback between memory and activism described above also entails a possible feedback into public memory at large whereby the memory of civil resistance and advocacy becomes an integral part of 'collective' identity. There is evidence here to suggest that movement memory sometimes spills over into public memory at large and interacts with it. Why and when this happens, and to what effect, should be the subject of future reflection. So far it would seem that the interaction between memory and activism is played out according to a dynamic that is particular to the movement in question, often in opposition to dominant public narratives and to a public culture of memory long dominated by war and its victims. The emerging interest among memory scholars in the memory-activism nexus, exemplified in this volume, marks a critical shift away from war. It offers new conceptual challenges at the same time as it gives the researcher a new responsibility in helping to bring to light the deep memory of civil life and non-violent contention.

Acknowledgement

Work on for this article was financially supported by the European Research Council under advanced grant agreement 788572 for the project *Remembering Activism: The Cultural Memory of Protest in Europe*.

Notes

1 Anna Reading and Tamar Katriel, eds. *Cultural Memories of Non-Violent Struggles: Powerful Times* (Basingstoke: Palgrave Macmillan, 2015); Yifat Gutman, *Memory Activism: Reimagining the Past for the Future in Israel-Palestine* (Nashville, TN: Vanderbilt University Press, 2017); Lorenzo Zamponi, *Social Movements, Memory and Media: Narrative in Action in the Italian and Spanish Student Movements* (Basingstoke: Palgrave Macmillan, 2018); most recently, Priska Daphi and Lorenzo Zamponi. 'Exploring the Movement-Memory Nexus: Insights and Ways Forward,' *Mobilization: An International Quarterly* 24, no. 4 (2019): 399–417.
2 Ann Rigney, 'Remembering Hope: Transnational Activism beyond the Traumatic,' *Memory Studies* 11, no. 3 (2018): 368–380.

3 Jenny Wüstenberg, *Civil Society and Memory in Post-War Germany* (Cambridge: Cambridge University Press, 2017).
4 Lorenzo Zamponi, *Social Movements, Memory and Media: Narrative in Action in the Italian and Spanish Student Movements* (Basingstoke: Palgrave Macmillan, 2018).
5 Charles Tilly, *Social Movements, 1768–2004* (Boulder, CO: Paradigm Publishers, 2004).
6 Marianne Hirsch in Ayşe Gül Altınay et al., eds. *Women Mobilizing Memory* (New York: Columbia University Press, 2019), 3.
7 Hayden White, *Metahistory: The Historical Imagination in Nineteenth-Century Europe* (Baltimore, MD: Johns Hopkins University Press, 1973).
8 Ann Rigney, 'Plenitude, Scarcity and the Circulation of Cultural Memory,' *Journal of European Studies* 35, no. 1 (2005): 209–226.
9 J.L. Austin, *How to Do Things with Words* (Cambridge, MA: Harvard University Press, 1962).
10 Red Chidgey, *Feminist Afterlives: Assemblage Memory in Activist Times* (London: Palgrave Macmillan, 2018).

INDEX

1 May celebrations *see* May Day
1921 riots 189
1945 generation (Germany) 10
1950s 248
1968 movement 6–7, 10, 203, 205, 264
1970s 133–40, 143, 149, 264
1989 generation (Germany) 10

Abendroth, Wolfgang 170
abolitionist movement 68, 221, 225
Aboriginals 96–8, 100–7; activists 103–5, 108; Advancement League 103; rights 103, 105, 107
Aborigines' Friends Society 103
action: focus of 272
Action Reconciliation/Service for Peace 266
activists: anti-racism 294; anti-globalization 70; black 289, 292; civil 68; cyber 8; existential 90; grassroots 101, 203, 211, 213–14, 260–2, 269–70, 274, 277, 288–9, 294; non-contentious memory 170; non-communist 157; pro-logging 127; professional 115; social 77, 105
actors: mainstream 274; network theory 4
Adenauer, Konrad 262, 264
Adult Franchise 46
advocacy 302; organized 301
aesthetics 135
affective relationships 27, 55
affirming beliefs 115
African Americans 13, 122, 280, 284–5, 287, 289, 293–4; civil rights of 280; empowerment of 294; history 286; political rights of 280; politicians 285; southerners 281; women 60, 85
Agartz, Viktor 248
agency 76, 261, 270, 278; long-term 139
agents 280
Aicher-Scholl, Inge 90–1
Aktives Museum Faschismus und Widerstand in Berlin e.V. 266, 277
Aldermaston marches 103
All India Peace and Solidarity Congress 54
All India's Women Conference 42–4, 52–4
All-German People's Party *see Gesamtdeutsche Volkspartei*
alliances 121, 141, 274, 302; retrospective 138
Alternative for Germany Party 252
American Historical Association's Committee of Women Historians 75
Ammann, Walther 170
amnesties 171–3
Amrit Kaur, Rajkumari 47
anarcho-syndicalism 181–2, 184, 246
Andrews, J.A. 223, 228
Angenfort, Josef 161
animal rights 127
Anniversary Demonstration Committee 230, 231
anti-capitalism 205, 248
anti-colonialism 97, 107–8
anti-communism 159–61, 163–4, 171, 174, 202, 262, 268, 291, 300
anti-conscription movement 200–1, 208, 210, 214

anti-environmentalism 115, 128
antifascism 157, 162–3, 166, 190, 247, 251; memory of 157, 174; struggle of 248
anti-gentrification movement 135
anti-imperialist movement 49
anti-monumentality 267
anti-nationalism 267
anti-nuclear movement 13, 95–7, 100, 105–6, 108, 137, 272, 300
Antis 199, 210
anti-Semitism 264
Anti-Socialist Laws 242
apologists 293
Arbeiterinitiativen 134, 145; *see also* workers' initiatives
Arbeitsgemeinschaft der Arbeidersiedlungsinitiativen im Ruhrgebiet 137
Argentina 6
artisans 225
Asia 41
Asian Women's Fund 33, 37
Assmann, Aleida 6
Assmann, Jan 6
associations: benevolent 282; for Christian-Jewish cooperation 267; civic 262, 280
atomic testing 97, 105, 300
Attucks, Crispus 286
'Aufruf an alle Deutsche' 90
Auschwitz 88; trials 264
Australia 13, 136
Australia's Nuclear Science and Technology Organisation 106
Australia's Security Intelligence Organisation 98, 103
Australian and New Zealand Congress for International Co-operation and Disarmament 103
Australian Communist Party 201
Australian Convention on Peace and War 103
Australian Imperial Forces 199
Australian Labor Party 98, 100–1, 105, 199–201, 206–7, 214
Australian Left 146
Australian Nuclear Forum 106
Australian Parliamentary Inquiry of 2006 106
Australian Peace Council 103
Australian Workers Union 207, 208
Australian-NZ-US alliance 101
Australian-US Joint Defence Space Research Facility 105
authenticity 273; quest for 135
authorization: dynamics of 62; strategies 62

autobiographical writing 201
autonomy, bodily 69

Baier, Frank 139, 147
Baldus, Paulheinz 165
Bari, Judi 120–2, 127–8
Barnes, Roy 292
Bastille, taking of the 9, 10
Battle of Waterloo 231
Bauer, Fritz 159–60, 172
Bautzen 268
BdV 268
Beauregard, P.G.T. 289
Befehlsnotstand 168
Begum, Hajrah 54
behaviour, collective 4
Bekennende Kirche 170
Bendler Block 262
Bergarbeiter proteste 254
Bergen-Belsen 261–2, 265; Jewish Committee 261
Berger, Stefan 2
Berlin History Workshop 265
Berlin Holocaust memorial 7
Berlin Wall 267
Berlin-Hohenschönhausen 268
Berufsschulen 240
betrayal: of revolutionary internationalism 246; of working-class interests 246
Beyer, Herbert 161
bias petitions 165–7
biocentrism 113–14, 125–7
Bitburg 268
black: accomplishment 285; activism 287; American women 71; community 284; complaints 288; empowerment 290; history 285–8; memory 284; power 3; southerners 280, 287, 294
Black Archives 77
Black History Week 288
Black Lives Matter 72, 292, 294
blitz-law *see Strafrechtänderungsgesetz, Erstes*
blockade 84–6, 90, 113, 115, 126; senior's 86–9
Böckler, Hans 247
Boland, Hilary 228
Bologna 138
Bolshevism 245–6
bombing 121–2, 127
bonding 118
Boot Makers' Union 207
boundaries 115
Bourdieu, Pierre 4
bourgeois state 161
Braunbuch 168

Brecht, Bertholt 225
Bright McLaren, Priscilla 67
Brissot, Jacques-Pierre 6
British Labor Party 241
British National Assembly of Women 51
brotherhood 230
Brown v. Board of Education decision 288–9
Brown, Freda 55
Buchenwald 268
buckaroos 124
Buergerinitiativen 134
Building Workers Industrial Union 137
Bundesgerichtshof 162, 164
Bundesverfassungsgericht see Federal Constitutional Court
Butalia, Urvashi 43
Butler, Josephine 67

Calhoun, Craig 2
Calwell, Arthur 201, 210
camaraderie 118
Campaign: for International Co-operation and Disarmament 103–4; for Nuclear Disarmament 98
capitalism 73, 182, 252
care for the weak 267
Catholic: education 246
Catholic church: persecution of 241; resistance 170
Catholics 242
celebrations 281; Cremorne Gardens 220
Center for Human Rights Memory 269
Central Council for the Protection of Democratic Rights *see Zentralratzum Schutzedemokratischer Rechte*
Central Security Office of the Reich *see Reichssicherheitshauptamt*
Central Working Community *see Zentrale Arbeitsgemeinschaft*
ceremonial splendor 280
change processes: long-term 270–1, 276; medium-term 276
Chapman Catt, Carrie 66–7
Charlottevilleneo-Nazirally 293–4
Charter of Women's Rights 54
Chartists 230
Chattopadhyay, Malabika 54
Checkpoint Charlie 277
Cherney, David 121–2, 126–7
Chicago martyrs' 243
China 13, 34
Chinese Comfort Women Museum and Research Center 36
Chomsky, Noam 33
Christian Democratic Party 249, 251

Chung-ok, Yun 30, 32
cities: Fordist 136; as object of contestation 135; planning 149; post-Fordist 136
citizens: action 136–7, 143, 267; participation 138; solidarity 136; of the world 55
citizenship: custodial 68
civic: effort 262; groups 267; spaces 290, 294; spirit 285
civil servants 246
civil rights 3; African American 287; activism 6, 70, 104, 205, 291, 300
civil society: 5, 261, 267; inclusion of 267; as supportive structure for state governance 263
claiming the streets 224
class: 167, 202, 243; identity 11; industrial 230; loyalty 206
Clifford, Dakota Sid 121, 125
Clinton, Hillary 32
Clothing Trades Union 212
CND 55
Coalition of Citizen Action Groups 136, 142
coalition-building 266
code of virtue 28
co-determination 249, 253; laws 249
coercion 84, 89–90
Coers, Mathias 147
coexistence of past and present 114
cohesive societies 281
Cold War 83, 87, 91, 95, 97, 101, 106, 156–7, 160, 248, 260, 263
collective action 2, 8, 115, 271–2; diffusion of 271; frames 272–3; repertoires 277; *see also* public action
collective identity 3, 7, 11, 33, 42, 85, 115, 134, 180, 190, 202, 232, 255, 302; weakening of 251
collective memory 1, 3, 42, 61, 85, 114, 118, 181, 190, 201, 286
collective movement: anchoring' 204
collective: purposes 232; singing 117–18; strength 243; ties 226
collectivization enterprises 182
colonial: archive 77; division 71; victimization 29
colonialism 13, 31, 42, 67, 70–6, 96, 124, 281; national memory of 31
comfort women 75, 300; advocacy movement 27, 29, 38
commemoration 39, 261–2, 264, 266, 268, 273, 282, 285; African American 286; annual 301; Confederate 283–4; decentralized 267; demands for 263; German-centric 264; of 'German

suffering' 268'; national 268; persistence of 227–8; public 234, 260, 274, 284–6
commemorative agenda 262
Commission on Memory Cultures of Social Democracy in Germany 240
Committee for an Amnesty – Defenders in Cases of Political Justice 169
common mind 286
communism 114, 181–3, 186, 188–9, 191, 201, 207, 246, 248
communist: communities 181; memory 158; parties 204; regime 268; resistance 160, 170
Communist Party: of China 35–6, 38; of Australia 98, 136; of Germany 136, 181–2, 186, 188–9; of India 45–6, 51–2, 56
communities 142; communist 181; imagined 191; national 185; political 180, 185–6, 191; preservation of 135; social democratic 181; syndicalist 181
Community Action for Windsor Bridge 147
community networks 205
compensation claims 102, 160, 251
competing 'pasts' 268
concentration camp 88–9, 162, 169, 248, 261, 265, 267–8, 274
conceptions: of the past 140; of the present 41, 140
conceptual: challenges 302; language 4
conciliation: strategy of 44
Confederacy 280, 282, 284, 293–4, 300
Confederate: flag 288–92; memorials 293–4; monuments 281; heroes 284; History Month 294; Memorial Day 283–4; symbols 289–90
Confederation of German Trade Unions 248, 250–2, 254
Confessing Church *see Bekennende Kirche*
conflict 261, 271
connection: feelings of 118
consciousness: changes of 44
conscription: campaign against 199–202, 209–10, 212, 214, 301
consensus 96, 275; simplicity of 108
conservation movement 118
conservatism 213; religious 128; white 292
Constitution, German 90
constitutional: complaints 84; democracy 171; state 174
Construction, Forestry, Mining and Energy Union 147
contention: acts of 299; circles of 261; cycles of 265, 270–1, 275; dynamics of

271; key success factors of 301; non-violent 302; trajectories of 271; wave of 275; women's 61
contentious: action 3, 9, 260, 268, 270, 299–300; arena 280; politics 96, 157; tactics 264, 270, 274
contingency 261, 278
continuity: of the movement 227
controversy 261
Convention on Indigenes and Tribal Populations 104
Cooper, Anna Julia 60, 65, 71, 74, 77
corporate executives 128
corporatism 249–50
Cosgrave, Jack 212, 214
Cottbus prison 268
counter-discourse 250
counter-memorialization 6, 91, 201, 255, 265, 281
cowboy mythology 114, 124
critical memory: institutionalization of 266, 272
Crow, Jim 287, 290
crucifixion 234
Cuban Missile crisis 103
cultural: appropriation 127; archive 77; change 108; epochs 270; forms 301; hegemony 191; memory 77, 85, 105; movements 45; policies 281; repertoire 300; representation cohorts 96; studies 61; voluntarism 281; work 284
culture: civic 295; Dutch postcolonial 77; historical 143; musical 114, 300; national 281; political 136, 268, 270; public 281–4; wars 294
Curtin, John 207
customs, trajectory of 271
Cycle Trades Union 212

Dachau 265
Daphi, Priska 3
David, Alice *see* Stertzenbach, Alice
Davis, Angela 71, 74, 287
Davis, Jefferson 289
debate 268, 301; culture of 143, 267
decision-making 92
Declaration of Independence 285
Declaration on the Elimination of Violence Against Women 32
deep ecology 114
defense strategy 161, 164, 174
deindustrialization 136, 145, 252
delegitimization 157, 165
Deleuzian analysis 4
demobilization, key patterns of 261

democracy 3, 161, 172, 174; economic 245, 249; political 245, 249; protecting 160; social 245
Democratic Labor Party 206
democratic society 270, 300; transition 29, 38
democratization 29, 38, 135; of politics 38; of the economic sphere 249; processes 135
Democrats, US 291–2
demonstrations: political 164; sit-down 84
denazification 159
depoliticization 162
desegregation 288–9, 291
destigmatization 30, 38
Deutscher Gewerkschaftsbund see German Trade Union Confederation
development 114
dictatorship 269
Die Linke 255
diffusion: conscious process of 114; processes 272
Diggers: English 123
dignity 42
Directive Principles 46
discrimination 213, 266, 287; economic 287; gendered 213
disruption 8
dissemination of information 221
diversity 136
Doerr, Nicole 3
Dolk, Michiel 143
Dolle Mina's 69
Douglass, Benjamin 231
Douglass, Frederick 285–7
dowry 53–4
Drucker, Wilhelmina 69
Du Bois, W.E.B. 287
Durkheim, Emile 4
Dutschke's revenge 84

Earth First! 113, 115, 117, 121, 128–9
Eastern bloc *see* Warsaw pact
Ebert, Friedrich 182
ecological networks 126
economic: development 133, 136, 149; independence for women 46; power 280; rights 233; sphere 249; transitions 136
ecoterrorism 121, 127
education: access to 245; historical 255
Edward VII, King 280
Eight Hours banner 227, 234; Demonstrations 220; League 220; memorial 253; pioneers 228–9
eight-hour day 219–20, 230, 232–4, 245

Eisenheim settlement 137, 140, 145–7
ELAS 170
emancipation 42; causes of 300; of African Americans 42, 284; movement 76; of labour 223
Emancipation Day 285, 287; Declaration 285
Emanuel African Methodist Episcopal Church 292
Emerson, Ralph Waldo 122
emotional: distance 268; dynamics 12; factors in interpretation of meaning 116
emotions 7, 42, 118, 122, 227; history of 12
Emu Field 97, 102, 106
Enabling Act *see Ermächtigungsgesetz*
endorsement 128
endurance of anniversary 227
environmental movement 13, 70, 101, 134, 137, 143, 240, 264, 272, 300
equal: pay 211; protection 289; society 191
equality 42, 46, 67, 136; of trades 226; universal 45
Erfurt 268
Ermächtigungsgesetz 89
Erskineville 143
establishment 264, 277
ethics, Christian 85
Eurocentrism 43
Eurocommunism 136, 146
Europe 3, 13
European Enlightenment 67; heritage year (1975) 140
events: catalogues 9; civic 294; impact 10, 181, 185; key 261, 271–2, 276–7; transformative 202, 270–1, 276–7
evidence: safeguarding 273
exclusion 61, 62, 69–70, 72–5, 118; racial 62
experiences: shared 201; thresholds of 44
expellees 262–3; *see also Vertriebene*
extraparliamentary actions 141
Eyerman, Ron 3

Fairskye, Merilyn 143
fascism 3, 73, 159, 166–7, 189–90, 264
Featherstone, Roger 119, 125
Federal Builders Labourers Federation 146
Federal Constitutional Court (Germany) 166–7
federalism 281
Federated Engines Drivers' and Firemen's Association 137
Federation of Homecomers, POWs and Relatives of the Missing 262
feedback between memory and activism 302

Female Operatives Hall (Melbourne) 233
feminism 2, 30, 60–2, 64, 70; American 68; Black 60, 69–70, 72–3, 76; first-wave 62; interpretations of 74; revision of 73; second-wave 74; universal 68
feminist: consciousness 30; historians 69, 72; internationalism 63, 69; movement 30, 70, 72, 137; publishing collectives 69; strategies 74; Indian 64
femo-nationalists 74
Fenian movement 211
field theory 4
fights 301
First Nations 126
Floez Dickebanck settlement 144
folk music 114, 127
forced labour 31
Foreman, Dave 119, 121, 124–5
forest campaign: California 127; Oregon 127
forgetting of the past, formal 232
Fourteenth Amendment 289
Fourth World Conference on Women 31–3, 36, 157
frames: macro-economic 249; of meaning 273, 275; of national memory 141
framing 273; biographical 212; of protest 2; of victimhood 27, 31
France 5, 10
Francis, May *see* Brodney, May
Francoism 10
Free German Youth 161
Free Workers' Union of Germany *see* Freie Arbeiter-Union Deutschlands
freedom 42, 49, 156
Freedom Movement 56
Free Riders 118, 122
Free Summer 118
Freie Arbeiter-Union Deutschlands 181–2, 184–8, 190
French Revolution 6, 10, 12
Friedrich-Ebert Foundation 252
Friends of the Earth 101
Fry, Elizabeth 67
Führer, Karl-Christian 250
Fukushima 107
Fundamental Rights 46
future: alternative 134, 205; ideas of the 136; post-capitalist 136

Gallagher, Norm 146
Gallipoli 99
Galloway, James 229
Gandhi, Mahatma 83
Gandhian: movements 41–2; repertoire 8

Garrett Fawcett, Millicent 63
gatherings for the purpose of memory work 273
gay liberation 3, 137, 203
Gedenkstättenbewegung see Memorial Site Movement
Gedenkstäthtenreferat 266
Gedenkstättenrundbrief 266
Gedenkstättenseminare 266
Geier, Friedrich Wilhelm 164–5
gender: definition of 72–3, 75, 211; equality 211; history 69, 74; justice 49, 62
General German Workers' Association 241
generational change 270; difference 220, 233; memories 44
generations 7, 10, 301; as carriers for memorial activity 44; sceptical (Germany) 10
genocide 5, 264
George V, King 280
Georgia state flag 292
German: Basic Law 90; German Labour History Association 255; Liberal Party 251; People's Union 252; Trade Union Confederation 240
German Socialist Party 169, 249–50, 255
Germany 13; division of 156; Imperial 241–4, 246, 249, 252, 255; National Socialist 255; reunification of 172, 251
Gesamtdeutsche Volkspartei 170
Geschichtsbewegung see History Movement
Geschichtsfeste see history festivals
Geschichtswerkstättenbewegung see History Movement
Gestapo 162, 170, 265–6, 277
globalization 270
goals: and strategies, recalibrating 301; common 286; shaping of 302
Gorbachev, Mikhail 91
Gottfurcht, Hans 247
grand narratives 76
Grayden, William 104
Great Recession 293
Green Bans 133–4, 141, 143, 145–7; Gallery 146; movement 133, 136
green fire, concept of 125
green spaces 136
Ground Zero 100
grounded theory 4
Gruzman, Neville 142
Günter, Janne 140
Günter, Roland 138, 141, 146–8
Guthrie, Woody 118
Gutman, Yifat 3

Hagen 184–6
Hak-soon, Kim 30
Halbwachs, Maurice 4–5, 11, 202
Hans-Böckler-Foundation 252, 255
Hartmann, Karl 160
Harvey, David 135
Hawke, Bob 101
Haymarket Riot of 1886 183
hegemonic: expression 199; memory 164, 204; methods 2
Heilbronn 88
Heimatvereine see homeland associations
Heimkehrermahnmal 262–4
Heinemann, Gustav 170, 173
Helms, Jesse 291
heritage 7, 11, 136, 138, 141, 145; activism 137, 141; alternative ideas of 148; Australian 142; commemorating 284; common understanding of 140; Confederate 290–1, 300; discourse 134, 140, 142; environmental 138, 141; immaterial 139; industrial 135, 137, 140, 144–5; institutionalization of movement of industrial 140; international heritage 138; labour movement 138; landscapes 146; legislation 141; material 142; movement 140; national 138, 141–2; protection laws 292; revolutionary 189; southern 280, 284, 290–1, 294; urban 34–5, 138, 140, 146; working-class 138–42
heroes: African American 285; of memory 1
Heyer, Heather D. 293
high treason 162
Hill, Joe 119
Hiroshima 86, 106–7
historical: accuracy 273; actors 61; alternative interpretations 294; American landscape 295; amnesia 26; authenticity 267; awareness 286; concerns 276; consciousness 147, 252; continuities 61; culture 134, 136, 138, 141, 146, 148; education 255; events 7; evidence 264, 274, 276; hypothetical 149; injustice 289; invocations 74, 294; justice 273; legitimacy 134; meaning 201; memory 220, 240, 252, 255, 280–1, 294; narrative 68, 74, 76; optimism 252; orientation 250; periods as focus of action 272; perspectives 61, 138; research 72, 76, 273; responsibility 266; revisionism 35; roots 270; sites 294; specificity 71; traces' safeguarding 265, 267, 275; traditions 270–1; 'truth' 294
historicism: new 61

Historikerstreit 13; *see also* History Wars
historiography 61, 76–7, 265
history: African American 288; as burden 255; as resource in contemporary struggles 255; as strategy 77; as whip to lash unions 252; Australian 142; common 302; digital 149; industrial 142; labour 301; national 1; of everyday life 264–5; of industrial workers 251; official 138, 204; oral 61, 76, 202, 264, 276; resources of 228; segregationist 288; urban 143, 146, 149; versions of 280, 285; working-class 142; festivals 264–5, 272; politics 253, 267; public 149; workshops 265, 275
History Movement 264
History Site Movement 267
History Wars 13
History Wars *see Historikerstreit*
History Workshop Movement *see* History Movement
Hitler's hanging judges 168
Hobsbawm, Eric 2
Hoffmann, Reiner 240
Holocaust 5, 87, 89, 262, 264, 268; commemoration 262; survivors 261–4, 270, 275–6; memorials 264
Holocaust Memorial Schöneberg 265
homeland: Anglo-Celtic 290; associations 267; white Euro-American 290
Horizon, Johnny 120; *see also* Koehler, Bart
House for the History of the Ruhr 145
House of Representatives Standing Committee 106
House of Sharing 31
housing: conditions 135; co-ops 238
Huber, Kurt 91
Hughes, Billy 200, 206, 208, 210
human rights 31–2, 36, 38
humour: sardonic 119

iaioflautas 10
identification 190; offer of 185
identity 215; black 287; civic 267; cohering 202–3; common 226; construction of 203, 301; fluid 138; national 188; of urban movements, objective 147; of urban movements, subjective 147; political 180–1, 270; profession as definition of 202; proletarian 202; regional 134, 137, 293; transforming 289
ideologies 133, 273; left-wing 135; New Left 137
IG Metall 250
Immerwahr Fränkel, Wolfgang 168
immigrants 290

impactevents 10, 181, 185
imperialism 67, 71, 73, 75, 124
impetus, uniform 64
inclusivity 300; strategies for 69
Independence Day 285
Independence movement 43
India 13
Indian National Congress 42, 45–6
Indigenous agency 103; Australians 108; communities 126–7, 300; cultures, romanticization of 127; empowerment 103; movement 137
individualization 202, 251
Indonesia 33
industrial: arbitration 199; bargaining 243; infrastructure 137; organization 212; relations system 249
Industrial Workers of the World 119, 121, 128–9
industrialization 270
Industriegewerkschaft Bergbau und Energie 137
inequalities 233; continuation of 228
information flow 271
Initiativausschuss für die Amnestie und der Verteidiger in politischen Strafsachen 168–74
Initiative Gedenkstätte Neuengamme 267
Institute for Social Movements 145
institutional: actors 274; allies 276; arrangements 260–1, 275; channels 264; environment 267–8; foundations of white power 288; impact 275; integration 269; repertoire of memory 139
institutionalization 1, 245, 275; dynamics of 272; of heritage 138; of scholarship 1
institutions 204, 274–5, 284; black-led 284; 'march through the' 275; regularized relationship of activists with 274
intellectual: life 286; traditions 4
interaction between memory and activism 302
inter-generational connections 42
internal: cohesion 255; differentiation 254; reconstruction 128
International Fourth 246
International Third 246
International Alliance of Women 63
International Camp Committee at Buchenwald 261
international cooperation 74
International Council of Women 63
International Federation for Research in Women's History 75
International Labor Office 246, 250
international: law 85; links 55; policies 246; relationship 41

International Transport Workers' Federation 248
International Woman Suffrage Alliance 66–7
International Woman Suffrage Association *see* International Alliance of Women
International Women's Decade 49
International, Second 181
internationalism 54, 67, 107–8, 244; national 244; proletarian 246; Social Democratic 244
interpretation: of events 10; of meaning 116; of the past 270
intersectional approaches 74
Iron Curtain 156; *see also* Cold War
ISIS 293
Islam 71
Italy 3, 6
IWW-EF! initiative *see Earth First!*

Japan 10, 13, 26, 33
Jennings, Waylon 124
Jewish art, destruction of 293
Jewish victims 261
Jones, Nancie 56
Juanita Nielsen Community Centre 143, 148
juridification of trials 164–5
jurisprudence 84
justice 42; political 157–8, 165, 169–71, 173; transitional 6

Kali for Women 43
Kantorowicz, Anton 172–3
Kapp Putsch 181, 183–4, 186, 188–9
Karachi Resolution of Fundamental Rights and Duties 42, 45, 54
Kaul, Friedrich Karl 166–7
Kelly's Bush 143, 149
key events 261, 271–2, 276–7
Khandvala, Kapila 47, 53
Kinemathek des Ruhrgebiets 145
King jr., Martin Luther 83, 291
kinship networks 205
kisaeng 30; *see also* sex tourism
Koehler, Bart 116, 120, 124, 126
Kohl, Helmut 251, 268
Korea Church Women United 30
Korean Council for the Women Drafted for Military Sexual Slavery 30–1, 33
Kristofferson, Kris 124
Ku Klux Klan 287
Kulturkampf 241–2
Kumar, Rajni 43, 51, 56
Kunga Tjuta people 107

laborites 227–8
Labour Day *see* May Day

labour: forced 31; historiography 135, 202, 234, 245; history seminars 255; politics 201, 206; propagandists 233; unions 136–7, 139–40, 180, 182, 185–6; unity of 226
labour market: access to 69, 73
labour movement 2, 13, 70, 133–4, 136–9, 141, 143, 180–1, 183–4, 186, 188–9, 190–1, 220–2, 228, 232, 245, 253, 300; Australian 232; German 181, 188–9, 191, 253; international 191; parlementarianism of 214; Social Democratic 242; traditions of 138
Lakshmi, C.S. 43
land use paradigms 113
landscapes: civic 293; inherited 294
Latour, Bruno 4
law enforcement officials 128
League of the South 290
Lee, Robert E. 284, 293
Lefebvre, Henri 4, 135
legend forming 209
legislative history used against privatization 139
legitimization 1
Leigh Kelland, Lara 3
Leistikowstrasse (Potsdam) 268
leitmotif 85, 88
Leopold, Aldo 122, 125
lesbian movement 137, 247
Leuschner, Wilhelm 247–8
LGBT movement 240
liberal: progress 64; rights 138; socialism 185; union movement 242; women activists 64
liberation movement 76
Liebknecht, Karl 189
lieux de mémoire 185, 246
lifecycle 230
life narratives 199, 201–2, 204, 210, 301
lifestyle 135
Li'l Green Songbook 116, 120, 123
limited government: tradition of 281
Lincoln, Abraham 285–6, 291
links: affective *see* emotions
Little Red Songbook 119
living standards: working-class 200
Living Without Armament 88
lobbying 266, 274
Loomba, Primla 43, 46–7, 51, 54–5
Loomba, Satish 51
loss 203
loyalty, maintaining 202
Lübke, Heinrich 168
Luddites 123
Lüttwitz, General 181

Luxemburg, Rosa 189
Lyons, Dana 116

macro-economic framework 249
Madres 6
Mahila Atma Raksha Samiti 45
Mammon 234
management decisions 245
manipulation 138
Mann, Tom 207
Mannheim agreement 244
Maoism 146
Maralinga 95–8, 101, 104, 106–8
Marburg History Workshop 265–6
Marburg Jäger Regiment 266
March Actions of 1921 186
'march through the institutions' 275
marginalization 70, 72, 118, 205, 248
Marquet, Claude 233
Marshall, Turgood 289
martyrdom 301
Marx, Karl 4, 76
Marxism 11, 135, 203, 207, 264
Mascrene, Annie 46
mass demonstrations 83, 184
Max Taut settlement 147
May Day 183–4, 191, 220, 243–4, 246, 254
McAdam, Doug 3
McClelland Royal Commission *see* Royal Commission into British Nuclear Tests in Australia
McClelland, James 98
meaning: contextual factors in interpretation of 116; intellectual factors in interpretation of 116; physical factors in interpretation of meaning 116
Mehta, Hansa 46
Meinberg, Adolf 188
Melbourne Peace Congress 103
Melucci, Alberto 2
Memorial Day 285
Memorial Site Movement 265, 267–8, 272–5
memorialists 294, 301
memorialization 39, 203–4, 211, 215, 220, 229, 232–3, 242, 244, 264–5, 283; agents of 215; counter- 6, 91, 201, 255, 265, 281; as political intervention 215; gendered nature of 211; of National Socialism 247; through song 127; of trade union history 255
memorials 265, 267, 274, 301; -institutional environment 267; aesthetics 268; associations 283; design 268; events 245, 265; hybrid institutions 267–8; initiatives 266–7, 275; institutions 266–7; practices

244; principles 267; sites 265–7, 276–7; sites' governance 274–5; as symbols of oppression 294
memories: affective collective 125; constructed 96, 204; contemplating 180; of crisis 242; generational 44; of history 228; of Holocaust victims 261; of injustice 108; of nationalism 97; of persecution 242; of struggle 242, 255
memory:1916 Australian 201; activism 1, 3, 13, 123, 135, 138, 204, 232, 281; -activism nexus 7, 302; activism, non-contentious 270; activism, reproductive function of 270; agents 204, 211; alternative 164, 274; as 'assemblage' 302; association 262; banalization of 135, 146; changing 299; of civil life 302; of civil resistance 302; of colonialism 31; common 284; communicative 117, 190, 252; construction 164; critical 266, 272; cultural 77, 85, 105; cultural repertoire of 139; developments 270; dynamics 61; dynamics of cultural 7; entrepreneurs 204; events 10; expedience of 215; of failure 300; formal 85, 91, 96, 127, 141, 201, 204–5, 209, 214–5; formal movement 205; framework 139; hegemonic 164, 204; horizon 250; 'hot' 135; implicit 300; initiatives 273; landscape 267; as legitimization 149; mobility of 251; national 5, 36–8; of Nazi past 174, 275; negative form of 300; of oppression 247; performativity of 302; of persecution 247; of perseverance 255; personal 201, 209; perspective 62; politics 181, 220, 251–3, 260, 261, 263–4, 266–7, 269–80, 273, 276, 278; -political area 164, 261, 264; political processes 261; politics activism 261; politics analysis 272; popular 96, 105, 234; practices 250; projects 268; protest 261, 270, 273–7; public 302; public expression of 281, 284; radical movement 124; reflexory 149; religious 140; of resistance 247; of revolution 245; scholars 302; shared 184; struggles 273; studies 157, 180, 203, 220, 261, 270; syndicalism 185; of the past 251; of totalitarianism 248; uchronic 204; by urban movements 146; work 184, 188, 191, 261–5, 270, 273, 275–7, 302; *see also* collective memory
memory culture 180–1, 186, 189, 191, 254–6, 260; democratic 267; differentiation of 181; Marxist 185; of the victims of the 1953 GDR uprising 262; of trade unions 240–1, 244, 250, 254–6; open 300; strengthening of 240–1; transformation of 276
memory discourse 242, 244, 246–8; German trade unions' 248; key agent of 254–5; on resistance 247; on suffering 247; post-war 248; unions' 249
memoryscape 143–4; urban 135
men of the "fifties" 222, 230
'mentality of the tower' 242
Menzies, Robert 97, 99
metamemory of activism 301
Midnight Oil 101
migration 75
militancy 119, 249
Militant Propagandists of the Labor Movement 200, 211–12, 214
Militants *see* Militant Propagandists of the Labor Movement
militarism 161, 199
Millers' Operatives Society 222
mine workers 53
'Mississippi Summer in the Redwoods' *see* 'Redwood Summer'
'Mississippi Summer Project' 122; *see also* 'Freedom Summer'
mnemomic: benefits of movies 105; cause 276; change 271; extension of the present 301; of failure 54; focal point 101; frames 273, 276–7; issue, visibility of 277; mainstream 277; narratives, change of 261; norms 270, 273–4; opposition 273; practice 62, 70; principles 275; repertoire, national 108; rhetoric 263
mobilization 1, 3, 5, 37, 64, 105, 199, 203, 205, 214, 260, 264, 269, 271, 277, 283, 286, 290, 293, 300; grassroots 260; key patterns of 261; medium-term patterns of 272; of oppositional groups 270; pattern of 272; social movement 261
Moderne Frauenbewegung 66
modernity 42
moments of madness' 300
Monkeywrench Gang 123
monkeywrenching 115
monuments 267, 281, 284, 293; Confederate 292, 294; German national 281
Moore, Fred 122
Morial, Ernest N. 289
mourning: conventions of 283
movements 301: abolitionist 68, 221, 225; anti-gentrification 135; anti-imperialist 49; anti-nuclear 13, 95–7, 100, 105–6, 108, 137, 272, 300; celebration 220; civil rights 6; conservation 118; culture 118; decline of 275; dynamics 209; elites 134;

Fenian 211; German syndicalist 180; histories 117; identity 203, 215, 221, 232; independence 43; knowledge 203; lesbian 137, 247; LGBT 240; liberation 76; memory 203, 205, 301–2; national 6; origins of a 61, 301; political 161, 180; pluralistic progressive 51; radicalization 273; right-wing populist 3, 241; Self-Respect 42, 45; sexually-focused 70; songs 139; squatters 137; strategies 203, 269; student 3; tenant 138, 140; theorists 269; Third World 240; urban 147, 151; US civil rights 114, 122; women's 10, 13, 41, 44–5, 54, 62, 64, 240, 264; workers' 199; working-class 181

movement's: sense of commitment 301; sense of numbers 301; sense of unity 301; sense of worthiness 301

Muir, John 122

Müller-Meininger Jr., Ernst 170

Mundey, Jack 136, 141, 144, 146–7, 151

Murphy, W.E. 232

Mururoa 103

music: as memory activism 128; as part of social movement culture 113; interpretation 116; rock 114

musical culture 114, 300

mythological moments 214

mythologies 203, 210, 215

NAACP 293

Nagasaki 86

Naidu, Sarojini 45

Nanking Massacre 34, 37

narrative 32, 62–3, 191, 203–5, 214, 233; of 1916 206, 210; alternative 158; anti-imperialist 36; of betrayal 301; Biblical 285; of colonialism 26; commitments 44; of defeat and martyrdom 301; developmental 64; dominant 260, 299, 302; feminist 73; first-wave 72, 74; formal 96, 127; German National Socialist 85; grand 76; of heritage 253; of heroes and villains 207–8, 211, 213, 242, 301; historical 1, 5, 60, 62, 72; ideological 242; of independence 41; Indian 41; of injustice 108; mainstream memory 270; media 3, 5; memory 243; meta- 96; mnemonic, change of 261; national self-congratulatory 135; national history 29, 37; of nationalism 108; of progress 243; personal 139, 209, 213; political 41; rescue 72; of resistance 301; of Soviet totalitarianism 85; of the 1970s 133; of the Freikorps 189; unsettling 266; of victimization 34; white Western 64; white women's 71; working-class 202; of workers' organizations 189; *see also* life narratives

National Democratic Party 251

National Federation of Indian Women 42–4, 46, 50–4, 56

National Front 158

nationalism 36, 41, 65, 70, 96, 101, 142, 144, 266; and rituals of remembrance 273; popular 99

Native Americans 126–7; resistance of 114, 125; traditions of 126

NATO 83, 85; Double-Track Decision 83, 86, 89, 91–2

nature: harmonious relation with 125–6; mystical link to 125; reconnecting with 125

Nazi: crimes 262–3, 265; Germany 86, 90–1; past 264, 267–8, 270, 275, 300; regime 163–4, 167, 173, 182, 293

Nazism 85, 157, 159–60, 165

Ned Ludd books 123

negative integration 242

negotiation: strategy of 44, 250

Negro history 286–7

Negro History Week 286–8

Nehring, Holger 2

Nehru, Rameshwari 42, 46–7

neighbourhood action groups 141

Nelson, Willie 124

neo-Confederates 290, 292

neoliberal: critique of corporatist models 250; urbanism 147

neoliberalism 73–4, 134, 136, 249, 251–2

neo-Nazism 264

Netherlands, the 33

networkedadvocacy 30

Neu Beginnen 170

Neuengamme 265, 274

Neumann, Oskar 162–3, 165

New Age 126

Newport Uprising 230

NFIW Congress Report 49

Nicholls, Doug 104

Nielsen, Juanita 143

Nightingale, Florence 67

NIMBY 135, 141

Nixon, Richard 291

Non-Aligned Movement 46

non-emotionality 267

non-monumentality 273

Nora, Pierre 1, 5, 42

Norden, Albert 168

Nötigung see coercion

NSDAP 172–3

NSW Builders Labourers Federation 137, 141, 144, 146
nuclear: armament 83, 88, 91; colonialism 96–7, 100; energy 101; missiles 84, 91–2; pacifiscm 103; war 88; waste 107–8
Nuclear Disarmament Party 100–1
Nuclear Non-Proliferation Treaty of 1968 103–4

occupying 115
Offenloch, Werner 90
official: forgetting of the past 232; history 138, 204; memory 85, 91, 96, 127, 201, 204–5, 209, 214–15; movement memory 205; narratives 96, 127
Official Secrets legislation 102
Old South': glorification of 280
Oliver, Bill 123
Olsen, Hinrich 86
Olsen, Luise 86–7, 89–91
On the Beach 103, 105
open society 300
openness 300
opportunity structure 35
opposition: groups formation of 270; between history and memory 61–2, 76–7; identity formation of 273; stories of 96
oppression 284, 294; of women 66, 71–2, 74
oral history 61, 76, 202, 264, 276
Ostrow, Cecelia 116
outlaw behaviour 124

parades 8, 285–6
Paris Commune of 1871 135, 183, 191
parlementarianism: of labour movement 214
parodies 120, 126
Partial Test Ban Treaty 103
participation 271; in commemoration 223; political 83
partisan: histories 67; politics 285
Pascoe, William 223, 227
past: critical approach of the 267, 272; defining the 127; practical 255; public representations of the 281
patriarchy 42
patriotism 242; symbology 114, 124
patronage 280–1
patterns 261
peace: groups 267; marches 105; politics 92; protesters 84–7, 90
peace movement 84, 86–8, 102–4, 240, 264; Australian 100, 103; German 83, 91
pentimento 49
Periyar *see* Ramasamy, E.V

persecution 242, 255, 264
perspective: medium-term 276; divergent 294; of the past 294; transformative 248
persuasion 221
philantropy 67–8, 73
Philippines 33
picketing 115
Pine Gap 105
Pioneers' Flag 231
Pioneers of the Eight Hour Day Association' 230–2; *see also* Eight-Hour pioneers
Pitjantjatjara People 107
places of memory 273; *see also* lieux de memoire
'Plea to all Germans' 90
polarization 199
political: action, shared 118; action, understanding of 72; argumentation 158–61, 165, 169, 174; change 271; communities 180, 185–6, 191; cooperation 77; culture 136, 268, 270; debates 60, 76; demonstrations 164; engagement 70; folk tradition 118; franchise 64; identity 180–1, 270; justice 169; landscape 180; liberalization 262; malaise 234; movements 61; network 54; organizations 3, 180; participation 83; power 44, 280; pressure 222; prisoners 268; rights 233; political song tradition 119; political struggle 174, 222; political topicality 90
politicization 27, 36, 159, 163–4, 174, 265
politics 261; carnivalized 8; of labour 214; moral force 221; pro-development 113; security 92
popular: memory 96, 105, 234; nationalism 99; remembrance 61; support 280, 282
Porta, Donatella della 2
Posser, Diether 170, 172
poststructuralism 1–2
postwar boom: break with the 136
poverty 234, 284
Power Cobbe, Frances 63–4, 69
power: discursive 92; relations 270
pre-Christian goddesses 126
presentism 255
preservationism: American 122
price controls 200
pride 225
professionas definition of identity 202
prognosis 255
programmatic orientation 255
projects, alternative 264
proletariat 187, 202

property rights 211
prosecution, political 172
prostitution 30
protections: regulatory 114
protest 2, 4, 265; framing of 2; cycle 273, 276; marches 107; normalization of 83; peaceful 83, 91; repertoires 266, 272; suicide 8
Protestant: heritage 66; ruling elites 242
Prussia 242
public: actions 115; activism 51; apologies 300; authorities 280–1; awareness 272, 283; commemoration 234, 260, 274, 284–6; culture 281–4; discourse 173, 205; enemies 161; expression of memory 281, 284; histories 149; interest 281; life 280, 293; life, black-led 286; opinion 221; performance 222; remembrance 275, 277, 283; representations of the past 281; schools 289; spaces 280, 284, 287, 289, 301; support 281
public memory 134, 136, 144–6, 174, 261, 270, 281, 294, 302; crafting of 281; inclusive 300; as mobilization source 105; revision of 280, 294
publicity stunts 277
publicly owned lands 114, 120
Purdah 71

quantative approaches 4

racial: equality 291; exclusion 70, 233; integration 291; prejudice 233; relations 293; sensitivity 104; state 246
racialized politics 199
racism 5, 71–3, 199, 233, 280, 285, 288–9, 293
radical: activism 119; environmentalism 123; left 201; movement memory 124; perspective 211; social movements 138; syndicalism 114; traditions 118
radicalism 120–1, 201, 232
radicalization 70, 273, 275; dynamics of 272
Railways Union 208
Ramasamy, E.V. 45
REACT 3
reactionaries 214
Reagan, Ronald 113, 291
rearmament 163
recollection: modes of 203
reconciliation 292; associations 263
Reconstruction 287
re-contextualisation 118, 128
Red Orchestra 160
red power 3

re-development 136–7, 142
'Redwood Summer' 122
Reed, Joseph 225
re-enactment 128, 227
Rees, J. 231
re-fascistization 156
referendum 199–200, 209
reflective learning process 268
reformism 246
Reichel, Horst 161
Reichsbanner Schwarz-Rot-Gold 159, 187–8
Reichssicherheitshauptamt 173
re-interpretation 301
remembrance 164, 181, 191, 202–3, 205, 260, 270; agents 204; of contest 95; creative 118; of human suffering 95; media of 106–7; organized 96; popular 61; public 270, 275, 277, 283; public, influencing 270; of repression 268; rituals of 283; varied 96; of war 184
remilitarization 162
Renan, Ernest 6, 107
repertoire: circulation 107–8; of contention 7–10, 123, 299; of memory 140, 147; protest 266, 272; shared 272; tactical 300
repetition of practice 227
Report of the Committee on the Status of Women 43
representation: of the past 77, 272; of workers 244
repression, sites of 268, 275
Republican-Confederate coalition 292
Republicans, US 252, 291–2
repudiation 128
research designs 62
Residents Action Group 143
resistance 76, 191, 247, 251, 295; fighters 90; groups 160, 162; non-violent 91, 122; women's role in 75
responsibility 302
reterritorialization 64
revolution 76, 180, 241, 244; of 1848/9 183; of 1918 182, 242, 245, 252; 1921 rebellion of Kronstadt Batavian 6; civil 29; French 6, 10, 12; October 181, 189; November 139; rights' 289; Russian 189
Rheinpreussen settlement 141
Rhenish capitalism 248–50
rhetoric 268, 274; governmental 36
Ricoeur, Paul 6
ridiculing 115
Rigney, Ann 3
'right to the city' 135
Riley, Betty 51, 55
Ritter von Lex, Hans 167

rituals 118, 203, 281; adaptations of 148; civic 280; of labour 202; of remembrance 283
Roadshows 117
rock music 114
Rocker, Rudolph 184–5
Rocks, The 142, 144
romance of achievement 301
Romania 8
Roof, Dylan 292–3
Rosa-Luxemburg Foundation 255
Rosa-Luxemburg-Bridge 265
Roselle, Mike 122
Rosemont, Franklin 119
Round River Rendezvous 117, 126
Route der Industriekultur see Route of Industrial Heritage
Route of Industrial Heritage 145
Rowan, Carl T. 287
Royal Commission into British Nuclear Tests in Australia 98, 100–2, 104
Royal Commission Report (1985) 104
Rudé, Gerard 2
Ruhrbanity 137
Ruhr-Volksblatt 137, 139–41
Runcie, Neil 142
Russell, Dora 51, 54
Russell, Edward 207–9
Russia 64
rythmanalysis 4

S.P.A.R.R.O.W. 43
sabotage 113, 115, 119, 122
Sachsenhausen 268
sacred country 108
sacrifice 228
Sagebrush Rebellion 120; *see also* Koehler, Bart
Sagebrush, Johnny *see* Koehler, Bart
Salt March 41
Sand County Almanac, A 125
satyagraha 42, 46
Scalmer, Sean 2
Schmid, Richard 172–3
Scholl, Hans 86, 90
Scholl, Sophie 86, 90
Schöneweidelabour camp Memorial 265
scientific reliability 4
Seamen's Union of Australia 137, 223
security politics 92
SED 159
segregation 285–6, 291; public 287
Seiffert, Wolfgang 161
self-censoring 27
self-critique 267

self-defense armed 187
self-definition 180, 202
self-determination 49
self-discipline of movements 301
self-government of unions 226
self-historicization 63
Self-Respect Movement 42, 45
self-sufficiency 66
self-victimization 162
senior demonstrators 87, 90–1
senior's blockade 87–9
settler nations 127
sex tourism 30
sexism 71, 73, 214; in slavery 71
sexual: norms 69; slavery 28; violence 30, 71
sexually-focused movements 70
shame: conferring 32
Shanghai Province 36
Shanxi Province 36
Sharma, Sarla 43, 47, 51, 55
sit-down demonstrations 84
slaveholders 294
slavery 60, 70–1, 77, 280, 282, 286–8, 294
slutwalks 8
social: activists 77, 105; chaos 283; codes 116; coding, collective 202; equality 243, 251; frames 42; identities 190; inequality 256; injustice 253; insurance system in Germany 246; justice 107, 253; lives 233; memory 85, 180, 281; model in West-Germany 252; partnership model German 248, 253; policy 249–52; responsibility' of unions 141; struggles 191, 271
social actors, primary 2
Social Democracy 180, 184, 190, 241–2, 244; movement in Germany 255
Social Democratic: organizations 181; Party 159, 241, 244; Party of Germany 186; Party of West-Germany 137–8
social democrats 160, 183–4, 186, 188–9, 191, 242, 249, 252
social movement 61–2, 70, 76, 85, 96, 114, 117, 128, 134–6, 141, 144, 146–7, 157–8, 180, 201, 203–5, 215, 261, 263–4, 272–3, 276, 299–300; activism 1; framework 302; memory 119, 122, 128, 203; new 133, 137; perspective 145; radical 138; repertoire 274; research 270; studies 261, 271, 299; theorists 270; tradition 128
social teaching: Catholic 241
socialism 183, 200–1, 207–8, 211–14, 243; movements 70; politics of 212; society of 167, 243
Socialist League 103

Socialist Party 208
Socialist Reich Party 251
Socialist Unity Party: East German 156, 158, 163–4, 167–9, 172–3; West German 156
Socialist Workers Party 100–1
socialization 274
societal: aims 255; changes 244; unrest 271
society: Imperial German 243; open 300; West German 248
sociology 4; of religion 204
solidarity 71, 209, 242, 266, 286; need for 242–3; proletarian 244
Sömmerda 181–2, 184–5, 187–8
songs: canon of 113; political tradition of 119
Sons of Confederate Veterans *see* neo-Confederates
sorrow 203
South Asia 41
Southern Europe 3, 8
Southern Historical Society 282
Southern Strategy 291
South-Korea 13
sozial-orientierte Stadterhaltung 138
Spain 3, 10
Spanish-American War 285
spatial-temporal markers 42
SPD *see* Socialist Party, German
spiritual: affinities 126; movements 125
spirituality 126; non-Christian 114
squatters movement 137
Stakhavonite 3
state: formation 270; governance 263; interests 36; rights of the 291
statues: tearing down 276
Stephens, James 221, 230
Stertzenbach, Alice 159–60
Stertzenbach, Werner 160
Stiftung Brandenburgische Gedenkstätten 268
stigmatizing 27, 29
Stone Mountain 284
Stonewall myths 11, 203
Strafdivision 999 170
Strafrechtsänderungsgesetz: Erstes 156–8, 161
Strategic Arms: 1972 Limitation Treaty of 104
strategic: interaction 8; memory 203
strategy 8, 73–4, 174; of conciliation 44; of confrontation 160; defense 161, 164, 17
strike 139–40, 145, 243, 249; 1889 miners' 243, 249, 253; 1905 miners' 242; 1974 public services 250; general 187, 214; history of German miners 253; hunger 141, 274; miner's 242; movements 243

structural dilemma 168
struggle 228–9, 233, 242–4, 251–2, 255, 261, 264, 273, 301; common 226, 242; import of 233; industrial 249; political 174, 222
student movements 3
suburbanization 290–1
subversion 158, 164
suffering 203; of Germans 276
suffrage 62, 63–9, 71, 73, 75, 211
suicide protest 8
Sydney 136
symbols 203, 222–3, 246, 273; Confederate 293; of white memory 280
syndicalism 119–20, 180–91, 207; radical 114

T4 Memorial 265
Taliban 293
Tarrow, Sidney 2–3
technological change 270
Technoseum (Mannheim) 253
Tell, Wilhelm 6
temporal: concepts 270; perspective 261
temporality 260, 269–70, 278; concepts of 261; immediate 276; medium-term 271; neglected 276; notions of 271
tenant movement 138, 140
terrorism 6
tertiary sector 136
Thälmann, Ernst 184
Theosophical Society 45
Third Reich 164, 171
Third World: movements 240; women 72, 76
Thirteenth Amendment 289
Thompson, Edward 2
Thoreau, Henry David 83, 122
Tilly, Charles 2–3, 7, 9
time regimes, perception of 255
Titterton, Ernest 99–100
tolerance 267
topography: of Nazi past 275; of Terror 265–6
Torgau 268
Touraine, Alain 2
trade, laws of 221
trade societies 226, 230–1; building 221
trade union movement 199, 241–3, 247, 251, 253; Catholic 243; German 246; memory of 301; united 248
trade unions 139, 208, 213–14; bashing 251; historians 252; houses 252; members 245; schools 252; secretariats 244; structures 243
Trades Hall Council: Melbourne 214, 224, 231, 233; Victoria 200, 207–8, 212

traditional neigbourhoods 136
traditions 114, 117–18, 181, 295; activism 274; civic 280; joint 11; radical 118; social 28; timeless 126
transcript: 'hidden' 205, 210, 215; 'public' 205
transfer: of capital 136; of ideas 136; of people 136
transformations: longer-term 277; medium-term 277; of cities and neigbourhoods 133; of memory through contentious action 260; of qualitative memory politics 261; of quantitative memory politics 261
transformative: episodes 260; events 202, 270–1, 276–7; perspective 248
transgenerational connectedness 301
transmission: of knowledge 49; of memory 203
transnational: developments 141; mnemonic repertoire 108; movement 63; overviews 62–3, 74; relationship 41, 75
transnationalism 103
trauma 5
Treaty on the Non-Proliferation of Nuclear Weapons 85
tree spiking 121–2
Trump, Donald 293
truth telling 118
Tudor, Frank 208–9, 213–14
tutelage 169, 244

UN resolutions 32
unanimity 286
unemployment 234
union: activists 212; Hirsch-Dunckersche 185, 242; imagination of 255; metalworkers' 249; miners' 249, 253; movement 207, 229, 233; Social Democratic miners' 242; social responsibility' of 141; women-led 213
Union of the Persecuted of the Nazi Regime/Association of Antifascists 261–2
Union of Victims of Stalinism 262, 268
unionism 157, 219, 221, 223, 226, 232–3; female 213, 233; new 223; pacification of 244
United Confederate Veterans 283
United Daughters of the Confederacy 283
United Nations Secretary-General 33
United Nations Sub-Commission on the Promotion and Protection of Human Rights 33
unity 248; excessive 191; of labour 227

universalism 61, 64, 67; methodological 72
uranium mining 95–6, 100–101, 106–7
urban: aesthetics 136; conservationism 138; crisis 133, 145; democracy 151; development 149; environment 136, 138; framework 142; heritage 134–5, 138, 140, 146; histories 143, 146, 149; memoryscapes 135; movements 147, 151; movements, objective identity of 147; movements, subjective identity of 147; political 180–1, 270; neoliberalization 134, 142; planning 145; structures 136
urbanization 134, 270
US civil rights movement 114, 122
USA 3, 6, 10, 60, 64
utopian thinking 95, 255

values: Christian 85; preservation of 139; values traditional 291
van der Capellen, Joan Derk 6
ventures: National Socialist 246; social imperialist 246
Verband der Heimkehrer, Kriegsgefangenenund Vermisstenange hörigen see Federation of Homecomers, POWs and Relatives of the Missing
Vereinigung der Opfer des Stalinismus see Union of Victims of Stalinism
Vereinigung der Verfolgten des Naziregimes-Bund der Antifaschisten see Union of the Persecuted of the Nazi Regime/ Association of Antifascists
Vergangenheitspolitik 262
Versailles conference 68
Vertriebene 262
veterans 263; as object of charity 282; Confederate 282–3; groups 262
victimization 28, 31, 33, 38–9, 72
victims: associations of 261, 265, 267, 276, 283; atomic bomb 31; Euthanasia 265; groups of 186, 262, 267–8, 272–3; Jewish 261; of Nazism 262, 276; recognition of 273; representatives of 265; of Stalinism 263; of war 302
Victoria, Queen 280
Victorian Labor Party 207–8
Victorian Socialist Party 207
Victorio 126
victory 227–9, 233, 255, 267
Vienna Declaration and Programme of Action 32
Viet Nam War 103, 201–2, 210, 291
violence 288; against women 38, 41; epistemic 76; imperial 34

voluntary associations 68, 280–1, 283
Von Weiszäcker, Richard 276
voting rights 68, 70, 222; Act of 1965 289

wages 73–4; agreements on 249–51; defending 252
Wagner, Walter 165
Walking Rainbow' *see* Moore, Fred
Wallace, George 288
Wallantinna station 106
war 5, 266, 302; crimes 35, 167, 265; nuclear 88; of Southern Independence 287
Warburg, Aby 6
Warburton mission 104
Warsaw Pact 83, 85, 172
Warsaw Peace Congress 103
Washington, Booker T. 287
weapons tests 95
Weber, Max 4
Webers' 'switchmen' 276
Weimar constitution 245; Republic 160, 242, 245, 248–50, 252
welfare state 249
West Commission 158
Western Europe 8
Western Germany 156
White Australia policy 199, 233
white authorities 288; memory 283, 287; nationalism 293; oppression 285; prejudices 288; supremacy 280, 287, 289–90, 292–4, 300
White Rose resistance group 90–1
white southerners 13, 280–4, 286–7, 290–1, 294; as latter day Israelites of the Old Testament 282; memory of 280–4, 286–7, 290–1, 294
Whitlam, Gough 98, 201, 210
Wiccan songs 126
WIDF Copenhagen Conference 46
Wild Mina's *see* Dolle Mina's
wilderness' 126–7
wildness' 125
William II, Emperor 281
Wintrich, Josef 166–7
witchcraft 126
Wobblies *see* Industrial Workers of the World
women: Asian 65; black 61–2, 65, 70–71, 74, 77; nurses 53; role of, in preventing world wars 54
Women's: Akron Convention 70; Committee of the Soviet Union 55; Declaration of Rights 54; Indian Association 45; Indian League 42; International Democratic Federation 43; International League for Peace and Freedom 103; March 73; Political Association 211–12
women's: activism 43–4; agency 72, 76; agitation 67; emancipation 54, 60, 67, 73, 75; groups, white 283; health care 69; history 69–70; liberation 3; movement 10, 13, 41, 44–5, 54, 62, 64, 240, 264; political activation 68; political awakening 64; progress 64; property rights 53–4; resistance 74, 74; rights 32, 57; role in imperialism 75; role in resistance 75
Woodson, Carter 286–8
Woolloomooloo 143; Residents Action Group 150
Woomera 102
workers': control 137; corps 182; emancipation 138; initiatives 133, 137, 144; interests 243; movement 199; non-White 233; party 138; representatives 245; rights 244; settlements 133, 139–41, 143, 145; struggles 138; uprisings 181; wages 244
working-class 135; culture 201; demands 184; interests 247; milieux erosion 251; past 135
working conditions 233, 242, 250, 252
works' council 248; 1921 Law of 245
World Anti-Slavery Convention 68
World Congress of Representative Women 60
World Congress of Women 54
World Fair, Chicago's 60, 65
World Federation of Democratic Youth Congress 54
world order 252
world proletariat 186
World War I 180, 183–5, 199, 233, 241, 246, 252, 283, 286; memorials 262
World War II 85, 87, 89, 91, 156, 162, 170, 207–8, 220, 265, 276, 286
World Congress of Influential Women 65
Wüstenberg, Jenny 3

Yayori, Matsui 30
youth centre movement 137
Yudhishter, Kumar 51
Yuha, Park 33

Zamponi, Lorenzo 3
Zentrale Arbeitsgemeinschaft 245
Zentralrat zum Schutze demokratischer Rechte 158–60, 163–4, 167, 169, 171, 173
Zhiliang, Su 35–7

Printed in Japan
落丁、乱丁本のお問い合わせは
Amazon.co.jp カスタマーサービスへ